Revolution without Revolutionaries

Stanford Studies in Middle Eastern and Islamic Societies and Cultures

Revolution without Revolutionaries

Making Sense of the Arab Spring

ASEF BAYAT

Stanford University Press
Stanford, California

Stanford University Press
Stanford, California

Printed in the United States of America on acid-free, archival-quality paper

Library of Congress Cataloging-in-Publication Data

Names: Bayat, Asef, author.
Title: Revolution without revolutionaries : making sense of the Arab Spring /
    Asef Bayat.
Other titles: Stanford studies in Middle Eastern and Islamic societies and
    cultures.
Description: Stanford, California : Stanford University Press, 2017. |
    Series: Stanford studies in Middle Eastern and Islamic societies and
    cultures | Includes bibliographical references and index.
Identifiers: LCCN 2017009148 (print) | LCCN 2017010826 (ebook) |
    ISBN 9780804799027 (cloth : alk. paper) | ISBN 9781503602588 (pbk. : alk. paper) |
    ISBN 9781503603073 (e-book)
Subjects: LCSH: Arab Spring, 2010- | Revolutions--Arab countries. | Arab
    countries--Politics and government--21st century.
Classification: LCC DS39.3 .B39 2017 (print) | LCC DS39.3 (ebook) |
    DDC 909/.097492708312--dc23
LC record available at https://lccn.loc.gov/2017009148

Cover design: Rob Ehle
Cover photo: Asef Bayat
Typeset by Bruce Lundquist in 10/14 Minion Pro

To the known and unknown heroes of the Arab Spring, those who put their lives on turning their uprisings into meaningful revolution

To be truly radical is to make hope possible rather than despair convincing

Raymond Williams

Table of Contents

Preface

People may or may not have ideas about revolution for it to happen. For the outbreak of a revolution has little to do with any idea, and even less with a "theory," of revolution. Revolutions "simply" happen. But having or not having ideas about revolution does have critical consequences for the outcome when it actually occurs. This book is about revolutions without "revolutionary ideas"— ones that are conditioned by the modalities of our neoliberal times. It focuses on the Arab Spring, the remarkable revolutionary uprisings that ironically burst onto the political stage at a time when the very idea of revolution had been dispelled. Thus, the book is neither a simple narrative of the Arab Spring nor a work of current affairs. Its central aim is to make sense of these extraordinary political happenings, primarily in Tunisia and Egypt, to understand their dynamics, analyze their mobilization process, examine their paradoxes, and highlight their promises from a global, historical, and comparative outlook. As much as it details the actual operations of these revolutions, the book is also a work of social theory, a modest attempt to introduce idioms and insights to better understand these political episodes.

The urge behind writing this book derived from my early fascination with and frustration over the unsettling novelties that marked the Arab revolutions, when I looked from the prism of a revolution that I had witnessed, experienced, and studied some thirty-five years earlier. Having lived in both Iran and Egypt just prior to their revolutions, I was struck by how different these experiences were. I was enthralled by the Arab Spring's more peaceful, open, pluralistic, and less repressive texture but was perplexed by its nonradical, loosely organized, exposed, and perilous quality. I wondered if the Arab revolutions were revolutionary enough to withstand the dangers of restoration. What made the political language, ideological makeup, and the broad trajectories of the Arab Spring so remarkably different from those of the revolutions of the 1970s?

In attempting to address such questions, I am hoping to highlight the nuances of the Arab Spring and complicate the meaning of "revolution."

This book is not a product of one-time research and writing; rather, its data, insights, and conceptual makeup originate from many years of reflections on the question of social and political change in the Muslim Middle East—long prior to the 2011 uprisings, when I was living and teaching in Cairo. In fact, my thinking about and experience of revolution goes back as far as the Iranian revolution of 1979, of which I was a participant-observer. I have reworked some of my earlier studies on the Iranian revolution to include in this volume for comparative purposes. However, the substantial part of the thinking, research, and writing that informs this book began as soon as the first protests broke out in Sidi Bouzid, Tunisia, and the subsequent developments that took the world by surprise. As uprisings surged in Egypt, Libya, Yemen, Syria, and Bahrain, I became deeply engaged in attempts to understand what was unfolding so rapidly. This involved multiple research trips to Egypt and Tunisia after the outbreak of the uprisings.

Of course, the import of the Arab uprisings has been far greater than the intellectual interests they stirred; the uprisings were poised to reshape the future of the region and remake the fortune of its people. I was aware of the challenges one faces in researching revolutions that are unfolding. How should one do scholarship in turbulent revolutionary times filled with struggles, sacrifices, intrigues, and passion, the time when people's lives, liberty, and material well-being are at stake? How can we observe and understand the events that are in the making, and what to do when the very act of observation could have the effect of intervention? And above all how should one navigate between a position of wanting to see the uprisings succeed yet retain the sobriety of critical scholarship and sincerity of judgment? I hope that this text has been sensitive to such concerns and succeeds in avoiding their potential pitfalls.

In Egypt, I had multiple discussions with observers, onlookers, secular people and Islamists, and revolutionary activists who included some of my ex-students from my teaching years in Cairo. I also collected valuable information by speaking to ordinary people, in particular the youth, women, and many unknown individuals at homes, neighborhoods, offices, universities, and especially in the streets; I visited poor neighborhoods in Cairo to observe their engagement with the revolutionary dynamics and followed the workings of new organizations in the localities, colleges, and public spaces that had emerged just after the fall of Hosni Mubarak. In Tunisia, I spoke to academics, intellectuals, activists, civil society organizations, both secular and religious, and many anonymous citizens in public places; I visited headquarters of political organizations, universities, and neighborhoods—both the posh Sidi Bou Said and the slums of Tadamon and Al-Menoubiya in Tunis. Speaking to ordinary people, both men and women, in the streets, neighborhoods, private homes, colleges, or during the rallies and demonstrations provided valuable insights into their ideas about revolution, change, role of religion, expectations, and obstacles they faced as a result of the uprisings in both Egypt and Tunisia. In referring to these informants in this book, I have used mostly fictitious names. Both in Egypt and Tunisia, I collected a considerable amount of written materials, beyond what one finds in the social media, in the form of leaflets, tracts, papers, reports, news items, and books. As fresh and more compelling data are becoming available, the future studies will, I hope, fill any gaps this study may contain.

.   .   .

I am indebted to many people who in different capacities and at different stages have helped bring this book to completion. The anonymous reviewers of the earlier drafts provided valuable comments and suggestions that involved two rounds of substantial revisions. In Tunisia, Professor Souad Halila and her family kindly hosted and facilitated a wonderful evening of discussion with a number of Tunisian intellectuals and academics. Habib Ayeb was most gracious in offering his intellectual insights as well as practical guidance during my research work in Tunisia. I also thank the numerous Tunisian activists and observers who generously shared their perspectives on the events, in particular Mabrouk Jebahi, Abdel-Haqq Zammouri, Mehdi Barghoumi, Nadia Marzouki, and Tareq Kahlawi, as well as Reda, Rasha, Fadwa, Delal, and many others. I thank Ozgur Gokman, who beyond translating my works into Turkish has supplied me with valuable ideas and sources on Turkish politics. In Egypt, I have benefited much from the support and insights of many friends and colleagues directly or through their writings; I am particularly appreciative of Ahmed Zayed, Hosam Bahjat, Omnia Khalil, Khaled Fahmi, Gamal Eid, Ala Abdel-Fattah, Abdelrahman Mansour, Samah Naguib, Rabab El-Mahdi, Ali El-Regal, Samia Mehrez, Mona Abaza, Hanan Sabea, Saad Eddin Ibrahim, Hani Shukrallah, Lina Ataallah, Hosam Hamalawi, Mustapha El-Sayyid, Reem Saad, Malak Roshdi, Hoda Sadda, Heba Rauf, Yahya Shawkat, Alia Mosallam, Nicholas Hopkins, Omar Nejati, Abdallah Erfan, Mona Seif, and Mohammed al-Arabi, to name only a few.

Preface

The Department of Sociology at the University of Illinois at Urbana–Champaign and the College of Liberal Arts and Sciences where I teach remain avid supporters of faculty research and writing. I am grateful to them for their support and encouragement while I worked on this book. I especially appreciate Antoinette Burton for her professional guidance and intellectual engagement. Some of the themes raised in this book were discussed with inspiring students in my graduate seminars, where they helped sharpen some of the arguments. I have been especially fortunate to have Heba Khalil as my student and research assistant. Heba has helped significantly both intellectually and in alerting me to relevant ideas and information. Her knowledge of Egypt together with Ahmed Elowfi's visions on the Persian Gulf States made possible lively discussions about the revolutions in the region. Kate Wahl, my editor at Stanford University Press, has consistently shown that her critical comments and counsel always benefit the outcome; I am grateful to Kate for not giving up. Finally, and as always, I am most indebted to my family, Linda, Shiva and Tara, for continuous love, intellectual engagement, and moral support without which this project might have a different destiny.

Revolution without Revolutionaries

1   Revolutions of Wrong Times

I happen to be an observer of two revolutionary episodes separated by roughly three decades. As a young activist in the late 1970s in Iran, I was engaged in a revolution that opened a new chapter in world politics, the effects of which continue to be felt even to this day. I am referring to the Iranian revolution of 1979, which unfolded almost in tandem with the Sandinistas toppling Anastasio Somoza's dictatorship in Nicaragua, followed by Grenada's New Jewel Movement (NJM) led by the left-wing Maurice Bishop, which ended the pro-US Eric Gairy's regime. Not long before, a socialist insurgency had given rise to the People's Democratic Republic of Yemen in the 1970s, while a Marxist-Leninist liberation front was seeking to alter the government in the neighboring sheikhdom of Oman. Arising in the midst of the Cold War, these revolutions spurred a powerful anti-imperialist, anticapitalist, radical democratic, and social justice impulse. I fervently followed these developments—intrigued by revolutionary politics, excited about the prospect of a better future for these nations that had endured repressive autocracies for so long, even though dispirited by their often authoritarian outcomes.

After a span of some thirty years, a new wave of political upheavals overtook the Middle East and beyond. Beginning with the Green revolt of 2009 in Iran, they peaked with the 2011 Arab Spring and were soon followed by a global wave of Occupy movements that raged in the heartland of the capitalist West and spread into some seventy countries. As a committed scholar and sometimes participant in social movements, I closely followed the events surrounding the Green revolt, experienced the political climate prior to the Arab uprisings as a longtime resident of Egypt, and observed the happenings associated with the Occupy movements in North America.

As I juxtapose these two revolutionary episodes, I cannot help sensing how remarkably different they are—not only in their modes of mobilization and organization but especially in their meanings and broader visions. I find the speed, spread, and intensity of the recent revolutions extraordinarily unparalleled, while their lack of ideology, lax coordination, and absence of any galvanizing leadership and intellectual precepts have almost no precedent. But even more striking is that they lacked the kind of radicalism that marked the earlier revolutions and that the ideals of deep democracy, equity, fair property relations, and social justice paled or were more rhetorical than driven by genuine concern anchored on strategic visions or concrete programs. Indeed, it remains a question if what emerged during the Arab Spring were in fact revolutions in sense of their twentieth-century counterparts.

What did happen over the course of the past three decades that altered the nature of radical politics? How and why did the meaning of revolution and the nature of transformative demands change? This book, built on evocations from the earlier revolutions, notably the Iranian experience of 1979, focuses on the Arab uprisings to address the questions of their distinctions and associated implications. At its core, the book aims to offer a new comparative vantage point from which to observe and examine the meaning of the 2011 political upheavals.

Revolutions of the 1970s

On February 11, 1979, a powerful revolutionary movement overthrew the regime of Shah Mohammad Reza Pahlavi, the last of Iran's twenty-five-hundred-year-old monarchy, replacing it with the first Islamic Republic in the modern world. The victory day followed some eighteen months of intermittent street protests, clashes with the police, labor strikes, and an eventual armed insurrection. The revolution toppled a regime that had emerged in 1953 from a coup engineered by the Central Intelligence Agency (CIA) against the secular democratic government of Prime Minister Mohammad Mosaddeq, who championed the nationalization of Iran's oil industry. With his return to power the shah, backed by the United States, began to pursue an aggressive policy of modernization, Westernization, and socioeconomic development. Women gained the right to vote, a literacy campaign covered rural areas, and a land reform turned sharecroppers into smallholders and poor tillers into rural proletariat, all set to modernize rural life. But the shah maintained a despotic rule anchored by the notorious secret police, the Organization of Intelligence and National Security (SAVAK), suppressing democratic voices, civil associations, and labor and left movements. Thus, when in 1977, US president Jimmy Carter, following his human rights agenda, called on the shah for openness, the opposition—college students, guerrilla insurgents, supporters of exiled Ayatollah Ruhollah Khomeini and the intellectual Ali Shariati—seized the opportunity to express dissent.

A number of liberal secular lawyers, opposition leaders, and intellectuals began writing open letters to the authorities, including the shah, demanding a free press, rule of law, and human rights. The intelligentsia began to regroup, organize, and mobilize. The evenings of poetry reading at Goethe Institute and Aryamehr University in Tehran brought thousands of mostly secular and leftist youths, including myself, into what became a forum to lash out at the government's repressive practices. Moderate clerics and Islamic figures, such as Mehdi Bazargan, who would become the first prime minister after the revolution, then launched their own evening lectures. Students at Tehran University organized street demonstrations once the academic year began. With the protests in the Qom Seminary concerning a disparaging newspaper article against Ayatollah Khomeini, who was in exile in Iraq for his opposition to the shah, revolutionary protests entered a new phase. Each death in a protest entailed further mourning and marches, generating a cycle of protests that continued for eighteen months. Even the imposition of martial law on September 8, 1978, did not suppress the protests, and demands for the downfall of the shah were voiced as early as February 1978.

The strike of some forty thousand oil refinery workers and the ensuing nationwide general strike in the key sectors of the economy and state administration, including state radio and television, encouraged the revolution and disoriented the regime. By now, the intransigent Ayatollah Khomeini, deported from Iraq to Paris, had become the de facto leader of the revolution; he communicated his messages and directives through personal networks; international media, notably the BBC; and recorded tapes that were widely distributed in Iran. Revolutionaries formed the Provisional Revolutionary Council as an alternative organ of power to that of the shah. The United States and Britain then urged the shah to leave the country for "vacation." Before his departure on February 1, 1979, the shah transferred authority to a Regency Council and a new prime minister from the liberal opposition, Shapour Bakhtiar, who held little legitimacy on the streets. Only days after the shah's departure, Ayatollah Khomeini returned from exile to a triumphant welcome. With the army in disarray and the revolution at its height, the ayatollah appointed an alternative government led by Prime Minister Mehdi Bazargan. It seized power following two days of armed insurrection led largely by the Marxist and Mujahedin guerrillas along with the air force cadets who had defected; they collectively defeated the notorious Imperial Guard, the last vestige of the regime's resistance.[1]

The revolution enjoyed widespread support from broad constituencies—modern and traditional, men and women, middle class and laborers—who were connected to a charismatic leadership and a revolutionary organization through the networks of activists operating in the seminaries, mosques, universities, and neighborhoods. The revolutionary strategy and ideology had an intellectual precursor, a body of ideas and visions rooted in both Marxism and political Islam. Many activists had been inspired by the Marxist Fedaian Khalq and Islamic leftist Mujahedin guerrillas, who like the Latin American guerrilla movements had established bases in the northern forests and urban cells. Islamists had sought inspiration from the revolutionary ideas of the Egyptian Sayyid Qutb as well as the Palestinian resistance movement. Ayatollah Khomeini had articulated his own vision of Islamic governance in the treatise *Islamic Government*.[2] But none matched the intellectual influence of Ali Shariati, a Marxian Muslim thinker whose ideas of "red" and "revolutionary" Islam garnered a widespread following among political youth and intelligentsia.[3] Thus, when the protests in Iran unfolded, many participants had already formed ideas about revolution and revolutionary strategy, even if their meanings and expectations differed. Yet sentiments concerning anticapitalism, popular democracy, and social justice remained key components of both the secular and Islamic intellectual compendium; they came to occupy a central place in the postrevolutionary deeds and debates.

The victory of the revolution coincided with the collapse of authority in the state administration and economic enterprises. Police control had crumbled, many businesspeople had deserted their companies, managers had left factories, landlords departed their large estates, and the rich abandoned homes hurriedly, leaving thousands of lavish properties behind. Thus, landless peasants confiscated large agribusiness estates, factory workers took over hundreds of workplaces, and government employees began to run the ministries and departments. In the cities, ordinary citizens launched a spectacular takeover of mainly public lands and illegal construction of homes, contributing to the rapid expansion of Iran's urban centers, notably the capital. Some 150,000 housing units—palaces, hotels, villas, and unfinished apartment blocks—belonging to the elites of the ancien régime went to the newly established Foundation of the Dispossessed. The new grassroots organizations, notably the "revolutionary institutions" such as the Pasdaran (Revolutionary Guards), paramilitary volunteers, rural Construction Crusade, and Housing Foundation, quickly moved to fill the power vacuum.[4] In the end, the Iranian revolution entailed a rapid and radical transformation of the old order; it opened a political future that embraced the republican ideals of popular sovereignty and distributional justice while paving the way for what was to be the long march of political Islam in the world.

Although dubbed "the last great revolution," the Iranian experience was not the only radical revolution in the region.[5] The late 1960s and early 1970s saw the emergence of a number of revolutionary movements in the Arab world that took their ideological cues from both Nasserite anti-imperialism and Marxism-Leninism. In Yemen, where Britain had forged a federal government run by the local amirs and sultans, a guerrilla group later called the National Liberation Front (NLF) began an insurgency in the early 1960s. Based in the port city of Aden with its militant trade unionism, these southern militants— including exiled workers, intellectuals, officers, and tribal leaders—fought British forces, mobilized the countryside and took territories, defeated the sultans and amirs who owned land, and inherited positions in the tribal hierarchy; by 1967 they had established the People's Democratic Republic of Yemen.[6] The new government nationalized the economy, created central planning, limited ownership of housing for rent, and carried out land reform with some success, as the gross domestic product (GDP) rose by 25 percent by 1973. Yet the poor economic base, scarce foreign exchange, meager skilled labor and inexperienced administrators, and hasty nationalization also had an adverse impact.[7] Nevertheless, social reforms proceeded with an impressive outcome. Income equality improved, corruption was reduced, and health and educational services expanded. Considerable efforts were made toward emancipation of women despite continuing conservative backlash—women became legally equal to men and were encouraged to work in public; polygamy, child marriage, and arranged marriage were all banned; and equal rights in divorce received legal sanction. Imams did continue their functions in mosques but lost their social power as education became secularized, religious endowment came under state control, and sharia was replaced with the state legal codes.[8] On the whole, emphasis was placed on the egalitarian tenets of Islam.

Like the Cuban revolutionaries, the NLF had transcended its early nationalist position to embrace Marxist politics and armed struggle. During their campaign in the mountains of South Yemen, the rebels read, reflected, and strived to learn from the international socialist strategies—notably Chinese, Vietnamese, and Cuban experiences—while shedding their "petty bourgeois" Nasserism and tribal mind-set.[9] But the more heart-felt inspiration came from the left-wing Arab intelligentsia centered in Lebanon, in particular those associated with the Palestine Liberation Organization (PLO), whose secular, pluralist, and progressive ideology had embraced such luminaries as the great poet Mahmoud Darwish, the author Elias Khoury, and the Marxist novelist and strategist Ghassan Kanafani, whom the Israeli secret police assassinated in 1972.

The victory of the NLF in Yemen boosted the insurgency in the neighboring Sultanate of Oman, where the nationalist youth in Salala had established the People's Front for the Liberation of Oman in the mid-1960s to free the southern province of Dhofar from the rule of Sultan Said bin Taimur and his British ally. Disenchanted by the Egyptian leader Gamal Abdel Nasser's defeat in the 1967 war and emboldened by the departure of Britain and the NLF victory in Yemen, the Dhofari liberation movement adopted Marxist-Leninist ideology and aimed to liberate "all of the Gulf from imperialism."[10] Political scientist Fred Halliday, who visited the liberated areas, reported that "wherever we went we saw people wearing Mao and Lenin badges, reading socialist works and discussing."[11] Works by Lenin and Bertolt Brecht and on Palestinian resistance and the Spanish civil war had special purchase, with discussions disseminated on the pages of the weekly *Sawt al-Thawra* and the monthly *9 Yunyu*.[12] The Dhofari revolutionary culture received its cue from the revolutionary movements in the Third World at the time, but it drew particularly on the nearby revolutions in Palestine and South Yemen, as well as the experiences of Cuban and Vietnamese revolutionaries.[13] Among the insurgents were ex-slaves, shepherds, fishermen, migrant workers in the Gulf, and fighters from richer families. The insurgency exhausted the sultan and his British ally, even though the fear of Marxist revolutions had caused the conservative regimes in the region—Abu Dhabi, Saudi Arabia, Jordan, Egypt, and Pakistan—to extend financial and military assistance to the sultan. But it was the shah of Iran who, by deploying thousands of troops, eventually forced the militants to consider a negotiated settlement.

The legacy of these liberation movements had become part of the intellectual universe of the Iranian revolutionaries—both Marxist and religious—who defeated the shah's Imperial Guards in their final push to topple the shah's regime.[14] When the Iranian revolutionaries seized the radio and TV stations in Tehran, the leftist Sandinista rebels in Nicaragua were preparing to take the capital, Managua, in a popular uprising that would end the US-backed dictatorship of Anastasio Somoza on July 19, 1979. Established in 1961, the Sandinista National Liberation Front (FSLN) undertook guerrilla operations against government installations, including the presidential palace, while building support among the rural and urban poor, middle classes, and progressive faction of the Catholic Church aligned with the liberation theology movement. But the revolutionary conflict had cost some thirty-nine thousand lives. The popular mobilization intensified after the 1972 earthquake in Managua and the revelations that the authorities had embezzled international aid funds, which compelled the government to impose martial law. The subsequent pressure by President Carter on the regime to lift martial law emboldened the insurgency to grow into a wider national conflict that eventually forced Somoza and his officers to leave the country once the United States retracted its support.[15]

Having just experienced our own revolution in Iran, the events in Nicaragua had special meaning for us. There was something peculiar about this experience—a radical revolution that simultaneously embraced political pluralism. The Sandinistas formed a government of national reconstruction that included moderate businessmen, intellectuals, conservative parties, and Marxists. They pursued political pluralism, a mixed economy, and nonalignment. But at the same time, the Sandinistas embarked on an ambitious social revolution. Their literacy campaign reduced the illiterate population from 60 percent to just 13 percent; health care became available to the lower classes, worker participation plans allowed workers to take control of industry and farms whose owners had fled or were involved in sabotage, and the land reform program granted land to the tillers for the first time in the country's history.[16] The Sandinista revolution represented an experiment to combine a project of national unity and the hegemony of popular classes: socialism and political pluralism.[17] It was partially this extraordinary political project that overshadowed the events in the nearby Caribbean island of Grenada where the NJM of Maurice Bishop launched an armed revolution against the government of Eric Gairy, who had come to power in fraudulent 1976 general elections.

These extraordinary upheavals had followed a series of anticolonial revolutions in southern Africa—Angola, Mozambique, and Guinea-Bissau—after the Portuguese rose to dismantle their own colonial dictatorship in 1974. Led by charismatic leadership and organization, all of these revolutions espoused powerful radical impulses expressed in anti-imperialist sentiments, anticapitalism, and distributive justice, even though only Nicaragua embraced inclusive multiparty democracy. They were all breaking away from global power relations in which the United States had been dominant. Informed by a blend of socialist, nationalist, and left-leaning religious ideas (Islamic and Catholic political theology), these revolutions entailed fundamental transformation of the states and societies and involved radical practices of popular control, civic engagement, nationalization, land distribution, and some forms of worker control and self-management in firms and farms.[18] Unfolding in the midst of the Cold War, however, they experienced deep hostility by the Western powers, led by the United States. Iran underwent economic sanctions that continued for some thirty-five years; the Persian Gulf revolutions faced a severe backlash from the conservative Arab regimes and the shah of Iran; the Sandinista strategy of socialist democracy was derailed by a devastating Contra War sponsored by President Ronald Reagan. And the US invasion in 1983 restored the old regime in Grenada after the four-year rule of the Marxist-Leninist NJM.

The Arab Revolutions

Some thirty years passed during which the Middle East went through a turbulent period of wars, globalization, economic restructuring, social change, demographic shift, religious revival, and technological innovation. Yet conventional wisdom deemed the authoritarian regimes resilient and stability was ensured.[19] But it was only to take the self-immolation of a poor street vendor in the hinterlands of Tunisia to reveal the scope of mass discontent and the fragility of the elites.

On December 16, 2010, Mohamed Bouazizi set himself on fire in the depressed town of Sidi Bouzid after the police abusively confiscated his scale and vegetables because he lacked a permit. Once the news spread, relatives and local youth poured into the streets in outrage. The clips of the protests found their way immediately into tweets and Facebook pages—one with seven hundred thousand participants—reaching the international media. Local activists and trade unionists quickly moved in to mobilize on the ground by helping organize more rallies. Within the following three weeks much of central Tunisia was involved in what came to be an uprising, with the citizens demanding jobs, dignity, and freedom. Bouazizi died in the hospital nineteen days later, and President Zine El Abidine Ben Ali's promise of jobs, reforms, and free elections went unheeded; if anything, his conceding tones emboldened the rebels, who now wanted the president to relinquish power. As the uprising stretched northward to the capital, Tunis, the trade unionists broke rank with the national leadership and staged labor strikes. The professional middle class that enjoyed a "comfortable" material and social life under Ben Ali's police state also joined in. The impressive march of eight thousand lawyers in support of the uprising sent a clear message that the uprising had garnered a broad national constituency. When on January 14, 2011, the protesters filled Bourguiba Boulevard in the capital and the army refused to shoot to kill, Ben Ali and his wife left Tunisia for good. The revolution seemed triumphant.

Activists in Egypt received the news of the revolution in Tunisia with great excitement. The April 6 youth movement and the coordinators of the Facebook page "We are all Khaled Said" had already planned a protest for January 25, National Police Day, to protest the brutal torture and murder of a young man, Khaled Said, by the police for alleged drug use. To the astonishment of the security forces and the organizers, tens of thousands marched from some twenty different points in Cairo, including the poor neighborhoods of Boulaq, Shubra al Khaima, and Dar El-Salam, flooding the iconic Tahrir Square. All sorts of people gathered—young and old, men and women, Christians and Muslims, a blind man with stick, a man in a wheelchair. Security used teargas, clubs, and rocks, and the government blocked Twitter and the Internet, but the protests spread in the following days to provincial cities such as Alexandria, Suez, Mahalla, and Mansoura. Friday January 28 saw the largest crowd in the nation's streets, where protesters fought the security forces, attacked police stations, burned government buildings, and chanted "bread, freedom, justice." The conservative Islamic Salafi groups generally did not participate, while the Muslim Brothers joined later after initial hesitation. As the police retreated from the public scene, protesters occupied Tahrir Square and began to erect tents, while citizens formed Popular Committees to protect their neighborhoods from potential acts of crime. When the police disappeared, the military took to the streets but signaled neutrality. Now that the protest had grown into a full-fledged uprising, protesters wished to end the thirty-year rule of President Mubarak, who was grooming his son to replace him. Mubarak signaled concessions but reaffirmed he was not leaving. During the Battle of the Camels on February 2, the revolutionaries repelled the regime's use of armed thugs riding camels, and when labor strikes escalated in the country, the balance of street power shifted. Eighteen days of spectacular uprising, which left 841 dead and thousands injured, forced Mubarak to step down on February 11, 2011; he transferred power to the Supreme Council of the Armed Forces (SCAF) to run the nation's affairs and preside over the "transition" process—to hold parliamentary and presidential elections and prepare a new constitution. Egyptians celebrated the victory of the revolution with ecstatic jubilance.

The demise of Ben Ali and Mubarak marked a new episode in the politics of the region—a region that had remained captive to the whims of autocratic kings, despotic sheikhs, and lifelong presidents for decades. As if Tunisia and Egypt had shown the path, popular revolts spread like wildfire to some seventeen other Arab states, notably Yemen, Libya, Bahrain, Syria, Jordan, and Morocco. In Yemen, where sporadic demonstrations over jobs and the economy had already been under way since 2007, more widespread protests targeted the corrupt president Ali Abdullah Saleh, who had ruled in opulence the poorest Arab country for thirty-three years. The opposition brought together diverse constituencies, ranging from the southern oil secessionist movement, to northern Shia Houthis who already controlled territories, youth and women's groups, and moderate Islamist groups such as the Islah Party. The mass rallies in the key city centers invoked the image of Tahrir as hundreds of thousands of protesters marched, clashed with police, and called for the end of Saleh's reign. After months of mass protests, during which top officials from the military and the ruling party defected, Ali Saleh eventually agreed on November 23, 2011, to a deal brokered by the Gulf Cooperation Council (GCC) to cede power to his vice president, Mansour al-Hadi, in exchange for immunity. Another dictator was forced to abdicate. In August 2011 Libyan Muammar al-Qaddafi was the fourth Arab despot deposed, following a bloody revolt in which NATO forces effectively determined how things should proceed.

In Bahrain only three days after the fall of Mubarak, tens of thousands of both Sunni and Shia responded to a call to protest unemployment, inflation, and repression in the center of Manama. But a deep-seated feeling of discrimination by the working-class Shia majority against the Sunni elites, chiefly the ruling clan, remained a key factor.[20] Thus, demands for more representative political reform faced the fury of the monarchy, who charged the opposition with being the fifth column of Iran. Playing the sectarian card, the regime asked for the military intervention of the GCC on March 14. Saudi Arabia was only too ready to dispatch thousands of army personnel and weapons to crush the uprising. The three-month Emergency Law declared on March 15 dampened the opposition, which was suffering from discord and dissension. The United States was inclined to keep both the monarchy and its naval base in Bahrain.

The speed and spread of these popular uprisings were truly extraordinary. Within six months they deposed four entrenched autocrats and seriously threatened others. With unusual bravery, persistence, and sacrifice these nonviolent rebels withstood the brutal violence of the adversarial regimes. As revolutionary movements, these were certainly spectacular. But the politics, vision, and broad trajectories of these revolutions showed remarkable difference from those of the 1970s. First, the Arab revolutions lacked any associated intellectual anchor. Revolutions usually both inspire and are informed by certain intellectual productions—a set of ideas, concepts, and philosophies—that come to inform the ideational subconscious of the rebels, affecting their vision or the choice of strategies and type of leadership. English revolution was associated with the political theories of philosophers such as John Milton on free speech, Thomas Hobbes on social contract, and John Locke on natural rights. The American Revolution was informed by the ideas of Thomas Paine; and the thinkers Montesquieu, Jean-Jacques Rousseau, and Voltaire informed the republican facet of the French Revolution. Figures like Václav Havel (Czechoslovakia), Adam Michnik (Poland), and György Konrád (Hungary) symbolized the intellectual face of the Eastern European revolutions; while the Iranian revolutionaries drew on Marxist-Leninist literature, Islamist thinkers like Sayyid Qutb, but above all the popular revolutionary intellectual Ali Shariati. But no visionary intellectual current seemed to accompany the Arab Spring.

Second, the Arab revolutions lacked the kind of radicalism—in political and economic outlook—that marked most other twentieth-century revolutions. Unlike the revolutions of the 1970s that espoused a powerful socialist, anti-imperialist, anticapitalist, and social justice impulse, Arab revolutionaries were preoccupied more with the broad issues of human rights, political accountability, and legal reform. The prevailing voices, secular and Islamist alike, took free market, property relations, and neoliberal rationality for granted—an uncritical worldview that would pay only lip service to the genuine concerns of the masses for social justice and distribution. Finally, and most important, there was no fundamental break from the old order. Except for Libya, little changed in the structure of power and the governing modes of the old regimes. The incumbent elites and their networks of patronage, along with the key institutions of governance such as the judiciary, police, intelligence apparatus, and the military, remained more or less unaltered.

In Yemen, the ruling families and tribal leaders mostly kept their status, as did the political networks and structure of power controlled by Ali Saleh. What the Saudi-led GCC had initiated was little more than an exit strategy for Saleh without any meaningful alteration in state power. Even Saleh's son retained his prominent position in the military. In the end, a civil and proxy war rattled the status quo when the Houthi rebels marched through the capital to unseat

President Hadi in September 2014, thus prompting Saudi Arabia to deploy its own massive forces to unleash a civil war to protect the president. In Egypt, President Mubarak's downfall opened the way for a new parliament, president, and constitution. But the institutions and the power base of the Mubarak regime, even though challenged, remained mostly immune; in fact, they harbored the forces of counterrevolution that ultimately took power from President Mohamed Morsi in a military coup on June 3, 2013. Only in Tunisia did a peaceful transition entail a political shift from the old autocratic rule into a pluralist democracy, which ensured a democratic constitution. Yet some key operators of the Ben Ali regime returned to power after the 2014 presidential elections, presiding over an economic system that inherited its neoliberal prerevolution legacy. More important, the old "parallel state," the de facto authority before the revolution, composed of the security sector, certain business elites, and local mafia, made a comeback.[21] Only a vocal opposition—vigilant civil society organizations, a powerful trade union movement, and a prudent post-Islamist current, al-Nahda—tilted the balance of power in favor of democratic transition.

Occupy Rebellion

The monumental uprisings in the Arab world, especially their remarkable politics of the square expressed in the Tahrir episode, inspired a series of Occupy movements whose rapid spread in the world reinforced the idea that we have entered a new age of popular politics. On May 2011, tens of thousands marched in Madrid to initiate what came to be known as Los Indignados—the movement of the indignant subalterns who camped out in the Puerta del Sol for a month; six million Spaniards joined in the protest in their support. In Athens one hundred thousand Greeks took to the streets, putting out tents in Syntagma Square for weeks. Protesters in Tel Aviv made some four hundred encampments on Rothschild Boulevard, protesting joblessness and the high cost of living, along with four hundred thousand demonstrators marching throughout the country. In the United States, the Occupy Wall Street (OWS) movement began with the occupation of Zuccotti Park in New York City in September 2011and soon spread across hundreds of cities. Within the next few months, the global Occupy movements had found echo in Britain, the Netherlands, Mexico, Chile, Russia, India, and later in Turkey's Gezi Park.[22] Even Brazil—a country that under a center-left government had enjoyed, according to Luiz Inácio Lula de Silva, "the lowest unemployment rate in our history, and unparalleled expansion of economic and social rights"—was not immune to the indignation of the citizens who wished to protect decent social services, demanding elite accountability and transparency.[23]

In the Western world, the Occupy movements emerged primarily to express outrage against the dominance of corporations in government, to "separate money from politics."[24] But almost all expressed dissent against the effects of neoliberal policies, notably staggering inequality, unemployment, precarious work, and uncertain life that had gripped a large segment of ordinary citizens, including the educated and professional middle classes. At the same time, it was a clear distrust of the liberal democracy in which the political elites aligned with money and business had drained democracy from its substance. A study by the political scientists Martin Gilens and Benjamin Page of some eighteen hundred policy initiatives from 1981 to 2002 confirmed that the US political system had descended from a democracy into an oligarchy, rule by the business elites.[25] Having lost confidence in the institutions of liberal democracy, protesters took to the streets to play politics.

Yet the Occupy movements refused to focus on any particular demand or put forth any "reasonable" alternative. Indeed, "no demand, every demand" summed up the movement's deliberate ambiguity. They lashed out at the rich 1 percent but left capitalism that produced it unconstrained. Activists were distinctly against any "ideology" and militantly disdained solid organization, recognizable leadership, not to mention any blueprint of alternative programs. Such a postideological posture and horizontalism did have the advantage of flexibility, "direct democracy," and a measure of innovation in mobilization. But they also incurred a precarious operation, uncertain commitment, vague message, blurred strategy, and quick breakdown of mobilization.[26]

Sociologists Manuel Castells and Sidney Tarrow suggest that the achievement of the Occupy movements was their very operation. Considering the process as the product, Castells and Tarrow focus on the way in which the movements conducted themselves as democratic, communal, horizontal, and without hierarchy.[27] This partly reflects the views of anarchists who saw the value of the Occupy movements in their very egalitarian operation. Suspicious of any engagement with the state and hierarchy, they put their hope in these movements as the possible model for the future—"future in the present."[28] My own observations in Toronto's St. James Park in October 2011 confirmed the communal, innovative, and egalitarian aura of Occupy assemblies. People sat down and sang, discussed politics, and shared food and water. Strangers connected, and boundaries of race, gender, and ethnicity seemed to dissipate. The occupied square appeared like a liberated enclave, free from the state, money, and greed. Earlier on Cairo's Tahrir Square had experienced a similar but more intense community of solidarity as well as sacrifice; it had offered a space where the revolutionaries were not only engaged in an ad hoc egalitarian community but also involved in barricading and battling the police, tanks, thugs, and teargas. Here was a place where ordinary daily lives—those of street traders, shoe shiners, or tea sellers— merged into extraordinary struggles for the revolution.

Such utopian order of solidarity and salvation would expectedly exude awe and passion; and the fascination with the romance of the square was not new. Inspired by the appeal of agora in the eighteen days of Tahrir Square, philosophers Alain Badiou and Slavoj Žižek imagined in these revolutionary arenas the prospect of a new social order that could serve as the foundation for a different future. But in truth square life of this sort, the Tahrir moments, is a liminal reality, a kind of fleeting egalitarian life that lies between the real and the unreal. These are exceptional episodes in great political mobilizations from which invaluable lessons can be learned, but they should not be mistaken for what activists can or cannot do in larger structures and national spaces after the dust settles and they all go home. Public squares of this sort can be cradles for democratic movements, but as the author Matt Ford points out, one cannot live in a cradle forever.[29]

The Occupy and similar movements were in a sense the child of our media-driven globalization—with half of the adults in the world carrying a supercomputer in their pockets—where the effects of an event may dramatically exceed its intent and the astonishing unforeseen effects may come not only as blessing but also as curse, since the initiators remain unequipped to manage them. Those in New York City who occupied Wall Street probably did not anticipate the explosion of similar concerns around the world, nor could they foresee the dynamics or offer remedies to alleviate the anxieties.[30] On a greater scale, such was the paradox of the Arab Spring—blessed by the startling response to the protest call and baffled by how to proceed with what had transpired.

Novel Revolutions?

Why did the revolutions of 2011 turn out to be so different from their earlier 1970s counterparts? What happened in the course of the past three decades that altered the nature of radical politics? How do we characterize the 2011 revolutionary episode and its distinct trajectory? Not everyone attributes anything distinct to the Arab revolutions, except perhaps their civil character, which avoided war and destruction as seen in the "classical" revolutions. Commenting on the Egyptian experience, the sociologist Saad Eddin Ibrahim argues that the remarkable revolt that overthrew the Mubarak regime opened the way for far-reaching social and political changes, including three free elections, a new government and parliament, and under General Abdel Fattah el-Sisi new economic projects, notably the new Suez Canal.[31] Yet most revolutionaries saw the post-Mubarak Muslim Brotherhood government as a barrier to rather than facilitator of deep democratic change. And only a few considered General Sisi, who forcefully seized power from the government on July 3, 2013, as the incarnation of the revolution; if anything, General Sisi's regime embodied a drive toward restoration.

From a broader perspective, the political scientist Jack Goldstone likewise suggests that the Arab Spring followed the same pattern as any other revolution, beginning with socioeconomic strain and elite opposition, followed by popular anger, shared views, and benefit of favorable international relations.[32] He predicted that they "will unfold as all revolutions do" with "ongoing struggles for power between radicals and moderates."[33] It is true that the Arab uprisings had similar preconditions, which tell us about *revolution as movement* or the way a revolutionary *mobilization* develops. They do not tell us about *revolution as change* or the *outcome*, nor do they reveal the ideology, vision, or choice of organization that has a crucial bearing on the outcome. Did the notion of radicals and moderates have any meaningful relevance in the experiences of Egypt, Tunisia, or Yemen? Where were the radicals, and was the role they played similar to those in the French, Russian, or Iranian revolutions?[34] In *Why Occupy a Square*, a book on the Egyptian uprising that builds on Goldstone's perspective, Jeroen Gunning and Ilan Baron express doubt whether Egypt's was in fact a revolution at all because there was little shift in the structure of the state and distribution of power.[35] But the question remains: Why was there no significant shift in the structure of power and state institutions or economic vision, even though a spectacular uprising did succeed in toppling an entrenched dictator? *Why Occupy a Square* does not address the question; its intended focus is on the causes and tactics of revolutionary mobilization rather than on strategic visions about how to wrest power from the incumbents.

Others consider the Arab Spring as true revolutions that were hijacked, manipulated, or stalled by the counterrevolution. What occurred in Egypt, Tunisia, and Libya was no less than a "political revolution" in Gilbert Achcar's assessment, because "the emergence of the people freed from the shackles of servitude, the assertion of collective will in public squares, and success in over-throwing tyrannical oppressors are the unmistakable works of a political revolution." Unfortunately, however, these revolutions "left the state apparatuses of the fallen regime intact," thus rendering themselves defenseless against the "conservative coup" or appropriation by such free riders as the Muslim Brotherhood.[36] In the view of Jean-Pierre Filiu, revolutions in Syria, Egypt, and Yemen were stalled not simply by the free riders but by the very counterrevolutionary "deep state"—that is, the secretive and extralegal apparatuses of the states, such as the police and intelligence service, which see themselves as the custodians of "saving" these nations at any cost.[37]

As I show in this book, the question is not whether the counterrevolution was responsible for stalling or hijacking the Arab revolutions; all revolutions carry within themselves the germs of counterrevolutionary intrigues. The question is whether the revolutions were revolutionary enough to offset the perils of restoration. The idea of "deep state" may be useful in highlighting the continuity of the old order after the revolutions.[38] But an overemphasis on its exceptional, "deep" character underplays the failure of the revolutionaries to address the question of state power per se, as if things would have been different had the revolutionaries confronted "normal" states. The shah's state also enjoyed a powerful military and the intelligence apparatus SAVAK yet was overturned by the Iranian revolution. Why were the Arab revolutions particularly more vulnerable in the face of the forces of restoration? As I discuss in Chapter 10, the geopolitical exceptionalism of the Middle East, shaped by oil and Israel, did play a part in undermining the revolutions, but the analytical lens deployed in these narratives allows little room to go beyond the notions of manipulation or hijacking to see something novel about these political upheavals.

Interestingly, those insiders to the upheavals seem to sense, even though in retrospect, something new about what they experienced. Tunisian novelist Kamal Zaghbani views his revolution as something "unique," one that "opens new horizons in human history."[39] According to the Egyptian revolutionary Wael Ghoneim, "Revolutions of the past have usually had charismatic leaders who were politically savvy and sometimes even military genius." Those were the "revolution 1.0 model." But the revolution in Egypt, according to Ghoneim, belonged to a new model, "revolution 2.0," a "truly spontaneous movement led by nothing other than the wisdom of the crowd."[40] In an attempt to give meaning to such particularities, the political scientist Ivan Krastev finds in the recent global protests, from Tunisia and Egypt to the Occupy movements, a clear departure from the twentieth-century experiences. The past protests were "about emancipation—advocating rights of workers, women, or minorities—and their street marches were aimed at gaining access to and representation within state institutions." The protests of 2011, however, were neither for revolution nor for reform; rather, they expressed a rebellion against the institutions of representative democracy, "without offering any alternative."[41] The recent revolts, according to Krastev, were not against government but against being governed.

This is an intriguing argument but raises important questions. Were the Arab revolts and the Occupy movements of the same breed? Were the rebels not truly interested in politics? The Arab revolts and the Occupy movements did share certain common roots—neoliberal economies, unprecedented inequality and precarity, unresponsive governments, and the use of new communication technologies for mobilization. But their different political settings—electoral democracies versus autocracies—entailed different political trajectories. Where neoliberal policies operated under an electoral democracy, as in the United States, Spain, Brazil, and Turkey, dissent took the form of Occupy movements; however, in places where neoliberal economies were mixed with autocratic rule, the outcome became revolutions. Yet Krastev, focusing on the centrality of social media, lumps all these together as the expression of a historic shift from politics to protest.[42] But in truth these activists seemed to be departing not from politics per se but from a particular kind of politics, the conformist party politics that had failed to offer a way out of malaise. On the contrary, the Syriza in Greece, Podemos in Spain, and Aam Aadmi Party in India garnered mass support because they were seen as political parties and programs that articulated unorthodox policies against neoliberal onslaught and corruption. In the Middle East, Iran's Green revolt of 2009 targeted those who deprived the citizens of participation in fair electoral politics, while the emergence of some one hundred new political parties in Tunisia and dozens in Egypt just after their uprisings pointed not to aversion from politics but a desire for meaningful politics.

"Refolutions"

What transpired in Tunisia, Egypt, and Yemen, I argue, were neither revolutions in the sense of the twentieth-century experiences (i.e., rapid and radical transformation of the state pushed by popular movements from below) nor simply reform (i.e., gradual and managed change carried out often from above and within the existing structural arrangements) but a complex and contradictory mix of both. In a sense, they were "refolutions"—revolutionary movements that emerged to compel the incumbent states to change themselves, to carry out meaningful reforms on behalf of the revolution.

Revolutionaries held enormous social and street power but failed to assume governmental authority; they did not actually rule. Revolutions stayed relatively peaceful and orderly but brought little structural change. The political and social realms remained relatively open and pluralist, favoring electoral democracy, but became susceptible to the danger of counterrevolution. The protagonists were rich in tactics of mobilization but poor in vision and strategy of transformation; they adopted loose, flexible, and horizontal organization but one that suffered from fragmentation; they espoused civil opposition but overlooked the danger of restoration; they were concerned more with democracy, human rights, and rule of law than reallocation of property and distributive justice. What came to fruition then looked like revolution in terms of mobilization but like reform in terms of change. These revolutions were reformist in the sense that the protagonists who spearheaded masterful mobilization were unable to imagine forms of organization and governance that departed from those against which they were rebelling; they were unable, unwilling, or uninterested in directing the process of change within state institutions; they conceptually separated the economy from those aspects of the political order that they sought to topple; and they hardly offered any exploration of how state power worked or how to transform it. In fact, most seemed to hold little preconceived ideas about revolution when they began their street protests and found themselves overwhelmed by mass revolts they never expected or had any clear idea how to handle.

The Arab revolutions occurred at an ideological time in post–Cold War history, when the very idea of revolution had largely disappeared from social thought and political struggles, when the three major postcolonial ideologies—anticolonial nationalism, Marxism-Leninism, and militant Islamism—that vigorously advocated revolution had vanished or been undermined. In their place was the powerful neoliberal paradigm and its normative frame. Thus, instead of the ideas of egalitarian ethos, fair property relations, welfare state, and popular control that marked the revolutionary discourse of the 1970s Cold War times, there developed in this postsocialist era an upsurge in the notions of the individual, freedom, rights, civil society, free market, and legal reform. The spread of postmodern thought in academia had further constricted efforts to imagine grand ideas, utopian orders, and universal values in a world in which the old utopias (communism, Islamism, national liberation, and revolution) were collapsing, while the postmodern preoccupation with fragmentation, ambiguity, and relativism ultimately served to depolarize. Unlike Frantz Fanon, who was invested in "genuine historical change," Michel Foucault emphatically rejected any preconceived "vision" for political transformation.[43] Foucault's idea of entrapment in disciplinary power, as Edward Said contended, ended up replacing "insurrectionary scholarship" with "quietism."[44]

If there was anything "grand" in these critical thoughts, it was the identity politics, the "politics of recognition" that transcended the politics of redistribution, with status and identity substituting for class politics. Even though scholars like Nancy Fraser wished to combine the two, according to sociologist Zsuzsa Gille, "identity politics came to dominate both the intellectual as well as in many places practical politics."[45] In the meantime, the new anarchist trends that had emerged at the turn of the twenty-first century—to join dissent against globalization and the US-led wars in the Middle East—continued disdaining the state and revolution as detrimental to democratic transformation, and organization as the harbinger of structure and authority; instead, anarchists, with their latent or explicit individualism, revered horizontalism and practices of self-rule on the margins of society, as though "structurelessness" was in reality free from internal authority.[46] Even though labeled "leaderless revolution," this horizontalism was "more evolution than revolution, for it is drawing on people across the world that in order to fix our problems, there is no one to look to but ourselves."[47]

Ironically, while movements became more fluid, open, horizontal, and ephemeral, the adversarial states turned more organized, secretive, "intelligent," and entrenched. Consequently, states came to possess far more knowledge about the dissenting movements than movements knew about the states.[48] Even though under neoliberal regimes the states lost much of their infrastructural power, they opted to monitor bodies, disrupt formal collectives, and atomize citizens more than before.[49] In these conditions of imbalance it seemed that only contentious acts of surprise, innovations, indefinable collectives, or sheer "people's power" could win political concessions; otherwise, movements were likely to fall prey to the manipulation or repression of the states if they did not disintegrate by their own inertia. For unlike ideological movements—such as nationalism, socialism, or Islamism—which cemented enduring loyalty and identity, postideological movements tended to vanish as rapidly as they came to fruition. Even the revolutionary heroes, if they ever emerged, fell from grace with the same speed as products traded by consumers in the aggressive markets.

In the end, none of these intellectual and political trends seriously challenged the neoliberal paradigm; if anything, some of their ideas—such as aversion of the state and class politics, flirtation with the market, and marketization of politics—found a selective affinity with the neoliberal normativity that came to inform much of the political field in the post–Cold War era; it simultaneously generated dissent and deradicalization.

Neoliberal Effect

There is a contention that "neoliberalism" is hard to grasp because, from its original coinage in 1938 by the German Alexander Rustow as a modern economic system with state intervention, it has come to refer to many different things—certain economic policies, an economic philosophy, or philosophy of society, describing at once "social market economy," "market fundamentalism," and "hyper-capitalism." Some even suggest that it is nothing but a bundle of ideas.[50] I understand neoliberalism both as an economic rationality that solicits contention and a form of governmentality that cultivates compliance.[51] Since the 1980s, the world has experienced an economic rationality that is distinct from its postwar economies, which were marked in varied degrees by an interventionist state, regulated economy, trade barriers, social subsidies, protectionism, unionized workers, and welfare provisions; these were known broadly as the New Deal in the United States, social democracy or Keyensianism in Europe, socialism in the Eastern bloc, and developmentalism in the Third World.[52]

The 1974 military coup in Chile against the socialist president Salvador Allende, however, inaugurated a new era in the world, where governments embarked on reversing most of the earlier trend in the economy and governance through deregulation, elimination of trade barriers and price control, privatization, shrinkage of the welfare state, and imposition of austerity.[53] Pushed by a relentless ideology couched in "human dignity" and "individual freedom," powerful agencies such as the International Monetary Fund (IMF) and the World Bank, and ruthless state policies or "shock doctrine,"[54] this hypercapitalist rationality came to be known as "neoliberal." As a consequence, a staggering disparity in wealth and life chances ensued.[55] An Oxfam study presented to the Davos 2015 economic forum found that the richest 1 percent in the world owned almost 50 percent of the world's wealth. In other words, eighty individuals owned as much wealth as 3.5 billion people.[56] In the United States, according to *Forbes* magazine, four hundred Americans possessed more wealth than half of the entire population; and one hundred British owned more than 30 percent of the wealth of the total populace. Countries as diverse as Canada, China, India, and even the social democratic Sweden also experienced a rise in the share of the national income taken by the top 1 percent. At the same time, almost half the world population, over 3 billion—according to the United Nations (UN) and the World Bank in 2013—lived on less than $2.50 a day, and 80 percent on less than $10 per day.[57]

The Arab world went through a similar process. As early as 1977, President Anwar Sadat's policy of *infitah* and its economic liberalization in Egypt had led to the first mass bread riots in the cities of the region. Before the arrival of liberalization, most countries in the Middle East were ruled by either nationalist-populist regimes (such as Egypt, Syria, Iraq, Libya, Sudan, and Turkey) or pro-Western rentier states like Iran and the Arab Gulf States. Funded by oil income or remittances, these mostly autocratic states pursued state-led development strategies, often attaining remarkable growth rates.[58] Most sponsored massive projects of state building, urbanization, industrialization, and educational development that by the 2000s had generated an increasingly urban, educated, and youthful citizenry. The rentier states were able to provide social services to many of their citizens, while the populist states dispensed significant benefits in education, health, employment, housing, and the like.[59] For these postcolonial regimes, this "social contract" served to build support among the peasants, workers, and middle strata at a time when the states were struggling against both the colonial powers and old internal ruling classes. The state acted as the moving force of economic and social development on behalf of the populace.[60]

The social contract, however, dwindled as the Arab states went along with the World Bank and the IMF from the 1980s to implement liberalization and structural adjustment policies. Even though Arab governments, weary of popular unrest, slowed down aspects of liberalization and facilitated safety nets such as social funds, welfare nongovernmental organizations (NGOs), or even Social Islam (Islamic charity), the strategy continued ceaselessly.[61] The *Arab Human Development Reports* of 2002–2009 invariably highlighted the Arab developmental deficits, underemployment, and mounting disparity gripping the region.[62] By 2008, food prices rose, increasing inflation to more than double the global rate; unemployment (11 percent average), especially among youth, reached the highest in the world (30 percent in Tunisia); exports declined because of the drop in global demand (7.7 percent in Tunisia; up to 22 percent in Yemen); workers' remittances plunged sharply (17 percent in Egypt) while income inequality grew.[63] By the early 2000s, 0.3 percent of citizens in Lebanon controlled 50 percent of the national wealth; of these just six men from two families (Hariri and Miqati) held most of the wealth.[64] In Tunisia in 2012, only 70 people held 20 percent of the national wealth, and in Egypt 490 individuals controlled 25 percent of national wealth.[65] Most of the new money went to powerful businessmen who, enjoying favoritism and monopoly, increasingly influenced governmental policies.[66]

As the old social contract collapsed, the new disparity found vivid expression in, on the one hand, a minority of globalized super rich with visible wealth, conspicuous consumption, and snobbery enclosed in the gated communities and, on the other, a majority of marginalized constituencies spreading across the urbanizing villages and ruralizing cities. Despite pushing for liberalization, the Arab states continued to remain at the center of economic activity, managing the neoliberal policies by facilitating, sharing its benefits, and attempting to handle its social costs.[67] It is no wonder that these autocratic states would become the prime target of any discontent triggered by developmental deficits, social problems, political repression, or corruption. An early popular reaction to austerity policies, notably cuts in consumer subsidies as the states tried to reduce their deficits, included a series of mass urban riots that extended from Morocco (1983), Tunisia (1984), and Sudan (1982,1985), to Lebanon (1987), Algeria (1988), and Jordan (1989).[68] Following a decade in the 1990s of safety nets, welfare NGOs, and Islamist involvement in social provisions for the needy, dissent assumed different dynamics and diverse forms during the years preceding the uprisings; the cost of living and social services protests merged with those of labor, democracy advocacy, and regional politics to form a single episode of mass street politics.

In the meantime, the neoliberal restructuring turned the Arab large cities into what I term "cities inside out," where a large number of urban subalterns were compelled, by necessity, to resort to the outdoor subsistence economy to survive and to public spaces to perform social and cultural rituals such as funerals or weddings. This then turned the urban space into a site of constant contention between the urban subaltern (the poor, youth, socially excluded, and politically marginalized) and the authorities. In Egypt between 2004 and 2009 there were some nineteen hundred protest actions, including labor strikes, social service unrest, and political protests.[69] Tunisia, under Ben Ali's police state, had seen a dozen large protests in the depressed central provinces within the few years prior to the uprising.[70]

A plethora of observers have confirmed that the neoliberal restructuring was at the root of the popular dissent that eventually burst into remarkable Arab uprisings. Some have detailed how these policies in Tunisia, Egypt, Syria, Lebanon, and the Arab Gulf States caused crony capitalism, extraordinary inequality, urban segregation, and deprivation along with unprecedented opulence.[71] What is missing, however, is an examination of how the neoliberal framework simultaneously deradicalized dissent. Neoliberalism does not just entail contention; it also structures compliance. The political clout of neoliberalism lies in its ability to serve as a form of governmentality, in its ability to structure people's thinking to internalize the methods of the market society, considering them to be a commonsense way of being and doing things, against which no concrete alternative is imagined or needed.[72] Treating it as "natural" is a key power of neoliberalism; when it is not talked about as a problem or as an ideology such as, say, communism, it becomes the natural way of life.[73] Indeed, the change in people's mentality is so crucial for neoliberal thinking that, in the view of Naomi Kline, it deploys the psychiatric method of "shock treatment" to erase memory and break resistance.[74]

In its ideal form, neoliberal normativity considers almost every social institution as if it were a business enterprise. Universities, schools, hospitals, art centers, and even the very state itself are expected to behave like corporations—with internalized hierarchies, working toward unlimited growth and efficiency to produce measurable products for their exchange value and in which individuals compete fiercely for self-interest.[75] In this perfect market society, the collectivist ideals of solidarity, common good, equality, and real democracy (rather than elections) are dismissed because they are deemed antithetical to the norms of such a society.[76] The neoliberal paradigm flatly discards talk about refiguring property relations, fair distribution of wealth and opportunities, or the welfare state as outmoded legacies of "failed socialism" and antithetical to individual freedom while it simultaneously incorporates the ideals of freedom, the common, caring, sharing (economy), or hospitality into its logic. It commercializes activism, human rights, civil society, gender equality, sustainable development, and poverty reduction, draining their radical intent.[77] Even the idea of "revolution" is up for sale.

Of course, the extent to which people in different societies have in reality incorporated and internalized neoliberal ideas differs. Certainly the degree of neoliberal norms practiced in the United States differs from those, for instance, in Latin America, which is considered to be an exception. The region, once at the forefront of neoliberal experiment, seemed to move toward a postneoliberal phase in which despite the indelible structural imprints of neoliberalism, many of its core principles have been cast aside.[78] This is quite a departure from the early 1990s when the region saw a dramatic process of deregulation, privatization, and decline in state traditional responsibilities toward its citizens. Thus, in the 2000s when neoliberal projects in the Middle East looked unstoppable, Latin America experienced a "left turn" as a number of elected "new left" governments came to construct development policies that rejected neoliberalist dogma.[79] Beginning with the Zapatista movement that galvanized the grassroots dissent in Chiapas against the Mexican government, these countries saw the rise to power of radical leaders such as Hugo Chávez in Venezuela, Evo Morales in Bolivia, Rafael Correa in Ecuador, and José Mujica in Uruguay. Explicitly rejecting neoliberal orthodoxy as the source of slow growth, poverty, environmental degradation, and inequality, these governments were deemed to represent the socialism of the twenty-first century. Correa's government changed the constitution to grant rights to nature; it aimed to develop the oil industry but also to preserve natural resources, to improve economic growth but reduce inequality. Correa campaigned to put an end to the "long and sad night of neoliberalism."[80] Evo Morales was reelected in 2014 for the third term for his rigorous socialist reform that has elevated Bolivia from an "economic basket case" into a country of both growth and equity. It is "one of the few countries that reduced inequality" while it attained "growth much faster over the last eight years than in any period over the past three and half decades." But along with growth there has also been redistribution: under Morales, poverty declined by 25 percent and extreme poverty by 43 percent; social spending rose by 45 percent and minimum wage by 87 percent.[81] José Mujica, the president of Uruguay and former socialist guerrilla leader, was described as the world's "poorest" president because of his austere lifestyle and his donation of around 90 percent of his twelve thousand–dollar monthly salary to charities that benefited poor people and small entrepreneurs. Broadly, leftist governments in Latin American strived to renationalize industrial and financial companies and take over those in crisis; they resumed government investments, established joint ventures, and returned to dispensing social services.[82]

Even though some remained skeptical about the actual achievements of these efforts, describing the new left turn as the "fashionable incarnation of dictatorship,"[83] or at best no more than an "intent" to transcend the core principles of neoliberalism,[84] regional experts such as Arturo Escobar acknowledged that Latin America had been the only region in the world where "some counter-hegemonic processes of importance" may have taken place at the level of the state.[85] Otherwise, neoliberal orthodoxy continued to gallop through the rest of the world, where its normativity became, in Doreen Massey's words, "part of our common sense understanding of life."[86]

In the Middle East, in the past two decades significant elements of neoliberalism have spread among the Arab elites, professional groups, and the political class, influencing their thinking about activism, change, and the image of a good society. This has had an undeniable deradicalizing effect. The political class, both Islamist and secular activists, took free market and neoliberal rationality for granted; their concerns, if any, became limited to some of its policy outcomes, such as unemployment. Any radical vision about redistribution, change in property relations, expropriation, or popular control was instinctively discarded. Thus, class politics and concern for the poor, workers, or farmers were largely sidelined in favor of the politics that centered on human rights, corruption, fair elections, and legal reform. Concerns for rights—human rights, women's rights, or personal rights—certainly had genuine relevance in the contemporary Arab societies. However, because the realization of rights is so deeply entangled in class, status, and political position, a disregard for class politics would strongly undermine the genuine struggle for such rights. Thus, against the real desire of the subaltern groups, "social justice" was reduced to no more than a phrase to be uttered without much clear political vision or programmatic backing. Youth activism centered largely on NGOs engaged in charity, development, poverty reduction, or self-help, often in conjunction with international donors or corporate funding. Such engagement, despite its civic values, was preoccupied with amending the existing order instead of one that devoted itself to political work—envisioning, strategizing, and working toward a different social order. "Civil society" activism then proved to be very different from forging social movements (such as labor, farmers', or student movements) for change. The most visible women's activism drew on the "gender and development" frame that was intimately linked to development aid, international NGOs, and the US Agency for International Development (USAID), whose "developmentalist" discourse has been described as an "anti-politics machine."[87]

This kind of deradicalization was not limited to liberal or secular citizens. The Islamist movements—which during the Cold War had adopted strong elements of revolutionary strategy, distributive justice, and collectivist values—moved to embrace neoliberalism by being at ease with the free market, inequality, and consumption. As I discuss later, the postsocialist conditions shaped a neoliberal Islam that promoted a cozy cohabitation of fervent morals and free markets, piety and profiteering. Thus, by the time the uprisings arrived in the Arab streets, few radical visionaries were planning in terms of revolution—a fact that differentiated the Arab Spring from the 1970s revolutions and their powerful anti-imperialist, anticapitalist, radical democratic, and social justice urge. Only the radical claims of the grassroots gave a revolutionary impulse to these otherwise nonradical revolutions.

In the following chapters, I elaborate on these propositions and discuss their implications for the way in which the Arab revolutions ensued. I show in Chapter 2 how the revolutions of the 1970s, unlike the Arab Spring, were informed by an intellectual component of which socialist ideas were a major element. Here I focus on the Iranian revolution of 1979, in which revolutionary ideas were articulated by the Marxist and Islamic leftist guerrilla movements, as well as the "ideologue of the revolution," Ali Shariati. The revolution saw radical strategies and repertoires to which revolutionary ideas lent support. Chapter 3 elaborates on these repertoires by examining the widespread (*shura*, or council) movements for grassroots democracy and self-rule in the neighborhoods, colleges, farms, and workplaces, focusing on the occupation of factories. With the fragmentation of labor and the end of actually existing socialism, radical ideas began to lose their clout. Chapter 4 examines the deradicalization of political Islam, showing how the Islamist opposition evolved from its strong anti-imperialist and social justice propensity to embrace reformist politics and neoliberal economy. By the time the Arab uprisings occurred, most Islamists and secular counterparts alike had been conditioned by the neoliberal climate. Despite the decline in revolutionary projects, popular dissent grew, as neoliberalism transformed the Arab economies and shaped an increasingly contentious urbanity.

Chapters 5 and 6 discuss how the Arab large cities became the spaces of popular discontent and how dissent found expression in the Arab squares, exploring what the urban setting of the uprisings tells us about their origin and dynamics. While the urban setting was by no means unexpected, the sudden and fierce eruption of the uprisings surprised observers and protagonists alike. Chapter 7 explores the way in which under the shadow of the authoritarian polity and neoliberal economy, the Arab subaltern were involved in discrete forms of everyday struggles to enhance their life chances; and in doing so, they had created their own opaque and illegible realities outside the radar of the state and scholars. Their struggles, often in the form of "nonmovements," assumed collective voice once the protests began and merged into what came to be known as the Arab uprisings. But the Arab Spring in Tunisia, Yemen, and Egypt had serious limitations in transforming into full-fledged revolutions. What transpired in the Arab world, I argue in Chapter 8, were not revolutions in the sense of their twentieth-century counterparts but a mix of revolutionary mobilizations and reformist trajectories. Yet I show, in Chapter 9, that the extraordinary acts of claim making by the poor, women, lower-class youth, and social minorities in pursuit of equality, inclusion, and recognition radicalized these otherwise nonradical revolutions. Indeed, as I demonstrate in Chapter 10, these subaltern struggles, in part, rendered the postrevolutionary transition acutely contentious, reinforcing the painful and paradoxical postrevolutionary moments. Defenselessness against the domestic and regional counterrevolution was one such anomaly; it left a devastating impact on efforts to achieve a just and free social order in Arab societies, feeding into the rising disenchantment with the experience and idea of revolution. The final chapter discusses the question of despair that came to afflict so many activists in postrevolutionary moments; it concludes by exploring grounds for hope and the renewal of revolutionary spirit in the post–Arab Spring Middle East.

2   Marx in the Islamic Revolution

Revolutions are not simply the spectacular modes of mobilization that exude awe and inspiration, nor are they limited to the art of insurrection. Revolutions are also associated with an intellectual feed—a body of ideas, strategies, and visions that inform the social order revolutionaries desire and the ways to achieve it. Even though revolutions (as movements) may in fact emerge without participants having preconceived ideas about them, ideas do matter on how the revolutions should proceed. As part of the radical political upheavals of the 1970s, the Iranian revolution was informed by and spurred a powerful anti-imperialist, anticapitalist, radical democratic, and Islamist impulse. Its intellectual articulation combined aspects of both Marxian socialism and political Islam—a kind of indigenous "third way" that at the time had become the standard thinking among the secular and religious activists and intellectuals in the Middle East and beyond. From Christian liberation theology in Latin America to African socialism, Arab socialism, and the Islamic liberation movements articulated by the Egyptian Sayyid Qutb and Iranian Ali Shariati, these third-way strategies represented diverse attempts to deploy a Marxian egalitarian ethos to particular cultural and historical settings. In Iran, the quintessential intellectual Ali Shariati, considered to be the ideologue of the revolution, offered one of the most elaborate revolutionary visions—one that would leave a profound impact on the thinking of Iran's political class. By focusing on Shariati and the associated radical thoughts of the time, I explore the broader moment of revolutionary theorizing across the Third World in general and the Muslim Middle East in particular at that historical juncture in Cold War history; I wish to emphasize how much a revolutionary vision matters to the outcome when rebels take to the streets and how its absence, as in the Arab Spring, may have adverse effects despite spectacular mobilization.

Marxian Spillover

In the late 1970s, the reading circles in the universities in which I was a part covered three kinds of materials—Marxist, Islamist, and those in between, broadly speaking. These genres largely reflected the ideological leanings of political opposition in Iran at the time. The Marxist circles were partly related to the defunct communist Tudeh Party—deemed at one time the most powerful communist movement in the Middle East until it was curbed by the US-sponsored coup in 1953, only to be revived after the 1979 revolution. But it was mainly the Marxist guerrilla movement, notably the Fedaian Khalq, which inspired a large segment of prerevolutionary students and intelligentsia. The guerrilla groups had emerged following the shah's suppression of a large pro-Khomeini street protest in Tehran in 1963; for some activists that event demonstrated that nonviolent political activism was no longer effective and that a revolution was necessary. Thus, college students and members of the professional class, those with origins in the Tudeh and the Marxist wing of the pro-Mosaddeq National Front, began to set up secret groups to read about and discuss the experiences of revolutions in China, Cuba, Vietnam, and Algeria. Some of these groups developed into guerrilla organizations. The Fedaian guerrillas established bases in the thick forests of the Caspian Sea province in the late 1960s, hoping to launch a revolution in the image of the Cuban revolutionaries.[1] Key leaders in the group, such as Bijan Jazani and Hamid Ashraf, as well as Amir Parviz Pouyan and Masoud Ahmadzadeh, elaborated on theories of revolution suitable to the Iranian condition. They published pamphlets like *How the Armed Struggle Will Be Transformed into a Mass Struggle* (Jazani), *What a Revolutionary Must Know* (Abbas Sorouki), *The Necessity of Armed Struggle and the Rejection of the Theory of Survival* (Pouyan), and the celebrated *Armed Struggle: Both a Strategy and a Tactic* by Ahmadzadeh, who had earlier formed his own group to discuss works of Che Guevara, Régis Debray, and the Brazilian guerrilla strategist Carlos Marighella.[2] They called for an armed campaign, both in the rural areas and cities, to undercut the repressive rule of the regime and open a political space for the masses to rise up. Many guerrillas had already gained military training by having to serve in the army. When in 1971, the "rural team" attacked a police station in the village of Siahkal to release an arrested comrade, a five-year guerrilla war had started. Even though the Siahkal incident resulted in a regime crackdown that eliminated the original leaders of the group, it became a watershed in the history of revolutionary struggle in Iran. The arrest of the guerrilla revolutionaries and their executions or cold-blooded murder by the police made them overnight martyrs, earning the groups new recruits who continued with deadly attacks against government installations, banks, police headquarters, foreign embassies, and US interests.[3] Even though their failure to spearhead a popular uprising caused a split within the group, with the offshoots favoring a more political mobilization, the Fedaian continued its operations in parallel with its sister organization, the Mujahedin Khalq.

The Islamic leftist Mujahedin Khalq had been established in 1965 by college graduates linked to the religious wing of the National Front.[4] Their secret cells in Tehran grew into branches spreading to other parts of the country, with some members traveling to Jordan for guerrilla training from the PLO. The group developed a detailed strategy of revolution informed by the culture and the "religious psyche" of the Iranian Muslims—a theory that was to find intimate resonance in the teachings of Ali Shariati. In his major work, *Nehzat-e Husseini* (Hussein's movement), the leading theoretician Ahmad Rezaei viewed the struggle of the Iranian people against the shah's tyranny in the same light as the struggle of Imam Hussein, the grandson of the Prophet, against the "feudal class," "big merchants," and "tyrannical caliphs" to establish the Nezam-e Tawhidi, an egalitarian united community.[5] This "classless society" would stand against all forms of oppression, imperialism, capitalism, and the conservative clerical class. The Mujahedin called on Muslims to rise up to establish such an ideal social order. To steer the masses, they began a series of military operations in 1971 targeting government personnel and facilities and US and Israeli interests, robbing banks, and attempting to hijack an Iran Air plane. Even though the regime struck back with arrests and executions, the group continued to grow, even sending volunteers to assist the Dhofar liberation movement in Oman. Interestingly, the crux of the Mujahedin's vision of Iranian society and postrevolutionary order differed little from that of the Marxist Fedaian. The Mujahedin saw Iran as a capitalist social formation dominated by US imperialism and ruled by a repressive regime. Their vision of revolution was to bring about a national economy, end dependency ties, redistribute wealth, give free voice to people, cause a deep social change, and ultimately create a "classless society."[6] Although sympathetic to Marxism, the Mujahedin kept their distance from materialist philosophy. But this was to change as the group increasingly identified its mission with the Cuban, Vietnamese, and Russian revolutions. As they began to mobilize the working class, the majority of the group opted by

1975 for Marxism as the strategy of popular revolution, rejecting Islam for what they considered its "petit-bourgeois ideology." This ideological shift entailed a split within the group into the Marxist and Islamic entities. Yet along with the Fedaian guerrillas both factions continued their campaign until the 1979 uprising opened a space for them to revitalize anew and play a vital role in the victory of the revolution. When the eighteen-month revolutionary uprising in Iran resulted in a dual power situation in February 1979—Ayatollah Khomeini's revolutionary government versus the shah's incumbent regime—these militant leftist guerrillas together with the air force cadets who had defected broke the deadlock through an armed insurrection; they defeated the shah's Imperial Guards, moving Iran toward a new horizon.

Even though the membership and actual operations of the guerrilla revolutionaries had remained limited, their repeated stories, mystique, radical literature, and inclusion of female fighters found considerable appeal among students and workers. The sentiments were translated into a dozen radical leftist organizations once the shah left Iran. While the Fedaian had fewer than fifty members in 1979 (341 guerrilla fighters had been killed between 1971 and 1977), they garnered over one hundred thousand active supporters.[7] The Mujahedin grew even larger and rapidly turned to an organized mass movement. The leftists established their presence in mass rallies, colleges, factories, poor neighborhoods, and the Kurdish and Torkaman provinces. Their May Day event of 1979 brought some five hundred thousand people into the streets.[8] The "epic of Siahkal," the symbol of Iran's guerrilla movement, had already become a favorite theme in the literary and artistic works of key Iranian intellectuals such as the poets M. Azarm, Shafiei Kadkani, and Ahmad Shamlou. Many of us among the students and intelligentsia in the late 1970s were fascinated by the heroism and mystical aura of underground politics these movements displayed. The images of the young female guerrillas holding up cumbersome Kalashnikovs had garnered much attention among the nonreligious youth and liberal intelligentsia.

Islamism

Such images were absent from the camp of Islamists, who were yet to forge a cohesive movement. Indeed, an Islamist movement was in the making when it was interrupted by an Islamic revolution.[9] Yet scattered pious clusters and sentiments did adhere to a broad "Islamic politics," whose growth occurred primarily after the revolution. They had sought inspiration from such clerics as Ayatollah Morteza Motahhari and Mahmud Taleqani, as well as Ayatollah Ruhollah Khomeini, whose opposition to the shah exiled him to Iraq in 1964,[10] where he articulated his theory of *vilayat-i faqih* (guardianship of the jurist) in the treatise *Hokumat-e Eslami* (Islamic government) in the early 1970s.[11] Even though this mostly unknown text was originally intended as a matter of Shia jurisprudence, Islamist zealots used it during the revolution as a blueprint for governance. Another intellectual inspiration came from the Egyptian Sayyid Qutb, whose well-known pamphlet *Ma'alim fi al-Tariq* (Milestones) had been translated into Persian by the cleric Ali Khamenei, who would become the supreme leader of the Islamic Republic of Iran.

In this text, Sayyid Qutb had articulated an elaborate vision of Islamic revolution.[12] He argued that since capitalism failed the majority of the people, liberal democracy had to borrow ideas from socialism to remedy the system. But socialism itself is no panacea. Marxism, which promised salvation and attracted much support, has been reduced to mere "thoughts" because the decline of the Russian economy displayed the failure of Marxism in practice, which after all is "antithetical to the nature of human instincts and its needs." Given the failures of both capitalism and Marxism, Qutb argued, the "leadership of humanity by Western man is close to an end . . . because it no longer has any of the 'values' that make such leadership possible."[13] Only Islam is capable of leading humanity toward salvation and prosperity, he proclaimed. With the failure of nationalism, patriotism, and territorial movements, no credible ideology remains but Islam. The Quran, according to Qutb, has already set the stage by recognizing the umma, the community of believers, as God's successor on earth. But to achieve this, the umma should be revived from its decline by European science, technology, and colonialism. To assume the leadership of humankind, Muslims should not focus on material achievements, in which Europe is certainly superior; rather, they should build on "faith" and "way of life." It is only these values that can overturn our current state of *jahiliyya* (a term Qutb borrowed from the Indian Abul A'la Maududi), where God's sovereignty has given way to that of man through the system of laws and norms. Muslims should reinstate the worship and sovereignty of God. This "absolutely perfect" model is totally new and needs to be put into practice. To this end, a dedicated "vanguard" unpolluted by jahiliyya values must be set up to prepare the way for an Islamic order. This vanguard should receive its "signposts" from the primary source of Islam—the Quran, the "way of life." All other sources—

Greek, European, Persian, or Chinese inspirations—must be discarded. This, according to Qutb, was the Prophet's way but has been ignored through centuries of innovations and additions. The vanguard, just like the early companions of the Prophet, must pursue "learning for action" while avoiding the pollution of the *jahili* ideas, culture, and leadership that has dominated our lives today. "We must return to the beginning," Qutb insisted, "to the unadulterated source from which [the first-generation Muslims] derived guidance, the content of which was unalloyed and free of defect."[14]

Clearly, Qutb envisioned a new social order for the Muslim world. In this sense, he was a revolutionary among the ranks of the "nineteenth Century Russian revolutionary Chernyshevsky, and later, Lenin," according to his biographer John Calvert.[15] Yet his idea of revolution developed on the global stage where revolutions were the common feature of the time. Thus, from being among the nationalist literati of Egypt's "liberal age," Qutb moved by the late 1940s to become the exemplary theorist of Islamism, especially after his return from a two-year visit to the United States with a dislike of the American culture—"superficiality," "hedonism," and "free sexual mixing."[16] From joining the Muslim Brothers after 1952 and supporting Gamal Abdel Nasser's revolution, Qutb continued to disparage anything that had to do with *jahili* society. Yet he maintained an admiration for a socialist economy, embracing the ideas of welfare, distribution, and justice; he considered labor as the sole source of value and the state as the regulator of the economy; he called for a national economy and denounced imperialism, accumulation of wealth, and business monopoly. While Qutb lamented the "absence" of moral values and spirituality in communism, he revered its egalitarian ethos. Yet he found social justice intrinsic to Islamic ethics, something that, unlike communism, was indigenous to Muslims' psyche.[17] His was a notion of social justice that combined the egalitarian tenet of socialism and the spiritual depth of Christianity.[18] Such a third-way strategy, exemplified in "neither East nor West," became a prominent theme in the thought of the postcolonial radical intelligentsia.[19] Qutb's economic ideas informed many other Arab Islamic writers, among them the Iraqi Shia cleric Ayatollah Muhammad Baqir al-Sadr (1935–1980), whose multivolume *Iqtisaduna* (Our economics) found much popularity among the Iranian revolutionary Islamists during the late 1970s, including the first president of the Islamic Republic, Abolhassan Banisadr, who developed his own *Divine Economics*. Qutb's notions of "neither East nor West," *tawghout* (tyrant), and *hizballah* (party of God) found powerful echoes among the Islamist rulers in postrevolutionary Iran, and his jahiliyya reflected the conservative philosopher Ahmad Fardid's "westoxification" but distanced him greatly from Ali Shariati, whose liberatory ideas had unparalleled impact on the youth and intelligentsia of prerevolutionary Iran.

Ali Shariati

Ali Shariati, not Ayatollah Khomeini, is considered the "ideologue" and "architect" of the Iranian revolution of 1979.[20] Shariati is reputed to be both an intellectual, who offered a scathing critique of Marxism and other "Western fallacies" from a radical Islamic point of view,[21] and a revolutionary who drew on "Marxist social ideas" to advance a biting critique of capitalism and traditional religion.[22] There is little disagreement about Shariati's role in transforming and redefining the ideological perspective of millions of literate Iranian youth. Shariati provided his audience with solid but complex ideological tools to envision a political project that transcended the rigid boundaries between Islam and the Marxian social and economic imagination. And he did so by reinterpreting Islam through "scientific" concepts employed by modern social theory—an interpretation that neither the traditional clerics nor the likes of Sayyid Qutb were capable of formulating.[23]

In the late 1970s, when the university students in Tehran were involved in Islamic and leftist debates, I could see that our rival Islamic students would rely almost entirely on the teachings of Shariati to advance their fierce discussions. At that time activism did not mean doing civil society or NGO work as in the Middle East prior to the Arab Spring; rather, it meant enacting and engaging in political education. So each ideological camp on college campuses developed its own organization, reading groups, library, hiking trips, dress code, and, most important, a distinctive language for everyday exchange. Both groups would compete avidly in their efforts to recruit new members. But at times they would make tactical alliances, for instance, during strike planning, handing out leaflets, and similar sensitive activities. We had our heroes, and they had theirs. The men we praised included Marx, Lenin, Stalin, Castro, Fanon, Che Guevara, and similar people. Their heroes ranged from al-Afghani, Iqbal Lahouri, and Imam Musa Sadr to Mirza Khuchik Khan Janghali, the Mujahedin Rezaei, and Ayatollah Khomeini. For them Shariati, however, was the greatest of heroes.

What defined Shariati's unique moral leadership was his ability to interweave his seeming intellectual sophistication with unrelenting revolutionary politics, which captured the spirit of his audience in those unsettled and repressive moments in Pahlavi Iran. Such a political-intellectual makeup at the time of the revolution was reflected in the perplexity among many observers about what kind of intellectual he was, if indeed they ever seriously engaged his disquieting ideas.[24] Shariati's political philosophy made him immensely popular during the revolution of 1979, when thousands of his lecture tapes and pamphlets were circulated among the Islamic youth. His reputation traveled beyond Iran, and the bulk of his works were translated into English, Arabic, German, Malay, Turkish, and other languages. He was regarded as one of the most prominent Islamic thinkers of his time.[25]

Yet his intellectual and political project was significantly different from the Islamist currents of the conservative Salafis, the violent jihadis, or the post-Islamist variants of the AKP (Justice and Development Party), which take neoliberal orthodoxy for granted. Shariati is too liberal for Islamists and too socialist for the post-Islamists. His revolutionary ideas on Islam particularly have inspired the groups of the Islamic left around the world, including the Turkish anticapitalist Muslims and their leader, Ihsan Eliacik. But his paradigm, just like Qutb's, developed at the cost of turning Islam as a religion and spirituality into an ideology of revolution.

Intellectual Life

Ali Shariati was born in 1933 in a village in the northern province of Khorasan, where he completed his primary and secondary school education.[26] His mother was from a landowning family, and his father was a well-known local Islamic thinker and teacher who introduced modern critical thinkers to his students. Shariati's father had formed a short-lived Movement of God-Worshipping Socialists, in which Ali was a member and through which he acquired his first critical Islamic education. During his college years in the Mashhad Teachers' College, he studied Arabic and in 1956 translated *Abuzar Ghafari: The God-Worshipping Socialist*, the story of the legendary companion of the Prophet who voiced dissent against the early caliphs and was a model combatant for justice. Shariati continued his studies at Mashhad University in Arabic and French languages. In the meantime, he was involved, together with his father's group, in reviving the outlawed National Front—a political coalition originally founded by the nationalist prime minister Mosaddeq in the late 1940s. For this activity, Shariati and his comrades spent eight months in prison.

He traveled to Paris in 1956, spending over a decade in this capital of a major colonial power. The journey proved to be a watershed in Shariati's political life and intellectual development. The Paris years had coincided with the escalating anticolonial struggles throughout the world, in particular Africa, where France had many colonies. He began to study philology at the Sorbonne, became engaged in anti-imperialist and student politics, and edited two antiregime Persian journals. Meanwhile, he worked on translating books by radical, Marxist, and Orientalist writers such as Che Guevara, Jean-Paul Sartre, Frantz Fanon, and Louis Massignon (a well-known scholar of Islamic mysticism) and developed a keen interest in Western Orientalism and radical Catholicism. He was also exposed to the ideas of French sociologists such as Raymond Aron, Roger Garaudy, Georges Politzer, and especially the eminent French dialectician Georges Gurvitch.

After his return to Iran in 1965, Shariati was immediately put into prison for eight months for his political activities abroad. In the following years he spent five years in the city of Mashhad teaching at the College of Literature and lived most of the remainder of his life in Tehran, where he began the most productive period of his political and intellectual life. From 1969 to 1972, he lectured at the Hosseinieh Irshad, a modern Islamic center located in the northern Tehran district of Gholhak. His lectures were mostly taped and then published in several dozen volumes; of these books the most important was the multivolume *Islam-Shenasi* (Islamology). They were circulated widely among Muslim youth in the 1970s.

The Hosseinieh center was shut down in 1972 by the government on the grounds that it had become a breeding ground for the activities of Mujahedin Khalq, a radical Islamic-Marxist group that had launched armed struggle against the shah's regime. For many the Mujahedin Khalq were the children of Shariati's political vision, and indeed Gholhak in my own experience had become a locus of underground activities associated with Shariati's ideas. This included the Forqan group, whose militant anticlericalism led to the assassination of one and an attempt on another prominent cleric just after the Iranian revolution. In the view of historian Ervand Abrahamian, however, the conservative clerics also played a crucial part in hampering Shariati's lectures at the Hosseinieh, for they suspected that Shariati was promoting not Islam but Western philosophies, in particular Marxist sociology. After the closure of the Hosseinieh center, Shariati was arrested and charged with having connections with the Mujahedin organization. This time he was to endure eighteen months behind bars. After his release, a series of essays titled "Insan, Islam va Marxism" (Man, Islam, and Marxism) appeared in the widely circulated official daily *Kayhan* and were attributed to Shariati. In 1977, a year before the beginning of the revolutionary protests, Shariati managed to leave the country for Europe. A month after arriving in England, he suspiciously died in London. His death brought a deep sorrow and sadness to Iran's opposition groups, including us, the leftists. Even though the British authorities attributed his death to a massive heart attack, SAVAK was blamed and Shariati was remembered as the first *shahid*, martyr of the revolution. Shariati's death, contrary to the hopes of those who shunned him, enhanced his reputation, rendering him a virtual legend among millions of enthusiasts.

Islamic Marxism

The key to Shariati's undisputable reputation, intellectual influence, his perceived danger was his Islamic Marxism—his attempt to implant major Marxist concepts—imperialism, exploitation, class struggle, classless society, infrastructure, and suprastructure—into the teachings of such Shiite leaders as Imam Ali, Imam Hussein, and Abu Zar Ghaffari (whom Shariati called the first "God-worshipping socialist") to articulate an indigenous radical project, an Iranian theory of revolution.[27] In those unnerving prerevolutionary years of the late 1970s, and against the background of the grand left-Islamic divide, Shariati's ideas provided the grounds for a possible discursive link between the two political trends, a strategy that was badly needed.

In the 1970s in Iran, two main radical political trends appeared to raise the banner of armed struggle against the shah's regime: first, the Islamic trend whose militant expression was embodied in the organization Mujahedin Khalq, on which Shariati's ideas had left deep imprints; and second, the Marxist trend identified with the organized activism of the Fedaian Khalq, a Leninist guerrilla movement. Despite their vanguardist makeup, the social reverberation of their armed operations on the political class was quite considerable. Apprehensive of the consequences, the regime attempted to prevent cooperation and alliance of any sort between the two political trends. The clerical leaders remained uninterested in forging or encouraging such an alliance. If anything, they would not hesitate to publicly denounce the Marxists, expressing the kind of mistrust to which a crude Marxism, dependence on the Soviet Union, and the political misdeeds of the Tudeh Communist Party had contributed. I can recall the systematic attacks against the "materialists" by the leading clerics of the Hosseinieh center, Ayatollah Mutahhari and Ayatollah Mofatteh, as well as Mehdi Bazargan, the first prime minister of the Islamic Republic, in the Qoba Mosque in Gholhak in the autumn of 1977.[28] But unlike the positions of these religious leaders, the overall position of the more influential Ali Shariati would be against sectarianism or denunciation of the Marxists as atheists or immoral. On the contrary, Shariati would praise the "revolutionary left" because they "work for the benefit of the deprived people."[29] At this time when pro-Western Muslim states (Egypt, Morocco, and Indonesia) were bolstering Islamism as the ideological enemy to undermine Marxist opposition, Shariati's vision to unite both forces was deemed politically dangerous. It is not surprising that the shah's regime attempted to generate suspicion and division. One such attempt was the fabrication in 1977 of one of Shariati's key texts in the state-run daily *Keyhan* in which Marxism was disparaged.[30]

Was Shariati, then, a Marxist who disguised himself under the Islamic mantle? Certainly Shariati was not a Marxist, but he did consider himself a socialist and was indeed influenced by Marxist social ideas. Reportedly, he even stated that "if I were not a believer, I would have been a Marxist."[31] The atheist Jean-Paul Sartre had stated about Shariati's religion, "If I were to choose one [religion], it would be that of Shariati's." Shariati drew considerably from Marxist concepts, applying them systematically in his critical works. As historian Ervand Abrahamian observes, Shariati's paradoxical attitude toward Marx originated from his identification of not one but three Marxes. First was the younger Marx, predominantly a philosopher who was seen by Shariati as a strongly antireligion economic reductionist and atheist. The second was the mature Marx, mainly a social scientist who discovered the laws of motion of societies, developed a theory of historical determinism, and promoted the notions of praxis and revolutionary practice. And the third, the older Marx, was chiefly a politician whom Shariati saw in a similar vein as other Marxist politicians such as Karl Kautsky, Friedrich Engels, and even Joseph Stalin, who in his opinion compromised the ideals of the oppressed classes in their political practice. Shariati rejected the first and third Marx but embraced the second one.[32]

In his *Insan, Islam va Marxism*, Shariati takes to task the Western humanist philosophies, chiefly Marxism, by drawing on a radical "Islamic conception of man." Shariati argues that Western philosophies, including liberalism, existentialism, and Marxism, do possess a humanistic perspective, but their

humanism is materialistic. Western humanism rests firmly on Greek myth-
ological perspective in which a constant struggle exists between humanity
and the gods who want to maintain man in darkness and ignorance. Here,
man is praised and given higher value than that of the gods. But, according to
Shariati, this kind of humanism establishes a distance between man and god.
All of the great Western humanists from Denis Diderot and Voltaire to Ludwig
Feuerbach and Marx have erroneously equated the tyrannical and antihuman
Greek gods with the spiritual gods such as Ahuramazda, Rama, the Tao, the
Messiah, and Allah. Thus, since these Western philosophers incorrectly gener-
alize the Greek distinction of human versus God/spirituality, their humanism
remains earthly, unheavenly, and materialistic. This explains why the "communist societies" are not much different from their bourgeois counterparts
in their understanding of humans; for in both everything culminates in man,
and both disregard "the spiritual dimension of the human essence."[33] Indeed,
Western humanism is atheistic in another sense, Shariati argues, in that it considers man by nature to possess a moral conscience that shapes his values and
therefore acts as a substitute for God. In establishing a distance between man
and God, the Western humanist philosophies exhibit ignorance of the Eastern religions such as Hinduism, Islam, and Sufism, which are grounded in
the *unity*, not distance, between God and man. Eastern humanism, unlike its
Western counterpart, is heavenly.

Whereas Marx, drawing on Greek humanism, perceives religion as an ir-
rational entity built on human helplessness, Shariati believes that religious
notions like heaven and hell are rational and scientific. In addition, Shariati op-
poses Marx's consideration of religion, ethics, morality, and virtues as elements
of a "superstructure" shaped by economic forces. In the Marxist paradigm man
has neither independent and noble reality nor any significant place in history;
lacking agency, he is the creation of his environment. Consequently, historical
events according to Marx are not the outcome of human acts but of the contra-
diction between the forces and relations of production. So, Shariati wonders,
where is the place of all those martyrs in history and all those social upheavals
and revolutions in Marxist thought? In truth, this Marxism that boasts of being
a ruthless critique of capitalism has ended up sharing the same values as its
enemy—productivism, mechanism, techno-bureaucracy, acquisitiveness, economic competition, and materialism.

Only Islam, Shariati contends, possesses true humanism. In Islam, humanism is the assortment of divine values that makes up man's morals and religious

and cultural heritage. In the Islamic concept of *tawhid* man is a contradictory being, possessing the dual essence of clay and divine spirit, of dust and God; he has the will to choose one over the other. It follows that, first, in Islam a human has nobility not on her own but only in relation to God; and second, humankind has a destiny as well as a choice. Possession of choice confers on man a "responsibility" to elevate himself from "dust" toward unity with God. This responsibility for Shariati is a highly critical concept, the implications of which he extends from philosophy and theology to political struggle. In this vein, Shariati implicitly calls on the Third World masses in general and Muslims in particular to elevate themselves from captivity to deliverance, to become "God's regents on earth."[34] "Responsibility to liberate ourselves" implies self-reliance—more precisely, cultural, political, and strategic self-reliance, which in plain Cold War language means "neither East nor West," neither capitalism nor communism, but "return to self"—to a historical, cultural, and religious self—an idea that resonates in Qutb.

While critical of Marxian humanist philosophy, Shariati embraced Marx's social theory, the theory of history. In his last two books, *Jahatgiri-ye tabaqati-ye Islam* (The class bias of Islam) and *Ommat va imamat* (Community and leadership), Shariati systematically employs Marxian concepts to elaborate on the political economy of Islam, even though he attempts to reformulate them to address the historical specificity of Iran and the Middle East. For instance, Shariati borrowed his theory of knowledge from Marxism, but he ultimately moved toward phenomenology.[35] He inverted Marx's ideological superstructure into ideological infrastructure to stress the role of ideas, faith, and the Shia doctrine in political and economic transformation. His envisioned classless society was rendered "divine"; his historical determinism appeared more like the will of God; and his notion of class, influenced by the prominent French sociologist Georges Gurvitch of the 1960s, was not limited to simply economic class formed by material interests but also political class shaped by religious beliefs, symbols, traditions, customs, and cultural norms. With such a political conception of class, Shariati suggested that in the Third World, especially in the Muslim Middle East, the only class capable of bringing about a profound change and providing leadership was not the proletariat but the intellectual class (*rowshanfikran*)—notably, university students and the literate milieu. He considered this formulation significant because Iranian class formation in the Marxian sense was only in its nascent stage—very different from the European experience where "the intellectual is dealing with a worker who has

41

gone through three centuries of the Middle Ages and two centuries of the capitalist system" and where the proletariat "has attained a higher degree of growth and self-consciousness." But in Iran, "we still do not have a working class in our society. What we have are groups."[36]

Just as Shariati refashioned certain Marxist concepts, he also redefined a number of fundamental notions of Islam. For him, the biblical story of Cain and Abel is only a symbolization of Marxian "historical determinism"—that is, the class struggle between the oppressors/exploiters represented by Cain and the oppressed/exploited symbolized by Abel. But these forces are not economic classes in the orthodox Marxian scheme; they are "political classes." In a sense, Shariati's emphasis on the primacy of the political over the economic and of masses over economic classes as the agents of historical change represents a redefinition of historical determinism when applied to the particular situation of Iran. It was particularly well suited to Iran's Shia Islam, which, according to Shariati, uniquely differed from other religions in its greater potential to serve as a revolutionary ideology. In other words, Shia Islam functioned as a key element in the "ideological infrastructure" to transform society and shape its economic structure.[37] In this understanding, the Shia belief in *intizar*, or anticipation of the resurrection of the hidden twelfth Imam, does not mean passively waiting for justice; it means an active involvement in struggle against injustice to realize justice. This is a struggle in which, according to Shariati's historical determinism, victory is a certainty. But Shi'ism itself is not free from contestation; it is subjected to an intense struggle between the oppressors and the oppressed. The oppressors tend to turn Shi'ism into a religion of domination, the "Safavid Shia," and the oppressed class renders it an ideology of liberation as manifested in the Alavid, or "red Shia," of which the historical Imam Hussein was a champion. Shariati places the heaviest charge on the ulema for establishing or nourishing the oppressive Shi'ism. Because of their simplemindedness, fatalism, and monopolistic control over the interpretation of religion, according to Shariati, the ulema have kept "true Islam" away from the masses, while their alliance with the political and economic elites has changed Shi'ism from a revolutionary creed to a conservative ideology in the service of power. While he insisted, against Fanon, on critically reviving religious legacy in the fight against imperialism, Shariati vehemently opposed any form of "religious government." For the "natural consequence of such a government is dictatorship, because the cleric views himself as God's representative who carries out His order on earth."[38]

Thus, what determined Shariati's stand toward political forces was not whether they were religious or nonreligious, but how *revolutionary* they were. Similarly in his view, *kufr* (blasphemy) should never apply to "those who deny the existence of God and soul"; rather, it should take to task those who are unwilling to take "concrete" action for the cause of liberation, that is, to establish a "divine classless society."[39] Consequently, Shariati, unlike most of the clerics, refused to disparage the Marxists on the grounds that they were philosophically materialists, atheists, amoral, and *kafir* (blasphemous). Instead, he developed a sustained critique of the clerical class and their raison d'être, the *fiqh* (Islamic jurisprudence). "Our mosques, the revolutionary left, and our [underdog] preachers," Shariati declared, "work for the benefit of the deprived people and against the lavish and lush." But "our clerics who teach jurisprudence and issue fatwas are right-wingers, capitalists, and conservative; simply, our *fiqh* is at the service of capitalism."[40] Shariati then presents a wholly different understanding of Shi'ism as an ideology of class struggle:

> It is shortsighted to consider Shi'ism in terms of the conflicts between Ali and Abu-Bakr or Umar. Rather, Shi'ism was the continuation of a movement that, in human culture, notably in the history of Abrahamite culture, fought against class disparity, exploitation, coercion, and injustice to safeguard *tawhid*; it fought for human unity against racism, for class justice against oligarchy and obedience, for rights against deceit, ignorance, and magic. In the history of Islam, this struggle expressed itself in the battle between the Prophet and the Quraysh oligarchy; then, between Islam and the Persian and Roman Empires. And when Islam itself turned into a system at the service of the ruling power, Shi'ism . . . now embodied in the person of Imam Ali continued this historic mission to struggle for freedom and justice.[41]

Third Worldism

Shariati's approach to acclimatize Marxism was by no means unique in that juncture in the history of the Third World. In fact, it represented a typical tendency among many postcolonial radical intellectuals and anticolonial activists in the developing world. Frantz Fanon, Aimé Césaire, Kwame Nkrumah, Julius Nyerere, Jomo Kenyatta, and Ahmed Ben Bella, among others, embarked on "alternative" politico-economic projects, which were based on a pronounced rejection of capitalism, with an emphasis on national and indigenous resources, values, and institutions. They embraced Marxian collectivist and egalitarian ethics to merge with their indigenous emancipatory values to forge a third-way development strategy. Julius Nyerere of Tanzania wrote in 1962:

> The foundation and the objective of African socialism is the extended family. ... "Ujamaa," then, or "familyhood" describes our socialism. It is opposed to capitalism, which seeks to build a happy society on the basis of the exploitation of man by man; and it is equally opposed to doctrinaire socialism which seeks to build a happy society on a philosophy of inevitable conflict between man and man. We, in Africa, have no more need of being "converted" to socialism than we have of being "taught" democracy. Both are rooted in our own past—in the traditional society which produced us.[42]

For the most part, this third-way strategy was eventuated in some kinds of "indigenous socialisms," including Arab, Ba'athist, and African socialisms, as well as the "non-capitalist path to development." Politically, it is embodied in "Third-Worldist populism," a regime type that adhered to a nationalistic ideology and development strategy, resting socially on the support of the popular classes (workers, peasants, and poor people) while promoting a state capitalist economic policy often within an authoritarian polity.[43] It represented an ideological package that blended nationalism, radicalism, and antidependency with anti-industrialism and anticapitalism. This way of thinking blamed the general underdevelopment of Third World nations wholly on the basis of their economic, political, and cultural dependence on Western imperialism. The radical intellectuals of the Third World in the postwar period broadly followed such an ideological outlook, although they differed in the degree of their adherence to socialism, anticapitalism, anti-industrialism, and democracy.

This ideological tendency was partly rooted in the "dependency paradigm"—initiated chiefly by the Latin American economists such as Raul Prebisch in the 1940s and later developed and popularized by such thinkers as André Gunder Frank, Ferdinando Cardoso, and Theotonio Dos Santos in the 1960s and 1970s. The dependency paradigm advanced a major critique of the modernization theory that had explained the "underdevelopment" of the Third World in terms of a natural stage in their eventual evolution to a higher stage of "mass consumption." It had further stressed that an organic relation of these countries with the Western capitalist economies would accelerate this "take-off."[44] The dependency paradigm, in contrast, attributed the underdevelopment of the Third World or the "periphery" to its incorporation into the world capitalist system, or the "center," through colonization, unequal exchange, and neocolonialism.[45] However, in regard to the relations of domination between the center and the periphery, the unit of analysis remained regions, nations, and countries rather than social classes. Countries or nations were deemed exploited or dominated by the advanced capitalist countries. This meant that in a dependent country, the struggle against imperialism would require a strategy of national unity in which all classes, including workers, peasants, the poor, students, the old and new middle classes, and the national bourgeoisie would join together in a united front.

Third Worldism was also a product of the socioeconomic conditions of these new states. Most of these countries were ex-colonies or had gone through a neocolonial dependency. Colonialism had a devastating impact on their social and economic fabric, distorting their indigenous culture, traditions, and value systems. In response, the political and intellectual class developed a strong resistance against capitalism as a socioeconomic system and against Western technology and industrialism as the embodiment of cultural dominance. In Iran, the earlier reaction came from the prominent author Jalal Al-e Ahmad in his powerful essay "Gharbzadegi" (Westoxification), which became the bible of the leftist, nationalist, and Islamic activists in those prerevolutionary times.[46] In this essay, Al-e Ahmad launched a powerful assault on capitalist industrialism and its distressing impact on the local economies. "Once the [modern] machine established itself in the towns and the villages," he lamented, "no matter whether it is an engine mill or a textile factory, it would lay off the laborers of the local industry, make the water mills obsolete, the hand looms redundant, destroying the production of carpets, rugs, and felt."[47] Once a member of the Tudeh Communist Party, he advocated the revival of Shi'ism as the only ideology that would withstand the spread of westoxification.

Capitalist colonialism also caused a strong feeling of national unity and resentment against foreign domination. This blend of nationalist and anticapitalist thought shaped the eclectic ideology of the radical intellectuals in the postcolonial world. The concepts of class and class struggle were deployed but were overshadowed by those of people, nation, and masses or were otherwise redefined to fit in with the nationalist/anticapitalist frame of thought. Thus, Shariati came to define class not only as an economic entity but primarily as a political formation, with the "committed intellectual class" as the driving force of society. And Julius Nyerere was convinced that the concept of class struggle did not apply to a society such as that in Tanzania, which had been organized along the principle of *ujamaa* (familyhood). *Ujamaa*, he argued, was marked by the convergence rather than conflict of interests between members. What further reinforced such an ideological eclecticism was the fact that most of these societies were still in the earlier phases of industrialization, so the masses of peasantry, urban poor, and state employees overshadowed the small industrial working class.

While Western imperialism and the Third World's internal dynamics pushed the radical intellectuals to embrace nationalism, anticapitalism, and Marxian social justice, the repressive policies of the Soviet bloc made many of them weary of Marxist-Leninist doctrine. This intelligentsia resented the subservience of their communist parties to the USSR and were horrified by Soviet suppression of democratic dissent in Hungary in 1956 and then Czechoslovakia in 1968, as well as the clampdown on oppositional voices in the communist bloc. Other segments of postcolonial intelligentsia either remained unaware of these developments or dismissed the claims of the Stalinist atrocities as bourgeois nonsense and imperialist propaganda. Many of them continued to embrace the orthodox Marxism of their own communist parties.

Ideas as Material Force

For some like Ali Shariati the idea of "return to self" came to articulate liberation from imperialism by return to national identity, indigenous values, and cultural heritage. In both Latin America and the Middle East, religion, as a deep-rooted cultural form, acted as the language of liberation, and in Africa the precolonial cultural and institutional norms served as the necessary elements for ideological self-reliance. While in Latin America radical Catholicism and liberation theology operated side by side with Marxist socialism and anarcho-syndicalism, in the Middle East political Islam emerged as an alternative language for nationalist and anti-imperialist struggles, in parallel with and often in competition with Marxian socialism. Like many of his Third World counterparts, Shariati had resorted to Shia Islam to articulate a political ideology and cultural form that, he thought, had profound roots among ordinary Iranians. He blended Islam and Marxian social justice to launch his Islamic reformation as a path to the liberation of his nation. His "red Islam" offered a frame within which both the Muslim and secular left could find a common trajectory in their revolutionary endeavors.

Indeed, it was this red Islam that captured the imagination of such secular revolutionary heroes as Khosrow Golsorkhi—a Marxist journalist and poet who before his execution by the shah's regime delivered a stunning defense in the military tribunal in 1974.[48] In a live televised trial, he stated, "I begin my remarks with a saying from Imam Hussein, the great martyr of the peoples of the Middle East. . . . I am a Marxist-Leninist, but I sought social justice first in Islam and then arrived at socialism."[49] Addressing the unyielding military judges, he proclaimed, "I will act as my own defense attorney in a court whose legality or legitimacy I do not recognize. As a Marxist, my plea is to the masses and history. The more you attack me, the more I pride myself; the farther I am from you, the closer I am to the people; the more your hatred for my beliefs, the stronger the kindness and compassion of the masses. Even if you bury me— and you certainly will—people will make flags and songs from my corpse." For the youth of the 1970s like myself who were watching such a remarkable performance live on television, Golsorkhi echoed the sentiment of scores of revolutionaries who transcended Islam and the left divide by drawing on the radical and progressive thrust that these intellectuals, most notably Shariati, projected.

It is no wonder that, during the Iranian revolution, Shariati emerged as an unparalleled revolutionary intellectual; his portrait was carried, and his nickname, "mo'allem-e enqilab" (revolutionary mentor) was chanted by millions of demonstrators. The anticapitalist chants such as "Saving the downtrodden: This is the people's slogan" (*nejat-e mostaz'afin shoar-e mellat-e mast*) or "The capitalist system must be dismantled" (*nezam-e saramaye-dari nabood bayad gardad*) reflected the radical sentiments that Marxists and Shariati had espoused. Shariati's writings and lectures, taped or transcribed, had already been widely circulated even to school pupils and rural dwellers. My father, barely literate, had his own copies, and a friend's mother read whatever she found from Shariati. Almost every student library in colleges carried Shariati's multiple works. A foundation was created after the revolution to print, publish, and circulate his works, now in forty-six volumes, worldwide. Ayatollah Khomeini had reportedly read all Shariati's (and Al-e Ahmad's) works,[50] and the conservative clerics eulogized this anticlerical intellectual in the 1980s because of his immense popularity. Shariati, who had translated Che Guevara's *Guerrilla Warfare*, nourished the ideology of the Mujahedin, the guerrilla organization that grew just after the revolution to become a mass movement with significant social and political influence. Shariati's notions of "return to self" and "neither East nor West" remained a key policy of the Islamic Republic, inscribed in the constitution. The anticapitalist thrust of Shariati's project informed the political thinking of many on the religious left who took charge of the new institutions in the Islamic Republic. And his Islamic socialism, along with the ideas and activism of the Marxist left, became the ideological anchor for the radical politics and grassroots movements that sprang up just after the Iranian revolution in the provinces, universities, neighborhoods, farms, and factories. Chapter 3 discusses these revolutionary repertoires.

3   Revolution in the Everyday

Revolutionary episodes typically involve the eruption of various popular movements to assert their claims and share the "fruits of the revolution." The collapse of the state machine and police control opens an exceptional space for the subaltern groups to embark on extraordinary efforts to pursue self-realization and redistribute power, property, and opportunity. In Iran, just days after the downfall of the shah, industrial workers, urban poor, humble farmers, the academic community, and air force cadets moved to take control or intervene in the organization of workplaces, urban neighborhoods, rural communities, universities, and the military units by establishing shuras (popular committees). The shuras embodied both the administrative organ and political ambition of these grassroots movements; their principles entered the constitution of the Islamic Republic. Similar radical democratic measures emerged in varied degrees in most revolutions of the 1970s—from the Sandinista revolution in Nicaragua to those in Portugal, Angola, and Mozambique, as well as in Chile under Salvador Allende. They aspired to alternative property regimes to reduce inequality in power and property.

These were the movements of exceptional times, the revolutionary moments of rupture—dysfunctional states, disrupted economies, novel popular consciousness, and utopian visions—that complicate the standard accounts of social movements deemed a "normal part of politics."[1] These repertoires of exceptional times were not simply sustained collective actions to compel authorities to make reforms in an organized way; rather, they embarked on direct actions to reorganize the social and economic institutions that shaped the people's collective lives. In depth and extent, they went beyond *horizontalidad*, the radical grassroots initiatives for self-rule that emerged in Argentina following its 2001 financial crisis.[2] These movements and the changes they ushered in symbolized the revolution in the everyday; they expressed what the revolution meant for the grassroots.

By retelling the story of the shuras, notably workers' councils, in Iran as an instance of the broader popular quest for grassroots democracy and redistribution, I highlight the dynamics of revolutionary repertoires and strategies that marked the revolutions of the 1970s.[3] Such radical repertoires found few inroads in the Arab Spring, pointing to a key difference between the Arab Spring and the revolutions of the 1970s. Whereas radical repertoires of this sort in the Iranian revolution received ample intellectual and practical input from the secular and religious Left (Marxists and adherents of Shariati), the reformist trajectories and neoliberal climate in the Arab revolutions stifled their drive.

Shura Movements

The fall of the shah followed eighteen months of mass protests and a nationally organized general strike culminating in two days of armed insurrections on February 10–11, 1979, which paved the way for the establishment of the Islamic Republic. Between the collapse of the old and the blossoming of the new order emerged an exceptional political opportunity that the subaltern subjects utilized to claim self-realization in the streets, farms, neighborhoods, universities, factories, government offices, and even in the army. These actions were not simply anarchy or chaos—in fact, there was little evidence of assaults on fellow citizens or property in pursuit of opportunistic self-interest. Rather, they reflected a powerful quest for self-rule, redistribution of social goods, and establishment of an alternative order in conditions where the old order of things had been tattered. Businessmen had abandoned companies; managers left factories; the rich deserted their properties in the frenzy of fleeing to the West, while agribusinesses and construction sites stood idle, and schools and colleges were in disarray. To fill the vacuum, the revolutionaries and the ordinary people moved to take over and run these enterprises by creating popular shuras.

Universities were the first to experience change. They had been a hotbed of revolutionary activities from the beginning of the protests in the fall of 1977. Student chapters of multiple Marxist, leftist Mujahedin, and Islamist groups established headquarters on college campuses. With office spaces, equipment, books, and pamphlets, they utilized the headquarters to hold meetings, discuss politics, organize extracurricular activities, and continue mobilizing. Once the shah's regime collapsed, students and employees called for the establishment of university councils with representatives from the faculty, staff, and students to make decisions democratically concerning university governance. To the dismay of the new government, students demanded to elect the presidents, participate in design of the curriculum, and be part of the governance structure.

While students were busy with campus and street politics, the migrant and urban poor had launched a spectacular takeover of mainly public lands that expanded the urban areas on an extraordinary scale. The land area of Tehran doubled in just two years; and some five hundred thousand hectares of land developed in this fashion between 1979 and 1983. Only days after the fall of the shah, many rural migrants had rushed into the cities to harvest the fruits of revolution—free housing—that some clerical leaders had promised to the downtrodden. In these turbulent times when the Islamic elites and secular leftist groups were intensely vying for popular support, the urban poor took advantage of the opportunity to advance their own claims to the city space, sidewalks, urban lands, empty apartments, and abandoned hotels. In the slums and squatter communities, the poor residents established neighborhood councils with the aid of the leftist organizations to manage and attend to local needs. Partly originating in the neighborhood committees that had surfaced during the revolution to tackle the hardship caused by the general strike, the neighborhood councils aimed to protect, manage, and upgrade the local communities through the participation of residents; they served as the embodiment of the civic dimension of the revolution.[4] In 1980, the city of Isfahan formally adopted the initiative, and Tehran and other urban and rural centers followed.[5]

Drawing on the idea of "land to the tillers," the peasant movements galvanized vast numbers of rural people, notably the landless peasants and smallholders (who owned less than five hectares) in the northern and western provinces, to appropriate farmlands belonging to the state and big landowners and demanded waivers on debt from banks.[6] Farmers launched collective petitions, protested at government offices, staged sit-ins and street demonstrations, and in this fashion brought the agrarian question to the top of the political agenda. Not only did the rural poor backed by the Marxist groups move to seize farmlands, but the Islamist state itself began to appropriate properties that belonged to prominent figures of the old regime, transferring their control to the newly established Foundation of the Dispossessed. Vast swaths of fertile land in Turkmen Sahra, Dasht-e Gorgan, and Kurdistan came under the control of the leftist groups that had already built support among the local population. The confiscated lands were transferred to the peasant shuras to run them collectively, while the local councils were given the task of managing civic affairs. When I visited the town of Bandar Torkaman in Turkmen Sahra in 1980, it was being run by a Marxist city council. The city clearly had a different, secular feel, with an uncommon cultural and political vibrancy expressed in the dress, posters, placards, and public arenas.

This is not to paint a rosy picture of the experience of popular sovereignty during the Iranian revolution. There were a number of drawbacks, including overzealous leftism, difficulty in reaching consensus, the problem of institutionalization, opportunism of some of those involved, and above all the crackdown by the new state. The students' initiatives continued for some two years before President Banisadr dispatched hundreds of armed Pasdaran militias to "liberate" college campuses from the opposition Marxist groups in an extraordinary show of force. In a Friday prayer ceremony in April 1980, Ayatollah Khomeini made it clear that "we are not afraid of economic sanctions or military intervention. What we are afraid of is Western universities and the training of our youth in the interests of West or East."[7] To consolidate power, the government shut down the universities for three years (1980–1983), giving time to the newly established Cultural Revolution program to "cleanse" higher education from "Eastern and Western influences." The peasant councils and land seizure caused a widespread reaction. Rich farmers and their supporters launched a campaign in the state media, forged collective response to defend their properties, and sought religious fatwas from leading clerics against unlawful land takeover, while the government attempted to appease the landless peasants with the promise of land distribution. But the more dramatic response came from Ayatollah Khomeini, who ordered a military operation to quell the leftist groups and their local allies in Kurdistan in 1980, waging a nine-day war in Gonbad Kavous.

What emerged were powerful social movements for local self-rule and collective responsibility embodied in the formation of popular shuras. Even though these progressive measures were undermined fairly rapidly, their long-term consequences came to the surface in later years. The peasants' movement to acquire land was partially effected in the land reform bill of 1986 after years of foot-dragging by the conservative clerics and big landowners, even though the Council of the Guardian diluted the reform project later.[8] In the meantime, efforts to transform rural life gained new momentum. I observed this change in my own home village in southeastern Tehran, which had experienced a remarkable transformation. In the early 1990s, I saw young people had taken charge of managing and developing the community through their elected village shura, which had worked hard to bring paved roads, electricity, and running water, while working to get natural gas connected to the village homes. Two new schools and a high school were turning the villagers into a literate public, while an impressive new mosque served as the cultural center of the community. Building a new library was on the agenda. Clearly the youth of the village had gained the trust of the elders, and people now favored competence over ageism. These developments were all new to me and to the village life. In fact, at the national level, the idea of shuraism and civic engagement resurfaced in the 1990s following eight years of war with Iraq (1980–1988) and grew further after Mohammad Khatami was elected president in 1997. In the freest elections for two hundred thousand posts on regional, city, and local councils in 1999, thousands of reformist councilors assumed the responsibility of managing civil life at various layers, expanding the practice of local democracy at the grassroots.[9]

All these were the long-term consequences of the progressive impulse the revolution had spurred. In 1979, the desire for shuraism as the embodiment of grassroots democracy was so powerful that few conservatives could contest it. Beyond the Marxists and the leftist Mujahedin, a most passionate defense of the idea came from the highly admired liberal cleric Ayatollah Taleqani, an associate of Shariati, whose unexpected death in 1979 and the widespread sympathy it engendered gave a dramatic boost to shuraism in the public sphere. Radio, TV, and print media all discussed the merits of the idea to the extent that shura as the organization of popular management in villages, cities, and workplaces found its place in the new constitution. The workers' shuras represented the most compelling experiment, expressing what the revolution meant for workers and how it unfolded in the factories. It embodied at once a strategy to save jobs, democratize working life, and intervene in the organization of production.

Revolution in the Factories

Just after the shah's downfall, when Iranian workers began to resume work following months of general strikes, many found their factories shut down, managers absent, supply of raw materials halted, and their jobs lost. These dire conditions along with the emergent ethos of self-determination propelled the working people to take over industrial plants to run them by creating workers' shuras. The religious and secular Left lent enthusiastic support.

In early 1981, in the midst of a resurgent civil society and political infighting in the government, I began seven months of research in fourteen industrial plants located around Tehran, Tabriz, and Arak to understand and document what the revolution had meant for working people and how it was manifested in their working life.[10] Workers had just completed extraordinary general strikes that had practically crippled the economy and state administration; in the process workers had gained new expectations and entitlements that they wished to exercise in their working lives. Even though workers as collective actors joined the revolutionary struggle later than students or bazaar merchants, their sporadic industrial actions since early 1978 had merged into a general strike after October 1978 following Bloody Friday in Tehran, which had forced the shah to impose martial law in the country. Thus, when seventy thousand workers in the oil sector, forty thousand steelworkers, and thirty thousand railway workers put down their tools, the dynamics of labor protests shifted, with the strikes spreading like wildfire to involve the key sectors of oil, communication, transport, public services, banks, customs, and even the movie industry and state TV in a short span of time.[11]

Once the shah's regime fell on February 11, 1979, laborers began to return to work only to find themselves locked out and their plants bankrupt or otherwise face the same polluted factories, same supervisors, and often the same bosses. The revolutionary disruption, the flight of businessmen, and the closure of foreign and domestic ventures had left millions of laborers without jobs ironically at a time when the revolution had boosted their expectations. Even though the Provisional Government (PG) provided some 85 billion rials in credit to boost production, only a quarter was utilized, thus forcing the new government to nationalize and supervise 483 production units. The moral outrage among workers caused an uncommon movement of the unemployed to demand jobs. Supported by student activists and leftist groups, the unemployed organized nationally and initiated mass street demonstrations, sit-ins, and hunger strikes; they battled with the Pasdaran militias and negotiated with the government to realize their claims. Workers were mobilized throughout the country, and their protest actions culminated on May Day 1979 when some five hundred thousand men and women along with the socialist forces marched in the streets of Iran's large cities. But the protests had declined by the outbreak of the Iran-Iraq War in September 1980 because of repression of dissent, internal discord, and largely by its own success since many jobless people received unemployment compensation, found jobs in the informal economy, or returned to work.

Those who did return to work, however, faced hostile and hierarchical management that often threatened them with closure and layoffs, thus spurring labor conflicts in places of work. Just in the first month after the revolution fifty thousand workers protested against layoffs and lockouts and demanded pay during the time when they were on general strike. Mass protests continued for the next five months.[12] In many plants, including some five hundred companies with foreign ownership or connected to the old regime, workers took over the administration fairly easily because the old management had collapsed. Yet the domestically owned enterprises also became the target of workers' takeover, despite stiff opposition from the owners; workers now wanted a new order of things. When I visited the Pars Metal factory in Tehran, for instance, the shura representing nine hundred workers was in the midst of a bitter conflict with the director over who were to have the authority to run the factory. The shura had rejected the government's mediation to appoint a new administrative management. "Those men have oppressed us so much; how could the government have appointed them as managers?" a shura leader objected. "We will never put up with it, never accept such a burden as long as we have blood in our veins," an old worker proclaimed angrily.

With the new insurgent awareness, workers now wanted to revolutionize their workplace, to purge the "oppressive" bosses and supervisors, identify the SAVAK informers, level off inequality in pay and positions, and "intervene" in running the workplace. The workers' shura was to embody and serve as the administrative structure to realize those claims. Investigation into the oppressive elements within the factories, including the shah's secret agents, became one of the first tasks workers undertook —and these committees of inquiry in some factories became the basis of later factory councils. In some plants, like Arj in Tehran, the general assemblies of all workers put on trial and sacked the "authoritarian elements" in the workplace. In the Yamaha Motorcycle plant in Ghazvin, the shura dismissed two production and administrative managers and later seven others. A delegation of workers even went to the central office in Tehran to fire the director and major shareholders. "The workers stayed there for three days to protect the available documents from access by the employees of the office," a shura member related to me.[13] In some factories, workers even used the intelligence of the Department of National Documents (DND) to identify the suspected elements. In the Iran Car Company, the inquiry resulted in identifying eleven SAVAK informers. In five out of twelve plants I investigated, the "worker's representatives" had been officially employed by SAVAK. In addition, many of the officially sanctioned workplace syndicates under the shah had been infiltrated by the secret police informers, and the Security Bureau, or factory police, constantly watched workers' activities. After the revolution, many of these worker-informers were identified and fired by the shuras. But the new Islamic regime reinstated some of the sacked employees. Indeed, to preempt the workers' initiative, the Revolutionary Council of the Islamic Republic and Prime Minister Mohammad Ali Rajai's government created its own "purging bodies" in August 1980 to "cleanse" the "production units from the conspiracies of the agents of the West, the East, and the defeated Pahlavi regime," a measure that came to haunt some of the militant workers who had initiated such initiatives.[14]

Purging the factories from the corrupt employees or elements of the past regime reflected a broader pursuit by workers of instituting an ethos of leveling in workplaces. The shuras were adamant to reduce the excessive inequalities in pay, position, and perks and to remove spatial segregation based on rank. They abolished the spatial hierarchy between managers, engineers, and manual workers so that all employees, irrespective of rank, dined, played, and prayed in the same sites. A number of shuras, such as that in the Caterpillar plant, cut down disproportionately high salaries and raised those at the bottom. It equated the allocation of parking lots and checked on the report of absenteeism of all employees regardless of rank.

This also included women, who constituted a small portion of factory workers. Left-wing shuras, in particular, recognized women's role in representing workers in the leadership. In the Zagros plant in Tehran, I attended a joint meeting of management and shura members of which a good number were women. In the Philips TV assembly plant, which had a higher proportion of female workers, an assertive pregnant woman, who I discovered later was a member of the Maoist Paykar Organization, worked side by side with male workers, including Akbar Agha, a follower of Ali Shariati's ideas, and was one of the most inspiring labor activists I met. Akbar Agha and I later developed a friendship outside the workplace. He invited me to his house in Narmak to meet with his wife and two teenage children, relating absorbing life stories, rare insights into the world of work and the working class during the shah and after. While egalitarian practices in pay, position, and space increased, gender segregation was enforced later by the new Islamist regime, compelling many women workers to stay home or join the struggle for gender equality.

Frontiers of Control

Surely the attempts to dismiss the oppressive elements were part of the broader question of who was to take the charge of the workplaces. The bylaws of the Pars Metal factory shura ruled that "it is the duty of the shura to intervene in the whole affairs of the factory, that is, in purchase, sale, pricing, and orders for raw materials."[15] To this end, workers elected a twelve-man shura, which then spoke with the finance department to learn about the financial situation of the company. It discovered and prevented the owner from transferring funds from the factory account. In late March 1979, the shura dispensed the year-end bonus. The clash with the owner and the PG entailed a series of reelections for members of the shura; but conflict with the factory's existing board of directors continued. At the time of my visit, the factory was controlled by the workers' shura, since the managers had gone on strike for twenty-five days to protest the shura undermining their authority. In the absence of the managers, the shura had a chance to exert a great deal of authority over various departments. Meanwhile, the shura's intent to control hiring and firing continued to challenge the authority of the board of directors, as well as the government, which viewed such interventions unlawful; the government consequently set up a "special force" to "prevent the strike committees and shuras from intervening in the affairs of the management."[16]

But intervention had become the order of the day. In the Philips factory, the shura set up a special Commission of Inspection to preside over and investigate administration and personnel affairs, including the rules of employment. In the Arj factory, the shura bylaws considered its objective to "preside over the financial situation and conditions of employment of the company." In the Eadem Motor Company in March 1979, the shura asked for the dismissal of eleven "antiworker" managers following an investigation. When the director refused, the shura ordered the factory security to arrest the two highest-ranking managers, who were forced to pay back their loan. The shura's desire to control employment issues aimed primarily at preventing nepotism in hiring and arbitrary dismissals; it also meant to have the authority to dismiss unwanted personnel (e.g., those linked to the old regime) and, most important, to protect shura members and militant workers from being dismissed for their activism.

Precisely because managers justified many of the layoffs on financial grounds, the shuras were adamant about holding the right to review the company's finances. In the Zamyad car plant, a shura member told me in March 1981 that when management refused, on the order of the government, to honor the profit-sharing scheme, the shura took funds from the company to pay off the workers' shares. In the Caterpillar plant, the shura transferred cash from the absentee director's personal account into the company fund, where it could be used to pay the delayed wages of the workers instead of laying them off. Indeed, monitoring the financial affairs of the company was enshrined in the shura bylaws of many factories that I reviewed, such as Azmayesh, Pars Metal, Philips, and Leyland Motors. The Philips workers' shura, through its Committee for Monitoring Finance and Administration, took as its task to create an inventory of the assets in order to cut superfluous costs and modify high (managerial) salaries. When in the winter of 1980 the shura found a corruption case concerning sales, it undertook an investigation and held a tribunal with all workers present in which two officials were tried and fired. Within three weeks, a trial was organized to investigate the director, and an official from the Ministry of Labor was invited. The verdict was to dismiss the director.

These seemed to be common practices in many plants, and workers felt very strongly about them. In March 1981, in a state-run Zamyad factory, an intense confrontation took place after the shura withdrew funds from the company to pay the workers' year-end bonus. The government detained a number of shura members as a result. In solidarity, workers of the plant all paid back their bonus in an attempt to have their shura members released. The day I visited Zamyad, the representatives from Ayatollah Khomeini and the prosecutor general turned up to settle the dispute. Feeling that the representatives were taking the side of management, workers became indignant. In a bitter argument, an articulate worker stood up and proclaimed in an Azeri Turkish accent: "Just as we brought down the shah's regime, we are able to bring down any other regime," to which workers reacted with audible applause and *takbir* (chant of "God is Great").

When I asked a shura activist in the Zamyad car plant what business the shura had to check the finances of a company, he reacted emphatically:

> Look, the reason why the revolution was made at all was because we wanted to become our own masters, to determine our own destiny. . . . We did not want the situation where one or a few make decisions for two thousand people. When we, twenty-five hundred workers, are working around these walls, we want to know what is going on here, what we'll achieve in the future, in what direction we are running the company, how much profit we get, how much we could take for ourselves, how much we could contribute to government for national investment. For this reason, we never let management employ somebody to make decisions. This would be a repetition of the same previous mistakes to the extent that it would violate the rights of the workers, which are in fact the rights of the Iranian nation.[17]

Such a powerful ethos of leveling and collective responsibility informed the spirit of many shuras and their pursuit of worker control. In the words of the Leyland factory shura, it expressed the "sovereignty of people over their own destiny"—the kind of popular authority that in some plants meant the shura's control over the processes of production and distribution but one that came about as a result of the exceptional conditions of revolution and improvisation. For instance, in the Earfo foundry, it all began with a series of workers' demands to ensure payment of delayed wages, profit sharing, supply of raw materials, dissolution of the "yellow" (government-sponsored) shuras, and appointment of a manager independent of the shareholders. The demands involved a long struggle in which the country's Revolutionary Council and the Pasdaran militias were drawn in and which entailed workers taking three managers hostage. It was settled when the director consented to the workers' demands. In the Melli Shoe Company, the shura simply expelled the existing board of directors, taking over the administration and production until the government appointed a new management team.[18] The Caterpillar factory shura ran the plant for five months, controlling "all economic, social and political aspects of this company," including employment, finance, purchasing of raw materials, sales, and coordination of work.[19] The shura reportedly dispatched a team of employees to Geneva to purchase raw materials. In the meantime, it formed a committee to settle disputes. It made decisions on all aspects of plant operation until the government nationalized the plant, consequently reducing the shura's authority to one of consultation. A number of brick-making workshops in Tehran and Azerbaijan province undertook a similar process of self-management for several months.

It is a mistake to assume that the experience of shuras followed an identical pattern. The shuras varied significantly across individual plants—in terms of the degree of control, ideology, and the political conditions under which they operated. Nor were the workers' desires necessarily translated into practice. The whole experience was one of complex disjunction, trial, and improvisation informed by extraordinary hope and a yearning for change in conditions of intense instability and uncertainty. There was no national coordination with a blueprint of ideas and models, even though a few industrial groups such as the Union of Factory Shuras of the Organization of Industrial Development or Union of the Shuras of the Gilan Province seem to have more integrated shuras. Otherwise, shuras remained dispersed across workplaces gripped in their own internal dynamics. The Ministry of Labor did develop a number of regulations regarding the workers' shuras, but they often did not fulfill the workers' expectations. The ministry's formulation defined shuras essentially as consultative entities rather than as institutions with authority to make decisions. Consequently, the degree of control the shuras exerted depended largely on the balance of power in the workplaces and in society at large. When labor had the upper hand, shuras would defy government regulations; and when the management could, it would repress the shuras even to the extent of preventing their elections.

Thus, the experience of the shuras varied from those at Philips, for example, which exerted a high degree of control over employment, finance, and management of production, to those such as the one at the Zagros refrigerator factory, which acted mostly like factory-based syndicates negotiating with management over better pay and conditions. The majority of the shuras navigated between these extremes. Indeed, their varied degrees of authority were reflected in the terms used by workers to describe them: They ranged from *kontrol-e kargari* (workers' control) to *modiriyyat* (management), *nezarat* (supervision), and *dekhalat* (intervention). The variation had primarily to do with the ideological makeup of the shura members, ownership status of the enterprise, nature of the labor process, and broader political conditions. Thus, the shuras with militant and leftist workers, in the state or nationalized enterprises, with simpler labor process or craft-based labor exercised more control in the affairs of the enterprises than those with less militant workers operating in private companies with a complex labor process. But all these were more or less subject to the broader political conditions, which boiled down to how the state behaved toward the shuras.

Challenges

The state hostility proved to be instrumental in shuras' subsequent trajectories. The regime's extensive assault in August 1979 to quell the multiple social and regional unrest changed the political mood in society and in the factories. Following the crackdown on left-wing organizations, peasant movements, Kurdish rebellion, and oppositional media, the militant shuras came under attack. The government, under the liberal-Islamic Mehdi Bazargan, then opted to appoint technocratic management to run the factories. The Islamist prime minister, Mohammad Ali Rajai, went further to "Islamize" the factories by establishing management that followed Islamic ideology, corporatist shuras, and

Islamic Associations to undermine both left-wing workers and liberal techno-crats and cement support for the regime in the workplaces. The Islamic Associations, the body of pro-regime workers, aimed particularly to transform the cultural aura of the workplaces. They instituted collective prayers, Quran recitation, and religious sermons with Islamic clerics on a regular basis. Many workers seemed to welcome the measures, especially as the latter offered some respite from work. On one occasion when I attended the prayer sermon in the Zagros factory prayer hall in the spring of 1981, only twenty of the seven hundred workers were in attendance; the rest were enjoying the sunshine outside or playing soccer in the factory yard. From then on, the authorities made collective prayers mandatory.

The regime's hard-liners would also bring victims of the Iran-Iraq War into the factories, usually at the end of the year, to shame workers who were de-manding year-end or profit-sharing bonuses—a benefit that most shuras were campaigning for. To ensure workers' commitment, the imams in such plants as a cement factory in Tehran advocated work as "*jihad* for the sake of God; God will pay for this jihad, the jihad of labor that you [workers] are carrying out in the barricade of the factory." It was not clear if such ideologization of work and production delivered. Earlier on Ayatollah Khomeini, exasperated by the wave of labor strikes and demands for a better life, had famously stated that "we have not made revolution for cheap melons; we have made it for Islam."[20] But workers seemed to have a different understanding. "They say we have not made revolution for economic betterment," angrily objected a worker at the Azmayesh plant. "What have we made it for then? They say for Islam! But what does Islam mean then? We made the revolution for a better life."

The ruling Islamists, notably Ayatollah Khomeini with his populist lan-guage, nevertheless did build support among segments of the working class. Even though the anticapitalist sentiments of these pro-regime workers brought them in line with the leftist and independent workers, their ideological loyalty to the Islamist regime caused a division among the workers and thus under-mined the power of genuine shuras. Many of the loyalist workers had been absorbed into the labor chapters of numerous Islamist institutions that were mushrooming in those decisive postrevolutionary moments. The Pasdaran militias, the Basij organization, the Organization of the Mujahedin of Islamic Revolution, and the ruling Islamic Republic Party all established labor chap-ters in the workplaces—recruiting, giving military training, and often serving as the eyes and ears of the regime. The Pasdaran in particular set up military guard commands in a number of plants, notably in auto and oil industries, as part of the securitization of working life that the conditions of the war (with Iraq) had instigated.

The loyalist workers constituted the support base for the Islamic corporatist shuras. Cooperating with the Islamic managements, the Islamic shuras followed the ideological lines of the populist wing or the "imam line" of the Islamist regime. From that position, they intervened considerably in the management of the enterprises but at the same time campaigned against both the leftist workers and the liberal technocratic administrators. In the Pars Metal factory, a loyalist worker stressed that the "shura must be Islamic, must be recognized by law." "But what should be its authority?" I asked. "It must be resolute against the board of directors and the like; it must intervene in everything and must run the factory," he replied. This sentiment reflected the position of Hossein Kamali, head of Workers House and a deputy in the parliament. "I believe that the shuras must be given the right to intervene in workplace affairs. But we do not believe that every shura is genuine. Because we believe that a shura member before everything else must be a true Muslim; otherwise it is not acceptable."[21]

Such Islamic corporatism reflected an image of a just Islamic society free from domination and depravities to stand as an alternative to both capitalism and socialism. Clearly Ayatollah Khomeini's rhetoric against the oppression of the dispossessed and dominance of the big capitalists had fed into the militancy of the loyalist workers and their corporatist image of a just Islamic order. "The deprived and oppressed should rise. They should not wait for the oppressors to save them," the Ayatollah often proclaimed.[22] Yet the support of the corporatist shuras for the regime policies and their exclusivist position often placed them at odds with the immediate interests of the general workers. The ensuing division and conflict between the loyalist and nonconformist workers was often bitter. I observed one such hostile encounter in the Saipa Citroën car plant in Tehran. It was my second day of interviews with the shura members. I was directed to the shura office where a few workers said they had been waiting for a long time with no one attending to their business. They expressed distrust of the shura, which they said did not represent them. After some twenty minutes four shura members arrived, who warned me not to interview workers collectively on the shop floor because "there will be chaos." As we sat in the meeting room engaged in deep conversation, I noticed through the glass door the mounting assembly of angry faces shouting and pointing at the nervous shura members. The indignant crowd swelled and the commotion rose, bursting into the meeting room, unleashing a barrage of charges against the shura members and me, demanding to listen to the entire interviews before allowing me to leave. "We want to know what these people have said to you; the radio and TV people come here and only interview them and ignore the workers," they protested furiously. I explained that I was not a journalist but a researcher and agreed that they could listen to the tape. When the listening ended, one of the workers requested in an Azeri accent, "Now, please interview me!"; and he began with "in the name of God; this shura is fascistic," continuing to deride the shura's "betrayal" of the workers' interests.

But state intervention proved even more detrimental. Controlling some 75 percent of the industry, the government could defeat the oppositional shuras by obstructing the flow of raw materials, parts, and credit. By halting production in this fashion, the shuras in such plants as Saka, Orkideh china, Naznakh, and Isfahan wool ceased operation.[23] The government had already created a Special Force in the industry three months after the revolution to neutralize plant takeovers by the strike committees and shuras. Once the universities were closed down in 1980, the authorities unleashed a wave of attacks against the militant shuras throughout the country. The shuras in such plants as Machine Sazi Tabriz, Tractor Sazi, Lift Truck, Pumpiran, the armament industry, the oil installations, and the railways became the target of physical liquidation and arrests. Of particular significance was the suppression of the Union of Factory Shuras of the Organization of Industrial Development, a conglomerate of a dozen industrial units in the country whose decision to hold a national congress caused the Ministry of Industry to dissolve the central shura.

Beyond state repression and the workers' division, the shuras also suffered from their own paradox. To exercise power, the shuras needed managerial knowledge that they largely lacked. Even at the height of the shura's "sovereignty" in the Pars Metal factory, both workers and the shura members were pleading with the striking managers to return to their position. Elsewhere, workers who had put on trial and sacked the old managers requested the government to appoint administrators. A shura leader at Zamyad explained this paradox:

> As soon as the [shah's] regime toppled, the shura was formed. The workers
> believed it to be their right to intervene in all operations. Management no
> longer made any sense for them. They replaced the managers. The halted any
> antiworker plots. They made efforts to provide raw materials. Foreign managers

were fired. The management had actually been paralyzed. . . . However, the level of output was pretty low. The shura would have to pay salaries and wages; they still would have to get raw materials to the plant. But it was a hard job. The shura then had to appeal to the government for help. You know, the shura wasn't able to pay the wages for even one month. Therefore, it had to come to terms with the state-appointed managers. In this way, the shura lost its genuineness.

Workers enjoyed exerting power, but to do so they felt they needed the expertise of the engineers and managers to be able to coordinate the technical aspects of production and administration. For instance, to order raw materials from abroad, workers needed to have the necessary know-how, knowledge of foreign languages, the skill of where to go or whom to contact. This was particularly crucial in enterprises with a complex labor process and division of labor.[24] To get around this, workers in some plants like Pars Metal "appointed" managers; even though this did not change the technical division of labor, it did modify the "rule of experts" by making it accountable to the power of the working people.

Things were easier in the establishments with less complex labor processes or craftwork where highly skilled employees could administer their institution. Unlike in the plants with the detailed division of labor, workers in the brick-making industry and craft-based works, for instance, could organize the entire operation reasonably well even without the managerial teams. In the same vein, college professors along with students and the staff were technically capable of making important decisions concerning college administration. This is precisely how worker control, or even in the less impressive shared governance, may become an indispensable component of democratic governance of working life in settings like universities, schools, or public administration, where authorities would depend on the knowledge and expertise of its members on crucial matters of governance such as evaluation, hiring, or planning.

Broader Resonance

The radical practices of this sort were not unique to Iran. They were the spirit of most revolutions of the 1970s. At the very same time that I was observing these developments in Iran, the Sandinista revolution against the Somoza dictatorship in Nicaragua had unleashed a number of initiatives by the subaltern groups to take the matters of their working lives into their own hands. Farmworkers were the first to seize control of enterprises whose owners and managers had fled the country, a process that had begun even before the Somoza regime was overthrown. On the liberated farms, a general assembly of workers, guerrillas, and peasants living on the properties ran the enterprises while tackling the broader issues of health, nutrition, and justice in these areas.[25] In the cities, when the business class began sabotaging the revolution through disrupting production, workers backed by the Sandinistas moved to seize the operation of the firms to ensure the flow of work and production. In the first two years after the Sandinista revolution, the extent of worker control navigated between full self-management in the agricultural sector and overseeing management decisions in the state-owned enterprises on a range of issues from production and sales to planning and international marketing.[26] Even though Sandinistas did lend support to such grassroots initiatives, the experience of worker control began to dwindle in the face of mounting social and economic instability and insecurity that the counterrevolutionary Contra War backed by the Reagan administration brought about.[27]

Earlier in 1970, the electoral victory of Salvador Allende's Popular Unity government in the Chilean national elections gave a big boost to the working people to begin an extensive expropriation of private and multinational enterprises, enhancing the already large social property sector. During the three-year government of the Popular Unity, workers set up organizations to coordinate the operation of enterprises, an initiative that Allende's socialist party had originally proposed. In the meantime, communal councils were set up to bring together workers, peasants, students, housewives, unions, and price-control committees to coordinate the services and needs of each sector when the bourgeois classes resolved to defeat the socialist government.[28] Their efforts produced results. Democratically elected President Allende was overthrown in a US-backed military coup in 1973, and with that came the end of the initiatives for popular governance. But the desire for self-rule and efforts to democratize working life found resonance elsewhere around the world.[29]

In 1974, a revolution in southern Europe brought down the colonial dictatorship in Portugal, ushering in a wave of struggles for self-management of the economy—a principle that found its place in the new Portuguese constitution.[30] In the meantime, the revolution in Portugal undermined its colonial grip over the colonies abroad—Mozambique, Angola, and Guinea Bissau— thus enabling the liberation movements to unravel their own revolutions in which local self-rule and popular participation assumed a prominent place. In Mozambique, the idea of popular control was pushed primarily by the Marxist president Samora Machel, who had advocated popular participation in "an active, collective and conscious manner in the discussion and solution of problems, as well as in the planning and control of production." But in practice the initiative was seen as a solution to the disruptions caused after the revolution by the departure of the Portuguese technocratic settlers who made up the bulk of the managerial class. The "production councils" as proposed by President Machel were to take charge of management and production. The project, however, encountered a number of obstacles. The vanguard party was adamant to mobilize workers, yet it also demanded discipline and higher productivity. In addition, the workers' desire for participation did not match their technical and administrative abilities; most workers were in fact illiterate.[31] But above all, the idea lost to the intense vulnerability caused by the Renamo counter-revolutionary guerrillas (backed by pre-Mandela South Africa and Rhodesia) and the eventual capitulation of the government in 1980s to the conditionality of the IMF in the face of dire economic downturn caused by war, drought, and flood.[32] Instead of gaining popular control and social justice, the economy was forced to undertake neoliberal restructuring.

Indeed, the story of Mozambique signaled the beginning of the end of an episode when radical repertoire of this sort marked most revolutions, when the popular struggles centered not simply on distribution—wage or welfare—but also means and organization of production. The gradual change in the structure of labor—growing privatization, informalization, fragmentation, and shrinking organizations—through the widespread neoliberal restructuring shaped the ideas about what kinds of demands were reasonable, realistic, or legitimate.

Even though General Augusto Pinochet's military coup in 1974 inaugurated the neoliberal path, the model of marketization that Mozambique, Angola, and other countries experienced came from Europe and the United States, where Margaret Thatcher and Ronald Reagan had championed a new phase of relentless liberalization since the 1980s. At the time when the quest for democratic working life was on the rise in the postcolonial regions, the Western working class itself was struggling hard to maintain its historic gains in welfare, employment, and organization. In Britain, strikes, picket lines, and street demonstrations became an everyday practice after the assaults on the miners and print unions, following Prime Minister Thatcher's policy of privatization. Eric Hobsbawm's *Forward March of Labor Halted* and André Gorz's *Farewell to the Working Class* were of the earliest explorations to capture the dynamics of the labor crisis.[33] Passing through troubling paths, neoliberalism continued to spread its rationale, projecting a narrative of society and economy in which the ideals of the common, compassion, egalitarian ethos, and democratic work became subservient to the whim of free enterprise, individual self-interest, and competition. The end of the Cold War and the "triumph of liberalism" deeply reinforced the trend, as the working people lost their critical allies when the communist and socialist parties changed course or abolished themselves. The Middle East witnessed extensive privatization and employment insecurity; the public sector shrank, labor further fragmented, and unions declined.[34] The resulting exclusion and inequality were bound to escalate social discontent. But while neoliberal policies caused dissent among the subaltern population, its normativity shaped deradicalization among the political class. Thus, by the time the Arab revolutions arrived, few showed awareness about or interest in such radical repertoires as worker control or self-rule that I have described in this chapter, as if struggle over property, production, or governance were off limits. Indeed, the entire political class took neoliberal reality for granted. And this included the Islamists, who were a key opposition against the Arab regimes and Western imperialism.

4   Not a Theology of Liberation

For over three decades, Islamism occupied a central place in the opposition against Arab regimes and their Western allies. It rose to prominence partly because Arab secular nationalism faced crisis following the 1967 Arab defeat by Israel, and the secular states shed much legitimacy because of their political repression and developmental deficits. With the collapse of communism, the decline of existing socialism, and the hegemony of liberal globalization in the 1990s, Islamism emerged as a formidable force to lead the mounting dissent against autocratic Arab rule, Zionist dominance, and Western imperialism, while championing revival of "cultural authenticity" and indigenous values. But questions remain: How revolutionary have Islamist politics been, and what has its anti-imperialism meant for the Muslim subaltern? Were Islamists fit to inspire and lead the Arab revolutions?

Rightist circles express a clear position that Islamism is a regressive, antimodern, and violent movement that poses the greatest threat to the "free world." Islamism represents, in their view, a "totalitarian ideology," a "cousin of fascism and communism" that is opposed to modernity and the Enlightenment values enshrined in the capitalist free world.[1] In a sense, the idea of a "clash of civilizations" captures the objective contradictions of Islam and Islamism with Western modernity and its universalizing mission.

Some groups on the left also express similar views, seeing Islamism as an "ideological enemy" or as "analogues to fascism" so that the best socialists can hope for is to break individuals away from Islamist ranks and lure them into progressive camps.[2] But most consider Islamism an anti-imperialist force with which the Left can find some common ground. For the British Socialist Workers Party, for instance, in the conditions of mounting Islamophobia in the West, an "internationalist duty to stand with Muslims against racism and imperialism" requires secular socialists to forge alliances with such admittedly conservative organizations as the Muslim Association of Britain,[3] whose misogynous stand on gender issues in Muslim communities is often overlooked on the grounds of "cultural relativism."[4]

Michael Hardt and Antonio Negri view "Islamic fundamentalism" as postmodern resistance to the modernity of Western hegemony, while Susan Buck-Morss considers Islamist critical thought as spearheading the contestation against global capitalist modernity.[5] Others suggest that "Islam has the advantage of being simultaneously an ethno-nationalist identity as well as a resistance movement to the dictates of capitalist world economy."[6] Thus, by mobilizing civil society against structural adjustment, by offering alternative welfare systems to the shrinking role of the states in fulfilling its responsibilities, Islamists present the most important challenge to global neoliberalism. Indeed, for some observers, the seemingly proletarian profile of Islamists and their populist rhetoric render them *the* movement of the dispossessed. In this sense, their anti-imperialist stand, combined with religious language, makes the Islamist movement analogous to the Latin American liberation theology of the 1960s and 1970s, which took the liberation of the poor as its central moral objective.[7] Mike Davis's influential survey *Planet of Slums*, for instance, portrays militant Islamism (along with Pentecostalism) as a "song of the dispossessed" who survive in the misery of slums, as in Palestine's Gaza Strip, or Baghdad, defying the empire's Orwellian technologies of repression by resorting to the "gods of chaos" or daily explosions and suicide bombings.[8] This argument finds a clearer expression in describing ISIS as a "revolution" in the face of intransigent and declining empire.[9] These accounts altogether seem to imply that Islamism represents an indigenous Middle Eastern version of global dissent against neoliberal imperialism.

The notion of anti-imperialism has traditionally held a normative significance, referring to a just struggle waged by often secular progressive forces to liberate subjugated peoples from the diktat of global capitalism and imperial (economic, political, and cultural) domination and to establish self-rule, social justice, and support for the working classes and the subaltern subjects—women, minorities, and marginalized groups. The Zapatista movement in Chiapas, Mexico, and the antiglobalization movement may be said to represent such anti-imperialist struggles.

Here the idea of empire is distinct from the liberal concept, where "leaders of one society rule directly or indirectly over at least one other society, using instruments different from (though not necessarily more authoritarian than) those used to rule at home."[10] In the liberal conception, empire is not all that bad;

the British empire spread the institutions of parliamentary democracy across the globe, and the US empire, as the Harvard historian Niall Ferguson stresses, not only seeks to ensure US national security and acquire raw materials but also provides crucial "public goods" such as peace, global order, and "Americanization" for the rest of the world through the export of goods and ideas.[11] In contrast, the left-critical concept of "new empire" is one that consists, in the words of David Harvey, of a mix of "neo-liberal restructurings world-wide and the neoconservative attempt to establish and maintain a coherent moral order in both the global and various national situations";[12] it results from the need of capital to dispose of its surplus, which by necessity involves geographical expansion. Put simply, capital needs the state to clear the way for a secure and less-troubled context for overseas expansion. Harvey's account is useful in understanding a notion of empire that is heavily invested in driving the neoliberal project across the globe.

What then is the relationship of Islamism to neoliberal empire? Does it pose a genuine challenge to its hegemony, or is it no more than a reaction that unintentionally furnishes unfortunate justifications for a deeper imperial expansion? After all, is Islamism—its view of work, individual self-development, inequality, production, or consumption—immune from the neoliberal normativity? I like to argue that, first, while Islamism has indeed remained relentless in its strong anti-imperialist posture, this anti-imperialism, which focuses primarily on culture, has been self-serving; it aims to preserve Islamist hegemony over local populations by sheltering itself from the influences of challenging notions and worldviews. Second, while the Cold War Islamism (of the 1970s and 1980s) did espouse quite a strong anticapitalist, distributionist (social justice), and anti-imperialist character—indeed, wanting to outdo its socialist rival—in the years after the Cold War it experienced a steady metamorphosis from its socialistic orientations to embrace a neoliberal outlook. The designation "Costa Salafi," frequenting Western cafés, to describe this neo-Islamism might sound too ironic, but it signifies well the submission of Islamism to the tantalizing allure of a free market pushed by the spread of global liberalization and consumer culture. In this sense, Islamism represents a project of hegemony that is neither revolutionary nor emancipatory.

Multiple Faces of Islamism

Conflicting views on Islamist politics are partly a result of its multiple faces and facets. Some observers focus on the political economy of certain Islamist trends, concluding that they stand against neoliberal orthodoxy;

some highlight Islamist movements' welfare operations, focusing on Islamism's proletarian character; while still others concentrate on Islamism's ideologies, moral codes, and religio-political visions, finding them conservative, regressive, or even fascist. Notwithstanding its variations, Islamism points to the ideologies and movements that aspire to build an Islamic order—a religious state, Islamic laws, and moral codes. Islamists' key aim is to establish a more or less exclusive ideological community drawn on an imagined "Islamic golden age"; secular concerns, such as establishing social justice, are only to follow from this strategic objective. But Islamist viewpoints vary concerning the meaning of this Islamic order and the ways in which it can be achieved. The gradualist and reformist Islamists such as the Jama'at-e Islami in Pakistan, Hizbut Tahrir in some fifty countries, or the Muslim Brotherhood and its offshoots in Algeria, Syria, Sudan, Kuwait, Palestine, and Jordan, have pursued nonviolent methods of mobilizing civil society through work in professional associations, NGOs, local mosques, and charities and have built legal political parties to compete in national elections. In contrast, the militant Islamists, such as the former Jama'a al-Islamiya in Egypt, Lashkar-e-Taiba in Pakistan, or the Algerian Islamic Salvation Front (FIS) resort to violence against state agencies, their own citizens, Western targets, and civilians, hoping to cause a Leninist-type insurrection to establish an Islamist order by decree.[13] Thus, militant Islamists also differ from the current jihadis, such as groups associated with al-Qaeda. Whereas militant Islamism represents political movements operating within the given nation-states and targets primarily the secular national state, the jihadis are transnational in their ideas and operations and represent fundamentally apocalyptic "ethical movements" involved in "civilizational" struggles, with the aim of combating a highly abstract West and all societies of "nonbelievers." They invariably resort to extreme violence against both the self (suicide bombing) and their targets.[14] Since 2014, the Islamic State of Iraq and Syria (ISIS) has come to represent a new brand of Islamism that combines the apocalyptic transnationalism of the jihadis, the pan-Islamism of the Muslim Brotherhood and Hizbut Tahrir, and the state-seeking strategy of the militant Islamists.

But many groups associated with Islamism are not in fact Islamist, strictly speaking. A growing trend that I have called "post-Islamist" wants to transcend Islamism as an exclusivist and totalizing ideology, espousing instead inclusion, pluralism, and ambiguity. In Iran, it took the form of the reform movement that partly evolved into the reform government of 1997–2004. In addition, a growing number of Islamic groups, such as al-Nahda Party in Tunisia, Jama'at-e Islami in India, the Justice and Development Party in Turkey at least until 2010, or the Tayar Masry Party in Egypt, are exhibiting aspects of post-Islamism. Post-Islamist movements aspire to a secular state but wish to promote religious ethics in their societies.[15] This notion of post-Islamism is different from the individualized, diffused, and Salafi-type active piety, or what Olivier Roy calls "neo-fundamentalism," in which adherents aim not to establish an Islamic state but to reclaim and enhance the self while striving to implant the same mission in others.[16]

Historically, Islamism has been the political language not simply of the marginalized but particularly of high-achieving middle classes who saw their dream of social equity and justice betrayed by the failure of both capitalist modernity (represented by regional monarchs and sheikhdoms) and socialist utopia (embodied in the postcolonial modernist secular and populist states). They aspired to an alternative social and political order rooted in "indigenous" Islamic history, values, and thought. Segments of the poor population may support Islamism when they think it can increase their life chances. Even though different facets of Islamism have adopted different ways to achieve their ultimate goals, they have all used a religious, Islamic language and conceptual framework, favoring conservative social mores and an exclusive social order; they have displayed a patriarchal disposition and often intolerant attitudes toward different ideas and lifestyles. Theirs, then, has been an ideology and a movement based on a blend of religiosity and obligation with little commitment to the language of rights.

In its diverse forms, Islamism has undoubtedly been oppositional. But as the sociologist Bobby Sayyid observes, the question is not whether Islamism is oppositional but why so much of political opposition in the Middle East takes an Islamist form.[17] The resiliency of Islamism—despite its failures, transmutation, and post-Islamization—lies primarily in its serving as an identity marker in a global time deeply invested in the politics of "who we are," identity politics. Even the more recent upsurge of the apolitical and peaceful renewal movements of Da'wa and Tabligh, which oppose political Islam, may be seen in terms of identity politics.[18] However, Islamism offers an ideological package filled with seemingly consistent components, clear responses, and simple remedies, thus automatically rejecting philosophical doubts, intellectual ambiguities, or skeptical probing. Finally, Islamism continues to project a utopian image of itself in a world in which grand ideals such as communism, democracy, and freedom have collapsed or are being questioned; it continues to project itself as a uniquely combatant, revolutionary, and emancipatory ideology.

An Anti-imperialist Movement?

But how revolutionary, anti-imperialist, and emancipatory has Islamism been? From their street marches and protests to their welfare programs in the back streets of the Muslim metropolis; from their defiance of Israeli occupation and the US role in the Middle East to their antiglobalization rhetoric—everything appears to point to the relentless opposition of these movements to Western global domination. What political force has in recent years inflicted more economic, geopolitical, and physical injury to Western powers than militant Islamism?

The victory of the Islamic revolution in Iran and the subsequent seizure of the US embassy and diplomats in 1979 heralded the advent of a new oppositional force. The revolution threw the major ally of the West, the shah, out of power and instigated similar movements that threatened to erode US interests and influence in the Muslim Middle East. The writings of the Sorbonne-educated Ali Shariati, a key anti-imperialist Muslim intellectual, had a significant impact on a generation of revolutionaries who presided over state power in Iran after the shah was overthrown. Shariati brought the modern concepts of imperialism, class struggle, and revolution from Marx into Shiite Islamic discourse, giving a scientific legitimacy to what he termed "red" or "revolutionary Shi'ism."[19] It was a position of this sort that informed the "Islamic Marxism" of Iran's Mujahedin Khalq organization, which staged armed struggle against the shah and his US imperial ally, acting as a major player in the immediate postrevolutionary situation of 1979.[20] Encouraged by developments in Iran and enraged by Israeli expansionism, the Lebanese Hezbollah in the late 1980s moved to center stage in world radical politics, thanks to its relentless struggle to oust Israeli occupation forces from Lebanon. Sheikh Hassan Nasrallah, the leader of Hezbollah and an avid reader of Frantz Fanon, Che Guevara, and other anticolonial figures, has led an anticolonial resistance in southern Lebanon.

This type of revolutionary Third Worldism resonated also with Sunni Islamism. The Egyptian Sayyid Qutb, a leader in the Muslim Brotherhood, the oldest and largest Islamist movement in the Arab world, brought the concept of *jahili* state and society from the Indian thinker Abul Al'a Maududi, who was himself influenced by Lenin's perspective on organization and the state. The concept of *jahili* society in Qutb reflected more or less what the Iranian militants, following the philosopher Ahmad Fardid, dubbed "westoxification," a concept that captured the imagination of generations of anti-imperialist Iranians. Islamists have been enraged by what they see as the domination of their economy, polity, and especially their culture by Western powers, US-led globalization in particular, which subordinates their Islamic core values. Muhammad Mahdi Akif, a leader of Egypt's Muslim Brotherhood, regarded the US design in the Middle East, its call for "democratization," with great suspicion, because the United States has invariably supported the region's secular dictators and spread its "corrupting" cultural products throughout the Middle East.[21] Even the Muslim Brotherhood's younger and more moderate leadership continued to lash out at the United States for its building of a "global empire" under the guise of globalization and because it subverted the Muslim Brotherhood's objective of establishing an Islamic international entity in Muslim lands.[22] Indeed, the very process of globalization is considered no less than a "trap" to subjugate through modern technology the downtrodden of the world, in particular the Islamic umma.[23] For Islamists, imperialism is embodied not simply in military conquest and economic control; it manifests itself first and foremost in cultural domination through the spread of secular ideas, immorality, foreign languages, logos, names, food, and fashion.[24]

Thus, Ayatollah Mesbah Yazdi, a major theoretician of Iran's hard-liners, formulates the dictates of the *kuffar* (nonbelievers or the West) over Muslims in four domains. *Military conquest* as occurred in the Crusades may be uncommon, but it is accompanied by *political control*, or ruling through cronies and proxy regimes, and *economic dominance*, which creeps in by changing the consumer culture and exploiting material resources and economic dependency. But the most ravaging aspect is *cultural command*, a sort of soft imperialism established through science, technology, films, entertainment, foreign ideas, and values that insidiously subvert Islam's hegemony. What instigates cultural domination is partly the Western fear of annihilation, a kind of Darwinian struggle in which cultures need to dominate if they are not to vanish.[25] The idea of "global village," according to Egyptian Adel Hussein, is nothing other than the world ruled by a single village head, the United States; it is simply summed up in the Americanization of the planet. Precisely because Islam believes in human diversity, it inevitably challenges the homogenizing tendency of US-led globalization.[26]

Self-Serving Anti-imperialism

It is certainly reductionist to attribute the rise of Islamism to Cold War politics, to the US support for Islamists aiming to undermine communism.[27] Yet the fact remains that Islamists and the "free world" have at times acted as bedfellows in making tacit alliances against anti-imperialist secular movements in the Middle East. The United States has gone along quite easily with Saudi Arabia's attempt to promote Wahhabism as an ideological bulwark against the sweeping secular nationalism and republicanism that the Nasserist revolution unleashed in the 1960s. In the 1960s and early 1970s, Islamists were deployed against the revolutionary movements (as in Oman) as well as against secular leftists, communists, and women's movements. It has now become an open secret that the United States and the United Kingdom allied with the Islamist Mujahedin in Afghanistan to combat the USSR, and especially that the US-backed government of Pakistan sheltered the Taliban in their formative years. The rise of ISIS and its uncommon atrocities is now attributed to the support of the US ally in the Persian Gulf, the Saudi kingdom. Indeed, as early as 2012, a declassified US intelligence report "uncannily predicts—and effectively welcomes—the prospect of a 'Salafist principality' in eastern Syria and an al-Qaeda-controlled Islamic state in Syria and Iraq," an entity that the United States hoped would isolate the Syrian regime.[28]

In other words, imperialism has often benefited from groups of Islamist militants in the quest for the global spread of its hard and soft power. These convergences should not, however, conceal the deep enmity between the two forces. Yet the key question is, what is there in this for the mass of ordinary Muslims and the social forces who seek liberation from the new empire? Certainly Islamists' struggles do undercut certain material and strategic interests of the West. But do they necessarily undermine its global ideological hegemony? Islamists' struggles may contribute to liberating Muslim nations from foreign domination, even ensuring a durable independence—a critical achievement. But in this struggle do they herald liberty, democracy, and well-being of the subaltern subjects at home? Islamists in Iran sided with a popular revolution in 1979 that overthrew the autocratic regime of the shah, backed by Western powers, and seriously undermined foreign influence in the country. But once in power the ruling Islamists established a religious authoritarian state, an exclusive social order, and a strict moral discipline that have subjugated a large segment of the population ever since. They systematically suppressed rival anti-imperialist forces—the socialists, leftist women's groups, independent labor organizations, and student activists—violating many civil liberties and establishing draconian social control. They undermined much of the radical progressive ideas and movements—such as the popular councils, independent media, and social movements—that the revolution brought about. Indeed, the labeling of any cultural practice disapproved by the Islamist authorities as a Western "cultural invasion" (in the formulation of Ayatollah Mesbah Yazdi) has meant severe repression and the systematic disciplining of both youth and women in particular.[29] Even after the Islamic Republic participated in a nuclear deal, opening its doors to political and economic relations with the Western powers, the hard-liners continued to warn of the danger of Western cultural influence and plots to "alter our ideals, beliefs, and life-style."[30]

It is true that factional struggles within the Islamist regime between in-house rivals have at times opened some breathing space for dissent from below. Yet Islamist factions have invariably forged an alliance at the top when opposition from below has mounted; they have opposed inclusive democracy, pluralist ideas, and independent voices. It was only with the ascendancy to power of reformists led by President Mohammad Khatami (1997–2004) that new hope arose for democratic governance. However, with the reformists' defeat by 2004, massive disqualification of their candidates, and popular dissatisfaction with their economic failures, Mahmoud Ahmadinejad's government brought a new round of repression. During his first term (2005–2008) scores of independent NGOs were closed down, key activists incarcerated, intellectuals and journalists detained, dissenting faculty and students removed, women activists put behind bars, and mass protests of teachers and bus drivers put down. The conservative Islamists forged what is believed to be an electoral fraud in 2008 to keep Ahmadinejad in power for another term. The resulting protests galvanized in the Green revolt and brought the Islamist regime to the brink but faced effective suppression that more or less continued through the 2010s. Ahmadinejad's populist electoral campaign focused on a fight against corruption, generation of jobs, and generous distribution of oil money. Yet under his presidency the number of Iranians below the poverty line increased by 13 percent.[31] His cabinet—closely linked to the military, intelligence, and security apparatuses—built a support base in the network of clients among segments of the provincial poor but also among military veterans and those benefiting from connections to the state—administrators of the Revolutionary Guards, informal credit associations, and the like.[32] However justified it is to oppose Israel's continuing subjugation of the Palestinian people, Ahmadinejad's anti-Israel rhetoric was another matter when it extended to a denial of the Holocaust, making him a bedfellow with the most grotesque white supremacists such as David Duke, a former leader of the Ku Klux Klan.[33] The Islamist hard-liners in Iran and the Lebanese Hezbollah expressed support for the 2011 revolutions in Tunisia, Egypt, and Bahrain in the name of "Islamic awakening" but sided with Bashar al-Assad's regime to brutally suppress the revolution in Syria.

The contradictory and self-serving nature of Islamist anti-imperialism is not limited to Iran or Hezbollah. Egypt's Jama'a al-Islamiya not only moralized its constituency and imposed discipline on its followers' behavior; it also terrorized unveiled women and non-Muslims and murdered scores of Christian Copts and foreign tourists, while fighting fiercely against the US-backed regime of President Mubarak. Even the anti-imperialism of the Arab Mujahedin, who in the early 1990s rushed to "help" the Bosnian Muslims against Serbian aggression, in the end meant little to the victims. These Islamist internationals had their own Islamization agenda—one that the Bosnian Muslims resented. Instead of focusing on humanitarian objectives, they concentrated on military operations and missionary work—spreading Salafi ideas through print, TV, and websites. They challenged the local religious authorities and attempted to turn Bosnia into a base against the West, and the Bosnian conflict into a war between Islam and Christianity.[34] It is understandable that these kinds of activities created among Europeans a fear of radical "white Muslims" in the heart of Europe, thus jeopardizing the legitimacy of the otherwise just Bosnian cause. All these pale next to the kind of anti-imperialist militancy and brutality that the neo-Islamists like al-Qaeda, ISIS, and Boko Haram have since displayed, with the overwhelming victimization of ordinary Muslims. ISIS and al-Qaeda's elitism, misogyny, and widespread violence against their critics, secularists, religious minorities, and Shia Muslims are too well known to elaborate here. The bombing, torching homes, beheading, and raping have inflicted far heavier damage to indigenous and innocent lives than the interests of the empire. Of course, such self-serving anti-imperialism is not restricted to religious, or for that matter Islamist, experience; one has only to note the sad destiny of the champion of socialist anti-imperialism, the Zimbabwean Robert Mugabe, who ended up leading a nation that had to endure twenty-hour daily cuts in electricity, triple-digit inflation, and a massive demolition of poor people's homes.[35]

Clearly the opposition between Islamism and imperialism has been real. The politics and value system preached and practiced by Islamists would allow little of the kind of freedom that the current neoliberal hegemons so deeply cherish. The puritanical and largely exclusivist image of social order projected by Islamists clashes with the free flow of cultural goods and ideas that globalization unleashes. Islamists lash out at what they see as the homogenizing onslaught of globalization against cultural diversity; yet they strive to enforce homogeneous thought and lifestyles in the societies they rule. They defend, as do most democrats, the right of Muslim women in Europe to wear what they wish; yet many of them deny such rights to both Muslim and non-Muslim women in their societies. Islamists offer a doctrinal justification for this by arguing that Islam does not accept Muslims being subjected to the dominion of nonbelievers.[36] However, the notion of nonbelievers is often interpreted so broadly that it would potentially include any non-Muslim Westerner, even those who may express solidarity with the "Muslim cause." In short, key to the anti-imperialist disposition of Islamism has been the struggle over hegemony, for self-preservation. Islamists' desire to cultivate an exclusive morality and culture to facilitate their authority over the Muslim umma is subverted by the spread of Western cultural and discursive practices. So the fundamental question is not whether Islamism challenges imperialist interests, which it does. Rather, the question is to what extent, if any, this struggle entails an emancipation of the subaltern population in Muslim societies. While the old Islamism of the Cold War period showed inclinations to articulate a discourse of justice, fair distribution, and care for the poor, the new Islamism of the post–Cold War has largely upheld neoliberal ethics. And this lies at the heart of the difference between Middle Eastern Islamism and Latin American liberation theology, notwithstanding their shared religious languages and anti-imperialist positions.

A Theology of Liberation?

Whereas Islamism takes the establishment of an "Islamic order" as its principal objective from which social justice and the advancement of the deprived may follow, liberation theology considers the "liberation of the poor" as its point of departure; the gospel is then reread and reinterpreted to achieve this fundamental goal. The principal question for liberation theology was "How can we be Christians in the world of misery?" "We can be Christians, authentic Christians, only by living our faith in a liberating way," they replied.[37]

Originally liberation theology was a reaction to, and a reflection of, the hideous imperial legacy of the Catholic Church in Latin America. In contrast to the Islamic ulema who were mostly involved in anticolonial struggles in the Middle East, the Latin American Catholic Church was an instrument of Iberian colonialism, which was to bring riches to Spain and Portugal and to Christianize the colonies. Not only did the church support colonial rule; it continued to back the wealthy conservative classes in society after independence was achieved. Even some rethinking during the 1930s, reflected in "New Christendom" and the subsequent emergence of Christian democratic parties, failed to overturn the church's old conservative disposition. Yet dramatic social and political events (poverty and oppression, military coups, American support of the holders of power and property, failure of the Christian democratic parties, the sudden victory of the Cuban Revolution, and the wave of popular guerrilla movements) had pushed the church to the brink of social irrelevance. There was a need to intervene to save Catholicism from the conservatism of the church's elites. In this sense, liberation theologians were similar not to Islamists but to post-Islamist intellectuals and critical clerics who were concerned with rescuing Islam as an inclusive religion from the exclusivist practices of authoritarian Islamism; "republican theology" became the central thrust in post-Islamist religious discourse.[38] But the post-Islamist embrace of the market was no match for the socialist developmentalism of Latin American liberation theology.

Thus, unlike Islamism, liberation theology was not so much an expression of cultural identity in the sense of self-preservation in regard to a dominating Western other; it was embedded in the indigenous discourse of development, underdevelopment, and dependency that Latin America was fiercely debating at the time. Gustavo Gutiérrez, during the Conference of the World Council of Churches held in Switzerland in 1969, when clerics were exploring a "theology of development," replaced that term with "theology of liberation," popularizing the concept through his book *A Theology of Liberation*. Central to this notion was, of course, the emancipation of the subalterns.[39]

Islamism had a different birth and birthplace. Broadly speaking, contemporary Islamism arose in the 1970s as a language of self-assertion to mobilize those (largely middle-class high achievers supported often pragmatically by segments of the lower classes) who felt marginalized by the dominant economic, political, or cultural processes, those for whom the failure of both capitalist modernity and socialist utopia made the language of morality (religion) a substitute for politics. In a sense, it was the Muslim middle-class way of saying no to those whom they considered their excluders—their national elites, secular governments, and these governments' Western allies. So they rejected Western cultural domination, its political rationale, moral sensibilities, and cultural symbols, even if in practice many of them shared those symbols, as in their clothing, food, and technologies. They attempted to offer an alternative utopian society and state for Muslim humanity. It was also a project that aimed to regain the self-respect of Muslims relative to Western cultural imperialism and to Zionism as a perceived component of the contemporary empire. And all these aspirations arose in the context of the Cold War, when the US fear of communism and secular nationalism drew the country close to Islamist movements.[40]

While Islamists aimed to Islamize their society, polity, and economy, liberation theologians never intended to Christianize their society or states but to change society from the vantage point of the deprived. Liberation theology, then, had much in common with humanist, democratic, and popular movements in Latin America, including labor unions, peasant leagues, student groups, and guerrilla movements, with whom it organized campaigns, strikes, demonstrations, land occupations, and development work. Here, as a partner of a broad popular movement, liberation theology intended not to proselytize or make the coalition partners Christian but to help advance the cause of the liberation movement in general. More important, liberation theology shared a great deal with humanist Marxism. Indeed, both Latin American Marxism and liberation theology had been influenced by the language of the radical *dependencia* of the 1960s and 1970s that originated primarily in South America. Prominent priests such as Clodovo and Leonardo Boff (Brazil), Gustavo Gutiérrez (Peru), José Míguez Bonino (Venezuela), and Camilo Torres (Colombia) were intellectual theologians who offered the discourse of dependency and Marxist humanism.

Their reinterpretation of Christian theology was that it facilitated the goal of emancipation. They began first with the practice of liberation and then formed their theology as a reflection of that praxis. "There is no truth outside or beyond the concrete historical events in which men are involved as agents," argued Bonino.[41] The protagonists refrained from projecting a blueprint for the future. What they could present was a general direction and basic structures, or "historical projects"—something halfway to utopia. This human project sought to transcend capitalism and to imagine a form of democratic socialism. And ordinary people, the grassroots, would carry it out. Such an imagined society was to be informed by the spirit of participation and cooperation. People were to move beyond struggles for equality and justice to a society in which they would achieve true social solidarity, organized around the concept of love. In this sense, liberation theology espoused a revolutionary project.

Islamic Left

Like liberation theology in Latin America, old Islamism conditioned by Cold War politics was also influenced—albeit to a lesser extent—by socialist ideas. The appeal of equality, social justice, and liberation of the working class among the political and intellectual class was so powerful that Islamists could hardly ignore it. Muslim intellectuals such as the Indian Asghar Ali Engineer, Ali Shariati, and the Sorbonne-educated Egyptian philosopher Hassan Hanafi, an ex-Muslim Brotherhood member, had been striving since the 1970s to build an Islamic liberation theology. Hanafi's project of the "Islamic Left" aimed to build an intellectual and political movement by drawing on the revolutionary tenets of Islam to fight against Western imperialism, Arab state tyranny, and unjust distribution of wealth in Muslim societies. He invoked the Quran as a full advocate of the oppressed—"And we desired to show favor unto those who were oppressed in the earth, and to make them examples and to make them the inheritors" (28:5). By highlighting the liberatory potential of Islam—a religion of the Muslim masses—the Islamic Left was to overcome the fanaticism of the Islamists, elitism of the liberal opposition, and aloofness of the Marxist-Leninist circles from the Muslim masses.[42]

Ali Shariati and his followers, the Mujahedin Khalq, had already adopted Marxian economic thought and critique of capitalism. They brought such concepts as "class struggle," "exploitation," and "classless society" into the mythology of Shia Islam, blending them with Third Worldist language drawn from Fanon, Césaire, and other anticolonial leaders.[43] One of the "God-worshipping socialists" of the late 1960s, Shariati nevertheless remained critical of the materialist conception of humankind in Marxism and other Western philosophies. For him the revolutionary struggle against capitalist imperialism, not simply religious identity, should guide political alliances. Similarly, in the "Second Message of Islam," Mahmoud Mohammed Taha, the Sudanese Islamic thinker and political activist, called for following the Quran of Mecca as the basis for today's Muslim society and politics because that stage in the Prophet's life and message focused on building community, participation, and equality of humankind, including gender parity. As the leader of the Republican Party, he and his group contended that "Islam represented the only system capable of reconciling the individual need for freedom and society's need for social justice through a democratic socialist system."[44] Not surprisingly, when he opposed Jaafar Numeiri's military government for taking a harsh version of sharia law to legitimize his authoritarian rule, Taha was charged with apostasy and executed in 1985.

Earlier, Abul 'Ala Maududi had drawn on ideas from the Indian Communist Party, applying them to his vision of Islamic polity. Maududi's notion of Islamic "theo-democracy" was not very dissimilar to a kind of communist state in which the capitalist economy was to succumb to the principle of "justice." Influenced by Maududi, Sayyid Qutb, student of the literary critic al-Aqqad and whom President Nasser had asked to serve as editor in chief of the national radio station, had strongly advocated social justice in Islam. In *Conflict between Islam and Capitalism*, the militant Qutb urged fellow Muslims not to wait for the "miracle of Stalin," communism, to save them but stand up and fight for their own liberation, social justice, and dignity.[45]

The Shia cleric Muhammad Baqir al-Sadr's *Iqtisadina*, advocating distributionist justice and a noncapitalist economy, had a great influence on Shia Muslim intelligentsia, including the Lebanese Hezbollah leader Hassan Nasrallah, who remained an enthusiast of Fanon and Che Guevara. In addition, since the 1980s, many Sunni Marxists in Egypt (such as Tariq al-Bishri, Mohammad Emarah, Mustafa Mahmoud, Adel Hussein, and Abdel-Wahab El-Messiri) turned to religion and brought Marxian vocabulary and visions into political Islam, offering it as an indigenous Third Worldist ideology to fight secularism, Zionism, and Western imperialism.

Clearly, those who espoused Cold War Islamism had largely populist and anticapitalist orientations, had ambiguous relations with private property, and were disposed to moral economy. The Islamists lived and were socialized in the global conditions where socialist ideology not only stood against the capitalist West; it also informed the social world of anti-imperialist forces. Even though few Islamist activists self-consciously incorporated Marxist notions into their ideologies—they were particularly adamant to keep their distance from the secularist and materialist predisposition of socialism—they nevertheless showed inclinations toward distributive justice. Indeed, as early as 1954, the Orientalist historian Bernard Lewis had wondered fearfully why communism had so much appeal among Muslims despite their disdain of atheism. In response, Lewis pointed to the "inherent totalitarianism" embedded in the "very nature of Islamic society, tradition, and thought," dismissing as "accidental" the otherwise powerful quest for social justice and equality deemed rooted in socialism.[46]

Neo-Islamism

Things, however, began to change with the collapse of communism and the advance of neoliberal orthodoxy. Just as the radicalism of Latin American liberation theology was lost to the astonishing growth of Pentecostal Christianity and its laissez-faire undertone, Islamism also gave in to the irresistible charm of free enterprise. By the late 1980s and 1990s, the small Marxist influence among Islamist intellectuals disappeared; it gave way to the nativist ideas and "authentic" canons expressed in the Quran, sunna, and the classic Islamic treatises. The attempts by such Muslim thinkers as Asghar Ali Engineer, Hassan Hanafi, and Ali Shariati to build the intellectual basis for an Islamic liberation theology faded before the rising laissez-faire economics of emerging Salafi Islamism, the neoliberal populism of the Ahmadinejad strand, and the politically inclusive but free-market post-Islamist trends. The Islamist currents called Hanafi's project of the Islamic Left Marxist, while the liberal opposition called it Islamist. The intellectual reference of this neo-Islamism became limited almost entirely to the Quran, hadith, and *fiqh*, with little engagement with and use of other intellectual and political thoughts and almost no alternative economic vision.

Many Islamist leaders became involved in business investment and financial speculation that included corrupt elements. In Iran, the case of financial corruption committed by a number of Islamist officials during the presidency of Ahmadinejad ended up in the courts. A business venture of the Turkish AKP leader Recep Tayyip Erdogan exploded in the media in 2013. Reportedly, Erdogan's son Bilal, a Harvard graduate and intern at the World Bank, is an owner of the marine transportation corporation BMZ Group Denizcilik.[47] The Turkish popular saying "mujahedin turned contractors" represents this new class of pious capitalists enjoying political rent.[48] The Muslim Brotherhood in Egypt and its key leaders, such as Khairat el-Shater, have been known for their vast business operations—endeavors that are seen to bear no conflict with their religious ethics. The Brotherhood ideologue Yusuf al-Qaradawi had already formulated his "Islamic discourse" to accord with the age and spirit of neoliberal globalization. Unlike Christianity, according to Qaradawi, Islam would see no clash between faith and fortune, if only Muslims abided by their obligation to pay the Islamic tax, 2.5 percent of their capital assets.[49]

The Islamists in power largely followed, if not extended, economic liberalization. President Morsi of Egypt (2012–2013) adopted the IMF conditionalities and sought advice from the well-known neoliberal economist Hernando de Soto, who had worked on several occasions with ex-president Mubarak on Egypt's informal sector. The Muslim Brotherhood government followed economic and social policies that differed little from those of the Mubarak regime.[50] Its Salafi partner, the Nour Party, rarely discussed, let alone elaborated on, principles for organization of the economy, the public or private sector, the place of the market, integration of Egypt into the global economy, or any rationale for taxation or subsidies. In effect the Nour Party took the economic status quo for granted.[51] President Ahmadinejad spearheaded a kind of neoliberal populism in Iran—cutting subsidies on basic goods while dispensing cash selectively to individuals and families to manage their own welfare. This is a sharp departure from the 1980s leadership when Prime Minister Mir-Hossein Mousavi managed a war-stricken economy on a far more egalitarian basis.

Post-Islamists, who arose within the global postsocialist discourse of the individual, civil society, and free market, have taken laissez-faire economy as a fact. The Turkish ruling AKP, for instance, has worked closely with the IMF since coming to power in 2001 to "cut public spending, control wages, roll back agricultural support, and privatize enterprises as well as natural resources." In this context Islamic civil society—the Islamic press, associations, and religious orders—helped sacredize neoliberalism.[52] The AKP proposed a three-generational family model as a remedy to the absence of a welfare state. By taking care of the elderly, disabled, children, and unemployed, family is to serve to transfer the responsibility of the state to the citizens.[53] The Tunisian al-Nahda Party, notwithstanding its political wisdom and respect for electoral democracy, largely took laissez-faire as the frame for the country's economic problems, including its serious inequality. A study on Tunisia and Egypt concluded that "the development visions and actual policies defended and pursued [by al-Nahda and President Morsi of Egypt] could easily have reproduced the conditions that had created discontent and contestation [that led to the uprisings]."[54]

Even civil Islam or Islamic charities did not remain immune from neoliberal adjustment. Instead of dispensing direct assistance to the poor, the charities came to embrace practices—as in secular NGOs or Christian faith-based entities—that are associated with Western thinking on development. In the logic of what the geographer Mona Atia calls "pious neoliberalism," religious practices are reconfigured to operate "in line with principles of economic rationality, productivity, and privatization."[55] Thus, Islamic charities blended religious sensibilities with capitalist rationality: they monitored beneficiaries, placed conditions on their provisions, and justified such policies on religious grounds. Operating in private mosques, private foundations, and markets of religious goods, the charities promoted entrepreneurship and self-sufficiency, integrating the poor into the circuits of financial capital through their microenterprise initiatives. Dispensing aid to the poor became conditional to "verifiability" and "productivity."[56] This kind of marketization has transformed the Islamic sectors in many Muslim majority countries, ranging from Egypt, Turkey, and Lebanon to Iran and Indonesia.

Thus, instead of social and economic justice for the subaltern population, Islamists focused on building an exclusive moral and ideological community. Da'wa, an invitation to Islam, became a key objective for the gradualist and legalist Islamists, whereas violent jihad remained the strategy of militant jihadism; but both converged broadly on the idea of a closed social order, a polity based on sharia, and adherence to "cultural nativism." Some Islamists, notably those raised in Europe, embraced what Olivier Roy called "de-cultured Islam,"[57] an abstract Islam devoid of national or local cultures, easily lending itself to instrumentalization. But for most protagonists, deploying certain authentic or traditional values served to secure identity and difference in conditions where neoliberal globalization has increasingly blurred identity markers. In these postsocialist neoliberal times, Islamists became extraordinarily similar to their political foes—on their ideas about property, accumulation, and poverty or in business methods, marketing, education, consumption, and dreams and desires.

ISIS

The same is true for jihadists like those in ISIS. Far from being simply medieval or traditional, as some have claimed,[58] ISIS may be said to represent an Islamism of the neoliberal order with which it has much in common—and that perhaps may explain its singular distinctions, including its uncommon savagery. An outcome of the US invasion of Iraq, ISIS originally embodied the grievances of the marginalized Sunni sect against the Shia rulers in Iraq and Syria; it was galvanized by the military skills of the Ba'thist army officers, built on an ideology of jihadi Salafism, and projected on an imagined Islamic caliphate—a unified totalitarian community tied to powerful leadership cult, obedience, and "pure" Islam without innovation.[59] Above all, ISIS is a child of our current globalization dynamics—the new communication and information revolution—that produces effects far beyond the intent. ISIS probably never imagined that it would cause such a sensation and receive so many volunteers—some seventeen thousand from ninety countries, including more than thirty-five hundred fighters from Europe, North America, and Australia.[60]

But key operators—the fighters, logisticians, propagandists, website managers, and the like—are very similar to their adversaries in their lifestyle, education, consumption, economic imaginations, and social world. A random survey of some of the activists reported in the press would include, for instance, a US blond Christian convert, an Australian male model, a British banker working in the city, a body builder, an Indian businessman, a French pizza delivery man, and five European soccer players. Imran Khawaja, nicknamed "Barbie," was also a body builder. Mohammed Emwazi, known as "Jihadi John," was a computer science graduate; and the Egyptian volunteer Islam Yaken had graduated from a private school and chased girls before he sought seclusion by joining ISIS after General Sisi's takeover in 2013. The Georgian ISIS commander, Abu Umar al-Shishani (Tarkhan), had worked in a Georgian military-intelligence unit trained by US experts.[61] The Belgian Abdelhamid Abaaoud, the mastermind behind the November 2015 Paris attacks, studied in an exclusive Catholic school, never went to mosque, and got involved in drugs and petty crime.[62] Mohammed Abdirahim Abdullahi, the leader of the al-Shabaab squad that slaughtered 148 people at the Kenyan Garissa University College in April 2015, was a law school graduate, son of a chief, a sharp dresser, and a pool player who ran a business.[63] In many ways these operators were Western or Westernized individuals, with a social existence as part of the neoliberal order. But in their political positions they differed profoundly from their adversaries, considering them as occupiers, arrogant hegemons, exploiters, tyrants, or their collaborators.

It is perhaps this similarity and coincidence of socioeconomic worlds that may ironically be the source of extreme differentiation and exaggerated emphasis on difference. In other words, when conflicts erupt between social groups with a history of similarity and coexistence, rival parties make an *exaggerated* attempt to highlight the difference and wipe out blurring and confusion. So, from this Simmelian outlook, ISIS's brutal beheadings, burning prisoners, taking enemy women as slaves, killing children for watching soccer, or destroying ancient artifacts may be intended to exaggerate difference in the face of their similarities to clear up ambiguity and blurring.[64] They are saying to their rivals (and to themselves) that when you claim human rights, we commit beheadings and burn people alive; if you speak of elections and democracy, we establish a model of a borderless top-down caliphate; you are Western and Westernized, but we are "authentic."[65] Why should the gay man Omar Mateen announce support for ISIS and brutally murder forty-nine people in an Orlando, Florida, gay bar (June 2016) but to exaggerate his difference from those whose "shameful" sexuality he shared? It is no surprise that ISIS strives to project itself as a moral order of a distinct nature completely different from what exists in the real world. The insistence by the ISIS magazine *Dabiq* that there is no "gray zone" in the holy war points precisely to their intent to erase ambiguity and clouding between "us" and "them."[66] In choosing rue Jean-Pierre Timbaud from which to launch their indiscriminate killings in Paris, the ISIS militants meant to obliterate what they saw as a gray zone, a neighborhood of unusual diversity—with Christians, Jews, Muslims, foreigners, expats, intellectuals, "bourgeois bohemians," and people of modest background—not knowing that those people who lived together on the same street, had in fact separate lives. "We are all together, on our own, waving to each other," stated a resident.[67]

But what drives these seventeen thousand young men from ninety countries to venture into a land, Raqqa or Mosul, with which they have little affinity? Is it religion? Interviews with ISIS rank and file seem to confirm that they are "woefully ignorant about Islam" and have difficulty answering questions about sharia law, militant jihad, and the caliphate.[68] Even superficial religious knowledge is not necessary to join movements like ISIS. Some may be driven by "desires for adventure, activism, romance, power, belonging, along with spiritual fulfillment,"[69] or even opportunism. It may be simplistic and even misleading to describe ISIS as a "revolution," considering the lack of almost any support among the Muslim masses;[70] an Arab Barometer survey showed Arab sympathy for ISIS ranged from 0.4 percent in Jordan to 6.4 percent in Palestine.[71] At best it may be a "revolution" of the vanguard in moments of agitation that has little affinity with the lives, desires, and demands of ordinary people whom the vanguard rules. But for many members of this vanguard, like the notorious Jihadi John, ISIS is perhaps the illusion of an ideological home, a community of selfless warriors for a just global order, brotherhood, and borderless caliphate; it is a quest for a utopia in a world that has shed all its grand ideals, no matter if this jihadi utopia turns out to be a nightmare for those ordinary Syrians or Iraqis who are trapped in its grip. Raqqa in Syria had a population of one million before ISIS arrived; in 2015 there were only four hundred thousand, despite restrictions on emigration, including confiscation of properties.[72]

Anti-imperialism or Emancipation?

At one level Islamism has shown a formidable opposition to the new empire, contributing to undercutting certain strategic interests of the Western powers, especially those of the United States. Islamists have spearheaded protracted public protests against US policies in the Middle East, especially its support for Israel, while the occupation of Palestinian lands continues. They have also opposed the region's secular authoritarian regimes and diminished or disrupted the normalization of US control in the region, particularly in Iran, Iraq, and Afghanistan.

But has Islamism been able to offer, either in practice or in vision, a viable alternative to imperialist domination? Despite its practical failures, socialism managed for some time to articulate a powerful theoretical model of social justice and liberation of the oppressed that offered a solid alternative to capitalist hegemony. For a long while, it undermined the ideological foundation of bourgeois values and the capitalist economic model. Its ideal of internationalism would galvanize, above all else, in the International Brigade, the heroic gathering of some forty thousand socialists from fifty-three nations to fight alongside their Spanish Republican workers, farmers, and comrades against the fascist coup led by General Francisco Franco that began the Spanish Civil War (1936–1939). However, the situation has been different with Islamism. The largely culturalist thrust of Islamists' anti-imperialism has meant that they have little to offer in the domain of political economy. Even the distributive populism of Cold War–era Islamism remained largely a feature of its *movement* phase. The macroeconomic policies of the Islamist states such as Iran, Saudi Arabia, Sudan, and Afghanistan, despite their variation, differed not much from those of other nonideological developing economies with comparable national incomes; and there is little in the Islamism of the neoliberal age to characterize as redistributive concerns.

A preoccupation with particularistic cultural and religious struggles has allowed little room to work with global movements that pursue broader concerns such as the environment, livelihoods, and welfare systems. This culturalism and ideological exclusion, instead of forging alliances, has caused division and hostility at both national and international levels. Although a populist posture, affordable welfare provisions, moral language, and fierce opposition to corrupt Middle East regimes have earned Islamist movements support, they have failed to set up a viable substitute because of their patriarchal, exclusivist, authoritarian vision of social order and lack of solid economic foresight. If anything, Islamism, especially its violent version, has played into the hands of imperialist circles; its policies have in practice justified and dignified the position of its neoliberal enemies who preach individual liberty and open social order. The undemocratic precepts and practices of most Islamist groups have provoked widespread Islamophobia, security measures, illiberal policies, and global surveillance, which taken together have victimized ordinary Muslims in the West and in the Muslim world alike.

The 1980 seizure of the US embassy in Tehran was bold and a blow to the US sense of self-importance, but it led to surveillance at home and hostility abroad. On the same day that the Muslim militants climbed over the embassy walls, a large group of unemployed marched in the streets of Tehran to demand jobs and social protection. But the desperate appeals of those marchers were stifled by the nationalist outcry of the militants who were preoccupied with "Islam against the Great Satan."[73] The hostage taking also pushed the United States to support a devastating Iran-Iraq War that cost millions of lives and massive economic destruction. Only recently have some critics openly wondered who benefited from this anti-imperialist act—the umma or imperialism? Again after some three decades history seemed to repeat itself. President Ahmadinejad's rhetoric over the Holocaust and his populist language played into the hands of the most dangerous warmongers in Washington and Tel Aviv, who had been fantasizing about massive air strikes against the Islamic Republic.[74] These acts and their damaging consequences appear modest when compared to the anti-West violence of al-Qaeda or ISIS. In its fight, ISIS has indeed resurrected the old ideal of internationalism, but in a murderous campaign whose victims have overwhelmingly been ordinary individuals and mostly Muslims.

Far from demagogy and voluntarism, a meaningful anti-imperialism is about building a hegemony that rests on the universal ideals of justice, inclusion, and human dignity. It is about winning the hearts and minds of global humanity to resist the diktat of the new empire through a patient, painstaking, and scrupulous strategy. This means opening up, connecting, negotiating, and developing a global platform with and for those in the world (from various races, religions, and genders) who struggle for liberation—not simply liberation from foreign, imperialist domination but also liberation from political, patriarchal, economic, and religious domination at home. This means transcending nativism, exclusivism, authoritarian codes, and xenophobia. The Zapatista movement in Mexico may perhaps represent this understanding of anti-imperialism. Emerging from the state of Chiapas on the day the North American Free Trade Agreement (NAFTA) was put into effect on January 1, 1994, the Zapatista movement campaigned against US imperialism, economic globalization, and NAFTA, favoring participatory democracy, economic justice, and inclusion, especially of indigenous peoples. Ideologically it combined Mayan culture with libertarian socialism. With its tactic of civil resistance, creative use of Internet mobilization, links with world progressive groups, and antiglobalization movements, it galvanized broad global support to help struggle against internal injustice and neoliberal empire, ensuring tangible change in the life of the locals, gender equality, and health of the deprived.[75]

Any struggle, however heroic, that replaces imperialist supremacy with domestic forms of oppression will not serve the well-being of the subaltern population. An emancipatory project may not deserve its name if it falls short of being inclusive, egalitarian, and universal. For decades in the Middle East, the majority of people and liberatory ideas have been held hostage to the crossfire between nationalism and colonialism, between Ba'athism and imperialism, and currently between Islamism and neoliberal empire, from which they are struggling to exit. The central question, then, is not just how to challenge the empire but how to realize liberation; for the ultimate end is not simply anti-imperialism but emancipation.

5   Cities of Dissent

Revolutions are not just about extraordinary rebels, astute leaders, or strategic visions, however indispensable they may be. Nothing promising is likely to transpire without the mass of ordinary people, those subaltern subjects struggling to make ends meet; their engagement is vital to bring revolts into the social mainstream. Urban life can push subalterns to engage in extraordinary politics not only by cultivating dissent but also by providing space for its expression. In the past three decades many large cities in the Middle East have experienced a neoliberal transformation, a kind of restructuring that added new depth and dimensions to urban dissent. Here I examine what the neoliberal city under authoritarian rule meant to urban space and its subaltern population—what sorts of strains it placed on the ordinary urbanites and what kinds of opportunities it offered for political engagement. Not only did this new urbanity furnish extensive marginalization; it also fostered new dynamics of publicness with important implications for "street politics" and the "political street" and extended the possibilities for popular dissent and insurrection. With a focus on the urban Middle East, my purpose is to show where the grassroots support for the Arab uprisings came from and how it was formed. This chapter introduces a broad analytical frame and language, which continue in the next chapter with the narratives of how dissent was produced and played out in the Arab squares.

Neoliberal Urbanity

The spread of neoliberal logic largely through the implementation of Economic Reform and Structural Adjustment (ERSAP) has since the 1980s had enduring effects on the economies and societies of the Global North and South.[1] It has resulted in lasting imprints on the urban space, engendering what may be called neoliberal cities. The neoliberal city is a market-driven urbanity; it is a city shaped more by the logic of market than the needs of its inhabitants, responding more to individual or corporate interests than public concerns. It is marked by an increasing deregulation and privatization of production, collective consumption, and urban space. Public amenities become subject to outsourcing while the logic of private business is brought into urban governance. In this logic, the urban space becomes the function of what Harvey calls "surplus-capital absorption" in that the city becomes the site of capitalist operation in pursuit of profitability rather than one that serves public needs.[2] This means that the state and public officials, as well as citizens, play a lesser role in shaping the city than before or act on behalf of the capitalist accumulation rather than the interests of city inhabitants. This new restructuring has in practice caused much change in the domains of work/production, collective provisions, and the life world (the way in which people subsist and operate in their daily existence), all with far-reaching implications for configuring the urban space and politics.[3]

With the gradual implementation of the structural adjustment in the Middle East since the 1990s, the ex-populist or socialist states increasingly retreated from public provision and collective welfare; public-sector firms have been rationalized, private enterprises increased, and urban employment structure experienced a dramatic shift. We have now seen the shrinking of the traditional labor-intensive public sector, which in the postcolonial era in the 1960s and 1970s was the dream of workers and the fairly educated middle layers. No other sector would match the perks, bonuses, job security, flexibility, and status associated with public-sector firms. It was, in addition, here that the most organized trade unions emerged and further boosted employment in this sector. However, with neoliberal rationalization, employment in this sector shrank; workers were laid off, transferred, or retrained for different jobs, while their perks, security, and welfare diminished or disappeared. Continuing rationalization further brought about unemployment, casual work, and an expanding informalization, which altogether has resulted in the fragmentation of urban labor.[4] Currently, a pervasive sector of dispersed informal and casual jobs and services marks the economic destiny of the neoliberal cities.[5] An estimated 180 million Arabs subsist in this sector.[6]

The partial retreat of public authorities from the provision of collective consumption like urban services, health, and education left people's everyday necessities to either the whim of private capital, the reach of the NGOs, or the mercy of religious charities, which are increasingly informed by neoliberal ideas. Not only were essential subsidies on basic staples like bread, oil, and gas cut back or reduced; the removal of rent control subjected scores of vulnerable households (in particular, the newly married and young families) to the dictates of the land market.[7] The predominance of private capital in urban operations meant that fundamental goods, services, and spaces—such as drinking water, electricity, transportation, garbage collection, green spaces, clean air, schools, clinics, and policing or security—were subject to privatization or were, at best, provided by a three-tier (state-private-NGO) system in which the affordable state provision was decreasing because of low investment or by "backdoor privatization." Thus, in this backdoor privatization, patients, for instance, have to bring their own medicine to public hospitals, or pupils have to have private lessons in public schools to compensate for the deterioration of public education.[8] The costly private sector kept expanding, and so did the NGOs wherein meaningful development remained minimal, while identity politics (e.g., Islamic NGOs versus Christian NGOs) was reinforced, deepening ethnic or religious divides.[9] In the Middle East, the NGO sector played a mediating role in transitioning to marketization and commodification.[10]

Today, the deterioration of working-class public housing, with its dilapidated structures and profound neglect, is essentially an extension of slum life.[11] Egypt's public housing, a vestige of President Nasser's distributionist socialism, differs little from the substandard informal settlements in their dereliction and disregard and are less flexible for expansion and innovation. In what Harvey calls "accumulation by dispossession," the states assist in pushing the poor, who have insecure tenure rights, out of the city center so they can grab high-quality land to hand over to the corporations in pursuit of mega projects such as shopping malls, leisure sites, or office buildings.[12] This is an extension of the age-old policy of gentrification, where dispossession takes place de facto by the invisible force of high prices and inhospitable social ecology. Thus, in place of public housing or the amenities of the welfare-state era, we see today the development of mega projects that cater largely to local and foreign elites.

Of course, these processes are not totally new; rather, they have been accentuated and intensified by neoliberal policies, which, in the meantime, herald decentralization, democracy, and citizen participation. The idea of a diminished role of the state has been predicated on the participation of the civil society in urban governance through NGOs, local councils, and municipalities to deliver services, organize budgets, or conduct local planning. Even though the civil society is unequal, and primarily the more privileged institutions are able to influence governance, some opportunities for subaltern mobilization may also open up. What did these remarkable processes mean to the urban space and its inhabitants? More specifically, how are the politics of the urban subaltern population articulated in these neoliberal times? Proponents of informality such as Hernando de Soto view the sector as the clear expression of the deep desire of people in the Global South to enhance free enterprise. Informality then stands as an alternative to the stifling state control over the economy.[13] De Soto even argues that the Arab revolutions were in part pushed by the "forces of the market" to "emancipate the entrepreneurial poor."[14] Here I do not wish to delve into discussing the merit of such propositions—in fact, a strong argument suggests that neoliberal policies have played a key role in the revolutionary dissent.[15] Rather, I suggest that the body of literature on informality has strikingly little to say about the spatial implications of informal life and even less on the effects of the neoliberal city and the kind of politics it engenders. These are crucial, for they have significant bearing on the formation of dissent, the raw material for the Arab uprisings.

The City Inside Out

I propose that a key spatial feature of the neoliberal city relates to double processes of "inside outing" and "enclosure." The neoliberal city is in part a city inside out, where a massive portion of the urban population, the subalterns, become compelled to operate, subsist, or simply live in the public spaces—in the streets, in a substantial "outdoor economy." Here public space becomes an indispensable asset, capital, for people to survive, operate, and reproduce life. Strolling in the streets of Cairo, Tehran, Tunis, or Istanbul in the middle of a working day, one cannot help noticing the astonishing presence of so many people operating outdoors in the streets—working, running errands, standing, sitting, playing, negotiating, or driving. One wonders why there are such inconceivable traffic jams at this time of day when people are supposed to be in enclosed spaces.

The increasing layoffs and unemployment (the Middle East–North Africa [MENA] region had the highest, 26 percent, youth unemployment rate in the world in the 1990s and 2000s),[16] which resulted from restructuring the public sector, removing job guarantees, and transferring from manufacturing to services and high-tech capital-intensive industries, boosted both casual and durable informal work. This work is embodied in street vendors, messengers, drivers, and carriers or in those laboring in street workshops (such as street laundries, car washes, mechanic shops, alleyway repair shops) and the spectacular pavement restaurants. Tens of thousands of motorcyclists make a living by illegally working on the streets of Tehran, transferring mail, money, documents, goods, and people in constant contention with the police. Some 100,000 such cyclists move around the Tehran bazaar area alone every hour. In 2009, the police confiscated over 78,000 motorcycles and fined some 292,000 in this same area.[17] Diminishing income and protection (such as food subsidies and rent control) have compelled many poor families to deploy more family members, like women and children, to earn a living, who often end up in the outdoor economy, if they choose not to seek state support and thus put pressure on the income of the relatives.

Of course, there has always been the option of pavement homes or simply homelessness. But given that space is also culturally constructed, the phenomenon may take varied forms. Middle Eastern cities have largely been free from the kind of stripped homelessness or "sidewalk life" that may characterize, for instance, Bombay or Delhi. For an exposed life under the public gaze of "friends and foes" constitutes the greatest of failures, thus obliging families to try at all costs to secure some sort of shelter to protect the inhabitants not only from cold and heat but especially from the public gaze, from being a spectacle. While adults may not be able to withstand the cultural agony of a bare life in the public gaze, children have a different reaction. Indeed, street children—three million in Egypt—as a dark side of neoliberal urbanity have now emerged as a salient marker of large cities in this region of the world. Here, in the cityscapes, under bridges, in graveyards, and side streets, street children have formed flourishing outdoor communities, some with elaborate order, discipline, and an outdoor economy of survival by begging, stealing, laboring, and prostitution.[18]

Slum dwelling, casual work, under-the-table payment, and street hawking are no longer characteristics of the traditional poor; they have spread also among educated young people with higher status, aspirations, and social skills—government employees, teachers, and professionals. Informal life and precarity have thus become a facet of educated middle-class existence, forming a new middle-class poor. By 2011, 30 percent of college graduates in Egypt, Tunisia, and Jordan were out of work. Taking advantage of the actually existing flexibility, and facilitated by overemployment, informality, and corruption in the public sector, many state employees subsidized their meager income by taking second or third jobs, often in the outdoor economy. Thus, it is not uncommon to discover that taxi drivers, street petition writers, or various kinds of traders are actually teachers, low-income bureaucrats, army personnel, or even professionals such as lawyers. I recall in Tunis in the spring of 2011 that a young man who offered to guide me to an address in exchange for two dinars was a college graduate who had studied literature.

Now that men tend to work in multiple jobs day in and day out, with the result that they are never home, women and housewives have to take on many of the tasks traditionally assigned to men—paying bills, attending to bank business, dealing with car mechanics, daily shopping, taking children to and from school, or going to government offices. Thus, women too, whether working outdoors or running errands, have increasingly been mobile and present in public spaces—streets, offices, buses, trams, and traffic. Contrary to the prevailing assumption about the Muslim Middle East, Islamic tradition, especially veiling, has not prevented women from public presence and visibility. If anything, it has helped their mobility by "protecting" them from the unwanted male gaze. Even though the rise in the expression of public piety in the form of the hijab has placed greater pressure on unveiled women in public places, it has allowed greater freedom for women from traditional families to be active in outdoor public places. It might seem surprising, but in 2011 some two thousand veiled women worked as taxi drivers along with their male counterparts in Tehran under the Islamic Republic. This kind of compelled and desired publicness stands in sharp contrast to André Gorz's notion of domestic or "home work" as the "sphere of freedom" and self-regulation in contrast to the discipline of social economy (or the sphere of necessity), where people have to work to survive.[19] In today's Middle Eastern neoliberal cities, the outdoor economy and public presence are both a necessity and (for some women) a space for self-expression.

The city inside out is not limited to the spatial features of working life; it resonates even more powerfully in the everyday life world. Simply, neoliberal logic expands and deepens the informalization of life worlds, of which outdoor life is a key attribute. Thus, the gentrification of city centers to accommodate global enterprises tends to push scores of low-income and middle-class families (state employees, teachers, professionals, or the workers) to live their lives in the expanding slums and squatter areas where outdoor life constitutes an underlying feature. Not only does informal subsistence heavily rest on the outdoor economy; the informal communities, slums, and squatter settlements rely greatly on outdoor public space that inhabitants utilize as places of work, sociability, entertainment, and recreation.

Strolling through the back streets of Cairo, Tunis, or Aleppo, one could not miss the spread of vast markets, mechanic shops, or pavement restaurants in packed neighborhoods; there might be the sound of happy music from colorful tents filled with families, friends, and neighbors attending a wedding ceremony; or a somber sound of Quran recitation signaling a death in the neighborhood; or the energetic commotion of teenage boys playing soccer. And all these are happening outdoors on the space of the streets and alleyways. Simply, the poor people's cramped shelters, as in Cairo's Dar El Salam settlement, for instance, are too small and insufficient to accommodate their spatial needs. With no courtyard, no adequate rooms, or a spacious kitchen if there is any at all, the poor inhabitants are compelled to extend their daily existence into public outdoor spaces—to the alleyways, streets, open spaces, or rooftops. It is in such places where the poor engage in cultural reproduction, in organizing public events—weddings, festivals, and funerals. Here, the outdoor spaces serve as indispensable assets to both the economic livelihood and social/cultural lives of much of the urban population.[20]

Unlike the rich, who can enjoy an expensive enclosed life, the poor cannot afford to frequent indoor restaurants, cafés, holiday resorts, or hotels. Anyone strolling in the streets of Cairo during such holidays as Eid al-Adha (the feast of sacrifice) or Eid al-Fitr (the end of fasting month) cannot help noticing overwhelmingly poor families, the young and the old, dressed up in their colorful outfits, on the Nile Cornish streets or the adjacent waterways, to enjoy affordable fun and festivity offered there. The unemployed male youth or elderly people, as in Cairo or Tunis, can afford only outdoor cheap coffee shops, where they can spend hours engaged in prolonged leisure activities or build "forms of intimacy" beyond family.[21]

In a striking contrast to the stretching out of the poor, there has been a simultaneous process of enclosure that represents one of the most glaring features of neoliberal urbanity. Along with the expansion of slums, with their real and imagined dangers of crime and extremism, has come the historic flight of the rich into the safe havens of private cities, gated communities—the Beverly Hills, the Utopias, the Dream Lands, and Sidi Bou Said of the large cities of the Middle East.[22] These super rich are among the new class of dot.com-like professionals and private developers who also aspire to live the life-styles of the private city dwellers. As the lower classes were encroaching and increasing their presence in public spaces, where it seemed "they were everywhere," the rich, now apprehensive of the physical presence and "social dangers" of the dispossessed, sought their own enclosed and exclusive zones— private beaches, exclusive neighborhoods, gated communities, and securely guarded bars, restaurants, and places of sociability, work, and even locations of worship and prayer. In cities like Cairo, the globalizing rich rarely attend the prayer halls of the ordinary people; instead, they generate their own private mosques, sermons, and religious teaching by bringing paid preachers and sheikhs to the secure spaces of their exclusive habitat. It is not just in Rio de Janeiro or Johannesburg that the elites' sense of security has been ensured by bodyguards, checkpoints, electronic monitoring systems, and barbed wire; the elites of Tehran, Tunis, and Istanbul also expressed profound anxiety about "urban dangers." Even their automobiles have not been spared formidable locks, bolts, and alarms.[23]

With such real and subjective checkpoints and barriers, neoliberal cities cease to be the spaces of flaneur, the free flow of inhabitants in the urban expanse. The privatization of streets and neighborhoods means that "outsiders" lose access to these exclusive places, while the threat of real and imagined crime and violence restricts the movement of the rich, as well as ordinary people, notably women, into many areas of these cities.[24] Moreover, the incongruous urban ecology and outsiderness, enforced by the piercing gaze of locals, would deter an uninvited "stranger" by making the person feel out of place. One then wonders what such urban landscapes with their pattern of "outdoorsing" and "enclosure" mean to the notions of public and private. If public space is understood broadly in terms of open, accessible, and inclusive space that is regulated by public authorities, then how public are such spaces when segments of the urban population lose access to them because of fear of being out of place? What happens to the public character of the spaces on which the poor extend their lives, turning them into private economic assets or avenues of sociability for weddings, funerals, or soccer games? What happens to privacy in its cultural and established sense—protection from public intrusion such as the public gaze? How private are the lives of tens of thousands of poor families who live—sleep, give birth, and raise children—on the rooftops of Cairo? These hybrid spaces subvert the rigid separation of private and public in the cities of the Middle East.

Subaltern Politics in the Neoliberal City

What are the implications of neoliberal urbanity in the Middle East for the politics of urban subalterns—particularly those who operate under authoritarian states and repressive regimes? The prevailing view on the Left seems to suggest that a neoliberal city is a lost city—where capital rules, the affluent enjoy, and the subalterns are entrapped. It is a city of glaring inequality and imbalance, where the ideal of the "right to the city," the ability of inhabitants to collectively restructure the urban, has all but vanished.[25] Evidence in a number of cities in the Global South, including the Middle East, seems to give some plausibility to this claim.[26] For instance, Mona Fawaz's studies on Beirut document how neoliberal policies have in the past three decades disempowered the "informal people," because urban land prices have increased (as a result of the presence of expats, foreign capital, and companies), police control on their encroachments has expanded, provision of social services has been delegated to nonstate agencies such as NGOs and political parties, and there is now greater competition for such meager services because their clientele now includes the impoverished middle classes.[27] This is in line with Harvey's argument that the poor are structurally entrapped in the logic of capital from which they have little chance to escape unless something is done to change the way that capitalism as a whole operates.[28] For instance, how can the poor deal with the deteriorating environment that affects their lives in a city where leisure, green spaces, and clean air are becoming privatized? While the rich may retreat into their green clubs, gated communities, weekend resorts, or secluded air-conditioned residences, the poor have few options. Even resorting to NGOs (which mediate between the poor and other social movements) without having allies with powerful institutions within the states cannot help. As Peter Evans suggests, only a synergy of the communities, NGOs, and the state may be able to address the problems of urban "livability."[29] In short, the neoliberal city is the victim of "urbicide" by global elites who kill cities such as Managua by disembedding and fragmenting them through zoning and expressways that connect the elites' work and leisure to their gated communities, leaving the rest to decay in the poverty, crime, and violence of slums.[30]

Quite distinct from this position are those of other thinkers such as Mike Davis, who seem to actually sense a stiff resistance on the part of the dispossessed in the "planet of slums." Indeed, for Davis, slums are like "volcanoes waiting to erupt," and their explosion might herald the emergence of "some new, unexpected historical subject" carrying a "global emancipatory" project. Even though slum dwellers do not constitute a Marxian proletariat, they are believed to have the potential to carry out radical actions.[31] Indeed, slums already constitute the highly volatile collective where the "gods of chaos," the dispossessed, the "outcasts," deploy their remarkable strategy of chaos—

suicide bombing and "eloquent explosions"—to counter the "Orwellian technologies of repression."[32] Other analysts like Jo Beall and Dennis Rodgers view the spectacular gang violence in Latin America as representing the response of the dispossessed to their excluded status. Gangs, in fact, correspond to vanguard forms of what James Holston calls "insurgent citizenship," attempting through violence to carve new spaces for possible alternative futures within the context of their wider exclusion.[33] Slums, in short, herald the "urban wars of the twenty-first century," similar to Eric Wolf's "peasant wars of the twentieth century."[34] Since the violence affects both rich and poor, Dennis Rodgers concludes that the subalterns have basically lost this war to the neoliberal political economy and its henchmen.[35]

While these analyses offer valuable insights into our understanding of the predicament of the ordinary urbanites in these new liberal times, they also raise important questions. For instance, if in Harvey's view, the solution to counter the process of dispossession lies in forging large-scale global social movements to undo or stop the neoliberal onslaught, how are the poor to carry this responsibility? If the dispossessed are to wait for a social revolution to reverse the course of capitalist encroachment, what are they to do in the meantime; what strategy they should pursue in their daily lives? In other words, for the foreseeable future, the urban disenfranchised are trapped in the structural web of the current capitalist system and the states that uphold it. Mike Davis, however, appears to be more optimistic. He seems to believe that a formidable resistance is already taking place, one couched in the rapid spread of Pentecostalism in African and Latin American slums and the language and violent practices of radical Islam in the Middle East—suicide bombing and spectacular explosions.

This, however, is a difficult argument to sustain. As I have suggested earlier in this book, radical Islam is hardly the ideology of the urban dispossessed; rather, it builds on the attitudes and expectations of the broadly educated middle classes who feel marginalized in the prevailing economic, political, and international domains.[36] When Davis speaks of spectacular violence emanating from slums, he seems to refer to the exceptional cases of Baghdad and Palestinian Gaza, where poverty and exclusion had been mixed with a blatant foreign occupation (the United States in Iraq and Israel in Palestinian territories). Almost nowhere else in the Global South, including the Middle East, do we observe the same type of violence as developed at times in Baghdad's Sadr City or the Gaza Strip in the mid-2000s. And Pentecostal Christianity, which has developed quickly in Latin America and Africa since the 1990s, has had little impact on mobilizing slum dwellers, and the Pentecostal political parties enjoy little support from the very poor.[37] In Africa, Pentecostal ethics, "wealth as a spiritual virtue," corresponds well with the spirit of aspiring middle classes who hear from their church that "you can be both rich and redeemed."[38] Finally, the accounts offered by Jo Beall and Dennis Rodgers on slum wars and violence remain by and large centered on Latin America. Their analysis of urban violence as the function of economic and political relations remains acultural. Why has such a high level of violence in many Latin American cities had little resonance in, say, the Middle Eastern slums, despite more or less similar economic and political exclusion? It becomes imperative to contextualize poor people's politics within their respective political cultures in relation to their specific subjectivities and the possible alternative venues that different dispossessed groups in different national settings often deploy to address (or not to address) their exclusion.

In fact, an exclusive focus on such postconflict social violence as gangs or on conventional large-scale mobilization and social movements may distract us from paying adequate attention to the intricate processes of "life as politics" among subalterns in the cities of the Global South. An exclusive preoccupation with such categorical dichotomies as passive-active or win-lose can entrap our conceptual imagination, preventing us from exploring further and discovering the intricate ingenuity that subalterns may discreetly use to assert and defend themselves. In this framework, I examine (beyond constraints) what possibilities the neoliberal city may have unintentionally furnished for subaltern struggles, those of not only the poor but also women and the young. I draw on the cities of the Middle East where neoliberal urbanity has been developing against the backdrop of illiberal regimes and conservative social and religious trends. I suggest that this new urbanity, the city inside out, not only exhibits a profound process of exclusion but also generates new dynamics of publicness that can have important implications for social and political mobilization—what I have described as "street politics" and the "political street."[39] While the subaltern groups may lose much of their traditional claims to the city, they tend in response to discover and generate new places to escape where they recover their claims in a different fashion and, in some cases, compel the elites to retreat. The social dimensions of the neoliberal city inside out in the context of the authoritarian state engender the type of grassroots mobilization that I have called "social nonmovements," which reinforce and deepen both street politics and the political street.[40]

Politics on the Street

When people are deprived of or do not trust electoral power to change things, they tend to resort to their own institutional power to exert pressure on adversaries to meet their demands—like workers or university students going on strike. But for those (such as the unemployed, housewives, and broadly the "informal people") who lack such institutional power or settings, streets become a crucial arena to express discontent. For such subaltern groups, however, the centrality of streets goes beyond merely the expression of contention. Rather, streets may actually serve as an indispensable asset or capital for them to subsist and reproduce economic and cultural life. In other words, not only do they resort to streets to organize rallies or protest actions; they also encroach on street space to conduct business, operate workshops, sell merchandise, prepare and serve food, organize funerals, entertain, and socialize. In all of these arenas, the actors are involved in a relation of power over the control of public space and public order. They are involved in street politics, which describes a set of conflicts and the attendant implications between certain groups or individuals and the authorities that are shaped and expressed in the physical and social space of streets—from back alleys to the main avenues, from invisible places to escape the city to main squares. The attendant conflict arises because the subjects engage in *active* use of public spaces, which under the modern state they are supposed to use only passively in the ways that the state deems through regulation. So the street vendors who carry out their business on the pavement, the poor people who extend their lives onto the sidewalks, the squatters who take over public lands, lower-class youths who appropriate street corners, or protesters who march in the streets are all involved in some way in street politics.[41] Daily tensions, if not physical confrontations with the authorities, mark the social world of the urban subalterns, keeping them in a constant state of insecurity and mobilization.

But streets are not just places where conflicts are shaped and/or expressed. They are also venues where people forge collective identities and *extend* their solidarities beyond their immediate familiar circles to include the unknown, the stranger. What facilitates this extension of solidarity is the operation of some latent or passive network between individuals who may be unknown to one another even though they share common attributes. Passive networks are instantaneous communications between atomized individuals that are established by tacit recognition of their commonalities and are mediated through real or virtual space. Thus, street vendors, who might not know each other, can still recognize their common position by noticing each others' pushcarts, vending tables, or chants. Similarly, young people who are strangers to each other, such as soccer fans, who have similar hairstyles, wear blue jeans, or act in a certain way, connect to one another and recognize their shared identities without necessarily establishing an active or deliberate communication and without being part of an organization. The unlawful motorcyclists in Tehran go further by informing one another of police crackdowns by hand gestures, blinking lights, or shouting "police."

Aside from shaping, expressing, or extending discontent and serving as an asset or capital for livelihood, streets signify a powerful symbolic utterance, one that goes beyond the physicality of streets to convey collective sentiments. This is the "political street," as in "Arab street" or "Muslim street," by which I mean the collective sentiments, shared feelings, and public opinions of ordinary people in their day-to-day utterances and practices that are expressed broadly and casually in urban public spaces—in taxis, buses, shops, sidewalks, or mass demonstrations.[42] For instance, the deliberative process of qat chewing in Yemen,[43] or even the undeliberate practice of public nagging in most of the Middle East where ordinary citizens speak out, vent, and exchange grievances in public, appears to be a salient feature of public culture in the region, serving as a crucial element in the making of public opinion and a component of political street. Political street then signifies the cognitive, intellectual, and affective domain of the city inside out—a domain wherein sentiments are expressed, emotions shared, and collective opinions formed informally in urban spaces. This has been important in Arab societies because when authoritarian regimes disallow institutional mechanisms of conveying public opinion, the urban street comes to serve as a measure of public sphere and locus of political expression.

This process of the city inside out becomes a crucial moment in street politics and political street. Reclamation by poor people of public space through encroachment, functioning, and subsisting constitutes an expression of street politics, while simultaneously feeding into and accentuating the political street. In other words, through this encroachment, the dispossessed are constantly engaged in struggles *in* and *about* the urban space; they become a party in the contest over shaping the urban form and molding the urban texture, the domains of the social, the cultural, and the sensory—noise, smell, and sight. This life-driven and constant nature of spatial politics among the Middle Eastern poor distinguishes it from that engendered by the Occupy movements, whose presence in the public space, the streets, was essentially deliberate and transitory rather than structural and enduring.

How do these contestations in and about urban texture take place where the authoritarian Middle Eastern states curtail the organized and sustained challenges to the political and economic elites? I have proposed that the political constraint under authoritarian rule compels the urban disenfranchised to resort to a particular form of mobilization, the unorganized and unassuming nonmovements. Nonmovements, or the collective actions of noncollective actors, are the shared contentious practices of a large number of fragmented people whose similar but disconnected claims produce important social change in their own lives and society at large, even though such practices are rarely guided by an ideology, recognizable leadership, or organization.[44] For instance, in Riyadh, Saudi Arabia, women challenge certain gender norms through the practice of what they call "pushing normal."[45] Groups of women stroll, frequent, and mix with men in the sex-segregated street cafés; ride bicycles in public places; or establish and visit art galleries that host both men and women. In pre-revolutionary Egypt, lower-class youths and soccer fans (ultras) who gathered and asserted presence in hostile urban locations operated as nonmovements, as did educated unemployed people in Tunisia in their pursuit of sustenance. In broad terms, the nonmovements reflect how such marginalized groups as Muslim women, youth, or the urban disenfranchised in the Middle East may succeed in making their respective claims for gender equality, citizenship, and the right to the city, despite their being dispersed, unorganized, and atomized. But the notion of nonmovement is particularly pertinent to the way in which the urban dispossessed become engaged in street politics and the political street.

The Dispossessed in Street Politics

Nonmovements represent perhaps the most salient features of activism by the urban dispossessed in the Middle East. I refer to the quiet, pervasive, and enduring encroachment of the poor people on the propertied, the powerful, and the public in their quest for survival and bettering their lives. Lacking a clear leadership, articulated ideology, or structured organization, these dispersed efforts represent the largely individual, everyday, and lifelong mobilizations that often involve collective action when the gains are threatened.[46] In the primate cities of the Middle East, the encroachment has been expressed by millions of rural migrants embarking on long migratory journeys to escape misfortunes and search for better livelihoods and new lives. They begin their new existence by grabbing plots of land to put up shelters in the seemingly abandoned, unnoticed, and opaque urban escapes—in the back streets, under bridges, on rooftops, or somewhere in the outer spaces of the megacities. Once the families are settled in, they acquire electricity by connecting their homes to the nearby power poles and then secure running water, often ingeniously, by installing underground pipes or using makeshift hoses to run water from a neighbor's supply or public pipes in the vicinity. Phone lines are obtained more or less in similar fashion. As more neighbors gather, they build roads and places of worship and manage garbage—efforts that of necessity become collective.[47] By 2011, over 65 percent in Cairo, 40 percent in Aleppo, and 25 percent of all Moroccans had crafted an informal life of this sort.[48] Some 180 million Arab breadwinners in such habitats, mostly without regular work and urban skills, strive to earn a living by encroaching by the thousands on the main streets, sidewalks, and squares as hawkers, vendors, or street workshop workers who then take advantage of favorable business opportunities that shopkeepers and rich traders created. They often freely market their diverse but affordable merchandise, including globalized but fake trade labels—Nike shoes, Gucci shirts, or Levi's jeans. In their life worlds, these disenfranchised groups manage their daily collective lives by coexisting, resolving disputes, and handling the outlaws and criminals who tend to inhabit such spaces. Yet they have not been able to escape constant insecurities of debt, illegal existence, and uncertain destinies.[49]

Such daily encroachments by multitudes of people have virtually transformed the cities of the Middle East and by extension the developing world. Over time, they have created massive communities with millions of inhabitants with complex life worlds, economic arrangements, cultural practices, and lifestyles.[50] By 2011, more than 46 percent of urban settlers in the Middle East were living in such a world. In these largely undefined urban spaces, the poor tried to live relatively autonomous lives, basing their relationships more on self-reliance, reciprocity, flexibility, and negotiation, traits that stood against yet negotiated with modern notions and institutions of bureaucracy, fixed contracts, and discipline. They carved off, claimed, and even pushed back the elites from sizable areas of the urban universe. By so doing, they posed the question of who owned, managed, and exerted power over the cities and who the players were in the urban governance.

I do not wish to depict a romantic vision of a resisting subaltern population, even though I realize that there is, as seen in the New Urbanism perspective, a temptation to idealize street and sidewalk life or to see in informality a
panacea for urban ills.[51] It is certainly valuable to recognize the agency of the
dispossessed in distributing social goods and opportunities for life chances
and in creating their vibrant communities. But who can deny that the neoliberal onslaught has brought much slum demolition, gentrification, and removal of street markets? How can one dispute the fact that the logic of control
in the modern state conditions the political authorities to turn any opaque
space—the slums, informal markets, underground lives, or even unregistered
humans—into transparent, quantifiable entities? Indeed, demolishing spontaneous settlements, deliberately burning street markets, and carrying out
programs of slum upgrading can establish transparency and knowledge that
can ensure social control.[52] Yet the truth is that the very logic of neoliberal
urbanity carries in itself the force behind generating such parallel, unknowable, and opaque life worlds. It renders both dispossession and repossession
a simultaneously parallel process, thus turning the urban physical and social
space into the site of a protracted battle for hegemony. The poor respond
to structural dispossession by not letting go easily—they often resist slum
clearance and demolition or make these measures politically costly. President
Mugabe did destroy the poor people's habitat, but this resulted in massive
resentment and opposition.[53] In Cairo during the early 2000s, selective demolition caused the furious settlers to wage street protests and demand resettle-
ment; in Tehran the poor in the early 1990s agreed to vacate only after being
compensated, and in Tunisia urban riots forced the government to embark
on serious upgrading. In general, slum clearance and demolition do happen,
but people still move to different, more remote, less visible, and less strategic
locations to reclaim what they have lost and begin life again. In this long war
of attrition, power reveals its limitations. It is therefore simplistic to claim that
the nonmovements serve as safety valves for the regimes of oppression. This
claim not only ignores the complexity of the state-nonmovement relation but,
more important, overlooks the norm-changing outcome and structural incremental dynamics of its encroachment—winning a position, reinforcing it,
and then moving forward to capture a new one. For instance, the squatters
do not stop after securing a shelter but continue demands for running water,
electricity, phone lines, garbage collection, paved roads, security, and official
recognition.

Poor people's encroachment concerns not merely physical space over land, street corners, or public parks; it also extends to social and political spaces—to domains of culture, urban order, mode of life, the sensory domain, "urban texture." In the city inside out, subalterns are seen and felt to be almost everywhere; in fact, they *are* everywhere. As carriers of a certain habitus—a mode of being, behaving, and doing things—the poor are present in the main streets, public parks, and alleyways; in buses, teahouses, and squares and on sidewalks. Where else can poor youngsters play soccer other than in the streets, alleyways, or other open spaces? Where else can they enjoy an affordable respite, when their cramped shelters allow little physical movement? So they wander, do business, sit about, hang around, and squat or sleep on any green spots available. In Cairo, the mass of the poor colonize every inch of public green spaces where they can rest or picnic, pavements along the Nile, and squares. Fences are installed around green patches but are unable to withstand the encroachment of the poor, when their own neighborhoods are likely to suffer from uncollected garbage, factory waste, and pollution. Thus, through their overwhelming presence in public arenas—with their overpowering bodies, gaze, behavior—and through their lifestyle, noise, and smell, the subaltern subjects unintentionally compel the disgruntled elites to retreat into their own safe havens.

Such modes of living in the cities of the Middle East are similar to how illegal migrants manage their movement and lives at the international level. There exist now massive border controls, barriers, fences, walls, and police patrols. Yet the migrants keep flooding—by air, sea, and road; hidden in the back of trucks and trains; or simply on foot. The 2015 wave of emigrants and refugees from Africa and the Arab world to Europe who literally forced their way through the borders tells us only the more mediatized form of this spreading out. They spread, expand, and grow in the cities of the Global North. They settle, find jobs, acquire homes, form families, build communities, and struggle to get legal protection. Indeed, the anxiety and panic that these subaltern groups have caused among the elites at national and international levels are remarkably similar. The Cairo elite lament about the "invasion" of peasants from the Upper Egyptian countryside; and the Istanbul elite warn of the encroachment of the "black Turks," meaning rural poor migrants from Anatolia, who, they say, have altogether ruralized and distorted "our modern cities." In a strikingly similar tone, white European elites express profound anxiety about the "invasion of foreigners"—Africans, Asians, and in particular Muslims—whom they see as having overwhelmed Europe's social habitat, distorting the European way of life by their physical presence and cultural habits—their behavior, dress, mosques, and minarets.[54] The encroachments, both at the local urban and global levels, is real and likely to continue. These protagonisms are more than benign practices of everyday life by the urban subalterns; they follow unintended political consequences. These subjects are involved in appropriating opportunities and social goods, asserting the right to the city. They are engaged, in other words, in a struggle for citizenship—a process similar to what Partha Chatterjee describes for India in his *Politics of the Governed*.[55] Thus, while the neoliberal city deprives many of its inhabitants of urban citizenship, it is also true that the disenfranchised do force the elites into socio-spatial retreat and enclosure—to the gated communities, private security guards, locked vehicles, partial governance, and parcelized hegemony. So in response to the neoliberal strategy of "accumulation by dispossession," the subaltern subject may resort to *survival by repossession*.

The Logic of Repossession

Why and how can such a response, that is, survival by repossession, happen? Two factors are crucial. The first has to do with the particular characteristics of the nonmovements and the second with the nature of the political settings (state forms) within which nonmovements operate. Nonmovements represent the collective action of noncollective actors, who are oriented more toward action than by being ideologically driven, concerned more with practice than protest.[56] Unlike conventional forms of activism, which by definition are extraordinary practices, nonmovements are merged into and are part and parcel of the ordinary practices of everyday life. Thus, the poor people's resolve to migrate, build shelters, or work, live, function, and stroll in streets and the illegal migrants' acts of crossing borders, finding work, and looking for livelihoods all represent instances of the ordinary practices of daily life, which unlike extraordinary acts such as attending meetings, marching, or demonstrating, remain mostly immune from repression. What grants power to these nonmovements is not the unity of actors, an effective force deemed to cause disruption and uncertainty and thus win concessions. The power lies in the consequential effects on society's norms and rules of many (even though dispersed) people simultaneously doing similar, albeit encroaching, things. Do these types of struggles echo the neoliberal notion of atomized individuals acting independently (even if simultaneously) toward self-interest? The dynamics of the nonmovements are too complex to be couched in neoliberal terms; even though nonmovements galvanize mostly individuals and families to undertake incremental claim making, the individual and independent nature of encroachment is not a *value* deriving from a desire to seek autonomy and self-reliance but a *tactic* stemming from a strategy to outmaneuver the adversaries as the encroachment moves forward. In fact, the individual actors are not atomized, strictly speaking, for they are connected to one another through their passive networks, and passive networks can be activated to form collective resistance or organized movements to safeguard the gains deemed under threat.

This, however, cannot happen under just any circumstances and state forms. Nonmovements usually work under the state forms that cannot, do not, or are perceived not to meet the social and material needs of the disenfranchised, who are then compelled to resort to direct action. Instead of forming collective protests to demand jobs or housing, the poor people may simply acquire them through direct action. The poor people succeed in doing so largely because the states under which they operate are "soft": despite their often authoritarian disposition and political omnipresence, they lack the necessary capacity, hegemony, and technological efficacy to impose full control over society. So there remain many uncontrolled spaces that the innovative subaltern groups can utilize to their advantage. Even though these states produce many strict rules of governance, the laws are often easily broken; or even though bureaucrats treat the poor harshly, they are often not difficult to bribe. Consequently, despite the seeming omnipresence, the reach (let alone the hegemony and legitimacy) of the state remains acutely limited, which leaves many free zones that the nonmovements can utilize to thrive.[57]

Equally crucial are the actors' civic virtues, their perseverance and innovative ability to assert their presence in society: that is, the subalterns' capacity to recognize their limitations while discovering new opportunities and deploying inventive methods of practice to take advantage of the available spaces to resist and move forward. I am pointing to the *art of presence*, the ability of the subaltern subjects to assert their collective will in spite of all odds, to circumvent the constraints, utilizing what is possible, and discover new spaces within which to make themselves heard, seen, felt, and realized. In normal times, this politics of presence serves as a mechanism through which subalterns strive to subvert their status of dispossession and make the best of what is perceived to be possible. But revolutionary times facilitate the grassroots journey toward more audible encroachment and organized mobilization. By definition, nonmovements imply already-active individuals who may emerge from their backstreets to join in the broader revolts and uprisings; they navigate between the everyday encroachments and revolutionary protests that take shape in the spatial expanse of the neoliberal city, the main squares. The squares represent the spatial locus and political form of subaltern struggles in the Arab revolutions.

6   Square and Counter-Square

The revolts of the 2010s in the Middle East—from the Green movement in Iran to the Arab uprisings in 2011 and the Gezy Park episode in 2013 in Turkey—took shape chiefly in the urban centers. What does this urban locus of uprisings in the Middle East, where some 45 percent of the population inhabits the rural areas, tell us about their origins and dynamics? More specifically, what aspects of urbanity render cities the spaces of contention; and why are certain urban sites, streets, and squares more conducive than others for mobilization? Observing such cities as Tehran, Cairo, Istanbul, and Tunis over the past two decades, I suggest that urban life consists of paradoxical dynamics that may potentially produce dissent. Urbanity generates in the inhabitants particular needs and obligations, while inculcating in them certain entitlements and rights; it enforces certain constraints on how to live an urban life yet offers extraordinary opportunities for networking, forging urban subjectivity, and voicing dissent. The particular political economy of the Middle East, expressed in the marriage of autocratic polity and neoliberal economy, in the past two decades gave a particular salience to these paradoxes, sparking in times of stress uncommon collective contentions that were often displayed in the urban streets and squares. They reached their zenith in the uprisings of the 2010s.

Cities in Revolt

People from different walks of life joined the Arab revolts—middle-class urbanites, youth, women, laborers, and slum dwellers, as well as people from provincial towns and villages. But the insurrections were remarkably urban in character. Millions poured into streets en masse, marching in the main streets, holding massive rallies in key strategic locations, and occupying central urban squares night and day. When the protests in Tunisia moved from the provincial towns of Sidi Bouzid, Bou Zayen, Kasserine, and others northward to the capital, Bourguiba Boulevard in the modern part of Tunis and the Kasbah in the Medina became epicenters of public protestation, just before Cairo's Tahrir Square came to epitomize the uprisings' street politics par excellence. Soon the idea of Tahrir traveled to other Arab cities—Yemen's Taghir Square in Sana'a, Tripoli's Green Square, and Manama's Pearl Square, whose spatial and symbolic power the Bahraini authorities could not bear so bulldozed it in a dramatic show of force.

The day after President Mubarak of Egypt was forced to relinquish power, the loyalists of President Ali Saleh of Yemen occupied Sana'a's Tahrir Square in the central business district to prevent protests like those in Cairo. It was only then that the opposition activists occupied the main street in front of the University of Sana'a, naming it Taghir Square (Change Square), which then became a key locus in Yemen's revolutionary struggles. In the south-central city of Aden, the *hirak* (activists) first gathered in the traditional *saha*s (courtyards), where men and women socialized, debated, recited, and listened to poetry. Then they congregated in what came to be known as Martyr's Square in al-Mansoura before it was demolished by the Yemeni regime. The popular al-Maidan, where many poor people congregated, received similar treatment on May 15, 2013, before the revolutionaries moved to Parade Square in Khormaksar, turning it into the location of the Southern Revolution by organizing the "One Million Rally." From here the protesters demanded not only the removal of President Ali Saleh but also independence for the south to return to their socialist past.[1]

Watching these developments in the neighborhood enthusiastically, Saudi youth, constrained by the repressive police, created their own Tahrir in the virtual world—where they came together, communicated, chatted, and discussed the nation's future. And in Libya, when the rebel forces entered Tripoli on August 21, 2011, in their last battle to overthrow the Qaddafi regime, they focused more than anywhere else on capturing Martyrs' Square (formerly Green Square), the heart of the capital city. Thus, police and revolutionaries battled over these urban squares as if the destiny of revolts rested on who controlled them.

Here in these monumental squares, Tahrir in particular, mass rallies were held, stages were erected, huge banners with revolutionary messages went up, and makeshift tents were set up to house those who spent the nights. Soon after medical teams, cleaning crews, and security groups were organized. In the headquarters around the square, multiple leaders discussed strategies, assigned tasks, and allocated resources—food, resting locations, communication tools, tract writings, and the like. In residential buildings surrounding Tahrir, a number of apartments offered rest and respite, the places where revolutionaries would take breaks from the strain of the events at the *maidan* (square), use lavatories, wash, rest, rejuvenate, and strategize their next steps. Young men and women spent sociable evenings together in the makeshift tents; Muslims and Christians assisted each other in their prayer services. As days passed and revolutionaries settled in their campsites, ordinary lives began to intermingle with these extraordinary episodes. Cairo residents—men and women, children and the elderly—descended into the arena, turning the battlefield of Tahrir into the evening hub, a carnival of conviviality and fun, where people enjoyed the magical energy, the light and sound of those intimate and extraordinary moments. In the meantime, street vendors continued shouting out what they were selling—hot tea, cold drinks, food, T-shirts, and protection masks—in the midst of rallies, shots, and teargas. A participant reported, "At Tahrir square you can find popcorn, couscous, sweet potatoes, sandwiches, tea, and drinks! Egyptians know how to revolt."[2] The maidan at once brought together fighters, friends, and families; vendors, barbers, and bystanders; music, poetry, and plenty of good humor. Young couples held their marriage ceremonies and spent their honeymoon in that monumental arena. Travelers came from provincial towns to visit Tahrir and participate in its unique historical thrill.

These squares then became a microcosm of the alternative order the revolutionaries seemed to desire—democratic governance, nonhierarchical organization, collective decision making, self-help, cooperation, and altruism. In Sana'a's Taghir Square the large banner "Welcome to the Land of Liberty" signaled entry into a different space and social existence, while the renaming of the surrounding streets as al-Adl (justice) and al-Hurriyya (freedom) spoke of a future the revolutionaries wished for.[3] Here in these squares strangers met and engaged, transcending at least temporarily gender, religious, and class divides. An extraordinary sense of solidarity, altruism, and sacrifice seemed to reign. On the evening of February 4, as tens of thousands decided to stay overnight in Maidan Tahrir after multiple battles with the police, a revolutionary tweeted from Tahrir that "my camera is stolen, my body is bruised and my eye is still black and blue; but I have never felt better in my life."[4] Another wrote, "Sunset over; Tahrir has never been so gorgeous."[5] During that extraordinary episode in Tahrir, everyone cried at some point, not just from teargas but from sheer emotion.

These were truly astonishing moments of revolution inscribed in the expanse of the city's key public arenas, where a community of uncommon character—something between real and unreal—had been born. As if they were the joyful, ecstatic celebrations of the birthdays of saints in Egypt (*mulids*), these revolutionary moments combined rituals of joy and conviviality with street battles and violence.[6] Even though the rituals of revolution were bound to be transient, the central concept of these Arab squares—the geographies of both contention and creativity, of alternative order—quickly traveled throughout the world, finding resonance in Tel Aviv, Madrid, Bangkok, São Paulo, and Istanbul and continuing with Ukraine's Maidan Square and Hong Kong's arena of the "umbrella revolution."

But revolutionary mobilizations were not limited to large and capital cities. Provincial small towns and "villages" also became the hotbed of revolutionary upheavals. In Tunisia, the revolt had begun not in the capital city but in the depressed town of Sidi Bouzid, spreading through Bou Zayen, Kasserine, Gafsa, Jendouba, Le Kef, and Thala, before it finally reached the streets of the capital, Tunis. The Egyptian uprising also engulfed Suez, Mahalla, Port Said, Ismailia, Tanta, Aswan, and other cities. Ferocious clashes in Alexandria's Sidi Gaber and Qaid Ibrahim Square equaled the heroic struggles in the working-class towns of Suez and Port Said. Abdeen Square in Suez saw the first violent battles of the uprising, where protesters torched the notorious Abdeen police station, an event that left a number killed and hundreds arrested. In Libya, the fiercest battles took place in the provincial towns of Misrata and Sirte, while in Yemen the small cities of Saada and Taiz competed with the capital city. In Taiz, protesters organized makeshift camps in Safir Square "with medical teams, cleaning crews, and security to protect them from outside attackers"; they pledged not to leave until President Ali Saleh stepped down.[7] In Syria the uprising took over provincial towns such as Der'a, Hama, Homs, Deir Ezzor, and al-Raqqa. In Hama, on July 2, 2011, some two hundred thousand Syrian protesters occupied Assi Square in the very city where in 1982 the Ba'thist regime had put down a rebellion by massacring nearly twenty thousand protesters. "We will remain in the streets until the regime's departure" had become the protesters' central strategy. Indeed, the experiences in Homs and Aleppo in Syria showed how crucial the geographies of the cities were in forging revolutionary battles. Both of these towns exhibited a sharp spatial divide between the poor, ill-serviced, working-class neighborhoods that spearheaded the revolts and the upscale, well-serviced bourgeois districts that opted for counterrevolution.[8]

Allure of the Agora

The revolts prompted an exceptional interest in the idea of urban space and politics and an extraordinary fascination with the image of the maidan as the locus of insurgent politics and an alternative social order. It seemed as though the early "digital turn," or uncommon attention to the centrality of social media, gave way to a "spatial turn," an unusual excitement about spatial contention. Yet much of the engagement remained at the level of fascination. While the city space is recognized as the crucial locus of contentious politics, we are yet to see serious analyses of why it is so.[9] The newness of this spatial perspective is not limited to the Arab uprisings. More broadly it is only recently that social movement theory has paid serious attention to the spatial dimensions of contentious politics. Even though ideas about space go back to Marx's insights on politics of urbanization and the modern factory system, to Henri LeFebvre's powerful notion of the "right to the city," and to the more recent upsurge of the Foucauldian take on space and power, social movement theory had until recently "downplayed the spatial constitution and context of its central concepts such as identity, grievances, political opportunities, and resources."[10] We are therefore confronted with some important questions. What, for instance, is particularly urban about urban contention? What processes in the cities induce insurgent citizens? What elements in certain urban sites make them Tahrir, or Taksim, or Taghir? What values do "Tahrir moments" espouse for emancipatory politics? Is it all about space? What about the broader impact of political economy? Should we not account for the role of social agents—those actors on the stages of the insurgent spaces?

Most observers point to the "symbolic power," meaning, and political history of certain sites like the roundabouts—for instance, Cairo's Tahrir and Manama's Pearl Square.[11] But it is crucial to determine what is behind such symbolic power—centrality, historical memory, architectural character, or morphology? And the symbolic significance of a site might change as the city itself transforms—during President Nasser's term, for instance, where the political crowd gathered more often in Abdeen Square than in Tahrir. Some studies place emphasis on the massive number of bodies in the streets of uprisings to question those who had deemed the Arab Spring a "Facebook revolution," arguing instead for a meaningful relationship between the digital and the spatial.[12] Focusing on the intriguing repertoire of actions and actors in the revolutionary squares, many have highlighted the "performative" feature of insurrections, "Tahrir as theatre," underlining the emergence of new democratic politics, horizontal organization, and cooperative order that the Arab Spring seemed to herald.[13] Egalitarian, intimate, and convivial—with gender, religious, and class lines dissipating—such an astonishing order of solidarity and salvation would expectedly exude awe and passion. Enthused by the appeal of the agora in the eighteen days of Tahrir Square, philosophers Alain Badiou and Slavoj Žižek saw in these revolutionary moments the promise of a new social order that could serve as the foundation for a different future—something similar to what Farha Ghannam characterized as "heterotopic space," which in Lefebvre's view offers the "seedbed of revolutionary moment."[14] Others saw it as an Arendtian Greek *polis* representing a "form of government that relied heavily on self-rule and common sense initiative, with no single sovereign ruler."[15]

The performative feature of the Occupy movements also conveyed similar sentiments. Similar to protesters in Tahrir, those in Toronto's St. James Park, as I observed in October 2011, had also created an innovative and horizontal community of engaged citizens who shared the place, passion, thought, food, and kindness. The occupied square resembled a liberated enclave, free from the state, money, and greed. It is perhaps in this spirit that most observers measured the actual achievement of the Occupy movements to be in their very operation. By highlighting the ideas of "process as the product" and "future in the present," emphasis is placed on the way in which these movements conducted themselves—democratic, communal, and without hierarchy.[16]

Surely, the innovative and egalitarian spirit of square activism merits intellectual attention and elaboration. But far from the Arendtian *polis*, the square life of this sort is a liminal reality, a kind of transitory egalitarian community that navigates between utopia and reality. Reminiscent of the carnivals of late medieval Europe, these square lives resonated more with Victor Turner's notion of *communitas* than Arendtian agora, representing an egalitarian community of equal individuals who break away temporarily from the everyday norms and structures of power to operate in an ad hoc state of liminality.[17] These are the social formations of exceptional moments in great political upheavals and should not be mistaken with what activists can or cannot do at larger structures and in broader national settings. Nor should the semantics lead us to confuse the "horizontal" organization employed in these squares with *horizontalidad*—that is, building popular power in society rather than seizing state power.[18] In Argentina, it was a practical response of the working people to the economic crisis of 2001–2002. Since people had lost trust in the state, they found their own solutions by taking over factories, initiating self-management, building autonomous associations, and undertaking neighborhood self-rule. They disdained state-centrism in favor of grassroots politics of affect and love.[19]

The egalitarian communities of those in the square may be cradles for a democratic movement, but as some have noted, one cannot live in a cradle forever.[20] In other words, an overemphasis on the *spatiality* of these "democratic moments" should not lead us to overlook their *temporality*—that is, the crucial fact that these democratic and egalitarian instants have typically ad hoc, exceptional, and liminal existence. As much as they are a function of space, they are also the product of history. Only in retrospect would an activist reminisce about "the astonishing Tahrir, where there were so many things, good people with good morals," but "I am shocked how we are changing from very good people into materialistic things."[21] Perhaps we need to take account of the political economy and structural dynamics in order to grasp the modalities of such uncommon social happenings in particular historical times. Only from such a position can we make sense of both the ephemeral revolutionary performances and the daily encroachments of subaltern subjects in their normal lives as they continue to claim their rights to the city and its livelihood. Whereas revolutionaries assert their presence in the large squares only provisionally, many poor families subsist by encroaching on the city spaces to make a living or engage in a cultural life. Space, after all, is not divorced from history, nor is spatiality from political economy.

Commenting on the Arab uprisings and the Occupy movements, David Harvey draws on a powerful political economy analysis but falls short of offering much-needed ethnographic insights into how the operation of capital and its spatial configuration actually creates urban insurgents battling in the neighborhoods or squares of the cities. In fact, there is little rebellion in Harvey's *Rebel Cities*, which appeared in the wake of the Arab Spring and Occupy movements. Its insights concern the aggressive encroachment of capital on cities and larger geographies to subordinate and dispossess the working people. In addition, Harvey's erudite and engaging interview in *Jadaliyya* (November 15, 2013) follows a similar mode of elaboration about capital's dispossession of the working class. Consequently, we do not learn much about how, if at all, the urban dispossessed fight back, nor do we know how these processes are related to the nature of the state. The state form (e.g., liberal democracy or autocracy) has much bearing on what the dispossessed can or cannot do in their struggles against capital's encroachment. Under a liberal democracy, citizens may be more or less free to mobilize and organize, but their political and business elites, embedded in the system, command more systematic (legal, technical, and social) control. However, repressive regimes such as that in Egypt, suffering from feeble hegemony, may by default allow for vast informal socioscapes—kinship ties, backstreet communities, or informal worksites—within which alternative norms counter to state logic may be instituted. Finally, since Harvey uses the city as an empirical lens to examine the broad processes of capital accumulation and dispossession—one that operates beyond the urban at national and international levels—the specificity of "the urban" remains obscure. We do not know what is particularly urban about the politics of capital accumulation or what type of urban dissent and agency—distinct from the broader movements against, say, corruption, dictatorship, or austerity—it may generate.[22]

Commenting on the Arab uprisings and the global Occupy movements, the sociologist Saskia Sassen makes an interesting point that the ecology of the city—the dense juxtaposition of lives, places, streets—complicates "powerlessness"; in fact, it enables the insurgent "powerless" to make history because in their acts of suppression, the states simply cannot pulverize a city and its insurgent inhabitants.[23] Even though the Assad regime in Syria did level the city of Hama, killing twenty thousand people to quell the uprising in 1982, and repeated similar urbicide in Der'a and Homs and then in Aleppo after the uprising began in 2011, Sassen's point remains important.[24] But the idea still falls short of spelling out how urbanity turns the inhabitants into insurgents in the first place. Nor does her deployment of the term "street"—something different from the European ritualized piazza—in these events reveal anything about how it may facilitate mobilization and insurgency.

Urbanity and Discontent

I have suggested that at least three inherent factors may potentially make modern cities the spaces of discontent: (1) the *urban problematics* related to urban processes, obligations, and entitlements that would stand at the roots of discontent; (2) the emergence of *urban actors* with particular needs, demands, desires, and subjectivities; and (3) the existence of *urban spaces*, both physical and social, that would facilitate political mobilization.[25] Modern urbanity generates particular needs, such as access to cash to conduct exchange instead of relying on trust and reciprocity, as was practiced in traditional village life; urbanites need to learn work discipline instead of enjoying flexibility and self-arrangement; they need to behave in their urban life according to certain set contracts instead of relying on negotiations or customary norms. In addition, while modern urbanity engenders certain desires and demands (like paid jobs, regular pay, particular norms of consumption), it simultaneously inculcates among urbanites a set of entitlements and rights, for instance, the right to have optimum urban services such as roads, schools, police, and broadly what the city can offer. It is crucial to bear in mind that these needs and expectations, as well as awareness about them, usually expand as societal standards shift or as mobility and information increase. If states are expected but are unable or unwilling to fulfill those demands, or if they are seen to violate those entitlements, urbanites are likely to feel and express moral outrage at the public authorities.

As an inhabitant of a small traditional village (about 250 people) in 1960s Iran, I can recall how my mother, like all other women in the village, would make her daily journeys to faraway water wells to bring water for drinking and preparing food; she would have to prepare a wood fire for heating or cooking and spend a long time washing clothes in the nearby creeks throughout the year. When eventually my family, like many rural migrants in the country, moved to Tehran for work and our schooling, my mother felt incredibly blessed by accessing water only by turning on a tap and having warmth and light by pushing a button. This was a tremendous change, indeed a liberation. But these amenities gradually became the reality of my illiterate mother's urban life, perceived as her new entitlements. So when at times we experienced power cuts or water shortages in the neighborhood, she would express strong outrage, swiftly lashing out at the government for failing to fulfill its obligations and for violating her "urban rights." My father, a bus driver, would often get enraged about uncollected garbage and especially about potholes on the city's paved roads, even though he earlier was operating with no complaints on the daunting dirt roads of our rural landscape. I could see such reactions on the part of many of our migrant relatives who had ended up living in the overcrowded slums of southern Tehran. Many years later, I would observe very similar attitudes among the poor families of Cairo's Dar El Salam, Ezbet Kheirallah, and Ramlet Boulaq neighborhoods, in their struggles to secure a power supply, garbage collection, or sewage services. Indeed, these very issues—garbage-infested streets and irregular supply of piped water—became key points of contention in Cairo, triggering what the press dubbed as Egypt's "thirst revolution" just prior to the 2011 uprising. In a survey of 2,956 Egyptians concerning their dreams just before the uprising, people overwhelmingly pointed to urban amenities, including drinking water (42.2 percent), and a better sewage system (42.2 percent) rather than solving unemployment (36.8 percent).[26] It is perhaps due to these urban entitlements and the associated possibilities of dissent that officials in Egypt have refused to recognize as urban many large urbanizing communities with ten thousand inhabitants in order to undercut the "rights" that such designations would generate for the inhabitants and obligations for the state.

While cities create in their inhabitants certain demands and desires, they also offer immense possibilities for forging collective identities, networks of solidarity, communication, and mobilization. Both social movements and nonmovements find a favorable environment for growth in the cities, not only because of the kinds of insecurities and vulnerabilities city life creates in its inhabitants but also because urban spaces can potentially bring subaltern subjects together, displaying their claims and extending their solidarity networks. Through latent, instantaneous, and unspoken communication among fragmented individuals who recognize their commonalities in real and virtual spaces, groups such as marginalized youth, street vendors, pious women, and ethnic migrants fashion collectives that may eventually act as a unit when the opportunity arises. Thus, it is largely in urban enclaves that fragmented young people forge collective identities. From being simply young individuals with similar attributes, they may become "youth" as a collective being with awareness about their shared concerns and capabilities. Schools, street corners, cafés, shopping malls, sport centers, and squares bring together fragmented but similar individuals through latent communication, making them a potential collective agent in the contentious politics of the city.

Contentious politics in the urban setting readily invokes the image of sites like Tahrir, Taksim, or Taghir in their revolutionary moments when dissenters battle the authorities and defy official order. But as discussed in the previous chapter, contention has become an enduring feature of the everyday urban life in cities like Cairo, Istanbul, Sanaʻa, and Tehran. For in their day-to-day subsistence, a large number of usually poor inhabitants are compelled by necessity to defy authorities and disrupt official order on almost a daily basis. Street vendors, subsistence workers, poor households, street children, the homeless, nonconformist youths, and women continue to infringe on public space and order, clashing with the police repeatedly as they carry on with their lives to earn a living, socialize, or organize social and cultural rituals. When women loiter in public arenas or lower-class youths hang out on the street corners, they challenge the dominant public sensibilities that are often sanctioned by official power. On the whole, these kinds of everyday contentions represent street politics during normal times.

Of course, such daily contentions do not change regimes or topple dictators; they may even be said to underscore some kind of tense compliance with little or no impact on the structure of power and the lives of the poor. But I contend that beyond being an inevitable facet of the working life and life world of millions of humble urban dwellers, these everyday acts of transgression do alter the urban configuration, establish alternative norms, and can serve as a catalyst for broader political mobilizations. Contentions of these types tend to intensify in the cities inside out. They render cities like Cairo, Istanbul, and Tehran highly contested and politically charged, where the street serves as the public sphere merged into the everyday of ordinary people as they struggle through their lives.

But there is more to these streets as public sphere. Where can the unemployed, housewives, casual workers, or migrants—those who are structurally absent from the institutional positions of power—express their discontent except the streets? What about those actors who have lost faith in the efficacy of their institutions, such as the unions, university administration, political parties, or even "representative" bodies? We see that students or workers may bypass their institutions to join ordinary citizens to express discontent on the streets. The Occupy movements and the maidan episodes in the Arab uprisings represent the most salient examples of this kind of political expression. Here, the significance of streets or squares is not just that they offer a physical place for congregations of so many like-minded people; it is also that protesters' presence in the streets extends signs of solidarity and acts of protest beyond the immediate circles to include others, the unfamiliar and strangers.

The element of the unfamiliar and stranger is central to maidan politics because it provides a sense of liberty of action that otherwise would be subject to social control. Living in cities all of our lives, we may underplay the fact that the large bustling streets and squares represent perhaps the defining marker of urban social space, something markedly distinct from the traditional village. Writing on late nineteenth-century England, Raymond Williams reflected on how both in literary works of fiction and real life, village represented a "knowable" place, where inhabitants knew the inside out of each other's lives.[27] But in the "unknowable" city, a sea of people, practices, ways of life, sounds, sights, and shifting events get meshed together to form a dense social whole in which

Chapter 6

anonymity rules. This was a familiar theme among the late nineteenth-century social thinkers such as Ferdinand Tönnies and Georg Simmel. But we do not need to go very far back in history to note this pattern. During the 2009 Green revolt in Iran, many residents in my small village would refrain from open expression of dissent against the government for fear of surveillance because they were intimately known to others; instead, they would travel to Tehran to merge into the opacity of large crowds. But today's cities of the Middle East are marked not just by modern unknowable opaque urbanity; they include many villagelike and knowable urban neighborhoods where the security of familiarity is intertwined with its surveillance and social control. Thus, Cairo protesters go to Tahrir Square not simply because of its symbolism and history but also for the anonymity and liberty of action it supplies.

Urbanizing the Rural

The Arab uprisings involved mobilizations not just in large cities and metropolitan areas but also in small provincial towns; not simply in massive central squares but also in villages. It is then reasonable to ponder, as some have, why small provincial towns have been the locus of revolutionary protests.[28] The question clearly presupposes a certain image about small towns as the traditional communities with provincial habits, customs, and environment that are presumably inimical to collective actions in pursuit of modern democratic polity. Such imagery invokes the well-known Simmel and Tönnies's dichotomy of "village/small town" versus "city/metropolis," where the former is identified as the place of traditional institutions, extended family, community, and consensus-based relations and the latter by the prevalence of cosmopolitanism, interest groups, individualism, and state control.[29] But the reality of the provincial towns in the Middle East is very different from Simmel's late nineteenth-century model of a small town. The Middle Eastern traditional towns and villages have been in the throes of profound transformation in the past three or four decades, as they have been experiencing increasing commodification, literacy and higher education, means of communication, consumer ethos, youth consciousness, urban needs, and opportunities.

Life in these provincial towns and villages, such as Mohamed Bouazizi's Sidi Bouzid in Tunisia, is not exclusively rural and agricultural, as it was in my childhood village in central Iran; nor are the inhabitants exclusively farmers residing in desolate traditional rural communities. Rather, the villagers

124

inhabit largely "urbanizing" rural settings, often with running water, electricity, phone lines, TV, mechanic shops, bakeries, services, day-care centers, and paved roads, as well as schools, banks, uniformed police, and other governmental offices. Above all, they are overwhelmed by the desire and demands of urban consumption patterns. These communities represent a novel formation of hybrid political economies. For the most part, these communities have been rural and agricultural but also subjected to intense processes of marketization, commodification, accumulation, and mechanization of large-scale farming colonies. Villagers may hold plots of land to grow vegetables or raise chickens, cows, or goats, but their surpluses are sent to market, and their life is dependent on cash, wage work, bank loans, and payment of (electricity, water, phone) bills on time. They may be rural, but their children are likely to go to college, be well versed in the new media, experience regular travel to large cities, and be in tune with the global consumer culture. In the Tunisian Sidi Bouzid, for instance, mechanization of large-scale capitalist farms was done at the cost of the smallholders' debt, dispossession, and proletarianization. In fact, farmworkers like Mohamed Bouazizi's father struggled on a small plot for "food security." His father's death left a three-hectare plot that depended on rainwater and produced barely enough to feed the family. His uncle, subsequently married to his mother, tried to build a new farm project to use irrigation water. To finance the project, the family took out a loan by mortgaging the land to the bank, but they were unable to pay the debt, and the bank seized their land. The young Mohamed then moved to work on his uncle's farmland but experienced the very same prevalent course of dispossession. Only then did Mohamed turn to becoming a vendor selling fruits in the streets. His possessions were taken away once again, this time by the police because he did not have a vending permit.[30]

These emerging social formations are bound to leave their imprints on the forms of dissent and political practice. The inhabitants do wish to have access to land and agricultural resources, but they also carry out wage work and operate in the urbanizing rural communities that produce dissent rooted in both rural and urban claims. In Sidi Bouzid, for instance, according to the scholar Habib Ayeb, for many years prior to the revolution, the farmers refused to pay for or subverted regular payment of electricity and water bills, which caused a sizable decline in the state's utilities revenue. In a sense farmers were involved in some kind of nonmovement in that thousands of them individually refused to pay, while keeping aware of what others were doing. In the meantime, some 150 families engaged in land squatting, occupying some four hundred hectares of state land near the Gabes chemical complex.[31] Once they occupied the land, the intransigent regime repression could do little to deter them from holding on to their new possession. In sum, such social changes have brought the provincial and rural into the circuit of the national society and politics, turning them into geographies of wider political dissent.[32]

Insurgent Squares

Despite the active participation of provincial communities in the Arab uprisings, only protests in the primate cities—with 10 to 25 percent of the country's population—led to regime change, as in Tunisia and Egypt. This is so, some have suggested, because a primate city "allows the possibility of rapidly assembled immense protests that paralyze the administrative and political life of the country."[33] But does the power of the square in the primate city, as in Tahrir or Bourguiba Boulevard, lie simply in its power of disruption? If so, why did the postrevolutionary protests in Egypt and Tunisia not bring down the postrevolutionary regimes? Effective disruptions are not caused by public protestations of this sort, which governments can enclose and isolate through blockade or traffic redirection, but rather from institutional protests—when, for instance, labor, civil servants, or bank or service employees go on strike. The power of the square lies in its visible and persistent defiance of authorities, for the square puts on display to both the people and politicians the power of opposition and the feebleness of the regime. In this fashion, the square opens the way for institutional dissenters to begin their institutional disruption; it empowers the opposition and poses a threat to the authorities, compelling them to concede.

But why did particular squares and streets become the location of monumental contention? Why are certain spaces more "insurgent" than others? What are their particularities? A number of factors are involved. First, spaces of insurrection are usually those that enjoy certain symbolic or historical significance—sites surrounded by governmental offices, presidential palaces, or memory of struggle. Emphasizing the historical significance of Tahrir, Atef Said connects the January 25 uprising to the earlier protest movements that took place here.[34] But beyond symbolism, governmental structures in the square may also serve as targets of crowd actions to cause disruptions. Second, the sites are usually in close proximity to intellectual and cultural happenings— sites close to university campuses, large mosques, bookstores, or cultural cafés. They are places that the cultural milieu, critical constituencies, nonconformists, or groups with alternative lifestyles may frequent. These uncommon sites, scenes, and milieus already mark these squares and streets as distinct enclaves in the cultural and political landscape of the city, making them potential spaces of contentious action. Third, they are a locus of mass transportation networks—terminals of buses, taxis, or trams—that can transfer a large mobile crowd and connect such central squares not only to the rest of the city but also to provincial towns and villages. Thus, the Egyptian government expectedly was quick to close down the metro lines passing through Tahrir Square during the eighteen days of the uprising. But in response, minibuses, mostly informal, parked in the nearby streets to transport protesters in and out. In these sites news is produced, exchanged, and spread beyond proximate localities to other sites and cities. Often those who seek news of the events would venture to these squares. Precisely because of their ecology and sociology, these sites serve as crossroads, as spaces where the rich and poor, lay and intellectual, rural and urban, men and women cross, assemble, cofunction, and meet if not mix. And finally, there is the crucial element of spatial flexibility, where a mobile and agile crowd can easily and rapidly assemble in the vast expanse of these squares but have the ability to disperse into the networks of surrounding streets, alleyways, barricades, business locations, and private homes in times of police assault. Accordingly, rivers and bridges can subvert the spaces of insurgency.

For example, Taksim Square in Istanbul has been the place for political crowds to gather for decades. Leftists and trade unionists have held May Day celebrations there at least since the 1970s, during which a number of protesters were shot dead. The square then was closed down, and the May Day celebration was removed from the calendar. But when a multiparty democracy was reestablished in Turkey, rallies and demonstrations returned to the square, with the Gezi Park episode being the most recent. An accessible roundabout intersecting multiple streets and alleyways, notably the Istiqlal promenade with its unique mix of bohemian and elite culture, the Taksim area accommodates many cultural venues—cafés, bookstores, music shops, taverns. Intellectuals, artists, anarchists, and people with alternative lifestyles have turned this area into an extraordinary enclave for unorthodox culture and campaign. The secular and liberal aura of this avant-garde Beyoglu neighborhood has stood in sharp contrast to the conservative moralism that the AKP regime wishes to establish in public arenas. But the Gezi Park episode brought the anti-AKP conservatives and secular activists into the same place of dissent.[35] The Turkish sociologist Berna Turam draws on the life world of Turkish citizens in Istanbul to show how spaces like Gezi encourage an ethos of solidarity and cooperation among divided inhabitants to fight the authoritarianism of the AKP in the wake of the Gezi Park upheaval.[36]

Cairo's Tahrir, part of the "Paris on the Nile" project of Khedive Ismail, was built in the late nineteenth century, but not until the late 1960s and early 1970s did it emerge as a key space of discontent in the capital city.[37] Earlier Al-Azhar courtyard served as the locus of anti-British protests during 1919–1920; and Opera Square, Bayt al-Umma, and Abdeen Square each hosted anticolonial demonstrations during and after World War II. During President Nasser's term, Abdeen Square, where the presidential palace is located, served as a ritualized piazza where the president stood on the balcony to deliver fiery speeches to the jubilant crowd. With the rapid change in the morphology of Tahrir in the late 1960s and 1970s—new buildings, bridges, the parliament, ministries, international hotels, the Arab League, the colossal Mogamma, headquarters of unions and syndicates, and the American University—Tahrir began to assume an unrivaled centrality and symbolism. After these changes, the square has witnessed mass demonstrations against the 1967 defeat in the war with Israel, riots over President Anwar Sadat's austerity measures, student protests against the Camp David peace accord, and rallies in support of the Palestinian Intifada and against the US Middle East policies. After construction of bus terminals and Cairo Metro, and with the multiple streets and bridges connecting the square to the rest of the city, including the rich Zamalek and the poor Giza, Tahrir virtually became the heart of Cairo. Some of its surrounding streets, notably Qasr El Nil Bridge, Qasr Al-Ainy, Sheikh Raihan, and especially Muhammad Mahmoud, became the epicenter of street politics during and after the 2011 uprising. Unlike Alexandria, a city that stretches forty kilometers along the Mediterranean Sea, where the lack of a central square made it difficult for protesters to determine where to congregate or end their protests, Cairo's Tahrir attracted protesters even from provincial towns.[38] Like Tehran's Revolution Square and Istanbul's Taksim, Cairo's Tahrir also interconnects the wealthy and the poor, parochial and cosmopolitan, secular and religious, locals and outsiders, and especially migrants from the provinces, which altogether mark these as potential sites of collective dissension.

Counter-Square

An irony of this politics of place is that these modernist vast squares and boulevards, inspired by the ideas of Baron Haussmann, were originally designed to prevent riots and revolutions, among other things, but they served precisely the opposite function. In the 1850s and 1860s, Haussmann redesigned the traditional ecology of Paris by modernizing its infrastructure. But a key in Hausmann's social engineering was to "fix" the insurgent central neighborhoods, where seven armed uprisings and revolts had occurred between 1830 and 1848, by demolishing their curvy and narrow (one to five meters wide) streets and alleyways, replacing them with vast boulevards, squares, and parks. This urban design was to make the unruly and opaque poor neighborhoods transparent; it aimed to facilitate easy movement of traffic and police in those areas, expose potential protesters to the police, and impede construction of barricades. Even though Haussmann's idea of spatial surveillance simply shifted the security problem from one urban area to another,[39] it left a lasting legacy on how space is controlled in today's cities.

But why did the revolutionary unrest in the Middle East take shape in the very modern squares and boulevards (Cairo's squares were built in the image of Paris and Bourguiba Boulevard by the colonial French) that in Haussmann's plan were supposed to offset revolts? Haussmann's plan was undertaken during a time when rioting and barricading were the main means of urban contention; it predated the prevalence of mass demonstrations that would require vast open spaces and streets to thrive and turn into a political force. The vast streets and squares then facilitate the movement and maneuvering of the police, as Haussmann had thought, but they also ease and accommodate the gathering of large protesting crowds in one place. In Cairo, Tunis, Istanbul, and Sana'a, protesters used these Haussmannian roundabouts precisely because of their centrality, symbolism, ease of movement, and above all, openness and magnitude—places that could contain a staggering number of human bodies. These massive squares displayed massive street power. But these particular Arab cities additionally exhibited a vibrant street life because beyond their urban culture they had become cities inside out. People were out in public working, walking, sitting, driving, loitering, praying, socializing, and being present, thus practically subverting any official prohibition and curfews. President Mubarak's Emergency Law of 1981 particularly targeted public gatherings, but it failed to undo the public presence of thousands who carried out their everyday lives in the city centers.[40] Women frequently disobeyed official restrictions; they would often deploy their maternal impunity as providers for and protectors of children, the sick, and the elderly to move through tanks and armored vehicles to attend to their daily necessities. Even at the height of the uprisings, no Arab regime could impose curfews, especially on Fridays, the Muslim weekend, when large groups of people would rush into the mosques and surrounding streets to attend collective prayers and then invariably march to the protesting squares. Thus, with their vast numbers and spatial protection—retreat and respite into the surrounding streets, shops, or houses—protesters in the Arab uprisings turned these ordinary streets and squares into extraordinary places of political meaning, compelling the authorities to resort to diverse counter-square strategies. The strategies ranged from violently dispersing the crowds, blocking roads, erecting barriers, to disfiguring the squares' physical and symbolic makeup or altering the urban design altogether.

In Riyadh, for instance, the Arab Spring caused much jubilance among dissenting youth and much panic within the Saudi ruling elites; but unlike in the social media and in largely Shia eastern provinces, notably Qatif, Riyadh saw no street unrest. Khaled al-Johani was the only person who protested in public when a "Day of Rage" was announced. This iconic lone protester remains in prison, and the organizer, Faisal Abdul-Ahad, was reportedly shot dead before the protest occurred. It is true that the Saudi regime quickly moved to criminalize street demonstrations as "against Islamic laws and our society's values" while dispensing a reward of thirty-six billion dollars (in the form of interest-free home loans, unemployment assistance, debt relief, and scholarship to students) to citizens to stay home. But the spatial reality of Riyadh itself impeded public protestation. Even though it is different from Pyongyang, North Korea, which has vast twenty-lane antipublic boulevards and colossal squares, modern Riyadh offers little outdoor public space that is social. The wide arteries in this decentered urban sprawl allow for fast streams of cars but barely favors individuals who want to stroll, spend time, or run errands along the sidewalks. The suburban residential neighborhoods with walled houses and concealed courtyards only reinforce atomization and diminish sociability and outdoor publicness. The central streets are often so empty of people that any small public gatherings would appear odd and suspect. Publicness is limited either to the traditional vibrant lower-class Al Batha, which largely houses South Asian migrant laborers and merchants, or to the impressive but enclosed shopping malls guarded constantly by the security and moral police. Reportedly, a few protest actions did take place in the shopping malls but were expectedly isolated and thus put down rapidly.

Watching Tunisia and Egypt, the regime in Syria was determined to prevent anything like Tahrir from emerging. Soon after April 18, 2011, when the revolutionaries took over the main square in Homs to put up signs and tents to settle in, security forces encircled the square and opened fire, killing some two hundred people, according to the opposition. Even though demonstrators filled the central squares in Douma, Zabadani, and Der'a, they had realized that the regime's uncommon brutality would not allow a Syrian Tahrir to materialize. The absence of a Tahrir in Damascus and Aleppo may have undermined the revolution, but the argument that the religious and ethnic culture of rural migrants in these cities served to deurbanize and militarize the revolt would need to address the peaceful protests occurring in many provincial communities.[41] In Sana'a's Martyr's Square (in al-Mansoura), police demolished the symbols of the uprising, such as the large billboard that carried the portraits of those killed by the regime. Sana'a's maidan, a popular site for the poor, faced the same fate when security forces ransacked everything that the revolutionaries had built. But more dramatically, the Bahrain rulers recaptured Pearl Square, Manama's Tahrir, in March 2011; bulldozed its ground and grass; and violently flattened the monument to erase the meaning that protesters had attached to that space.

In Egypt, an antiregime retired police officer instructed the protest coordinators not to descend into Tahrir directly on January 25 but to mobilize and march first in five separate districts, such as Bulaq and Imbaba, and only then advance to Tahrir. His pamphlet became a guide to outmaneuver and offset the usual police tactics to control the square.[42] During the eighteen days of the uprising, the regime's attempts to undo the Tahrir political life—including the violent attacks by thugs on camels and horses on Mawqi'a Gamal Day—all failed; but as street politics continued ceaselessly into the postrevolutionary years, the new (military) rulers began their counter-square plans. First they blocked some of the key intersecting streets to Tahrir by placing massive concrete blocks; a number of these barriers inspired artists to inscribe some of the most memorable murals of the revolution. The attempts by the pro-Mubarak counterrevolutionaries to make Mustafa Mahmoud Square in al-Mohandessin and Abbasiyya Square in Heliopolis rivals for Tahrir went unheeded. But the military authorities went ahead with diminishing the image of Tahrir as space of insurrection through neglect—by allowing the square to fill with garbage and construction debris—and then under General Sisi through new architectural interventions. The new dismal and remarkably unspectacular "monument of the revolution" constructed in Tahrir Square under General Sisi just after the military takeover reflected much about how the counterrevolution wished Tahrir to (not) be remembered. The monument became the target of immediate vandalism by revolutionaries who saw it as an insult to their revolution. The

Figure 1. Tahrir flag; photo by the author

monument lasted only a few months before being replaced by an excessively lofty Egyptian flag (higher than the nearby Mogamma building), which said more about military power than a memory of the revolution. These unsettling makeovers in Tahrir were a sharp contrast to the days after the fall of Mubarak, when the revolutionaries turned their attention to "their city" and that endearing Tahrir roundabout by cleaning, painting, removing garbage, and washing the square as if they were paying back the city for embracing, enduring, and nurturing their insurrection. The move also represented a closure to a chapter in the odyssey of the revolution and its remarkable street politics, not knowing that square politics would continue incessantly, culminating in the June 30, 2013, rebellion against the Islamist president Mohamed Morsi.

Concerned about the "congestion," it came as no surprise that in 2014 President Sisi's government entertained the idea of relocating the capital with all its state institutions into a new forty-five-billion-dollar city in the desert. The initial design, with investment from the United Arab Emirates (UAE), was for a city similar in morphology to those in the Persian Gulf but with no apparent public squares and central spaces. Spatial relocation of this sort in fear of urban insurgency is not new. The Burmese junta moved the government from Yangon, with five million people, to a new capital, Naypyidaw, where the inhabitants lived in isolation in a city with vast boulevards and no public space. When in 2007 the "Saffron Revolution" erupted everywhere in Burma, Naypyidaw remained calm.[43] In a similar vein, President Ahmadinejad of Iran just after the 2009 Green revolt also planned to relocate half of Tehran's population and its universities into different towns to secure them from the danger of an "impending earthquake," but in fact to dilute the potentiality of urban insurgency.[44] General Franco of Spain did succeed in transferring Barcelona University, a bastion of antifascist street politics, to a different location, but relocation plans of both President Ahmadinejad and General Sisi encountered difficulties because of their massive social and economic costs.

. . .

Clearly, square politics of revolutionary times represents the most crucial political acts by ordinary people—those who lack institutional clout, excluded from the centers of power, or have lost trust in the efficacy of institutional politics, including liberal democracy. In these exceptional episodes, revolutionaries become the master of streets not only to battle the powers that be but also to experience moments of unique grassroots democracy and egalitarian order.

They craft a liminal community in the urban arenas, acting as if they live the "future in the present." But the street politics of revolutionary times exhibits its constraints when the exceptional episode comes to an end, when the ordinary people long for normalcy, expecting rewards for the hardship they have endured in the revolutionary battles, and when reforming or building institutions becomes necessary. This means that political engagement and mobilization cannot remain only in the main squares for long but have to be adjusted to the everyday of people's lives, in the backstreets, neighborhoods, households, workplaces, schools, and villages. The ways in which the revolutionary movements come to fruition, and the ideas and strategies they carry, greatly influence the shape of mobilization beyond the streets.

7   The Spring of Surprise

How did the Arab Spring come to fruition at a time when few suspected the fortitude of the Arab regimes and their "authoritarian durability"? It is widely acknowledged that almost no one had anticipated the Arab revolutions, not even those whose business was monitoring such events. Intelligence agencies, political establishments, and think tanks were reportedly taken by surprise by the monumental events that began in Tunisia and Egypt and then spread like wildfire throughout the region. Even the US intelligence services seemed to be confident that the Mubarak regime was safe enough not to be toppled by a handful of the "usual" demonstrators who appeared in the streets of Cairo every so often.[1] The well-known review of scholarly literature on Middle East politics over the past decade by the political scientist Gregory Gause similarly concluded that almost no social scientist was able to systematically foresee what happened.[2] Perhaps more than anyone it was the protagonists who expressed disbelief in what they experienced in the streets of discontent. How surprising were the Arab revolutions? I suggest that surprise lay less in the unexpected arrival of these revolutions than in their particular character—ideological makeup, strategic vision, and political trajectories. Revolutions always come as a surprise, but for some people disbelief runs parallel with a vague sense of anticipation—anticipation not in the sense of systematic prediction but in the broad feeling that things cannot continue like this. This chapter explains how the Arab revolutions unfolded despite the clear resilience of the regimes. While the regimes appeared to govern with a strong hold on society, large segments of the Arab population had discreetly created within the same governance their own realities. When these largely unassuming segments joined the political opposition, a revolutionary breakthrough was created. Yet against expectations, the revolutions did not follow an Islamist path, nor did they have a liberal outlook; theirs was a patchwork of different (non)ideological cues tilted more toward a post-Islamist orientation.

Every Revolution Is a Surprise

Clearly the Arab revolutions came as surprise, but in a sense every revolution is a surprise, no matter how convinced the protagonists or observers may be that they will happen. Alexis de Tocqueville famously wrote that the French Revolution caught everyone off guard, finding the whole episode surprising even though he thought that it was "inevitable."[3] Even a revolutionary strategist like Vladimir Lenin, who was involved in years of preparation, stated to an audience one month before the Russian February Revolution that he would not live to see Russia's great revolution. Nor were the Bolsheviks, Mensheviks, or foreign observers expecting the fall of the czar.[4] Views on the Iranian revolution of 1979 followed a similar pattern. Just a few months before the fall of the shah, President Carter at a dinner in Tehran announced that Iran, based on the CIA's assessment, was an "island of stability" in a troubled region. Ayatollah Khomeini in 1970 thought it would take two centuries to topple the Iranian monarchy; even by 1978 he still doubted that the shah would relinquish power.[5] I recall that my revolutionary friends and I were utterly surprised by the unfolding of the Iranian revolution, even though we never shed our teleological conviction that "history is on our side." The story of the 1989 revolutions in Eastern Europe seems not much different. Only 5 percent of East Germans had anticipated a revolution a year before it actually happened. The vast majority of Germans were in a state of total disbelief.[6] Similar sentiments were expressed when the Soviet Union collapsed in 1989. And the uprisings in Tunisia and Egypt stunned the most revolutionary protagonists, in particular when they had barely thought about or organized the revolutions in any systematic fashion.[7]

So, why the surprise? Economist Timur Kuran has argued that revolutions come as a surprise because those in the dissenting population do not reveal their discontent in public. Consequently, the opposition remains hidden from the eyes and ears of both adversaries and observers, who then assume that things are stable. But when an accident triggers a protest, the hidden dissenters join forces to create formidable public protestation that may undo authoritarian systems.[8] This is an intriguing argument but raises questions. What if people actually speak out instead of hiding their grievances? Does any dissent necessarily translate into political action and, if so, under what circumstances?[9] In my own experience of living and working in both Iran and Egypt prior to their revolutions, I could not help noticing that people publicly complained about a range of issues—from high prices and power cuts to police brutality and traffic jams—and they mostly blamed the government for these misfortunes. Under Ben Ali's police state, Yusra, a working-class woman from Monastir, would "angrily recount the unsavoury behaviour of the local despots to her fellow passengers" during "her commute to and from [the] capital every Monday through Friday."[10] Indeed, the practice of "public nagging" or venting and voicing grievances in public places remains a salient feature of public culture in the Middle East, serving as a central element in the making of public opinion; it constitutes an important component of what I have described as "political street"—the collective sentiments, shared feelings, and public opinions of ordinary people in their day-to-day speech, sarcasm, and acts that are usually expressed casually in urban public spaces, in taxis, buses, shops, main streets, backstreets, or deliberately in mass demonstrations.[11] Whether or not the autocratic regimes and political elites were able or willing to hear these dissenting voices may be open to question. But given the regimes' vast intelligence operations, it was likely that the elites and authorities could hear them but dismissed them as the commoners' "usual bickering" or a cultural trait of the pitiable but "cunning poor" that had little to do with politics.

What transpired in the Arab Spring, I suggest, resonates somehow with what the anthropologist Alexei Yurchak considers the paradox of the Soviet collapse, which came as a surprise yet was expected. Yurchak shows that while the Soviet system—its values, institutions, and discourse—appeared to be normalized and stable, it nevertheless offered spaces within which the Soviet citizens functioned, interpreted, altered, and subverted the meanings by creating their own different reality. Socialism espoused values like equality, justice, community, friendship, selflessness, and a future that citizens genuinely embraced, but at the same time it imposed the party's command over most aspects of people's lives. The system induced citizens' attachment but also their alienation; it seemed stable and durable but in fact remained fragmented and fragile.[12] Beatrice Hibou's account of citizens' obedience under Ben Ali in prerevolutionary Tunisia reveals a number of similar dynamics. Ben Ali's regime had crafted a system of a "security pact" and social integration in which the citizens displayed obedience not only because of state surveillance and repression but more pervasively through their "inclusion" in the state provisions of protection, consumption, and modernity. The state's coercion was rife and rampant, but it also came with the good things the state provided, albeit unequally—welfare, a high standard of living, access to a modern and consumer society, and national unity.

Under the Arab autocracies in Tunisia and Egypt ordinary citizens imagined the state in paradoxical ways both as provider and punisher, virtuous and villain, abler and oppressor—an image that informed their paradoxical relations with the state. They respected, feared, expected service, yet were relentless in their criticisms. They appeared to go along with the state discourse, bought into the dominant narrative of the nation and progress, consumed state TV, participated in its rituals, and hung the images of national leaders on their walls. But in their everyday lives, they carved off spaces in the socioscapes of kin and cliques in private homes, backstreet assemblies, worksites, mosques, alternative art galleries, Internet cafés, or even in the state-sponsored popular committees (Libya), student or labor unions (Tunisia), or the ruling parties, wherein they operated, produced sustenance, reproduced culture, built trust, and created their own realities. Here in these vast and practically normalized socioscapes, ordinary citizens interpreted, produced alternative meanings, and subverted what they apparently complied with—the state narratives and its governmentality. These masses did not directly confront the regimes in the way the militant activists did; rather, in the manner of nonmovements, they got involved in discreet practices of alternative life making and norm creation. So even though people "nagged and moaned," they still looked "passive"; and while the regimes appeared unchallenged, they in fact remained fragile, especially when their neoliberal policies had enhanced highly visible marginalization and inequalities. Thus, merged into the process of everyday life, these popular practices became by the 2000s increasingly contentious in the political arena; they rendered the ordinary and marginalized Arab citizens, chiefly unemployed young people, as critical players in the 2011 uprisings.

Yet the popular politics of this sort received little recognition from the political elites or the academics, who overlooked them altogether or considered their actions as survival strategies with a slight political meaning. As Greg Gause's survey of the field suggests, the mainstream Middle East studies was preoccupied with the accounts of politics that fetishized the elites, the state, and political society, focusing on such matters as elections, Islamist subversion, or relations with the United States.[13] Of course, considering the state, the elites, and international relations is indispensable to understanding the dynamics of domestic politics, but it becomes less helpful when the elites or the state is examined in isolation from the broader field of popular politics. The elites are in the business of governance, but governance would fail if it overlooked societal sensibilities, and its hegemony would fade in the face of any alternative mode of life citizens may construct. It is equally unhelpful to reduce politics, as Hannah Arendt does, to town hall meetings, organized civic activism, or mass demonstrations where conscious deliberation for freedom occurs, dismissing the realm of life, labor, and work as simply apolitical struggles for survival or apolitical endeavors.[14] One wonders where Arendt would place activities and institutions like factory shuras in the Iranian revolution of 1979, the Zapatista movement in Chiapas, or the Saudi women's initiative of "push normal" to augment gender equality, all of which navigate through life, labor, and politics. In fact, what people do in their daily lives can produce surprises in the most critical revolutionary moments, as in the Arab revolts.

Activists and the Ordinary

Pre-uprising Arab politics displayed a complex mix of organized activism embodied in political parties, Islamist insurgency, and social movements with the type of politics that were merged in everyday life and labor. In Egypt, legal activism focused largely on traditional party politics, a tired method that had lost much of its efficacy and appeal by the early 2000s. But in the extralegal domain, radical Islamists such as al-Gama'a al-Islamiyya and al-Jihad resorted to Leninist-type underground organization and struggle, and the reformist Muslim Brotherhood combined its civil activities with electoral competition when allowed. While student activists were forced to remain on campus sites, laborers, going beyond conventional organizations, launched wildcat strikes to push for their claims, and middle-class professionals resorted to expanding NGOs. And all embraced street politics when permitted, for instance, during demonstrations in support of the Palestinian cause or protests against the US invasion of Iraq in the early 2000s. Unlike that in Egypt, the police state in Tunisia permitted little independent activism or street protest; the Tunisian Islamic opposition remained limited, underground, and suppressed; the leadership of the highly organized trade union movement was allied with the regime; and no meaningful intellectual opposition was on the political stage.[15]

But beyond audible and organized activism, a plethora of disconnected activities were under way in the lower strata of society. The urban poor made sure to secure shelter, consolidate their communities, and earn a living by devising work in the vast subsistence and street economy. Muslim women strove to assert their presence in public, go to college, and ensure justice in the courts. And youths took every opportunity, often through "subversive accommodation," to affirm their autonomy, challenge social control of elders and political authority, and worry about their future, even though many remained atomized and dreamed of migrating to the West.[16] In other words, a large number of the urban poor, marginalized youth, women, and other subaltern groups were involved in nonmovements—the dispersed but contentious practices of individuals and families in everyday life who struggled to enhance their life chances. Even though many of these activities were carried out individually or through family and friends, they would turn into larger networks and collective actions when their gains were threatened.

What is crucial to point out is that Arab societies were marked by innumerable small (ten to fifteen members), informal private or semipublic cliques (*shillas*) and collectives within which ordinary people connected, socialized, deliberated, developed trust, and often generated alternative norms and narratives. These "uncivil societies" lay somewhere between the Habermasian binary of "private" as the domain of family and intimacy and "public" as the sphere of civil interaction and rational deliberation.[17] Very different from the static and singular image of a "social mosaic," these hybrid collectives offered a clue about what went on between the upperside and underside of Arab societies. The Yemeni qat-chewing assemblies, Kuwaiti *diwaniya* and Iranian *doureh* (both referring to male private gatherings), are too well known to elaborate; nor do we need to detail the Iranian *patouqs*, the place-based collectives of intellectuals, friends, or workmates who may assemble regularly in coffee shops, malls, or restaurants to socialize or discuss political or literary matters.[18] But in Saudi Arabia, where political control was embedded in an intransigent patriarchy justified on Wahhabi Islamic doctrine, young Muslim women generated their own spaces within the system to challenge sex segregation, while the young devised ways to assert their youthfulness through associations with their shilla or in open public spaces. Amelie Le Renard's ethnography gives us a glimpse of how educated Saudi women have been transforming urban societies by creating their own professional, consumerist, and nonconformist life worlds.[19] Groups of women initiated the "push normal" campaign to challenge sex segregation in public by, for instance, strolling in male-only spaces: in art galleries, in work areas, and at home. A young male who lived in Riyadh related that "we were trying to make our own youthful spaces, shillas, in clubs, schools, or friendship gatherings in homes to watch movies, play games, discuss issues, and make friends with girls."[20] Pascale Menoret, reporting from the Saudi Arabian activist world, shows how "groups of ten or twenty friends who share a common goal and meet regularly in a given place, apartment, coffee shop, or private rest house [*istiraha*]" had created their own world under the shadow of the regime's surveillance.[21] During my visit to Riyadh I could see that groups of young boys and veiled girls hung out in the malls, eyeing each other and sending messages in the restricting spaces. The boys told me that they had formed their own societies in malls, gymnasiums, and private homes where they socialized, watched banned movies, and deliberated social issues.

Under Tunisia's police state, the intelligentsia typically refrained from direct opposition and instead deployed metaphors for political expression. Thus, when the literature professor Samiyah chose to teach George Orwell's *1984*, "everyone understood and related to it."[22] But the young often resorted to underground communities of cultural activities, music and art groups, tattoo users, or LGBT associations, all of which espoused a fundamentally oppositional spirit.[23] Amin Allal reports of the unemployed youths who formed their shillas in affordable cafes, and those in the working-class suburb of Tunis met, socialized, discussed, and carried out subversive actions against the police and local authorities.[24] In Egypt, students formed informal circles within official high school and college unions and clubs. Even though under the watchful eyes of the secret police, these activities "gave me a lot of experience and a lot of connections," an activist recalled.[25] Many used youth clubs as places to assemble, play, watch films, and discuss; while others formed groups in the Internet cafés to surf and chat with youth groups from other countries.[26] In the initiative called Lamma (Gathering), some youths gathered in public places such as parks to chat, discuss politics, and read books; someone might initiate a point of research or introduce a discussion on a topic in which young men and women, Muslims and Christians, would participate.[27] Others, like the very young Ala Abdel-Fattah, who would become an icon of the Egyptian revolution, did volunteer work with the children of the poor Zilzal area of Mokattam or engaged in al-Nusur al-Saghira summer camps to help enhance the deprived children's creativity, awareness of their communities, and their value as individuals. Later in the mid-2000s, group members inspired by the April 6, 2008, labor strikes formed discussion and reading circles.[28] By this time a new strand of activists with new thinking and literature (on human rights, social movements, and civil disobedience) broke from traditional party and nationalist politics.[29] Many ex-communists who had disengaged from party politics of the 1970s worked individually or formed their own small shillas in the cultural clubs, literary magazines, or informal gatherings and joined in the Kefaya democracy movement when it emerged.[30]

Figure 2. Clique in Dar El Salam, Cairo; photo by the author

These disparate networks, cliques, collectives, and nonmovements, often immersed in the practices of everyday life, kept the participants engaged or offered opportunities since the repressive regimes prevented them from forging open and organized mobilization. While the regimes were able to subdue "collective actors"—political parties or organized movements—they were unable to prevent "collective actions" forged through these diffused socioscapes in which parallel institutions and alternative norms against the official ideologies developed. But some of these initiatives became coordinated with the organized work of activists when the opportunity arose. Thus, President George W. Bush's unleashing of his "democratization" rhetoric after the US invasion of Iraq created a political opening. The second Palestinian Intifada—the Israeli aggression and the images of a father protecting his little son from Israeli gunshots—brought youth into a new political realm through the growing social media. They moved from the quieter activities of street gatherings, friendship networks, and informal NGO work into more direct political engagement with regional politics and democracy at home. The upsurge of the Arab street against Israeli incursions, the occupation of Iraq, and expanding social media configured the region's "new politics"—one that emphasized decentralization, broad alliances, street politics, and democratic language. In Egypt solidarity with the Palestinians moved from elitist "antinormalization activism" to a popular movement by feminist groups, human rights centers, labor unions, student associations, mosques, and churches to offer concrete support—donations, food, and medicine—to the besieged occupied territories.[31]

The second opportunity came with the Kefaya movement in Egypt, which significantly put the demand for democracy on the agenda and further served as a precursor to broader protest movements, notably the April 6 youth movement, laying out opportunities for ordinary actors to become engaged. Thus, the urban poor protested collectively against the high price of food, especially bread, and against the demolition of illegal homes and the shortage of drinking water in the neighborhoods. Cairo's garbage collectors waged a series of unprecedented collective protests in 2009, leaving piles of trash in the streets and at homes, exposing the failure of the state to ensure a modicum of sanitary urban life. More significantly, labor protests against the eroding traditional perks and security reached new heights in 2009 and 2010, while the young became involved in civic activism and voluntary work on a scale never seen before. When social media became available for them, the young began to connect and build network groups, with some engaging in mobilizing protest actions. In Tunisia, self-immolations and labor unrest had previously occurred in the central provinces of Gàbes, Qasarain, and Sidi Bouzid; small farmers had shown their public indignation against the lending banks and the government over credit, land, water, and subsidies.[32] And the Tunisian younger generation—some 40 percent of them unemployed—were already in the business of online networking and building political identities. Young bloggers began to defy Ben Ali's dictatorship. "We had long been working against censorship and the obstruction of free speech," said a prominent activist; "we tried to talk about opinion prisoners, torture and dictatorship."[33] These largely disparate voices and practices seemed to coalesce by the end of the 2000s to form the backbone of what came to be known as the Arab Spring.

Structural Change and Dissent

All these activities were happening against the backdrop of some remarkable structural changes that Arab societies had been undergoing since the early 1990s, for which the autocratic Arab states operating according to neoliberal globalization were responsible. In a sense the autocratic regimes created environments and actors that came to challenge those very regimes. Middle Eastern societies since the late 1980s had become more urban and globalized, with nearly 60 percent living in cities. In the meantime, certain urban institutions, means of communication, and education permeated into the countryside, producing opportunities and constraints that are the markers of urban subjects. Urban life generated desires, demands, and rights (such as paid jobs, decent shelter, optimum amenities, respect, basically the "right to the city") that autocratic regimes failed to address in regard to a large portion of urban inhabitants. Cities then inculcated in the urban dwellers a sense of entitlement, making them increasingly insurgent citizens. Second, a dramatic demographic shift made these societies excessively young, with an estimated 70 percent of the population under the age of thirty-five. While in those overcrowded habitats, the young encountered tremendous constraints—economic deprivation, social control, and moral pressure. In fulfilling their youthful claims, they utilized the opportunities that these very cities offered (such as street-corner gatherings, teashops, schools and colleges, and recently social media) to forge collective identities and demand social inclusion. Indeed, it was in these cities that fragmented young persons turned into becoming *youth*, collective agents.

In the meantime, these urbanizing and youthful societies became increasingly literate, so that over 90 percent of people between fourteen and twenty-four years of age could at least read and write. With the explosion of higher education institutions in recent years (more than 280 universities), thousands of graduates poured each year into the highly segmented labor markets, which became aggressively liberalized by the policy of structural adjustment pushed by the World Bank and IMF since the early 1990s. In this neoliberal restructuring, those smart and well-connected groups in such globalized sectors as high-tech, entertainment, real estate development, communication, and import-export thrived, while disproportionate numbers were unable to achieve their expectations.[34] It is no surprise that prior to the uprisings the MENA region suffered from the highest rate of unemployment in the world, particularly among youth (more than 25 percent). The diminishing subsidies, job insecurity, and deteriorating social provisions had caused massive urban riots in Arab major cities in the 1980s and 1990s. To offset the destabilizing effects of social exclusion, most Arab states have assigned since the 1990s a good portion of their development and welfare tasks to the rapidly growing NGOs, religious charities, and microcredit projects. But these arrangements, often framed in neoliberal logic, failed to address welfare needs and the deep inequality generated by the end of the social contract and the diminishing role of the states.

One outcome of such an uneven development was the growth of the middle-class poor, a class that played a key role in the Arab revolts of 2011. This class had college degrees, knew about the world, used electronic media, and expected a middle-class lifestyle. But this group was pushed by economic deprivation to live the life of the traditional urban dispossessed in shanty towns and slums and undertake jobs in the largely precarious and low-status parallel economy—as taxi drivers, fruit sellers, or street vendors. The middle-class poor constituted a segment of the 36 percent of Arabs who lived in slums and of the 40 to 50 percent who subsisted on the insecure informal economy in the late 2010s.

The middle-class poor was not a new formation. It had existed since about the 1980s but expanded as the Arab economies liberalized excessively in the 1990s. Just before the revolutions, unemployment among youth, in particular the highly educated, in the Middle East had reached roughly twice the world average. In Egypt college graduates were ten times more likely to remain without jobs than those with a primary education. In the 1980s and 1990s, much of this stratum had merged into a political class absorbed by the nationalist and Islamist sentiments, even though in their daily existence, many were involved in everyday struggles to subsist, make claims, and generate alternative norms.

A great deal, then, was happening in the lower strata of Arab societies, which remained unnoticed by Middle East observers, who were concerned less with the theme of change than continuity, less with exploring internal forces of transformation than explaining how authoritarian rules endured. Many in the policy circles, looking through the "exceptionalist" lens, focused on a narrow, static notion of culture—one that was virtually equated with the religion of Islam—to explain the status quo. Others who found little explanatory power in the "culturalist" paradigm pointed to oil and the rentier state as factors that presumably ensured stability and continuity. Certainly, oil money does matter in buying off dissent by helping establish social contracts, creating labor aristocracies, funding efficient surveillance, and creating a "regime class" of loyalists who support incumbent regimes in exchange for state handouts and compliance, as in Islamist Iran or Qaddafi's Libya. But the rentier state is also developmental; it modernizes, helping establish the infrastructure of economic and social change and classes of political actors who may come to question the very authoritarian states that helped create them. The development processes in Iran, Saudi Arabia, Oman, Kuwait, and the United Arab Emirates exemplify the regenerative facet of oil income, even though the exclusive control of oil by the states also had repressive consequences.[35] Kaveh Ehsani has demonstrated the developmentalist potential of oil in Iran's twentieth century in terms of modern urbanity and the formation of a modern working class; and Timothy Mitchell has complicated our understanding of the role of fossil fuels in the history of democracy.[36] Whereas using fossil fuels involves laborers and labor processes that made oligarchies vulnerable to democratic demands, the desire for cheap energy pushed the Western powers to keep authoritarian rule in the Middle East to ensure the flow of cheap oil. Such structural factors barely figured in the analyses of the prevailing scholarship on the Middle East.[37]

Consequently, those who did point out the potential of popular dissent as a source of change could not find much potency in the activities of ordinary people. If anything, they viewed popular activism as little more than sporadic angry protestation, with most of it directed by Islamists mainly against the West and Israel rather than their own repressive states. Even the celebrated *Arab Human Development Report* could not envision any other alternative to the depressing state of Arab development but a "realistic solution" of a "western-supported project of gradual and moderate reform aiming at liberalization."[38] If there was any formidable dissent to reckon with, it was to come only from the ranks of the Islamists.

Post-Islamist Orientation

In truth, Islamist politics was so prevalent prior to the uprisings that, for many observers and policy makers, any real challenge to the despotic regimes would unleash some form of "Islamist revolution" in the region. Indeed, once the Egyptian uprising sent a shock wave through the region, concerned voices about an impending Islamist revolution surfaced. The idea did not come just from a segment of anxious Egyptians; Hosni Mubarak's regime was frantically attempting to dissuade its Western allies from supporting the uprising. At the same time, Israel's Benjamin Netanyahu and the Iranian hard-liners claimed that Egypt was experiencing an Islamist turn. The Israeli government projected the revolution as a new menace to its interests, while the Iranian Islamists were attempting to present it as the continuation of Iran's "Islamic awakening."[39]

But contrary to expectations, the Arab revolts espoused the kind of aura, idioms, culture, and constituencies that radically distinguished them from earlier Islamist movements. Of course, most participants in the uprisings were pious Muslims who fought along with seculars, leftists, nationalists, and non-Muslims. And many protesters appeared to perform religious rituals, such as praying in streets and squares and utilizing religious times (Fridays) and places (like mosques). But these religious rituals have all been part of the regular practices of all pious Arabs who perform them in everyday life rather than carry them out to Islamize the uprisings. Rather than Islamist revolutions, the uprisings embodied largely post-Islamist orientations. Even though the Islamists were certainly present during the uprisings, they never determined the direction of these movements—after all, there was hardly any central leadership in any of the uprisings. Some Islamist groups initially were even reluctant to join in the protests, and the major religious groups in Egypt—Salafis, al-Azhar, and the Coptic Church—initially opposed the revolution. The mufti of Egypt, Ali Gomaa, proclaimed that rising against the lawful ruler—President Mubarak— was *haram*, not permissible. And the Muslim Brotherhood's old guard joined in protests reluctantly only after being pushed by the group's young people, who defied their leaders to cooperate closely with the liberals and leftists. In Tunisia, the Islamic al-Nahda showed great hesitation in joining the uprising when it flared up. Al-Nahda remained mostly silent initially; it did not wish to antagonize the Ben Ali regime at a time when some of its members were being released from prison. In an interview with the al-Jawar al-Londoniya channel, Rachid al-Ghannouchi reportedly called the early demonstrations "rebellion against the ruler and thus *haram*."[40] But when al-Nahda eventually sided with the revolution, the exiled leader Rachid al-Ghannouchi insisted that his party did not want a Khomeini-type religious state; he favored a nonreligious civil state. The leadership of the Libyan uprising, the National Transitional Council, was composed not of Islamists or al-Qaeda members but doctors, lawyers, teachers, and some defectors from the Qaddafi regime who suddenly found themselves leading a revolution. In Yemen, the key participating religious group (Hizb al-Islah) in the revolutionary coalition remained moderate, while al-Qaeda used the disruption in security only to launch its own sporadic anti-government attacks in the provinces. Even in Bahrain, where conflict appeared religious in terms of Shia opposition against the Sunni ruling family, the opposition rejected a religious takeover of the state. Broadly, the Arab revolts called not for a religious state but for freedom, dignity, and social justice.

These overwhelmingly civil and nonreligious revolts represented a sharp departure from the region's politics of the mid-1980s and 1990s, when the political class was preoccupied by a mix of nationalist and Islamist politics. But

Islamist politics had begun to lose its dominance in the post-9/11 Middle East. The Iranian model had faced a deep crisis for its repression, misogyny, exclusionary attitudes, and unfulfilled promises. It had spurred a widespread opposition and then a formidable movement to mobilize a broad spectrum of the population to bring the post-Islamist Mohammad Khatami to power in 1997.[41] Al-Qaeda's brutal violence and extremism had caused widespread Islamophobia from which largely ordinary Muslims suffered. The challenge faced by Turkish Islamism—expressed originally in Millĭ Görös and then in a series of political parties such as Refah and Fazilet—in its encounter with strong secular sensibilities and the Turkish military had caused the emergence of a post-Islamist Justice and Development Party (AKP). In Morocco, the 1970s Islamism of Shabab al-Islamiyya had evolved in a turbulent process into the legal and moderate Justice and Development Party (PJD) whose leader, Abdelilah Benkirane, became the first Islamic prime minister of Morocco in 2011. Thus, Islamist politics in the region encountered serious challenges from without and within—from seculars and faithful alike who felt the deep scars Islamists' disregard for human rights, tolerance, and pluralism had left on the body politic and religious doctrine. The faithful could no longer accept Islamists' exploitation of Islam as a tool to procure power and privilege. It was time to rescue Islam and the state by abandoning the idea of the Islamic state.[42] This line of thinking broadly underscored the post-Islamist orientation of a "new Arab public"— young, educated, postideological, and variously marginalized—who utilized expanding electronic communication, notably satellite dishes, mobile phones, and social media, to initiate the uprisings.[43]

Islamism in Power?

But a surprising element here is that on the morrow of these overwhelmingly civil and nonreligious uprisings, it was mainly the religious parties that assumed parliamentary and governmental power. In Morocco, the Islamic PJD earned the highest number of votes, and its leader, Benkirane, became prime minister. The Tunisian Hizb al-Nahda won 40 percent of the seats in the parliamentary elections and became the dominant power in the Constituent Assembly; and Hamadi Jebali of al-Nahda became prime minister (2011–2013). In Egypt, the Muslim Brotherhood and the Salafi parties together captured 60 percent of the seats in the parliament, and Mohamed Morsi of the Muslim Brotherhood became president. It was as if the Middle East were on the verge of yet another wave of Islamism, reinforcing the ideas of those who feared the Arab Spring would turn into an "Islamist winter."[44]

The anxiety over "Islamist resurgence" had largely to do with the common practice of lumping together under the rubric "Islamism" quite different kinds of religiously inspired trends, as if any Muslim man with a beard and wearing a *jalabiya*, or woman wearing a *hijab*, or a volunteer in a religious association was an Islamist. In fact, many of the religious parties that seemed to cause anxiety in the mainstream media were not Islamist, strictly speaking; they were post-Islamist, even though they all self-consciously remained Islamic. As discussed earlier, Islamism describes those ideologies and movements that seek to establish some kind of an Islamic order, including a religious state, sharia law, and moral codes, in Muslim societies and communities. Islamists insist on controlling state power, not only because it ensures their rule but especially because they consider the state to be the most powerful and effective institution that is able to "command good and forbid wrong." Consequently, Islamist normativity places more emphasis on people's obligations, on what people must or must not do, than on their rights and choices. Islamism perceives people more as dutiful subjects than rightful citizens, so it embodies a duty-centered religious polity. This type of polity informs the perspectives of diverse Islamist movements in the world, ranging from the Iranian hard-liners led by the supreme leader Ayatollah Khamenei, the Jamaat-e-Islami and Lashkar-e-Taiba in Pakistan to Laskar Jihad in Indonesia, al-Shabaab in Somalia, and Hizbut Tahrir in many parts of the world.

Post-Islamism is different. It is neither anti-Islamic nor secular but wants to transcend Islamist politics by emphasizing people's rights rather than just their obligations. It views people more as citizens than mere subjects; hopes to mix religiosity and rights, faith and freedom (with varied degrees), Islam and democracy; and favors a secular/civil state but a pious society. In short, post-Islamism represents a critique of Islamism from within and without. The Iranian Reform Movement under Mohammad Khatami, the Indonesian Prosperous Justice Party (PKS), and the Turkish AKP between 2002 and 2012 exhibited a few variants of the post-Islamist trends in the Muslim world.[45]

What unfolded in the aftermath of the Arab Spring in these countries was not Islamist resurgence per se but a new religious polity with a broadly post-Islamist proclivity. In the Algerian and Libyan post-uprising elections, the religious parties lost to their secular and liberal counterparts; in Libya Abdel Hakim Belhaj's Islamist party did not win any seats in the General National

Congress in 2012, which elected the secular Mustafa Abushagur as prime minister. It is true that by early 2015 the self-declared Islamist militias defied the officially elected parliament and government by establishing their own ruling bodies in Benghazi, but it remained unclear how much popular support their polity enjoyed. In the cases of both Morocco and Tunisia, the religious parties that captured most power did not push for Islamist polity but worked toward a post-Islamist vision. Morocco's PJD remained committed to Morocco's new constitution as Benkirane formed the government for the first time. In fact, PJD did not consider itself an Islamist party per se but a party with an "Islamic reference." Al-Nahda in Tunisia remained steadfast about forming a civil and secular state, while it continued to profess religion as a major player in civil society. In the words of its spokesperson, Samir Dilou, in al-Nahda "we are not an Islamist party, we are an Islamic party, that gets its inspiration from the Quran." Inspired by the Turkish AKP and the Christian Democratic Parties in Europe, the religious al-Nahda rejected theocracy and embraced "a democratic state that is characterized by the idea of liberty."[46] In 2016, it formally declared a "complete separation" of its religious and political activities.[47] Indeed, al-Nahda worked with liberal, leftist, women, and labor constituencies to produce one of the most secular and democratic constitutions in the region. These parties were conservative but not necessarily Islamist.

In Egypt the situation was more complex. The Egyptian revolution drove the Muslim Brotherhood, the largest and most organized Islamist movement, to undertake a crucial test of its history, revealing the group's profound ideological and strategic quandaries. Whereas the Brothers kept their low profile during the uprising, vowing not to field any candidate for the post-Mubarak presidency, the group nevertheless rushed to ascend to governmental power later when it saw the opportunity. Earlier in the mid-2000s, the Brotherhood seemed to discard the Quranic idea of shura in favor of elections, people's power, and democracy.[48] But this discursive shift had been pushed more by events than being a result of a systematic evaluation of its Islamist ideology. The Brotherhood's concept of democracy proved to be no more than majoritarian rule. Conflicting statements and diverse positions at different times reflected the group's ideological discord. The old guard continued to speak of Islamism and sharia, with the leaders, such as Muhammad Badiʿ and Mahmoud Ezzat, subscribing to the ideas of the radical Sayyid Qutb, while many of their young people embraced post-Islamism of the AKP orientation. When the followers of Qutb dominated the leadership in the elections of the Shura

Council in December 2009, the indignant "youth of the Brotherhood" rebelled, proclaiming "no allegiance, no obedience, and no leadership to the putschists [old guard] of the Maktab el-Ershad."[49] The discord and differences of vision within the Muslim Brotherhood led to multiple splits with prominent leaders such as Abdel Moneim Aboul Fotouh, who was expelled from the group and formed his own Strong Egypt Party. Younger members lashed out at the old guard for their authoritarian rule, gender bias, and secrecy.[50] Many left the organization; among them were those who established five different political parties, including Tayar Masry and Hizb al-Adl. Another group defected, forming the Society of Revival and Building for Development, because it claimed Muslim Brothers were "secretive" and invested too much in politics rather than Da'wa.[51] In the end, the short two years of the Brotherhood regime cost the group an unprecedented loss of sympathy and a dramatic rise in opposition against the Brotherhood. State institutions under Morsi, such as the Ministries of Interior, Culture, and Tourism, were fraught with tension and discord, not only because of counterrevolutionary sabotage but also because of their mismanagement and exclusionary policies that in the end instigated citizens' discontent. The opposition to the Brotherhood's rule reached its peak in the June 30, 2013, rebellion, which many Egyptians called the "second revolution," while General Sisi used the occasion to forcefully end the rule and the organization of the Brotherhood once and for all.

Beyond the change in the formal organizations, Arab publics seemed to undergo an ideological shift toward post-Islamist sensibilities. A values survey conducted in June–August 2011 in Egypt, Iraq, Lebanon, and Saudi Arabia showed that some 85 percent of Egyptians perceived the aim of the revolution to be democracy, economic prosperity, and equality, while only 9 percent believed the goal was an Islamic government. Egyptians favoring democratic polity had increased from 68 percent in 2001 to 84 percent in 2011.[52] A different poll by TNS Global Market Research, reported in *Al-Masry al-Youm* in 2011, suggested that 75 percent of Egyptians favored a civil rather than religious state.[53] Expressing a typical post-Islamist sentiment, a taxi driver stated his dislike of the Ekhwan, preferring a nonreligious state, one that could handle domestic and international affairs. "But we want a moral society; we don't want people having sex in the streets . . . we don't want people drinking alcohol in public," he stated.[54] Indeed, in the first round of presidential elections in Egypt, the Brotherhood's Islamist candidate earned less than 25 percent of the votes, and in the final round (against the pro-Mubarak Ahmed Shafik), just over 50 percent. Even though there are no clear data, it is well known that many Egyptians had voted not in support of Morsi but in opposition to his rival, Ahmed Shafik, whom they saw representing the sentiments of the counterrevolution. Nevertheless, the surprising visibility of Salafis in the public arenas in the postrevolutionary period caused grave concern. Even though Salafism remained a heterogeneous entity—some preferred the status quo, others focused on enhancing the ethical self, while still others embraced a militant *takfiri* path—the sporadic and violent intrusions into free expression, artistic products, and women's rights instigated serious disquiet and debate about the future of Salafi groups in the new Arab political landscape. Widely detested and isolated, ISIS came to embody the kind of extremism that ordinary Muslims had feared jihadi Salafism could unleash.

But where were the revolutionaries—those who initiated and carried out the uprisings—when the religious parties ascended to the helm of governmental power? Why were the protagonists, including the leftists, liberals, and post-Islamists, predominantly pushed to the margins instead of rising to rule? The revolutions in Egypt, Tunisia, and Yemen did topple dictators and opened the space for new social forces, including the Islamists and Salafis, to openly mobilize, but they failed to cause a radical transformation of the state—a step necessary to realize the revolution's objectives. While the protagonists succeeded in creating the magic of Tahrir and Taghir, little changed in the institutions of the old order. This "half revolution" marked the key surprise, indeed the chief peculiarity of the Arab Spring—a theme discussed in the following chapter.

8   Half Revolution, No Revolution

In 2011, the Arab uprisings were celebrated as world-changing events that would redefine the spirit of our political times. The astonishing spread of these mass uprisings, followed soon after by the Occupy protests, left observers in little doubt that they were witnessing an unprecedented phenomenon—something totally new, open-ended, a movement without a name, revolutions that heralded a novel path to emancipation. According to Alain Badiou, Tahrir Square and all the activities that took place there—fighting, barricading, debating, camping, cooking, and caring for the wounded—constituted the "communism of movement." Posited as an alternative to the conventional liberal-democratic and authoritarian state, this was a universal concept that heralded a new way of doing politics—a true revolution. For Slavoj Žižek, only these "universal" political happenings, without hegemonic organizations, charismatic leadership, or party apparatuses, could create what he called the "miracle of Tahrir." For Hardt and Negri, the Arab Spring, Europe's *indignado* protests, and Occupy Wall Street expressed the longing of the multitude for a "real democracy," a different kind of polity that might supplant the hopeless liberal variety worn threadbare by corporate capitalism. These movements, in sum, represented the "new global revolutions."[1]

New, certainly, but what does this newness tell us about the nature of these political upheavals? What value does it attribute to them? Just as these confident appraisals were being circulated in the United States and Europe, the Arab protagonists themselves were anguishing over the fate of their revolutions, lamenting the dangers of counterrevolutionary restoration or hijacking by free riders. Five years after the fall of the dictators in Tunisia, Egypt, and Yemen, not a great deal had effectively changed in the states' institutions or the power bases of the old elites. Police, army, and judiciary; state-controlled media; business elites and the clientelist networks of the old ruling parties—all had remained more or less intact. The fact that Egypt's provisional military rulers in 2012 could impose a ban on strikes and bring more than twelve thousand revolutionaries before military tribunals suggests that there was something peculiar about the character of these revolutions.

I suggest that the key marker of the Arab revolutions lay in their painful paradox in coupling revolutionary mobilization with a reformist trajectory. "Half Revolution, No Revolution" is how a protester's placard in Egypt captured the spirit of this anomaly. Indeed, the contrasting reactions to the Arab Spring—lauding and lamenting—reflected precisely this paradoxical reality of the Arab revolutions, if we take revolution to mean, minimally, the rapid and radical transformation of a state driven by popular movements from below. The polarities of opinion echoed the profound disjunction between two key dimensions of revolution: *movement* and *change*. The celebratory narratives focused predominantly on "revolution as movement"; on the dramatic episodes of high solidarity and sacrifice, of altruism and common purpose; on the *communitas* of Tahrir. The attention here is centered on those extraordinary moments in every revolutionary mobilization when attitudes and behavior are suddenly transformed: sectarian divisions melt away, gender equality reigns, and selfishness diminishes; the popular classes demonstrate a remarkable capacity for innovation in activism, self-organization, and democratic decision making. These outstanding episodes, which for anarchists represent the "future in the present," certainly deserve to be highlighted and documented. However, the overemphasis on revolution as movement served to obscure the peculiar nature of these revolutions in terms of change, with little to say about what happens the day after the dictators abdicate. It even served to disguise the paradoxes of these upheavals, shaped by the new political times in which grand visions and emancipatory utopias had given way to fragmentary projects, improvisation, and loose networks and when the possibility of revolution as change had been drastically undermined while revolution as movement was in spectacular supply.[2] The Arab upheavals expressed this anomaly. The trajectories of the Arab revolutions—barring those in Libya and Syria, which assumed the form of civil wars mediated by foreign military intervention—resembled none of the known pathways for political change about which the literature has informed us: reform, insurrection, or implosion.[3] They had a character of their own, marked by a mix of revolutionary movements and reformist change, "refolution," and shaped by the dynamics of our postsocialist and neoliberal times.

Transformative Strategies

Historically, social and political movements following a reformist strategy usually organize a sustained campaign to exert pressure on the incumbent regime to undertake reforms, using the institutions of the existing state. Relying on its social power—the mobilization of the popular classes—the opposition movement forces the political elite to reform its laws and institutions, often through some kind of negotiated pact. Change happens within the framework of existing political arrangements. The transition to democracy in countries like Brazil and Mexico in the 1980s was of this nature.[4] The leadership of Iran's Green movement in 2009 attempted to pursue a similar reformist path.[5] In this trajectory, the depth and extent of reforms can vary: change may remain superficial, but it can also be profound if it takes the form of cumulative legal, institutional, and politico-cultural reforms.

However, the insurrectionary path requires a revolutionary movement, built up over a fairly extended period of time, that develops a recognized leadership and organizational structure along with a blueprint for a new political order. While the incumbent regime deploys its police or military apparatus to resist any change, defections begin to split the governing bloc. The revolutionary camp pushes forward, attracts defectors, forms a shadow government, and builds alternative power structures. This challenges the state's ability to govern its own territory, creating a situation of "dual power" between the regime and the opposition, which usually possesses a charismatic leader in the mold of Lenin, Mao, Castro, Khomeini, Walesa, or Hável. Where the revolution is successful, the situation of dual power culminates in an insurrectionary battle in which the revolutionary camp takes power by force; it dislodges the old organs of authority and establishes new ones. Here there is a comprehensive overhaul of the state, with new personnel, a new ideology, and an alternative mode of government. The Russian, Chinese, and Cuban revolutions of 1959, the Sandinista revolution in Nicaragua, and the Iranian revolution in 1979 exemplify the insurrectionary course.[6] Qaddafi's regime faced a revolutionary insurrection under the leadership of the National Transitional Council, which with NATO backing eventually advanced from liberated Benghazi to capture Tripoli.

There is a third possibility: that of "regime implosion." A revolt may gather momentum through strikes and other forms of civil disobedience, or through revolutionary warfare progressively encircling the capital, so that in the end the regime implodes, collapsing amid disruption, defection, and total disorder. In its place, alternative elites hurriedly form new organs of power, often in conditions of confusion and disorder, staffed by people with little experience of public office. Nicolae Ceauşescu's regime in Romania imploded amid violence and political chaos in 1989, but it was succeeded by a very different political and economic order under the newly established body, the National Salvation Front, led by Ion Iliescu, following the dictator's execution.[7] In both insurrection and implosion, in contrast to the reformist path, attempts to transform the political system do not operate through the existing state institutions but outside them.[8]

The Egyptian, Tunisian, and Yemeni revolutions bore little resemblance to any of these paths. A first peculiarity to note is their speed. In Egypt and Tunisia, powerful mass uprisings achieved some remarkably swift results. The Tunisians in the course of one month, and the Egyptians in just eighteen days, succeeded in dislodging long-term authoritarian rulers and dismantling a number of institutions associated with them—including their political parties, legislative bodies, and a number of ministries—while pledging themselves to policies of constitutional and political reform. These gains were achieved in a manner that was, by relative standards, remarkably civil and peaceful, as well as swift. But these rapid victories—unlike the prolonged revolts in Yemen and Libya, or those in Bahrain and Syria—left little time for the opposition to build their own parallel organs of government, if indeed this had been their intention. Instead, the revolutionaries seemed to want the regime's institutions—including the interior ministry, judiciary, and the military, for example—to carry out substantial reforms on behalf of the revolution: to modify the constitution, hold elections, guarantee the freedom of political parties, and institutionalize democratic government. Here lay a key anomaly of these revolutions: they enjoyed enormous social prestige but lacked administrative authority; they achieved a remarkable degree of hegemony but did not actually rule. Thus, the incumbent regimes continued more or less intact; there were few new state institutions or novel means of government that could embody any vision of deep change.

It is true that the Central and Eastern European revolutions of 1989 were also astonishingly swift and, for the most part, nonviolent: East Germany's took ten days; Romania's, only five. And unlike what occurred in Egypt, Yemen, or Tunisia, they effected a complete transformation of their national political and economic systems. In these Eastern European countries, the difference between what the people had—one-party communist state, command economy—and what they seemed to want—pluralist democracy and more open economy—was so radical that the trajectory of change had to be revolutionary; halfway, superficial reforms would easily have been detected and resisted. In the German case, the imploded state institutions of the German Democratic Republic (GDR) could easily be dissolved within the governmental functions of the Federal Republic of Germany (FRG). This was quite unlike the pattern in Egypt or Tunisia, where the demands for change, freedom, and social justice were so broad and loosely defined that they could even be claimed and appropriated by the counterrevolution.

The revolutions in Tunisia, Egypt, and Yemen were also different from those of the Philippine Revolution of 1986, when a popular movement toppled President Ferdinand Marcos, who since 1973 had retained ultimate power over all public institutions, including the military, by relying on a crony business class and US support. The revolution enjoyed a fairly unified organization and charismatic leaders such as Corazon Aquino, the widow of the popular senator Ninoy Aquino, who was assassinated by Marcos, as well as the military leaders Juan Ponce Enrile and General Fidel Ramos. More important, organized dissent and defections from the military, galvanized in the Reform the Armed Forces Movement (RAM), Soldiers of the Filipino People, and Young Officers Union, offered crucial protection to the anti-Marcos opposition. Like those in Egypt, Yemen, and Tunisia, the Philippine revolution enjoyed mass support with millions demonstrating in the streets, particularly in the EDSA, Manila's Tahrir; but the popular mobilization followed only after an appeal to the people by Cardinal Vidal to offset the threat by Marcos to arrest the dissenting military leaders. Finally, the rebels held coercive military power, which they deployed when necessary, such as taking over the national TV stations to communicate with the citizens. Such resources were absent among the rebels in Tunisia, Yemen, and Egypt. It is true that protesters in Egypt attacked or set fire to many police stations—half of all units in Cairo, 60 percent in Alexandria, and eighty-four throughout the country. But most of the attacks took place after the police killed individuals in particular districts, a familiar scenario dating back to years before the uprising.[9] There is no evidence that the attackers tried to acquire arms or ammunition to seize strategic state institutions when needed.

The Egyptian and Tunisian experiences seemed to bear a closer resemblance to Georgia's Rose Revolution of 2003 or Ukraine's Orange Revolution of 2004–2005, where a massive, sustained popular movement brought down the corrupt incumbents. In these instances, the trajectory would, strictly speaking, be more reformist than revolutionary. Nonetheless, there was a more promising side to the Arab upheavals, a powerful revolutionary drive that made them farther reaching than the protests in Georgia and Ukraine. In Tunisia and Egypt, the departure of the dictators and their apparatuses of coercion opened up an unprecedented free space for citizens, above all for the popular classes, to reclaim their societies and assert themselves. As in most revolutionary situations, enormous energy was released and an unparalleled sense of renewal transformed the public sphere. Banned political parties emerged from the shadows, and new ones were established—at least twelve in Egypt and more than one hundred in Tunisia. Social organizations grew more vocal, and remarkable popular initiatives began to emerge. With the threat of persecution lifted, working people fought for their rights; unofficial industrial actions and protests raged. In Tunisia, the existing trade unions took on a more independent and prominent role.

In Egypt, workers pushed for new independent unions; the Workers' Coalition of the January 25 Revolution asserted the principles of the revolution: change, freedom, social justice. Small farmers called for independent syndicates. Cairo's slum dwellers began to build their first autonomous organizations; youth groups fought to upgrade slum settlements, took on civic projects, and reclaimed their pride. Students poured onto the streets to demand that the Ministry of Education revise their curricula. New groupings were formed—in Egypt, the Tahrir Revolutionary Front; in Tunisia, the Supreme Body to Realize the Objectives of the Revolution—to exert pressure on the postrevolutionary authorities for meaningful reforms. Of course, these represented levels of popular mobilization specific to these exceptional times. But the extraordinary sense of liberation, the urge for self-realization, the dream of a just social order, in short, the desire for "all that is new"—this was what defined the very spirit of these revolutions. Yet as these mass social groups moved far ahead of their elites, the major anomaly of these revolutions was exposed: the discrepancy between a revolutionary desire for the new and a reformist outcome that could lead to harboring the old.

Refolutions?

How, then, are we to make sense of the Arab Spring? What kind of trajectory did the uprisings experience? In the immediate postrevolutionary period, the monarchies of Jordan and Morocco opted for minor political reforms. In Morocco, constitutional change allowed the leader of the majority party in the parliament to form the government. The Libyan regime was overthrown in a violent civil war. And in Syria the regime's repression propelled the uprising to take an insurrectionary path and bloody proxy war, the outcomes of which remain to be seen. But the uprisings in Egypt, Yemen, and Tunisia followed a particular trajectory that can be characterized neither as revolution per se nor simply in terms of reform measures. Instead, it may make sense to speak of "refolutions": revolutionary movements that, instead of seizing power to usher in a new social order, opted to push for reforms in, and through, the institutions of the existing states.[10] In a sense, they were revolutionary in terms of movement and mass mobilization but reformist in terms of strategy and vision for change. These revolutions were reformist in the sense that, first, they had almost no intellectual inputs to articulate a vision of revolution in the ways they did with respect to their twentieth-century counterparts—Nicaragua, Cuba, and Iran. Second, the protagonists who initiated the uprisings seemed to be unable to envision modes of governance and institutions different from those against which they were revolting; they seemed to be reluctant or unconcerned about directing change within the state institutions. In fact, no group or organization had before the uprising proposed any serious appraisal of the state power or articulated ways to transform it. Third, most protagonists conceptually separated the realm of the economy from polity, from those aspects of political order that they wished to undo.

Few Arab intellectuals, if any, had in recent years elaborated any serious perspective on revolutionary politics in the region, as if revolution were an idea whose time had passed.[11] They were preoccupied more with the questions of authenticity, nativism, cultural nationalism, and Islam.[12] Those such as the Egyptian Amr al-Shobaki, who did speak of revolution, warned against the "illusion of revolution," and called instead for "reform."[13] While Tunisia's intellectual life had been squeezed by state repression, the Egyptian intelligentsia (editors of newspapers, magazines, writers, and artists) was operating, according to Sabry Hafez, in "bleak conditions."[14] Pushed by the powerful "Islamic mode" since the 1990s, the intelligentsia had tacitly formed a discursive bloc with the state and religious establishment to the detriment of critical thought and radical politics.[15] Serving as state employees since the time of President Nasser, the intellectual class left no revolutionary ideas that could be deployed in the uprising. Rather, the key ideas included political reform, responsive government, human rights, and employment. The massive banner of demands in Tahrir Square—calling for the toppling of the president, forming a transitional government, modifying the constitution, and prosecuting the corrupt officials and those responsible for the death of revolutionaries—somewhat invoked the

Figure 3. Tahrir protesters' demands; photo by Mona Seif, used under Creative Common license

"transition from authoritarian rule" through "political pact." It is not surprising that some analysts described the Arab Spring as "negotiated revolutions," except that revolutionaries had in effect little part in the "negotiations."[16] In truth "during a decade of vibrant activism, no activist group or network had entertained the thought of assuming state power," confirmed a local observer. "They had neither seen the need to create institutions that could mobilize and lead towards capturing power, nor worked on articulating a set of long-term political objectives."[17] Few had any systematic knowledge about the concept of revolution prior to their street protests when they found themselves caught by spectacular mass revolts they had never imagined or had any clear idea how to handle. "When we went out [on January 25], we didn't plan or think of revolution," explained a young activist. "We thought there would be a few hundred people as usual; but in a few hours thousands came out, and we lost control of the crowd who did their own slogans."[18]

In prerevolutionary Tunisia, organized activism was severely constrained. "People were so fed up with politics that the idea of being organized was somehow rejected," remembers a cyberactivist.[19] While police confined student activities to college campuses, provincial youths had formed shillas, street-corner associations, and fraternities that could be used for collective action. At times local leaders, such as Bouaziz, Gamal Bu-Elaby, or Ghazal, a lawyer, would engage in protest actions, for instance, in Sidi Bouzid. When the protests broke out in Sidi Bouzid, the "commission of citizenship and defending victims of marginalization" emerged to relay information about the events to cyberactivists, who would then circulate it via social media. Youth groups in Tunis created a "news agency of Tunisian street movements."[20] As social media expanded by 2010, some sort of nonmovements developed among the youth through electronic networks. But the local trade unionists of the corporatist Tunisian General Labor Union (UGTT) were quick to deploy their organizational skills to coordinate the protests in Sidi Bouzid and elsewhere. On January 11, they held a meeting authorizing a general strike.

The unexpected downfall of the Tunisian dictator Ben Ali on January 14, 2011, brought the idea of revolution and its possibility to Egyptians. Activists who had called for a day of protest against police brutality on January 25 began to utter the word *thawra* (revolution).[21] When three men attempted self-immolation, as did the Tunisian Mohamed Bouazizi, activists stated they would rather see police stations set on fire than people. On the eve of the Day of Rage, someone went so far as to call for a "sacrifice."[22] But these sentiments still reflected what Herbert Blumer called "general movement" rather than "specific movement," which involves a vision, organization, and coordinated efforts to pursue concrete goals of how to undo the injustice.[23] Reflecting on the European revolutions, Charles Tilly concludes that the "presence of a coherent revolutionary organization makes a great difference" because it "facilitates the initial seizure of control, spreads the news, activates the commitments already made by specific men."[24] Even though the Arab rebels showed commendable ability in spreading the news and mobilizing street protests through online and offline methods, they felt unprepared for what to do once the massive crowd poured into the streets. Lacking preconceived plans, the Tahrir activists had to improvise. As they held meetings on January 25 to decide how to proceed, some protesters called out, "Increase the minimum wage"; "Dismiss the interior minister; and "Remove the Emergency Law." At 1:45 p.m., the crowd cried "Freedom!"; by 3:00 p.m., when the protests had spread throughout the provinces, the calls for *erhal* (leave) could be heard. Only at such moments did the protagonists realize that something extraordinary was happening—"This is fucking happening!!"; this was something they had never anticipated and was terrifyingly difficult to manage. Stunned by the passion and immensity of the protests, a well-known activist who worked to organize the event tweeted, "Protests are like watermelons and it seems I opened the wrong one."[25] The fundamental question then became where to go from there, what the objectives were, and how to achieve them.

The absence of a unified leadership did allow for horizontal networks and multiple voices, but it also made incongruity of demands, expectations, and ways of operation inevitable. While most protesters seemed to want Mubarak to step down, others appeared satisfied with his pledge not to run again; some favored marching to the presidential palace, but others insisted on staying in Tahrir; indignant crowds decided to take over the heavily fortified state TV, but others opted for peaceful actions.[26] At times the discord alarmed the protesters. "The country seems to be splitting apart," said an activist; "fissures in my own family have already started." [27] In fact, Mubarak's second speech after the uprisings started, when he made significant concessions, brought the Tahrir occupation to "the verge of collapse" as parents pleaded with young people to end the siege.[28] The need for a revolutionary organization became more evident as the regime vowed to negotiate. But who were to represent the revolution? The Muslim Brotherhood backed the "council of wise men" who wished to see power go to the vice president, Omar Suleiman.[29] Reportedly, they had agreed to halt protestation in exchange for concessions, including the release of jailed leaders such as Khairat Shater.[30] But on the ground protests continued. The Revolutionary Youths blasted the "council" for its elderly male politicians similar to those in the Wafd Party; they were dismayed by "unrepresentative youths,"[31] as well as "negotiators" who "had nothing to do with what was going on."[32] The regime negotiators seemed to sense the discord, treating the revolutionary youths during the negotiations with polite contempt and derision.[33] It was at this juncture that rebels felt the "lack of organization will be used against us in every way possible."[34] This realization modified earlier enthusiasm about the "absence of organization,"[35] even though it may have thwarted the regime's crackdown on the protest movement.[36]

Despite the lack of organization, the protests did enjoy a good degree of coordination and multiple local leaders known on the ground and in their communities for their activism, bravery, or wisdom. In Tunisian town of Sidi Bouzid, young people from different neighborhoods met in the city's cafés to decide how to organize protests, what to target, where to march, and what to chant. In Egypt, local activists divided tasks and made sure to link to people in the poor neighborhoods, like Cairo's Imbaba, where local youths and opposition parties organized the street demonstrations.[37] Yet this type of coordination and leadership concerned predominantly the tactics of protests, not the strategy of a revolution; it focused more on winning the battles rather than the war. Local leaders were no doubt instrumental in mobilizing the protests, outmaneuvering the police, and battling the regime thugs. But establishing an alternative political order would require a strategic vision, understanding the workings of state power, a united voice, and some degree of hard power. Lacking these resources, the rebels had no choice but to rely on their street power to pressure the regimes to reform themselves, to undertake a "transition" in which the revolutionaries, however, would have little or no oversight. Even though the rebels soon realized that "only forms have changed" and "everything remains the same,"[38] there was little they could do to achieve a rapid and radical transformation of the state.

Lower Hopes

Why did the revolutions encounter such impediments? These were revolutions without revolutionaries, in that few protagonists had really strategized for a revolution, even though they might have dreamed about it. Wael Ghoneim, who came to be a celebrated persona of the Egyptian uprising, acknowledged that he was hardly a political person, let alone a revolutionary. "I was not politically active" before the revolution. He "was not optimistic about the impact of the activists' efforts" and basically "busy with work, where I spent all my time."[39] Earlier in the decade he had sympathized with the Muslim Brothers before becoming Salafi and creating the website Islamway while in the United States before he returned to Egypt to work for Google.[40] Only with the support of Mohamed ElBaradei did he engage in politics, but mostly for "my marketing and Internet experience," working on a "promotional marketing campaign." Otherwise, "I was no more than a guy with some marketing experience who started a Facebook page that snowballed into something greater than any of its thousands of contributors." Clearly there was no prior interest in the idea of revolution per se. "January 25 began as a reaction to the events in Tunisia," Ghoneim recalls. "It was a simple invitation on Facebook that unexpectedly spread like wildfire across the entire web and moved into the streets. . . . There were no master plans or strategies."[41]

Likewise for Mustafa Ibrahim, an Islamic liberal and member of the Coalition of the Revolutionary Youths (CRY), the uprising's leadership network, "revolution came without anyone planning it." As one of the many thousands Mustafa joined the protests on January 25 and saw a small group chanting "bread, freedom, and dignity." As he and others marched and approached Tahrir Square, he saw "people were coming from all over," some 125,000, chanting "People want the downfall of the regime."[42] But his group had still not determined what they really wanted. "What will be our demands?" one of them wondered. In truth, "we had not thought of making revolutions," Tamer al-Sadi, an April 6 activist in CRY confirmed. "We realized that just around us revolution made itself by itself." What they had done as activists in the previous two years, Tamer recalls, "was too easy." "In all our movement and our abilities, we didn't do anything, didn't create any political movement; we were just happy to be able to gather one hundred or two hundred people with us going to demonstrations." Such small gatherings seemed enough to make Tamer and his colleagues "overwhelmed by joy." "Even in Tahrir Square with so many people and the rising level of demands, we were very surprised by the people wanting the downfall of the regime; and not a single one of us had expected this."[43]

For activist groups and networks such as Kefaya or the April 6 movement of which Tamer was a member, the horizon of change did not go beyond "reforming" the "tyrannical rule of the NDP [National Democratic Party]." The April

6 platform had called for the "coalition and cooperation of all factions and national forces to reach the reform and peaceful change of the situation in Egypt." Responding to a claim that the April 6 movement resembled the Lebanese Hezbollah, the group made it clear in April 2010 that "there are no parallels between us and them; we are a peaceful organization looking for reform."[44] While the *modawwana* (platform) discussed the details of tactics, organizing protests, educational matters, and nonviolent resistance, there were no deliberations on state power, structure of vested interests, and international players beyond acknowledging that the "corrupt National Democratic Party has brought Egypt to the present miserable state of affairs." Politics of change appeared more a matter of technicality than the idea of transforming the structure of governing power. Only in retrospect would a leader reflect on the "errors," "contradictions," and "identity crisis" of his April 6 movement, describing it as a "protest cry" with no "means to offer any political project or an ability to design or implement such a project."[45]

The events of the two years prior to the revolution had certainly radicalized segments of the citizenry; the workers' strike of 2008 and the subsequent urban social protests brought the vague idea that "we can change things." The prospect of a Gamal Mubarak presidency and the torture of Khaled Said convinced many that a change was needed; "it felt like you could die at anytime anywhere," an activist recalled.[46] The day the Tunisian revolution toppled Ben Ali, the word "revolution" entered the popular conversation in Egypt, but protesters became "revolutionary" mainly when they experienced the power of mass protests in the streets. "It was in Tahrir and precisely in Muhammad Mahmoud street that I learnt politics and became a revolutionary," stated eighteen-year-old Abir.[47] Indeed, it is at such momentous junctures that individuals experience a distinct feeling of collective effervescence, camaraderie, and selflessness—a sudden shift in consciousness as if they had undergone a religious experience. This was the moment of revolution as movement. But what did revolution mean in terms of change? When the call for "leave" overtook the streets of Egypt, revolution came to be synonymous with the departure of Mubarak; the break with the past and radical change in the structure of power still seemed of lesser concern. Most continued to revere the military as a "learned and cultured" institution that unlike the oppressive central intelligence services remained neutral or sided with the revolution.[48] On the day President Mubarak resigned, a known activist expressed this general sentiment with jubilance—"The military statement is great. I trust our Egyptian army"—not imagining that it would play a decisive counterrevolutionary part in post-Mubarak moments.[49] The Muslim Brothers maintained their reformist position, signaling the departure of Mubarak as the end of the revolution. While the Islamists' idea of change meant the rule of sharia, some in CRY could still imagine such establishment figures as the billionaire Najib Sweiris, the ex-prime minister and the champion of privatization Kamal Ganzouri, or Mubarak's last prime minister, Ahmed Shafik, as their postrevolutionary presidents. While some favored Mohamed ElBaradei, others opted for technocratic transitional governments to reform the intelligence services and to address police brutality and the Emergency Law.[50]

Whereas the Egyptian political class took revolution to mean what transpired in Tunisia, Tunisian revolutionaries expressed profound misgivings about their own experience.[51] "When I emerged from the cells," wrote a militant protester after his arrest during the uprising, "I found everybody talking about the 'January 14 Revolution.' . . . I was wary of the word 'revolution' itself, not just because true revolution means establishing a new political awareness and creating a break with the past, but also because the most fervent champions of this 'revolution' had been the biggest beneficiaries of Ben Ali's regime." When he looks back at the revolution, he notes that the "youths and district activists who were its original architects are almost entirely absent from public life."[52] In Tunisia also, scarcely any group had entertained the idea of revolution before the uprising—the time when Ben Ali's police state had severely subdued oppositional politics. Only with the hosting of the international conference on communication in 2005 did an opening seem to emerge. A campaign of hunger strikes for prisoners' rights brought the secular and religious opposition together; this was followed by the working-class protests of the mining areas of Gafsa in 2008, leading to the emergence of cyberactivism in 2010. Otherwise, the intelligentsia had suffered a "political death," as an academic told me, forced to lead a passive life of going to work, socializing with friends, and taking their vacations but avoiding the lethal affairs of politics. "Everything was good except we could not speak about Ben Ali's politics," said a college professor.[53] "The middle and upper middle classes were bought off by a relatively good life, good education, health care, travels in exchange for political apathy," admitted an activist.[54] It was no wonder that the outbreak of the uprising left "us, the political class surprised." For the Tunisian political class revolution was over when the dictator abdicated, even though many ordinary citizens were still pushing for a real change of regime.[55] Likewise in Yemen, the activists' idea of change, as the anthropologist Bogumila Hall reports, seemed to hinge on "development and self-empowerment" that the "civil society" organizations promoted.[56] Such a perspective, which relied on the transformative power of individuals, avoided tackling state power.

Marxist-oriented activists seemed to be more in tune with projecting a realistic, if pessimistic, appraisal of the regime's power, the military, imperialism, and the meaning of revolution. A Tunisian leftist recalled, "It seemed to me and others like me that the dictator's departure had not resulted in the departure of dictatorship."[57] In a similar vein, and minutes after Mubarak stepped down, a Marxist revolutionary wrote, "We got rid of Mubarak. Now it is time to get rid of Mubarak's regime."[58] But this strand of political imaginary had been minimized by the discourse and institutions of the postsocialist period, chiefly the neoliberal paradigm, where piecemeal technocratic reform was the norm.

As a consequence, not much changed in the institutions of the old regimes. Insofar as new structures did emerge, they were soon taken over not by revolutionaries but for the most part by "free riders," those traditionally well-organized political currents whose leaders had largely remained on the

Figure 4. A protester's sign reading "Half Revolution, No Revolution"; photo by the author

sidelines when the struggles against the dictatorships began. In Yemen, the key elements of the old regime persisted, even though the new openness promised to enforce political reforms, as new president Hadi tried to weaken Ali Saleh's base by bringing new recruits to the Security Service.[59] But along the way a pact initiated by the GCC retained much of the power of the old elites under President Hadi, until the northern Yemeni Houthi rebels captured Sana'a in early February 2015, forcing President Hadi out and prompting Saudi Arabia to launch a civil war in Yemen.[60] In Egypt after Mubarak, the SCAF's rule involved widespread repression, incarceration of revolutionaries, virginity tests, and shutting down critical opposition organizations. Counterrevolutionary restoration gained further momentum as popular frustration grew over unfulfilled expectations from the government of Mohamed Morsi, who was then removed forcefully by General Sisi to rule Egypt more repressively.

In Tunisia, the revolution did establish free speech, press, elections, and organization; the right to protest was recognized, and the Truth and Dignity Commission promised to bring human rights' violators of the old regime to

Figure 5. A sign reading "Overthrow, Not Reform"; photo by Mona Seif, used under Creative Common license

justice. Yet "the networks of the old regime are all there," an activist recounted in July 2011.[61] The Ministry of the Interior rebuffed the reforms that the revolutionaries had demanded and continued with arrests, torture, and killing of the opposition.[62] The elites and economic mafias of the Ben Ali period then organized into some forty-seven political parties supported by another seventy organizations that began to fight back and block the path to genuine change. They retained their dense network of political factions, friendly media, and business organizations.[63] Even though a national alliance of the Islamic, secular, liberal, and labor groups neutralized the initial move, the victory of the rightist Nidaa Tounes in the 2015 presidential elections consolidated the position of the old "parallel state"—the security sector, business elites, and local mafia that had served as the de facto authority before the revolution. In January 2016, Amnesty International reported that the prerevolutionary violation of human rights had fully returned to Tunisia. One could only expect the indignation of youth over the fate of their stalled revolution. "When young people took to the streets, they were asking for freedom, dignity and employment," stated a prominent activist, "but almost none of these objectives were fulfilled."[64]

Different Times

Why did the Arab uprisings in Tunisia, Egypt, and Yemen assume this refolutionary character? Why did key institutions of the old order remain unaltered, while revolutionary forces were marginalized? In part this had to do with the very swift downfall of the dictators, which gave the impression that the revolutions had come to an end, achieved their goals, without a substantial shift in the power structure. As we have seen, this rapid "victory" did not leave much opportunity for the movements to establish alternative organs of power, even if they had intended to. In this sense, these were self-limiting revolutions. But there was something more profound at play: revolutionaries remained outside the structures of power because they were not planning to take over the state; when, in the later stages, they realized that they needed to, they lacked the resources—unified organization, powerful leadership, strategic vision, and some degree of hard power—that would be necessary to wrest control both from the old regimes and from free riders who had been reluctant to join the uprisings when they began but were organizationally ready to take power. A principal difference between the Arab uprisings and their twentieth-century predecessors was that they occurred in quite altered ideological times.

Up until the 1990s, three major ideological traditions had been the bearers of revolution as a strategy of fundamental change: anticolonial nationalism, Marxism, and Islamism. Anticolonial nationalism, as reflected in the ideas of Fanon, Sukarno, Jawaharlal Nehru, Nasser, or Ho Chi Minh, conceived the postindependence social order as something new, a negation of the political and economic domination of the old colonial system and the comprador bourgeoisie. Even though their promises far exceeded their ability to deliver, the postcolonial regimes did make some progress in education, health, land reform, and industrialization—measures that were affirmed in such national-development pacts as Al-Mithaq in Egypt (1962), the Arusha Declaration (1967), and the Mwongozo guidelines (1971) in Tanzania. Their major achievements lay in state building: national administration, infrastructure, class formation. However, because they failed to tackle fundamental problems of unequal ownership of property and wealth distribution, the nationalist governments began to lose their legitimacy. As former anticolonial revolutionaries turned into administrators of the postcolonial order, they largely failed to deliver on their promises; in many instances nationalist governments devolved into autocracies, were saddled with debt, then pushed into neoliberal structural adjustment programs, if they had not already been overthrown by military coups or undermined by imperialist intrigues. In fact, few Third World states have avoided revolutions and counterrevolutions of some sort since their formation.[65]

Marxism was undoubtedly the most formidable revolutionary current of the Cold War era. The Vietnamese and Cuban revolutions inspired a generation of radicals; Che Guevara and Ho Chi Minh became iconic figures, not only in Asia, Latin America, and the Middle East but also for the student movements in the United States, Paris, Rome, and Berlin. While Fanon's *The Wretched of Earth* (1961) theorized revolutionary violence, the experience of revolution in Cuba virtually rendered it the practical guide for the transformation of the Third World, with guerrilla movements coming to symbolize the revolutionism of the 1960s. They surged in Africa after Patrice Lumumba's assassination and with the hardening of apartheid in South Africa. Following the collapse of the dictatorship in Portugal in 1974, a wave of Marxist-Leninist revolutions overthrew colonial rule in Mozambique, Angola, Guinea-Bissau, and elsewhere. Although the "foco" strategy promoted by Guevara did not bear fruit in Latin America after Cuba, there were successful insurrections in Grenada and Nicaragua toward the end of the 1970s, while El Salvador appeared to be another likely candidate for revolutionary advance. By this time, Latin American radicals had found a new ally in

Christian liberation theology, which inspired lay Catholics and even members of the clergy to take arms to join the struggle. In the Middle East, the National Liberation Front drove the British out of Aden and proclaimed the People's Democratic Republic of Yemen. Up until the 1970s, left-wing groups and guerrillas played a significant role in Iran, Oman, Kurdistan, and the occupied territories of Palestine. The Dhofar Liberation Front launched a ten-year insurgency against the Sultanate of Oman to create a Marxist state in this Arab country; the Fedaian and its Islamic counterpart Mujahedin Khalq launched a guerrilla struggle against the shah of Iran; the Marxist Democratic Front for the Liberation of Palestine kept up combat against the Israeli occupation; and the Kurdistan Workers' Party (PKK) emerged in 1978 to establish a socialist republic in Kurdistan.

The impact of these revolutionary movements on the intellectual climate of the West was undeniable, helping to detonate the worldwide rebellion of youth, students, workers, and intellectuals in 1968. Even though, in Hobsbawm's words, few in the West really believed that old-fashioned revolutions were possible, the Carnation Revolution overthrew the dictatorship in Portugal in 1974; and sympathy with the idea of revolution lingered among the radical Left, notably the Trotskyist organizations, that held elaborate theories of state takeover. While some communist parties in Europe (Eurocommunism) and the developing world (those pursuing a "noncapitalist road to development") took an increasingly reformist course, significant forces within the Marxist-Leninist tradition remained committed to a strategy of revolution.

But the picture shifted dramatically with the collapse of the Soviet bloc. The concept of revolution had been so integral to that of socialism that the demise of "existing socialism" following the anticommunist mobilizations in Eastern Europe in the late 1980s and the West's victory in the Cold War effectively implied the end of revolution and of state-led development. Statism was disparaged as inefficiency and repression, leading to the erosion of personal autonomy and initiative. This had a profound bearing on the notion of revolution, with its focus on state power, now identified with authoritarianism and the failures of the communist bloc. "Revolution" became a dirty word. The advance of neoliberalism, beginning with Pinochet in Chile in the 1970s after his anti-Allende coup, and then in 1979–1980 with the victories of Margaret Thatcher and Ronald Reagan, later expanding as the dominant ideology across much of the world, played a central role in this change of discourse. In place of embracing "state" and "revolution," there was now an exponential growth of talk about NGOs, public spheres, rational dialogue, nonviolence, civil society, and managed change. In these postcommunist moments gradual change became the only acceptable route to social transformation. Western governments, aid agencies, and NGOs promoted this new gospel assiduously. The expansion of the NGO sector in the Arab world and in the Global South more generally signified a dramatic shift from social activism, informed by collective interests, to an emphasis on individual self-help in a competitive world. In these neoliberal times, the egalitarian spirit of liberation theology and its Marxist strategy gave way to a global surge of evangelical Christianity of Protestant and Catholic variants informed by the spirit of individual self-interest and consumerism. Whereas liberation theology took the liberation of the poor as its point of theological departure, the new evangelicalism ensured the marriage of faith and fortune.[66]

Marxism-Leninism and its idea of revolution had declined, but it had left its imprint on its ideological rival, Islamism. Militant Islamist movements since the 1970s had drawn on the ideas of Sayyid Qutb in their battle against the secular states of the Muslim world; Qutb himself had learned much from the Indian Islamist leader Abul A'la Maududi, who in turn had been impressed by the organizational and political strategy of the Communist Party of India. Qutb's 1964 pamphlet *Milestones*, arguing for a Muslim vanguard to seize the *jahili* state and establish a true Islamic order, became the Islamist equivalent of Lenin's *What Is to Be Done?*, guiding the strategy of militant groups such as Jihad, al-Gama'a al-Islamiyya, Hizbut Tahrir, and Laskar Jihad.[67] A number of former leftists—Adel Hussein, Mustafa Mahmoud, Tariq al-Bishri—defected to the Islamist camp, bringing ideas from the Marxist-Leninist tradition with them. The 1979 Iranian revolution was informed both by leftist ideas and Sayyid Qutb—*Milestones* had been translated by Ayatollah Khamenei, the current supreme leader, into Persian. The Marxist-Leninist Fedaian Khalq and the Islamic-Marxist Mujahedin Khalq played a significant role in radicalizing opposition to the shah's dictatorship. More important, perhaps, was the popular theorist Ali Shariati, who as a student of the French left-winger Georges Gurvitch, had spoken passionately about revolution in a blend of Marxist and religious idioms, invoking a "divine classless society." The concept of revolution had thus been central to militant Islamism, in both its Sunni and Shia forms. This tradition always stood in clear contrast to the strategy of electoral Islamists such as the Muslim Brotherhood, who aspired to build up sufficient social support to capture the state through peaceful means. It also differed from the strategy of al-Qaeda and ISIS, the most militant and violent of jihadi groupings; notwithstanding its relentless violence, Bin Laden's al-Qaeda remained in essence nonrevolutionary due to its multinational form and diffused aims, such as "saving Islam" or "fighting the West," and the idea of jihad as an end in itself.[68] ISIS may look like a revolution, but its nihilism reflects precisely the absence of revolution-as-change in the region.

By the early 2000s, the Islamist revolutionism also had begun to change. With the growing crisis of Islamism and the rise of post-Islamist trends, the belief in the idea of revolution had substantially run out of steam. The inability of Islamists to address economic disparity and their exclusionary politics, misogyny, violence, and abuse of religion as political ideology had alienated vast Muslim constituencies, supplying the post-Islamist critics with substantial support. Thus, AKP in Turkey, PJD in Morocco, al-Nahda in Tunisia, PKS in Indonesia, and Iran's reformists had all transcended their Islamist past by articulating new ideas on religious politics and society. The post-Islamists had departed from the Islamist discourse of violence, militancy, and revolutionism, instead embracing nonviolence, legality, and reformist strategies. Whereas Islamism and its idea of revolution had roots in Cold War politics, post-Islamism has been informed by the ideas of the post–Cold War era—the idioms of civil society, accountability, free enterprise, and gradualism.[69] Thus, in Iran during Mohammad Khatami's presidency (1997–2004) the once-cherished idiom of revolution became associated with destruction, extremism, and violence. Instead of revolution, "reform" had become the catchword of the day. Like their Iranian counterpart, post-Islamist currents in other parts of the Muslim world had transcended the idea of revolution as a path toward political and social change. In a world dominated by neoliberal rationality, both Islamist and post-Islamist currents, as had their secular counterparts, embraced both reformist politics and free-market economics. In the Arab world, perhaps nothing was more telling about the neoliberal effect on religious speech than the discourse of the highly popular Egyptian televangelist Amr Khaled, whose preaching blended piety and privilege, faith and fun, competition and consumerism, morality and the market.[70]

Neoliberal Climate

The Arab uprisings thus occurred at a time when the decline of key oppositional ideologies—anticolonial nationalism, Marxist-Leninism, and Islamism—had delegitimized the very idea of revolution and its radical components so that activists and the political class in general ceased to entertain change in terms of revolution. This was a very different era from the late 1970s, when my friends and I in Iran would often invoke the notion, even though it seemed far-fetched; cycling through the opulent neighborhoods of northern Tehran, we speculated about how the shah's palaces could be taken over and the lavish mansions redistributed among the poor. We were thinking (and reading) in terms of revolution—an idea that embraced not only political freedom but also equity and economic justice. But in the Middle East of the new millennium, hardly any group imagined change in these terms; few Arab activists had really strategized for a revolution, even though they might have dreamed about it. The postsocialist neoliberal ideas and practices had structured the conduct of and deradicalized much of the political class.

At the same time that marketization caused social exclusion and dissent among the grassroots, it conditioned the activism of groups like youth, women, and political opposition, including the Islamists. In pre-uprising Yemen, for instance, activism largely meant "civil society work" in NGOs concerned with human rights, empowerment of women, charity, and development (up from five thousand in 2008 to more than thirteen thousand by 2013).[71] Yet such "NGOization of resistance," instead of shaping public policies or meaningful change at the grassroots, remained limited to "elite advocacy" with the effect of depoliticizing activism and deradicalizing the idea of change.[72] While the Tunisian police state had since the mid-2000s restricted concerned youth to college debates and cyberactivism, "civic activism" absorbed scores of young Egyptians in NGOs, charity work, sports clubs, or cultural and student events in colleges. A typical civic activist like Ahmed from Alexandria kept busy in a young writers' association, human rights education, civil work training, the Model American Congress, and in charity NGOs like Life Makers. But "I was not involved in politics, like Kefaya," he explained candidly. "It was very difficult; we even did not have a place to assemble. . . . We had lots of problems with the security."[73] Civil society activism of this sort was a double-edged sword. On the one hand, it would help the young build networks, share responsibilities, acquire skills of mobilization, and even form opposition within the state system. On the other hand, it would fragment activism, discard or deradicalize social movements, and override revolutionary efforts like organizing discussion clubs, reading radical literature, being involved in dissident theater and art groups, scouting and mountain climbing, or undertaking combat training—the kinds of activities that the 1970s revolutionaries embraced.[74]

In Egypt, youth activism had received great input from the lay popular preacher Amr Khaled, whose sermons on ethics of self-enhancement and the morality of everyday life had made him a household name among the affluent and middle-class milieu in the Arab world. As harbingers of "neoliberal Islam,"

Khaled and the "new televangelist preachers" had since the 1990s advocated an Islam that was thick in rituals but thin in dissent, pronouncing a piety that accommodated privilege and power.[75] Khaled's 2006 initiative Life Makers, with some twelve thousand projects, intended to push Arab young people to help themselves—raise entrepreneurial spirit, civic engagement, income generation, and employment in partnership with such corporations as Coca-Cola, Vodafone, Samsung, and Nestlé. Funded privately with some partnership with governments, the projects ranged from assisting small businesses, bringing Internet to schools, to turning empty rooftops into gardens. Somewhat similar to the new Pentecostal church activities in Africa and Latin America, Life Makers was premised on the spirit of individual self-help articulated in religious ethics and operating within the free-market paradigm. Wael Ghoneim and most of the religious young activists had been an avid audience for Amr Khaled's sermons.[76]

Likewise among women activists, the strand with the loudest public voice, women's empowerment came from the "gender and development" frame that was intimately linked to development aid, international NGOs, and USAID, whose discourse was fundamentally developmentalist and antipolitics.[77] In many ways, the "NGO-ization" of the women's movement signaled and materialized the decoupling of "gender issues" and popular struggles.[78] In Egypt, Tunisia, and Yemen this strand had partially merged into what the scholar Mervat Hatem called "state feminism," whose concerns at best focused on quotas for women in parliament, personal status, and similar liberal concerns,[79] and at worst, served as a "liberal progressive" veneer to conceal the illiberal and authoritarian character of autocratic regimes. Such elitist state feminism did help with some legal changes in favor of women in prerevolutionary Egypt, Tunisia, Yemen, and Morocco, but it mostly remained oblivious to the plight of lower-class women and their manifold marginal positions (such as the one-third of Egyptian households that were headed by women or those millions who lacked even national IDs).[80] When it campaigned against the repressive secular regimes, state feminism mostly sided with the status quo.

Broadly speaking, the political class treated politics and the economy as if they were separate domains of social life. While the socially excluded people insisted on bread and social justice, the political class gave only lip service to such vital subaltern concerns. In Egypt, both secular and Islamist political parties and movements uttered the rhetoric of social justice, minimum wage, health care, education, corrupt privatization, subsidies, and social services in their platforms. But their political practice, social bias, and actual strategies rendered these claims no more than what they really were—"mere rhetoric, not demands to struggle for"; there was no strategic vision, let alone articulated policies, to realize them.[81] Having internalized market rationale, these political forces were preoccupied instead with the "struggle against the person of Mubarak . . . without directing the battle towards the heart of the governing system itself."[82]

For most political forces in Tunisia, the claims of social justice were to follow from "achieving the goals of the revolution," a disclaimer somewhat similar to the way in which Presidents Ben Ali and Mubarak would subject social justice to "achieving development."[83] The secular Nidaa Tounes and its pro-business allies remained the "staunch enemies of the economic rights of the popular classes,"[84] and the Islamic al-Nahda, instead of having a specific strategy to address the demand for social justice, subjected it to the broad goal of "fighting poverty and raising the standard of living of citizens."[85] When it was in the government, al-Nahda froze hiring in the civil service, broke its promise to raise the minimum wage in industry and agriculture, and failed to establish a fund for the unemployed. In April 2013 it agreed to the IMF demand to extend "structural reform," and its government ratified an austerity budget to freeze wages, increase taxes, and decrease subsidies.[86] Perhaps the angry reaction of the poor, like residents of the al-Sayyida al-Menubiyya slum in Tunis, was no surprise. "No one has come to see us here; the revolutionaries have never come here," one protested. "They are afraid of us and think that we are monsters. . . . They are no better than Ben Ali." Another agreed: "I don't even feel I belong to this country. . . . The revolution was not for us."[87]

In broad terms, the economic and social policies of the postrevolutionary governments in Tunisia and Egypt did not differ much from those they replaced.[88] Failing to explicitly address socioeconomic grievances that led to the uprisings, their ambiguous platforms and policies reflected among other things "the dominant position of neoclassical and neoliberal economics."[89] Even the well-organized Tunisian UGTT, notwithstanding its many rank-and-file militants and prominent role in national politics, did not propose any fundamentally different economic order. Limiting its campaign to improving wages and labor conditions, the UGTT generally accepted the continuity of neoliberal policies inherited from the Ben Ali period.[90] In general, there was scant sensitivity among the political class with respect to meaningful distribution of wealth, amending property relations, land redistribution, or self-management. In Egypt only twelve plants were taken over by employees because the managers had left, but they were returned to the owners on legal grounds. The media, politicians, and unions dismissed "unlawful" practices that violated the principle of property ownership.[91] In short, the political imagination of the political class had been constricted by the ideas and institutions of the neoliberal order.

Even though uninterested in the idea and experiences of revolution, some activists had read the nonviolence advocate Gene Sharp, mainly *From Dictatorship to Democracy*. They had also obtained training in the US-sponsored "democracy promotion" initiative in the United States, in the Qatari Academy of Change, and by the Serbian Otpor on election monitoring, network building, youth leadership, change via elections, and tactics of nonviolence. The April 6 movement's logo emulated that of Otpor. But the training focused on the technical aspects of the campaign rather than a strategic vision and alternative social order.[92] While these activists expressed outrage at official corruption and despotic rule, they seldom offered ideas to address the structure of power and neoliberal order. In fact, some key protagonists used the idioms of the free market in their language of mobilization. Wael Ghoneim, a leading activist of the Egyptian uprising, for instance, was an MBA graduate and a Google marketing executive who deployed marketing techniques to sell the protest. He would use the jargon of marketing to "brand," "advertise," and "sell" the "products" of democracy and freedom.[93]

Market mobilization of this sort was not new; it originated from the "brand" that the Serbian opposition movement Otpor had deployed in its 1998 campaign against the dictator Slobodan Milošević to undo the communist economy and polity in favor of a liberal and market society. Operated by activists from NGOs and universities, Otpor pushed for political reform through nonradical, electoral, and market-driven language and practices. Resorting to music, street art, chic branding, and fun, they wanted to make revolution "cool" and "sexy." Otpor received funds from the American National Endowment for Democracy, USAID, and the International Republican Organization. The US State Department enhanced such activities in 2006 under its new "public diplomacy" and "cyber-dissident diplomacy" projects to promote US interests abroad by linking to foreign citizens, including the youth of the Muslim Middle East. At the end of the Bush administration, the US State Department with the support of Google instituted the Alliance of Youth Movements to focus on Muslim youth to counter Islamist radicalism by promoting values of democracy, moderation, and entrepreneurship.[94] The US support seemed crucial in making Otpor's model available to dissidents in Georgia, Ukraine, Belarus, and later Tunisia and Egypt during their uprisings.

Such a mode of mobilization, in sum, reflected new political times when instead of the ideas of egalitarian ethos, welfare state, and revolution, the focus shifted to the individual, identity, freedom, competition, and free market; in place of revolution as fundamental change, "civil society" had become the panacea for both democracy and development. But this was a different kind of civil society— different from the Gramscian notion that in effect meant revolution before the revolution. Rather, it was a reinvented civil society that ironically both the dreamers of change and the institutions of the status quo simultaneously embraced. This "reinvented civil society," according to the Slovenian philosopher Tomaz Mastnak, originated from the Eastern Europe of the 1970s and 1980s, where the anticommunist intelligentsia reconstructed civil society as a cure to all ills of communism, but one that left postcommunist societies with no defense against the onslaught of neoliberalism.[95] Now devoid of a class dimension, this civil society stood as the remedy against the tyranny of the state and party; it was premised on the aversion of structures and allure of fluid and free forms reflected in the much-valued notion of "human freedom."[96] Assuming an ethical inference as "truth" (against the "political society" representing "interests"), this notion of civil society then spread across the globe following the demise of the communist bloc.[97]

It is tempting to reduce the Arab revolutions, as some have, to a series of plots designed by foreign institutions or states to manipulate dissent, generate partial and trivial change, or shape "color revolutions" acceptable to Western powers.[98] Foreign states, no doubt, do project elaborate strategies in pursuit of their national and international interests; in this sense, they are always in the business of "conspiring." The exceptional geopolitical position of the Middle East—shaped by the presence of oil and Israel—has for decades rendered the region susceptible to international intrigues. And this geopolitical exceptionalism did play a significant role in impairing the revolutions after they occurred. However, defining the Arab revolutions simply in terms of foreign manipulation betrays the genuine desires and demands of ordinary citizens for deep and meaningful change. In fact, irrespective of the vision of the political class, the subaltern groups, the urban poor, rural tenants, women, and social minorities were engaged in a real grassroots struggle for social justice, redistribution, inclusion, recognition, and dignity. Indeed, these grassroots activities marked the radical impulse of the Arab Spring, which deepened its revolutionary character.

9   Radical Impulses of the Social

What did these refolutions mean for the ordinary people? As extraordinary actors, young activists of the new Arab public played a critical role in initiating the uprisings. But youth or the political class on their own could never cause a breakthrough in revolutionary struggle. The breakthrough came only when ordinary people (such as parents, elderly relatives, or children) joined in these extraordinary struggles—when the slum dwellers marched, workers downed tools, and unlikely citizens publicly spoke out. Besides aiding the revolutionary breakthrough, the subaltern acts of claim making in the social domain radicalized these otherwise nonradical revolutions. Often through direct actions marginalized women, social minorities, and lower-class youths pushed for equality, inclusion, and recognition, while the urban and rural poor launched extraordinary efforts to reclaim dignity and enhance their life chances, contesting the logic of neoliberal orthodoxy that the political class had largely taken for granted. These radical claims, away from the state institutions, marked the social dimension of the revolutions. Thus, even though falling short of fundamentally altering state power, the Arab revolutions nonetheless unleashed significant social claims as citizens challenged entrenched interests and established hierarchies.

Counter-Norm Currents

The revolutionary performance, the downfall of deep-rooted dictators, and the subsequent political opening prompted Arab citizens to imagine their nations as if everything were now possible. Change in consciousness remained one of the most enduring, if invisible, legacies of the Arab uprisings, one expression of which was the sudden outburst of both highly conservative and liberal ideas in the Arab public sphere. Thus, only days after the downfall of Mubarak, Ben Ali, and Qaddafi, the sudden appearance of ultraconservative bearded men wearing traditional garb and women with their faces covered gave a new character to public spaces. Bands of militant Salafis with long black beards and white *jalabiyas* roamed the cities of Egypt, Tunisia, and Libya to herald the coming of their divine social order. In Libya, they attacked the US consulate in Benghazi, killing the ambassador, assaulted and vandalized Sufi shrines, and demanded that women be covered. By 2015, the unruly Dawn militias had captured the capital, forbidding women from traveling without male chaperones; dismantling statues, Sufi mosques, libraries, and art colleges; closing beauty salons; and wanting to segregate the schools.[1]

In Egypt, the newly founded association of Amr be Marouf wa Nahy an al-Munkar and its agents stopped women in the streets to impel them to observe "proper" moral behavior and dress code. Even though the passersby, shopkeepers, and women themselves, for instance, in the city of Suez, struck back at these new moralizers, many felt apprehensive at these conservative shockwaves.[2] In 2012, a Salafi sheikh in Egypt called for the death of the opposition leader, Mohamed ElBaradei; and the infamous Wagdi Ghoneim called for a jihad on those who were protesting against President Morsi.[3]

The Tunisian religious radicals seemed even more intransigent. Shortly after the revolution, hard-liners demanded female circumcision, marriage of underage girls, and polygamy. In July 2012, in the capital's coastal suburb of La Marsa, Salafi groups attacked an art exhibit and destroyed artworks they deemed "offensive." Earlier others had ransacked a police station and bars selling alcohol in the El Kef region.[4] Extremist groups further made a public uproar against airing the Iranian film *Persepolis* on TV because it was considered blasphemous—a claim that a Tunisian court upheld. Other groups replaced the national flag of Tunis with what came to symbolize the Islamist ISIS, whose horrific brutality in Iraq and Syria took the world by surprise. Others raided the US embassy in Tunis, while their likes assassinated the leftist activist Chokri Belaid in a cold-blooded murder in the early morning. Even though these incidents remained sporadic, their shockwaves reverberated across the Arab nations and beyond, fortifying the idea that the Arab Spring was receding into an impending Islamist takeover, and all this at a time when the religious parties were poised to assume governmental power.

But this was only one side of the story. In parallel with and bolstered by these very conservative onslaughts emerged a series of contrapuntal, liberal sensibilities that shook conventional beliefs. Tunisia, already the most liberal Arab society, saw an upsurge in women's fury against the aggressive Islamist and Salafi trend. To protect their rights, they organized into associations, staged street marches, carried out sit-ins in the prime minister's offices, and campaigned on college campuses. The international FEMEN movement found participants among some Tunisian women. Images of their bare chests stirred much controversy at home and praise in the West, at a time when "saving Muslim women" had become part of the imperialist agenda of military intervention and regime change. No less dramatic was the public kissing of a dozen Moroccans in front of parliament as a defiant protest against the arrest of three teenagers who had posted their affectionate photos on Facebook. "Our message is that [detained teenagers] are defending love, the freedom to love, and kiss freely," said one protester. Thousands supported the move.[5] And then came a campaign of "free hugs" in Saudi Arabia by groups who offered hugs to passersby in the streets to "brighten up their lives." The morals police would not tolerate these mundane public acts, which had caused moral panic over their possible implications. "Today it's one hug, tomorrow it's a free kiss, and the next day it'll be free sex," imagined a blogger.[6]

In Egypt where religious sentiments and modesty, shown by wearing the *hijab*, *khimar*, and *niqab*, had dominated the public arenas since the 1980s, a new wave of deveiling came to life. It is not known how prevalent this was, but it seemed to become a trend, as scores of veiled women, including TV presenters and those in the "poor areas like Imbaba," began to take off their headscarves.[7] "There is a wave of my friends doing it," as a deveiled woman said.[8] Hala, for instance, was from a very religious family, with a grandfather who was a Sufi sheikh. Hala was recruited by a Muslim Brotherhood group, which looked "cool and upper middle class." But she found them "such class snobs," so "I was traumatized and totally lost religion." But the turning point was just after the revolution when the Muslim Brothers came to power, when "they became a total failure." After grappling with the ideas of religion, freedom, and Muslim identity, eventually "I took off the veil." Of course, undergoing such dramatic change in identity, beyond personal trauma, became socially painful when family members, friends, or neighbors displayed disapproval. "Some people didn't talk to me anymore," Hala said. Yet the women continued in their new convictions, "because [after the revolution] they felt so empowered."[9] Only a revolution could cultivate such courage and daring among Muslim women in a society where taking off the *hijab* remained by far harder socially and religiously than putting it on. The revolution made these women believe that rules could be broken and norms could be altered, while the dispirited rule of the

Muslim Brotherhood made them question the very logic behind that type of religiosity. Thus, women in particular exhibited a strong quest for autonomy and selfhood. "For me not wearing veil," stated Meshraf, a deveiled woman, "I feel like myself for the first time in my life. Only when men accepted this right for women could we say that we have a revolution," she claimed.[10]

The desire for selfhood and autonomy also found expression in many girls deciding to live on their own, separate from their families. Unmarried women living on their own or with friends became "quite a phenomenon," according to Hala, who knows many who do so. The checkpoints, curfews, and general decline in the feeling of security after the revolution offered grounds for young women to justify their new counter-normal lifestyle by arguing that commuting was unsafe, so they would be better off to live near work or school even though away from the family. Others had already experienced the single-household lifestyle because their families had migrated to the Gulf States for work. But once the family returned, "the girls hated it" because they felt they were losing their independence.[11] It took some three decades after the revolution for a third of Iranian unmarried women (between twenty-five and thirty-five years of age) to live on their own; it seemed to take only a few months for the Egyptian revolution to unleash such ideas of autonomy. The shocking display of twenty-year-old Alia el-Mahdi's nude self-image on her web blog to protest social control epitomized this profound frustration yet showed the courage and selfhood that many women expressed in these revolutionary moments. As the scholar Laleh Khalili put it, Alia's act at once challenged the long-standing gender norms, body discipline, and its commodification.[12]

But women were not alone in uttering such an overt counter-normal position. Bolder expressions came from people who were gay, whose lifestyle was deemed in the conventional moral codes as a Western disease, cultural threat, and something counter to religion. Even though as collectives gay people did endure before the revolution—frequenting certain bars, hangout places, or virtual space—they became extraordinarily vocal and visible in just days after the revolution. So when an activist began an antihomophobia campaign on Twitter, thousands joined within hours, with further support coming from other activists and celebrities. The move was to begin the foundation for a "distanciated" community.[13] Like others, gays had taken part in the revolution, fought street battles, and stayed in Tahrir Square for days and nights. The liminal space of Tahrir offered them respite to venture "out," become visible, and set up headquarters to congregate and connect. Not long after Mubarak's downfall, both gay men and women in Cairo and Alexandria held gay nights in bars and private parties; met in cafés, in gyms, and on beaches; and through the Internet linked to wider communities beyond Egypt.

Being openly "out," however, could not ensure tolerance. On the contrary, precisely because they became more visible and vocal, gays had to face increasing official witch hunts of both Islamist and military-backed governments. In October 2013, police raided a medical center and arrested fifty-two gay people, while in November a Valentine's Day party in Alexandria Road came under police assault and detainees were forcefully sent for "forensic examination."[14] In April 2014, police arrested four men at a gay party, and later others were detained for same-sex marriage on a boat in Cairo.[15] In the euphoria of exalting General Sisi as the "lion of Egypt" and the "real man" of the nation, the depiction of gays as "femalelike" or "half men" certainly served the new national chauvinist narrative that the post-Morsi counterrevolutionaries championed. But neither this nor any other onslaught was able, of course, to stop gays from being gay; rather, they would push the members from open activism to nonmovements, in which they would go underground as noncollective actors to engage in passive networks, waiting for the next chance to "come out" as collective agents in organized communities.

Such public expression of personal liberties and lifestyle was unprecedented in scale and scope in the societies in which patriarchal sensibilities and conservative religiosity had gained extraordinary momentum since the 1970s. But the revolutions of 2011 shook many of the established ideas. "After taking down Mubarak," opined an activist, "I cannot think of anything that is not possible."[16] The revolutions made the subalterns believe that rules could be broken, norms altered, and sacred beliefs questioned—even the very idea of God. And they could. In fact, a burgeoning "atheist movement," as it came to be known, emerged ironically at a time when the religious parties (in Morocco, Tunisia, and Egypt) had ascended to governmental power. Reportedly, some two million "closet" Arab atheists began to speak out in public—talk to journalists, organize debates, and voice opinions on the web.[17] Multiple websites such as Egyptian Atheists, Atheists without Borders, Atheist Brotherhood, Atheists against Religion, Atheist and Proud, and I Am an Atheist sprang up. In February 2013, a packed Cairo mosque hosted a debate between a group of atheists and a cleric. Others were aired on television.[18] In the Persian Gulf area, at least two television talk shows discussed atheism.[19] Mostly the young expressed doubt about the credibility of a religion that "says we don't have free will, but we will still be accountable for what we do." A cleric testified that every day parents brought their disbelieving children to him, seeking a remedy.[20] A group of Egyptian atheists called on the prime minister, asking that "atheists' rights" be recognized in the constitution. The movement also spread to the Arab world at large. Saudi atheists became so vocal and visible that the state issued a decree criminalizing any call for "atheist thought" and "questioning the fundamentals of Islam."[21] Some accounts spoke of more than sixty Arabic-speaking atheist Facebook groups that emerged after the revolutions, ranging from Yemen with 25 followers and Sudan with 10,344 followers.[22]

This coming out had costs. Open disbelievers often faced insult, isolation, and even violence by family members and others. Basma Rabei (eighteen years old) was locked up for three weeks, receiving death threats from her brother, while Asmaa Omar's (twenty-four years old) father broke her nose for "insulting Islam" and becoming a "loose girl";[23] and police arrested young people for advocating atheism through Facebook.[24] Many continued to reject the idea of God, while others held their God but rejected religion, whether Islam or Christianity. The gender bias of actually existing religions seemed to drive more women than men to question religious dogma.[25] The aggressive rise of Salafis in public spaces and of the religious parties in governments had placed religion at the center of the social struggle precisely at the time when the revolutions had made the underdog unafraid to express unorthodox views. As a Tunisian atheist claimed, "Before the revolution, people didn't see Islam as the problem, but after the revolution, they saw what political Islam was, and what Islam is."[26] In Egypt this "atheist movement occurred, for the first time, in the history of Egypt, during the time that Morsi and the Muslim Brotherhood were in power."[27] In 2014, the Egyptian Ministries of Youth and Endowments (Religious Affairs) convened to create a national plan to combat the atheist phenomenon through educational, religious, and psychological means.[28]

Defying Organized Power

While atheists were defying God, the emergent anarchists defied organized power. The mysterious Black Bloc—with members wearing masks, hoods, and black clothing—surfaced on the streets in January 2013 to fight President Morsi and his "armed militias"—when nonviolent tactics were seen to be unable to halt the government's attacks against protesters, especially women.[29] The bloc operated in eight Egyptian cities, in the streets, and on several dozen Facebook pages. Suspicious of any type of systemic power, the bloc opposed all post-revolutionary governments whether secular or religious. As a novel subculture of lower-class male youths, the bloc arose first to avenge the killing of a comrade known as Jika during the Muhammad Mahmoud battles with the military. But at its core, it expressed an indignant claim by subaltern youths to public space controlled by the police and the privileged; like the Brazilian graffiti *pichadores*, it was a defiant proclamation of "I matter," an expression of rejecting authority in all forms. It reflected the rebellion of the subaltern but globalizing youngsters who had been operating under the heavy-handed command of fathers, elders, teachers, and rulers. Appearing in public and then vanishing mysteriously, just as the mythical image of Robin Hood, the Black Bloc inspired awe and admiration. But for the state intelligence service, these do-gooder outlaws were a source of deep anxiety, prompting the secret police to infiltrate their ranks to control them or to invent fictitious versions as a means to impair the Muslim Brotherhood and its rule. In Tunisia, the anarchist trend was taken on more often by the feminist group Feminism Attack, whose members met in cafés, in public places, and on Facebook to campaign and build collective identity. Sympathetic to FEMEN and close to the green anarchist current Beck 7es, Disobedience, and Alberta, but critical of the more established feminist organizations like the Tunisian Association of Women Democrats, the group aimed to raise awareness in favor of a culture of self-management and equality between men and women and to oppose "the system and the police generally" and the "extremist political parties that are all in the service of the same system."[30]

The public display of such counter-normal ideas—whether deveiling, alternative sexuality, atheism, or anarchism—exemplified a broader phenomenon typical of most postrevolutionary moments, a phenomenon whose enduring manifestations could be traced only in the long run. These are revolutionary moments that give rise to new ideas, values, and trends in society—when new perceptions and practices unsettle established hierarchies, when citizens challenge the rulers, youth the elders, women men, workers the bosses, pupils the teachers, and laymen the clerics. These new subjectivities, if sustained, would serve as the precursor for a social transformation—change in social roles, relations, values, and expectations; they inspire a quiet revolution in those layers of society that often remain invisible and undetected.

In the Arab postrevolution, the young who initiated and carried out the uprisings assumed a new exalted image rising from "inexperienced and emotional" youth changing into "brave and responsible" children of the nation. Perhaps for the first time in decades, elders appreciated and admired their youth, who in return charged their parents' generation with complicity and apathy that had sustained the Arab dictatorships for so long. Hours after President Mubarak was forced to step down, a female young activist reported, "My dad hugged me after the news and said, 'Your generation did what ours could only dream of. I am sorry we didn't try hard enough.'"[31] These youths described the current models of rule as belonging to the old generations: "The very idea of 'Islamic rule' and even the 'military coups' are from the 1980s," wrote the blogger Sandmonkey (Mahmoud Salem). For him, the current establishment represented "a generation holding on to the 1980s as tenaciously as a playboy holds on to his youth."[32] In truth the young people had taken charge of street politics; they stunned and gained the respect of elders by their dedication, self-discipline, and wisdom. Self-confident and empowered during the revolutions, they began to demand institutional respect and accountability. In Egypt, pupils formed and launched waves of strikes in the schools, demanding their "rights" and teacher accountability. Student representatives of six major universities publicly called for the dismissal of the ministers of higher education and interior for mismanagement.[33] Teachers complained about "uncontrolled pupils," "chaos, disorder, and disrespect" in schools. President of an Egyptian University complained privately and with humor that "everyone in the university—staff, workers, drivers and especially students all want 'their rights.'"[34] Apprehensive about the defiance of the pupils, the army warned students that it would raid schools to restore order if they did not end their protests. Thus, the low turnout of the young, including young women, for the constitutional referendum in January 2014 caused an uproar in the establishment media and government.[35]

The Arab uprisings brought millions of young women onto the streets for days and nights, during which they marched with men, chanted slogans, formed groups, battled with the police, and helped the injured. As part of the struggle to occupy public spaces, many spent nights away from home and family in the streets along with male comrades. Often they did so in defiance of their anxious fathers, brothers, and elders. Disobeying her parents to participate in the anti-Mubarak protests, young Heba joined the revolutionaries and in the process acquired a new self-confidence: "I can do whatever I want, because I did what I wanted [during the revolution], and I went through a lot of confrontations," she stated. "[Now] my family is starting to realize that I am actually responsible." And she was not just challenging ageism; she also questioned the religious authorities when she "lost respect for 95% [of the sheikhs]."[36] Indeed, women's unprecedented voice and visibility had caused grave anxiety among conservative men, especially statesmen, who reportedly sanctioned the alarming wave of sexual harassment to drive women off the public squares. In response, women forged one of the most genuine movements of their own, compelling the government in June 2014 to criminalize sexual harassment in Egypt.[37]

Perhaps more significantly, the revolution redefined and brought to public scrutiny the relationship between religion and politics. The short two years of religious rule—Muslim Brotherhood in Egypt and al-Nahda in Tunisia—caused a remarkable change and misgiving in popular attitudes toward the merit of a religious state. In Tunisia, al-Nahda responded by renouncing the idea of a religious state, pursuing instead a post-Islamist line of promoting a secular state and pious society. But in Egypt, the intransigent Islamism of the Muslim Brotherhood faced formidable dissent from Muslim citizens and from within the organization as scores of prominent leaders such as Abdel Moneim Aboul Fotouh and Mokhtar Nouh defected or were expelled. Along with the youth of the Muslim Brotherhood, they formed a half-dozen political parties, such as Misr al-Qawiya, Tayar Masry, and Hizb al-Adl, which espoused a broadly post-Islamist outlook.

These subversive counter-norms did not mean that Arab societies in the 2010s suddenly moved into a liberal, secular, or democratic mold. Indeed, such trends as deveiling, atheism, anarchism, alternative sexuality, and an antihierarchy ethos were the preoccupation of minority groups. Most people, however, retained their religious beliefs and the fundamental social norms and valued order and stability. Yet they also disdained authoritarian rule and governing in the name of religion and wished to enjoy personal liberties, social rights, and local self-rule. What the postrevolutionary societies in the Arab world were experiencing was not liberal or secular but societies in flux, unsettled by emerging trends, entitlements, and social dislocation—societies polarized between the highly conservative and highly liberal margins, between stubborn elitism and subaltern radicalism, with a large mainstream subject to a growing sociocultural fusion and hybridity. This represented a historic rupture in the Arab societies and offered abundant potential for new openings.

Insurgent Poor

The new subjectivities and insurgent endeavors were not limited to youth and the middle class. The urban and rural poor emerged from their neighborhoods, factories, and farms to challenge their bosses, managers, and patrons in pursuit of enhanced life chances and dignified lives. The revolution and the collapse of police control cultivated an extraordinary self-confidence and entitlement in the poor, who took the opportunity to make claims, wage direct actions, and govern themselves in popular committees, neighborhoods, and villages.

On the Day of Anger, just three days after the start of Egypt's January 25 Revolution, the massive informal community of Imbaba in the heart of Cairo joined the uprising in earnest. A small fifty-person march, half of them children, following a Friday prayer, rapidly grew into a mass demonstration so large that "one could not see the beginning and the end." The crowd called for the downfall of the regime, invited others to join, battled with the riot police for hours, and continued their march toward Tahrir Square.[38] Imbaba was known for its Islamist past when in the early 1990s hundreds of al-Gama'a al-Islamiyya militants had penetrated this opaque neighborhood—with unmapped narrow alleyways without home numbers—creating an "Islamist state within the state."[39] But by the time of the revolution things had changed. "The last thing youth are talking about is religion," said Ahmed Metwalli, a son of an ex-Islamist. "It is the last thing that comes up. They need money, they need to get married, a car. . . . They will elect whoever delivers that." The poor population in Imbaba had risen up because of their outrage at their denigration as poor, having to pay bribes to go to the hospital, to get ID cards, and to please the police. "We don't need prayers, sheikhs and beards; we have had enough of the clerics."[40] On January 25, some two hundred activists had managed to mobilize up to twenty thousand demonstrators in the slum community of Naheyan over the issues of police brutality and the price of bread,[41] while a small crowd of one hundred demonstrators soon swelled into thousands in the slum of Dar El Salam.[42] In the meantime, artistic youths inscribed the symbolic images of the revolution—murals, slogans, and images of martyrs—on the walls of these poor neighborhoods.

Of course, not everyone joined the revolutionary protests. Many remained unsure about the dynamics and outcome of these upheavals, preferring to engage in local struggles that they found manageable and meaningful. Yet the very heterogeneity of these neighborhoods, where residents held diverse educational backgrounds, tended to facilitate the link between the parochial and the cosmopolitan. The *'ashwa'iyat* communities (informal settlements) like Imbaba and Dar El Salam housed not merely the rural, illiterate, and abject poor but also segments of the middle-class poor—government employees, newly married and educated couples, as well as professionals such as lawyers or teachers who could not afford to secure housing in the formal market. The members of this class, traversing between the middle-class world and that of the poor, critically linked the local struggles of their dispossessed parents, relatives, and neighbors to the world of the universities, cyberspace, associational activism, and main streets.

Beyond joining the big revolutions, the poor also carried out their own local mini-revolutions. In Cairo's Manshiyat Naser, where falling boulders from the hills had demolished several homes, residents attacked and set fire to the Neighborhood Council and the police station, which they deemed responsible for corruption and evictions.[43] Indeed, when the police retreated and disappeared from the public arenas on January 28, "revolution was over for the poor," as if an insurmountable victory had been achieved.[44] The absence of the police diminished poor people's daily anguish and humiliation and opened the opportunity for their aggressive encroachment. Thus, hundreds of poor families occupied some 510 apartments in the Wahayed public housing in Duweiqa. "These apartments were for us, for the families from the Duweiqa slums," they claimed. To ensure security of tenure, they reported to the municipality and visited the Ministry of Defense, which temporarily permitted them to stay.[45] However, under the postrevolutionary military government, the residents soon had to fight eviction by security forces, who fired guns and threw the people's belongings over the balconies. As usual, the government pledged alternative housing. But refusing the offer, the squatters set up temporary tents until they got what they regarded as "proper homes." At this juncture, the illegal construction of homes and informal additions continued throughout the country. Half-built vacant apartments were taken over, and public lands on the periphery of cities were occupied so homes could be constructed. The sudden rise in the price of cement (compared to unchanged price levels in general) pointed to the widespread illegal construction during the revolution. The struggles of this sort were to assume an unmatched momentum in the immediate postrevolutionary period, when poor people's heightened expectations were rapidly dashed by disruptions in the state machinery and lack of response.

Tunisia saw an upsurge in informal settlement and extension or consolidation of previously built extralegal homes. Communities such as al-Sayida al-Menubiyya and Tadamon in Tunis became the subject of elite stigmatization as the bastion of anarchy, extremism, and social strife, not only because of the memory of their 1982 riots but also because of the new fear about poor people's support for the Islamic Nahda Party.[46] To the dismay of the elites, the poor took over dozens of sidewalks in the central districts adjacent to the Medina, turning them into vibrant marketplaces—scenes that reminded me of the central areas of Tehran just after the 1979 revolution in Iran and of Cairo's central streets just after Mubarak's downfall. The fact that Bouazizi, the hero of the Tunisian revolution, was a street vendor brutalized by the police had given street vending an unprecedented legitimacy and immunity, which the poor utilized to enhance their lives. In fact, before the departure of the dictator Ben Ali, local activists in Sidi Bouzid had deliberately (mis)represented Bouazizi as an "unemployed university graduate" to connect his spectacular drama to the plight of some 250,000 jobless college graduates—Tunisia's most likely revolutionaries, the middle-class poor.[47] The postrevolutionary political and economic turmoil, however, left little chance for substantial progress in poor people's lives. If anything, many of these educated young people hung around in the local cafés, dreaming of migrating to the north, while the urban poor and the working class felt that the "old order has continued" even two years after the fall of Ben Ali. They responded by stunning waves of social protests so that by 2013 Tunisia was poised to become the nation with the highest number of labor strikes and social protests—some forty-five thousand, or ninety per day.

In Egypt, land grabs and illegal construction largely on agricultural plots went on in earnest. Within the first six months, January to March 2011, some 110,000 hectares of land were taken over illegally for construction, mainly of homes. In June 2013, the Awqaf authorities reported 9,335 encroachments on 2.5 million square meters of land, of which more than one million square meters were agricultural parcels.[48] Most of these encroachments were carried out by the needy (but also by some opportunistic developers) in an aggressive fashion, at times involving violent confrontations with security forces. In the coastal town of al-Arish, families took over lands (military property), claiming that they had belonged to their ancestors for hundreds of years. The claim led to violent scuffles, injuries, and hospitalization.[49] On Quorsaya Island in Giza hundreds of residents battled with the military over rights to five hundred feddan (over two hundred hectares) of land that the army had claimed since 2007. Soldiers fired gunshots while residents fought back fiercely, injuring a number of soldiers and succeeding in overturning the eviction. Activists, artists, and intellectuals gathered to celebrate the people's victory.[50]

Thousands of the urban dispossessed waged collective campaigns throughout the country to obtain state housing, fight gentrification, and contest rent increases. The residents of Duweiqa, who had been relocated from their unsafe shelters to tents and then into government rental flats during the early postrevolutionary period, joined forces with other poor residents from areas such as Medinah Nahda, Ezbet Abu Qarn, and Estable Antar to demand ownership of these rental flats; they had already resisted paying rent for months. Backed by the activist-initiated campaign "Upgrading Only in Name," (Ehya' Bel-Esm Faqat) they organized angry sit-ins at the Cairo governorate headquarters, chanting, "Oh Governor, tell the truth; are we not the priority?" Warning that they would launch the "the revolution of the 'ashwa'iyyat," they cut off a main road, causing noisy traffic disruptions while fighting the security forces that were trying to disperse them.[51] In Alexandria, residents of the Imam Malik neighborhood protested in outrage at the governorate office because the authorities had evicted them, citing their unsafe shelters.[52] And others in the northern city of Ismailia staged a hunger strike at the city's Housing Department, demanding that the government grant them apartments because their shelters had been demolished; because a hunger striker was hospitalized after losing consciousness, activists got involved in boisterous protests in front of the governorate office.[53] Tent residents of Cairo's Shubra al-Khaima, whose dwellings had been demolished, threatened an indefinite sit-in and hunger strike at the district court if they were not relocated to government flats.[54] And where authorities warned residents would be evicted from "unsafe" dwellings (as in Falaki in Alexandria), families refused to relocate in an attempt to get governmental housing.[55]

Figure 6. Street vendors in downtown Cairo, 2011; photo by the author

Figure 7. Street vendors in Tunis, 2011; photo by the author

Figure 8. Al-Sayida al-Menubiyya community in Tunis; photo by the author

Figure 9. Poem written on the wall of a ransacked villa belonging to the relatives of ex-president Ben Ali, Sidi Bou Said, Tunis, 2011; photo by the author

They are the ones who looted the country
They are the ones who robbed the People
Ben Ali, Leila [his wife] and Imad
Bel-Hassan, Monsef, Mourad [Leila's Brothers]
What a group [they are] like Locusts!
They spared neither flatland, open space, nor valley
Not al-Marsa, nor Halq-Al-Wad
Not Gammarth, nor the Rowad

But claiming state housing, a diminishing trend since the 1980s, involved its own set of conflicts—over bureaucracy, ownership claims, and rents. For instance, dozens of Samanoud city residents in southern Egypt attacked the city council and chained its doors in a protest over what they considered an "unjust" lottery method to allocate government flats for which they had been on the waiting list.[56] In Port Said, in a highly dramatic show of force, some six thousand people from families eligible for the National Project of Mubarak Housing attempted to disrupt the flow of ships in the Suez Canal. Angered by the authorities' failure to clarify the conditions of occupancy, the protesters descended on the canal and threatened to halt navigation. So ferries ceased operating, causing hundreds of cars to wait on both sides of the canal, while a giant 190-kilometer line of waiting ships revealed the extraordinary impact of the protest.[57]

Collective Outrage

While some segments of the poor population were engaged in aggressive encroachment, others collectively resisted the claims made by authorities on their gains. This became evident immediately with respect to the gentrification policies, in particular Cairo2050, a massive project from Mubarak times that would overhaul central Cairo and lead to the relocation of hundreds of thousands of poor families into desert towns.[58] Even though the project was tabled after the revolution, some aspects of it were tried. Thus, when the developer Sawiris offered to buy the dwellings of some six hundred families in the Ramlet Boulaq squatter settlement adjacent to the luxurious Cairo towers, most residents refused to sell, at least not for the price offered, when the real value hovered around ten times that amount.[59] Resisting moving to the desert town of Medinah Nahda, people looked to one another to form a solidarity network. "We are like fish; this is our water; if you take us out of here, we will die," an elderly man stated.[60] The neighborhood exploded when an incident (a fight between a resident and his employer in the towers over pay) led to one death and twenty-two injuries by the security forces. People smashed windows, set fire to cars, and blocked the main Corniche Avenue.[61] Following a number of arrests, the case attracted activists' attention, notably lawyers, who mobilized to assist residents by defending their right to stay.[62] A year later when I visited the area, the case was still in court and the mood tense. Yet life seemed to go on as vibrantly as ever in the neighborhood, with people feeling a new sense of empowerment by the revolution and their own cultural capital. As a colleague and I walked through the narrow alleyways that linked lines of fragile dwellings, people surrounded us, inviting to their homes. Unlike the shabby and makeshift exteriors, the interiors were a different world full of life, energy, and hope. Family members navigated between the tiny kitchen and small but clean and orderly rooms decorated with religious symbols and family photos; they brought drinks, talked, cracked jokes, discussed politics, and watched TV. Friends and neighbors joined in, and the young showed off their baggy pants, gelled hair, and mobile phones. Yet beneath this hidden world of hope, humor, and humanity, there was also a deep-seated anxiety about the fate of their habitat. But they stood firm in their determination to win the battle and not be forced to leave.[63]

Postrevolutionary Egypt saw remarkable social protests when basic urban services perceived as rights, such as power, water, and the sewage system, faced disruption. A drastic energy crisis involving two-hour daily power cuts due to increase in consumption (e.g., over three million new air conditioners had been installed since 2011) and mismanagement brought millions into streets in Egyptian cities and urban villages. Even though the government subsidized 22.5 piasters of the 35-piaster cost per kilowatt-hour, the Socialist Popular Alliance launched the "We Won't Pay" campaign in Imbaba in August 2012 to combat power cuts.[64] Residents of villages in Luxor gathered in front of the power stations to express outrage, while dozens in Kafr El Sheikh warned they would set the power station ablaze.[65] In Alexandria, residents in Sidi Bashar and Syria Street, among others, assembled at power stations, blocked roads, and caused many traffic disruptions.[66] Summer 2013 was a particular turning point in the eruption of protests when thousands poured into the streets, blocking highways, occupying power stations, and refusing to pay their bills in Cairo, Giza, Doqliyya, Sharqiyya, Tanta, Qena, Qalyoubiyya, Kafr El Sheikh, Minya, and other governorates.[67]

Water shortages had continued intermittently since the late 2010s, prompting protests that came to be known as the "thirst revolution." With the rising demand and disruption in provision, social protests escalated and reached new heights in the summer of 2013. In July 2012, residents of the poor Giza district of Saft Al Laban staged a sit-in at the governorate building, holding signs that read "We Are Thirsty." Following their demands for job security, state housing, and compensation for physical damage during the revolution, they now wanted to overturn the daily water cuts, sometimes twelve hours per day, they had endured for the past six years. They expressed outrage, especially over what they considered an unequal distribution of water cuts that privileged affluent areas.[68] Residents of a community in Qalyoubiyya mobilized, chanted slogans, and blocked the railway, objecting that they had not had water for the previous four days and had to obtain it from other villages. Security forces dispatched to end roadblocks and water authorities promised to attend to the problem.[69] In the village of Fars in Aswan, residents blocked the Cairo-Aswan highway because sewage water had disrupted life in their community. Again police and local authorities intervened to end the crisis.[70]

Protestation of this sort reflected an aspect of broader developmental deficits that had gripped the subaltern population. Indeed, claims for social provision, a de facto call for the return of a social contract, underlay a widespread dissent that contributed to the fall of President Morsi's Islamist government in July 2013. Villagers of Meris in Luxor set out to close down the local council to bring attention to the "terrible services," which ranged from power cuts and water shortages to poor schooling and waste management.[71] Thousands from Alexandria slums formed a mass protest in front of the city's wastewater offices because the authorities had neglected their faulty sewage system. Joined by activists from the April 6 and Kefaya movements, slum dwellers derided Morsi's "el-Nahda project" that was supposed to tackle such social problems.[72] Similar neglect caused similar opposition in Aswan, where residents of a district took to the streets to block roads, causing disruptions, and in Minya, they occupied the power station whose defective sewage system had polluted their neighborhoods; only when security forces and authorities pledged to address the problem did they go home.[73] Some, like villagers of al-Shaqib in Aswan, stopped rail traffic to demand installation of proper rail crossings, whose lack had caused fatal accidents,[74] while others, such as those with disabilities in Minya who thought that city authorities had neglected them, stopped trains from running.[75] Then pensioners erupted en masse, with some going on hunger strikes in central Cairo to demand a 25 percent increase in their pension. Aligned with the Tamarod (rebellion) movement to impeach President Morsi, one protester stated that after thirty-seven years of work he received only 340 Egyptian pounds.[76] While most protesters blocked roads, caused traffic disruption, staged sit-ins, and undertook hunger strikes, others resorted to legal means, writing petitions to authorities about their plight and publishing them in daily papers.[77] But collective outrage, in particular cutting off highways and rail traffic, became the order of the day. During 2012, Egyptians held 500 sit-ins, 581 local protests, 414 labor strikes (up from 335 during 2011), and 558 street demonstrations.[78] The next year, during Morsi's presidency, social protests increased to a staggering 7,709 and street demonstrations and clashes to 5,821.[79]

Most of the protests took place in urban areas. But many occurred in provinces and villages, where the infusion of urban but unreliable amenities (electricity, running water, means of communication, and service wage work) into these rural agricultural areas had merged the claims concerning urban collective consumption with the demands over agricultural subsidies, irrigation water, bank credit, and especially access to land and security of tenure. This creeping urbanity had brought the villages into the political discourse of the nation, positing welfare rights and distribution of property as major subjects of social struggles in these postrevolutionary yet neoliberal moments.[80]

In Tunisia, just after the departure of the Ben Ali family, smallholders began to seize land from large landowners, many belonging to relatives of Ben Ali and his cronies. About one hundred large farms were subject to forceful occupation by landless and small tillers. In 2011, groups of farmers organized a campaign to prevent large landowners from preparing to cultivate some ten thousand hectares of farmland they deemed illegitimate. Farmers pushed for the purge of the old Tunisian Union of Agriculture and Fishery (UTAP) of its corrupt and complicit pro-regime leadership. Hundreds of farmers and fishermen traveled to Tunis on April 28, 2011, to demonstrate against the slow progress of change, demanding reorganization of UTAP.[81] In February 2012, the landless and small farmers formed their first independent union to address the problems associated with the costs of agricultural input and access to land, water, and other resources.[82] Besides access to land, access to affordable irrigation water drove farmers (for instance, in Testour and Medjez el Bab) to "steal" water and refuse to pay electricity bills to the Tunisian Electricity and Gas Company, which supplied energy to pump irrigation water. Only the government intervention of forgoing half of its electricity debt brought some peace between the parties.

Likewise in the rural communities in Egypt, where big landowners used the opportunity to expel poor tenants, small and evicted farmers and landless tenants occupied lands they considered theirs, began to cultivate, and filed lawsuits against the current owners who had benefited from the 1997 tenancy law to the detriment of tenant farmers. They formed their first union in November 2011 to secure access to land and land tenure, agricultural input, and health care and ensure representation of farmers in parliament. The union emerged when the relentless workers' campaign informed the legislation by the Ministry of Manpower to allow the formation of independent unions. Some nine hundred syndicates, including two hundred by small farmers, were formed after the declaration, covering farmers from Fayyoum, Kafr El Sheikh, and Mansoura to

Ismailia and Giza; access to land and security of tenure remained the prime objectives of the campaign.[83] And when they felt they had the opportunity, villagers took the initiative to manage the affairs of their communities.

In an Upper Egyptian village, as reported by the anthropologist Lila Abu-Lughod, youths took over local responsibilities. They formed a popular committee, protected their village from "thugs," and formed a Facebook page; tackled the distribution crisis (of bread, cooking gas), high price of meat, and garbage collection; and continued organizing literacy programs. They set up a weekly market, helped the displaced people in the community, and fought the corrupt village council. The villagers, especially women and girls, developed a sense that they could now freely talk about and discuss matters of their community as well as engage in local and national politics; they enthusiastically participated in all elections. For the villagers, this represented a new consciousness and language, a product and producer of revolutionary movement. "They did not speak of democracy; but in tackling problems directly and personally, they were living democracy."[84]

Specter of Bouazizi

The specter of Mohamed Bouazizi had haunted the autocratic Arab states, but it empowered the urban poor to test their fortunes in undertaking livelihoods during a time when economic hardship and postrevolutionary disruptions had put millions, including college graduates, out of work. Thus, once the uprising erupted, dictators abdicated, and police control collapsed, the cities saw an extraordinary spread of informal activities, notably street economic livelihoods. In Tunisia where Mohamad Bouazizi ignited the revolution, street vendors rapidly proliferated in the central districts and strategic locations in large cities. In Syria, police ignored unlawful street trade, and in Morocco the urban poor aggressively occupied key streets in Rabat and Casablanca, as well as in provincial towns to carry out business. Rather than outlaw informal street trade (despite the bitter animosity of local shopkeepers), authorities outlawed the sale of small gasoline containers for fear of self-immolations.[85]

Egypt experienced a spectacular expanse of hundreds of thousands of street vendors in key locations of large cities and small towns throughout the country. In Cairo, Tahrir Square, Nile Cornish, downtown streets, and Ramses Square saw the largest concentration of stalls, kiosks, and mobile vendors. The uprising and the presence of millions of protesters on the streets offered a lucrative market to boost vendors' businesses. Tahrir Square, where large rallies and demonstrations continued for months, became at times a surreal space of contention and commerce. While the revolutionaries battled the police, built barricades, chanted slogans, and dodged teargas canisters, the square vendors carried on with their routine work of preparing tea, cold drinks, food, and fruits and chanting for their merchandise. The street vendors became an integral element in Tahrir's spatio-political fabric, selling watermelons carved with words "Down with Military Rule" or trading "January 25 Tea" and "Tahrir Liquorice Juice."[86] Tahrir vendors catered to visitors and protesters, who often spent day and night in the square, and others traded goods that ranged from food, books, and domestic appliances to cheap clothing and revolutionary souvenirs.

Each vendor seemed to have his or her own story. Nagwa, a female seller, left her abusive husband to come to Tahrir to support her children; many men had lost their previous jobs, and others had just joined the job market. They did not pay tax and enjoyed a good degree of autonomy and flexibility but often felt insecure and dispensed bribes of up to 70 to 250 pounds to police for their unlawful practices.[87] Yet, as part of the vast informal economy that produced 40 percent of the GDP ($218 billion), they all were seizing this new opportunity to better their lives, even though their plebeian livelihoods carried out on the streets invited the fury of local merchants, disdain of the elites, and hostility of the state. Local merchants complained that they could not compete with the cheap offerings of the vendors; the elites whined about the image the street vendors projected, public sanitation, and (for some) "sexual harassment"; and the authorities expressed concern over traffic congestion, illicit trade, and public disorder. Both SCAF and Morsi's government moved to crack down on street trade. In fact, little had changed in the official policy of criminalizing the unauthorized vendors since Law 33 passed in 1957. Under President Mubarak, they were to receive a three-month prison sentence and a fine of up to one thousand pounds. The Islamist Morsi's government increased the penalties to six months in prison and a fine of five thousand pounds. In the meanwhile ministries joined forces to "cleanse" the central districts of Cairo, Giza, Daqahliya, Mansoura, and Alexandria of the "parasitic vendors," which the prerevolutionary governments had tried but largely failed to achieve.[88] Street subsistence workers resisted through an everyday war of attrition—temporarily retreating and then returning and regrouping. It was a war that continued relentlessly thanks to vendors' persistence, police complicity, and bribing. When in October 2012, a twelve-year-old fruit seller working in the heart of Tahrir was shot dead by a sniper, thousands of vendors staged a powerful demonstration from Tahrir to the Supreme Court. The captivating scene of marching vendors with pushcarts and mobile stalls in the main streets of Cairo remains one of the hallmarks of Egypt's street politics.

This act of solidarity served as a prelude to serious attempts to organize the street vendors in a national syndicate at a time when unemployment had reached 31percent (from the prerevolutionary 9 percent), or 5.3 million unemployed people, of which 72 percent had lost jobs and one out of three had college degrees.[89] With their proliferation and visibility, street vendors felt they needed to unite to deter eviction threats and ensure security. By December 2012, activist vendors, led by Ramadan al-Sawy, had collected four thousand signatures from colleagues in Cairo and other cities to set up a union. Before long they established an office and obtained support from counterparts in Helwan, Giza, Suez, Alexandria, and Asyut. Assisted by lawyers from the Egyptian Initiative for Personal Rights, they set out to obtain legal recognition. Their struggle for urban citizenship was coming to fruition. "Just give me a reasonably priced and strategic spot that I can rent—even it is only one meter—then I will happily pay rent and taxes," stated a vendor.[90] Indeed, forming organizations at this juncture had become a common feature of poor people's politics after years of restriction. Thus, following Mubarak's downfall, a citywide Association of 'Ashwa'iyat was formed in Cairo to work toward securing and upgrading slum communities and calling for the dismissal of corrupt local officials. Numerous Popular Committees, formed during the uprisings to protect neighborhoods, turned into local associations for development after the revolution. Thus, in Cairo's Mit Uqba neighborhood, the youth of the Popular Committee initiated a negotiation with the local authorities as well as ministries to upgrade their neighborhood. Being dismissed as "these young activists," the young people resorted to mobilization, petitioning, sit-ins, and public protests, as well as involving and discussing the matters with the locals. After impressive research, organizing, discussing, and lobbying, they succeeded in persuading authorities to connect their homes to natural gas and pave their streets, a process in which they fully participated and supervised.[91] The waste collectors demanded that the new government systematize their work by assigning districts to specific groups who would then charge a fee of five pounds (one dollar) per month per household for their service; they also demanded that the government should cancel its contract with the multinational company that carried out 40 percent of waste collection.[92]

Industrial workers purged the corrupt union bosses (in Tunisia), made them accountable, or set up new independent unions (in Egypt); they battled neoliberal employers who had violated their traditional entitlements such as a decent minimum wage, perks, and employment security. Many demanded expulsion of managers, renationalization, and reinstatement of benefits and perks. They called for the return of job security and the traditional benefits and entitlements. In Egypt workers occupied and ran a number of industrial plants whose managers had deserted or opposed workers' rights. The occupation of the giant Egyptian Iron & Steel Company (EISCO) in 2013—because the management withheld the annual bonus—cultivated a new awareness among young workers, who would no longer accept precarity but wished to restore stability in their working lives.[93] Indeed, the whole experience of strategizing and operating a steel mill with thirteen thousand workers would come with new values, a "refashioning of self," and radical desire in a revolution that had faced many setbacks.

Activists played an important part in these collective endeavors. Just as lawyers assisted street vendors to obtain legal protection and slum dwellers (like Cairo's Ramlet Boulaq) to fight evictions, the youth organizers of the campaign Upgrading Only in Name went to slum neighborhoods such as Gezira al-Forsaya, Bab al-Nasr, al-Salam, al-Nahda, Ramlet Boulaq, and similar locales in Suhag to help bring basic services. Residents understood these attempts as fulfilling their "right to enjoy a minimum standard of living" and the "right to live in decent housing," as one articulated.[94] Other groups organized a We Want to Live campaign to help remedy poor people's livelihood at a time when the persistence of neoliberal policies had made public provisions such as trains, hospitals, or drinking water more costly. The We Will Not Pay campaign advocated that poor residents not pay their electricity bills unless a clear schedule for power cuts in different districts was supplied, and an equal distribution of power supply (or power cuts) with affluent neighborhoods (such as Maadi and Mohandesin) was guaranteed. Beginning first in Giza's Saft Al Laban, the campaign moved to towns and villages in the delta and Upper Egypt and was adopted by the leftist Popular Alliance Party.[95] Reminiscent of *Masakhane* in post-Apartheid South Africa and the Chilean slum dwellers' "refusal to pay" campaigns in 1990s, these reflected a struggle for *leveling*, equality in what a city can or cannot offer to its citizens.

Radicalism Meets Neoliberalism

Poor people's struggle for (urban) citizenship has been truly remarkable in the Arab revolutions. Reinforced by a strong sense of entitlement, it embodied attempts to secure shelter, claim state housing, battle eviction, contest high rents, demand collective provision, and realize leveling. Urban citizenship also meant that the poor wished to be an integral part of the city—not only their low-status work and habitat but also their physical being and habitus. They disdained policies and people that considered them "outsiders" or "intruders." They wished to extend their horizon of the city beyond their backstreet localities by forging access to the larger community. Thus, in Cairo, people in the informal settlements located around the inaccessible Ring Road (designed to detach and halt the further encroachment of these settlements) took the matter into their own hands just after the revolution to construct access to the highway. Micro-taxis (tuktuks) could then bring people from the nearby settlements to these "transfer points" from which they could move throughout the rest of the city. Others built exit ramps to facilitate car access to the highways. In one settlement, the residents paved the road, opened a police station, produced a CD about the initiative, and invited the governor to officially inaugurate their access ramp. In these ways, the poor ensured their physical entry into the city at large. Still others, like the residents of the Ard Al-Liwa informal community, mapped their neighborhood; a local tailor drew an elaborate sketch of streets, alleyways, slopes, bridges, and homes, giving their community a life on paper, to give it recognition that it officially lacked.[96] In the meantime, the revolution eased more than ever poor people's mobility and presence in the cities' public spaces where they were usually shunned. Places like Bourguiba Boulevard in Tunis and Tahrir Square in Cairo became places for people with different class backgrounds to mix, briefly subverting the diktat of the spatial structure and elite attitude about where the poor could or could not go, sit, shop, or loiter. More than anything, the important role of the Black Bloc and ultras in the revolutionary streets pointed to the unusual presence of poor youth in the city's strategic locations. The public drama and display of these mostly lower-class youths reflected not only a form of subaltern male fun but also an enunciation of "I exist" in a public arena in which the underdog felt scorned and castigated.

Such a feeling of self-determination is a common feature of immediate postrevolutionary times when people, freed from state control, take initiatives to assert their will. Empowered as "free citizens," as "owners of their nation," yet facing a disrupted state and economy, they move to exercise self-rule. They embark on self-management in farms, factories, universities, workplaces, and neighborhoods. Such radical politics have a long history in most revolutions. In the aftermath of the Iranian revolution of 1979, workers occupied hundreds of factories to run them through factory committees; farmers took over agribusinesses; the urban poor grabbed land to build homes, occupied apartments and hotels, acquired urban services, and demanded security of tenure; they colonized central street sidewalks to conduct outdoor businesses; they formed organizations of squatters, street vendors, and the unemployed.[97] Segments of the lower classes dominated the urban streets, squares, and mosques with great confidence and boldness. For a while, spatial hierarchies crumbled, replaced by the scenes of managers and workers dining together in the nation's workplaces. The poor were further empowered by the intense competition between various left and Islamist groups to secure their support; and their radical measures were backed by the idioms of "equality," "social justice," and "socialism" that held currency in most of the twentieth-century revolutions.

But as discussed earlier, Arab revolutions were different; they occurred in an ideological age when the very idea of revolution had been discredited, a time when neoliberal ideas had seeped into the common sense of our political classes. So while the Arab revolutions embodied *in practice* radical impulses and initiatives on the part of the subalterns, no serious intellectual articulation, ideological frame, or social movement anchored them. If anything, the commonsense neoliberal thinking among the political elites, both secular and Islamist, dismissed such radical endeavors as out of place, extremist, utopian, and above all illegal, as if revolution were a legal enterprise. Thus, in Egypt, factory takeovers and workers' control did take place but only in twelve plants whose owners had left, given up, or gone bankrupt. The media, politicians, and even the unions dismissed the practice that violated the principle of property ownership as "unlawful." In the end, only one factory with 250 workers remained self-managed, and the rest were settled in some sort of "comanagement."[98] The urban poor did engage in remarkable social struggles to enhance and defend life chances, yet structural discrimination against them continued. Despite their aversion to the complex bureaucratic institutions, the poor still had to grapple with government agencies, schools, municipalities, agencies that handled ID cards, police stations, or hospitals in which they often received unequal treatment.

Once again, the fear of the poor as the spoilers of public order, as culprits of violence, insecurity, and sexual harassment, kept rendering them as outsiders. In these neoliberal conditions, the poor had lost their traditional ideological anchor. Except for a few activist groups that did give support to the poor, the urban subalterns were left largely on their own, dependent on their social networks and cultural capital. Nor did the postrevolutionary governments concretely address the plight of the poor, despite the rhetoric of social justice, which remained the most unattended demand of the revolutions. With no radical rethinking in social and economic policies, the poor were poised to continue with their collective contention or resort to the familiar strategy of quiet encroachment. The specter of Bouazizi continued to haunt. Indeed, the radicalism of the grassroots, the reformism of the political class, and the sabotage of the counterrevolution came to shape the highly volatile and paradoxical dynamics, the "agony of transition," in the aftermath of the uprisings.

10   The Agony of Transition

Few revolutions appear to have experienced such a disheartening aftermath as the Arab Spring, so much so that many began to question the very wisdom behind the making of those otherwise monumental uprisings. It might be hard to feel otherwise when Syria sank into a civil war, creating one of the most tragic (7.5 million) refugee crises since World War II; Bahrain's revolution stalled by the intervention of Saudi Arabia; and little changed in the power structure in Yemen in favor of the subaltern groups before it turned in 2015 into a front for a civil war between the Houthi rebels and the deposed president Ali Saleh on the one side and the Saudi regime, which backed the central government, on the other. While post-Qaddafi Libya was torn by civil strife between an elected government and the Dawn militias, the military ouster of President Morsi in Egypt in July 2013 paved the way for the counterrevolutionary restoration. The Egyptian military annulled the constitution, installed an interim civilian government, and violently cracked down on the defiant Muslim Brotherhood. In an orgy of national chauvinism, misinformation, and self-indulgence the old guard—the security captains, intelligence agents, big businessmen, and media chiefs—gained fresh blood, extending the witch hunt against the left, liberal, and other revolutionaries. The 2015 parliamentary elections, with only a 22 percent turnout, brought mainly the pro-Sisi and pro-Mubarak elites to the legislature, and military officers took control of seventeen of the twenty-seven governorates; the opposition crackdown within nine months after Morsi left some three thousand killed, seventeen thousand injured, and nineteen thousand arrested, while thousands of civil associations were shut down, and freedoms of speech, protest, and organization were severely restricted.[1] Even the most hopeful transition in Tunisia suffered setbacks. Despite the success of political forces in negotiating a democratic constitution, recognizing freedom of expression, and establishing an electoral democracy, official neglect on key revolutionary demands—

jobs and justice—dispirited many ordinary Tunisians, prompting thousands of youths with Islamist inclinations to join ISIS. In the end, Arab uprisings cost the Arab economies a staggering eight hundred billion dollars by 2104 and a 35 percent drop in their GDP (compared to that in 2010),[2] while social divide seemed to expand, and the prospect for democracy seemed remote.[3]

Why did the Arab revolutions face such an unfortunate destiny? Were they an anomaly, the unavoidable casualty of their own making? Most observers have pointed to the domestic and regional counterrevolutionary intrigues—"conservative coup," the "deep state," and foreign meddling.[4] There is certainly a truism in this. The region's geopolitical exceptionalism, shaped by oil and Israel, rendered the revolutions more vulnerable to geopolitical diktats. Foreign meddling took the form of protracted and devastating proxy sabotage, causing much instability and destruction. NATO forces used the Libyan revolution to crush Qaddafi's rule, to secure close ties to a post-Qaddafi government, and to access its oil. Deeply apprehensive of the spread of the Arab Spring in its cities and surrounding regions, the Saudi regime rolled its tanks through the streets of Bahrain to obstruct the revolution in the Persian Gulf. Intervention by Iran, Russia, and the Lebanese Hezbollah in support of Assad's rule and of Turkey, Saudi Arabia, and the United States to topple the regime turned Syria into a war theater to settle geopolitical accounts. Qatar backed Islamist groups in Libya and Egypt as well as ISIS, whereas the UAE led a campaign against them in support of the military regime in Egypt and anti-Islamist factions in Libya.[5] The Yemeni revolution fell victim not only to its own serious limitations but also, and more destructively, to the geopolitical competition between Iran and Saudi Arabia, which deployed military force to fight the Iran-backed Houthi rebels in support of the central government.

Most of these acts of sabotage happened before the popular uprisings managed to unseat the dictators. But in Tunisia, Egypt, and Yemen, where the long-standing dictators were toppled, foreign actors, in particular Saudi Arabia and the UAE, pursued a strategy of destabilization, sectarianization, and influence through economic leverage. As the major counterrevolutionary power, the Saudi regime continued to subvert any democratic openings or footprints of Iran that it deemed would jeopardize its hegemony. To this end, Riyadh supported extremist Salafis, provoked sectarian discord, backed an early ISIS, intervened militarily in Syria and Yemen in 2015,[6] and used financial blackmail to dissuade Egypt's post-coup government from any reconciliation with the Brotherhood. The United States simultaneously supported and sabotaged the revolutions, depending on which regimes and what interests they were threatening. The United States was caught off guard in Tunisia, remained ambivalent on Egypt, supported the uprisings in Syria and Libya, but disavowed revolutionary change in Bahrain and other Arab oil states. Washington consistently remained subservient to the counterrevolutionary course of its close ally, the Saudi regime at home and in the region.[7] The United States and its Israeli ally were only happy to find the sectarian war in Syria benefiting the neighboring Jewish state.[8]

But most revolutions, not just the Arab counterparts, have suffered counterrevolutionary interference—whether subtle sabotage or flagrant war waged by rival states whose fear of impending hostility or revolutionary contagion pushed them to crush the revolutionary regimes and the social order they heralded.[9] Half a dozen countries targeted revolutionary Russia in 1918; Cuba has remained under constant US threat since the 1950s, and its economic embargo continued until 2016; backed by the West, Iraq invaded the Islamic Republic of Iran in 1980, causing an eight-year devastating war; and the US-backed Contra War ravaged the Sandinistas in Nicaragua in the 1980s. Only the 1989 Eastern European anticommunist revolutions remained immune from foreign threats, primarily because the likely foe, the USSR and its allies, were themselves crumbling and because the capitalist West made every effort to ensure the smooth victory of these anti-Soviet revolutions in a bid to drive the world to the "end of history."

Thus, all revolutions invariably carry within them the germs of counterrevolutionary intrigues waiting for a chance to strike. But the counterrevolutionary attempts often fail primarily because they lack sufficient popular backing. The infamous Coup of 18 Brumaire by Louis-Napoleón Bonaparte did not last long, and the French Revolution reasserted itself. The 1848 revolutions in Europe succeeded in overcoming the wave of formidable counterrevolutions as the new democracies defeated the old orders over two decades. Internal intrigues and international wars against the revolutions in Russia, China, Cuba, and Iran all failed, even though they rendered these revolutions deeply defensive and security conscious. In the Philippines, the military's consecutive coup attempts against Corazon Aquino's government following the anti-Marcos People's Revolution in 1986 were all neutralized. Only in Nicaragua, a rare experience of democratic polity after the 1979 revolution, did counterrevolution succeed through electoral means, as the US-backed Contra War profoundly undermined the Sandinista government, thus ensuring the electoral victory of the rightist Violeta Chamorro in 1990.

What aspects of the Arab revolutions made them more vulnerable to counter-revolutionary restoration? What was peculiar about the Arab Spring transition? I suggest that beyond the regional geopolitics, the peculiarity of the Arab refolutions in Tunisia, Egypt, and Yemen shaped a transition dynamics that differed considerably from the prevailing models.

Transitions

The transition debates are preoccupied primarily with the process of shift from authoritarian rule to democracy, focusing predominantly on nonviolent and nonrevolutionary experiences, such as those in the early phase of Huntington's "third wave" of democratization in Latin America or the more recent political change in Burma.[10] Revolutionary transitions, when addressed, are often examined within the same conceptual frame as a nonrevolutionary shift.[11] In this model, transitions are carried out largely from the top by political elites through "political pacts" between authoritarian regimes and the democratic opposition. Descriptions of the transitions are often mixed with prescriptions and preconditions to achieve "successful" transition. A report by the Brookings Institution on "Egypt's difficult transition," for instance, calls on democrats and international partners to "work on ensuring that clear steps are taken toward establishing a true democracy, focusing initially on institution-building and changing political culture. This needs to be underpinned by a growing economy with a much fairer distribution of income."[12] The preconditions range from pursuit of elections even if flawed, nonviolent mobilization, and inclusive growth to bring about an effective legal system and decentralization.[13] Some have focused on the determining role of key and capable individuals such as Ferdinand Cardoso (Brazil), Ricardo Lagos (Chile), Fidel Ramos (Philippines), and Thabo Mbeki (South Africa) to manage the transition.[14] Otherwise, emphasis is usually placed on the attitudes and interplay of political groups and institutions, such as government and opposition, reformers and standpatters, or moderates and extremists.[15] Those aspects of social and political life that remain outside institutional politics or established groups seem to play little role.

Crane Brinton's *Anatomy of Revolution*, examining the English, French, American, and Russian experiences, remains perhaps the only classic work to explore the logic of revolutionary transition after the seizure of power—which may not necessarily entail democratization. Brinton examines the stages through which the revolutionary mobilization unfolds and leads to regime change, as well as how power continues to shift in the aftermath. Immediately following the regime change, the dominant groups that were poised naturally to inherit power from the old government are pushed aside by the rivals on the left. The power is taken away again, this time by the "extreme radicals" or "lunatic left," who then begin to centralize their rule—in particular in times of war—unleashing a "reign of terror" and "asceticism." This period of crisis shifts according to the nature of the society, the network of interactions, into the phase of effervescence, anti-asceticism, and joy, eventually ending up in equilibrium, at which point the revolution comes to an end.[16]

Thus, whereas transition studies focus largely on nonrevolutionary change from the old into new regimes mainly through political pacts, Brinton's exploration centers mostly on the struggles, negotiations, and change within the new revolutionary regimes after the collapse of the old order. How do we account for the dynamics of transition—in Tunisia, Egypt, or Yemen—that lie somewhere in between, where powerful revolutionary mobilization forced dictators to abdicate but failed to capture the governmental power, thus leaving the interests and institutions of the old order largely unaltered? How should we read the logic of transition in such political upheavals that were both revolutionary and nonrevolutionary, reflecting both a transition to democracy and revolutionary desires for economic distribution, social inclusion, and cultural recognition? To spell out the specificities of transition in the Arab Spring—primarily in Tunisia and Egypt—I discuss the painful paradoxes of postrevolutionary moments, shaped by the particular character of the refolutions, where the story of transition is not just what happens within the new regimes but also the intense struggles to transform the old ones.

Paradoxical Moments

A key paradox of immediate postrevolution relates to the extraordinary rise in popular expectations, ironically in conditions where even minimum resources to fulfill them diminish. So while people expect to be unusually better off, they instead end up becoming worse off. Having gone through a period of hardship and sacrifice for the sake of revolution (street battles, labor strikes, altruism), the citizens emerge feeling exceedingly entitled but suddenly face disrupted states, dysfunctional institutions, and crumbled economies for which their own struggles have contributed. Working people who had gone on strike to cripple the economy, students who caused disorder in colleges, and citizens who remained vigilant day and night to dismantle the old order—all those involved in these "creative disruptions"—find on the morrow of the revolution their wages unpaid, jobs lost, garbage uncollected, public services undelivered, and security diminished. It is not surprising that in Tunis, a medical intern "hated the revolution" because she was frustrated by her injured patients who would attack her for "delay in treating them" in a disrupted hospital.[17]

There is yet a second paradox. People express a common desire to keep order, functioning institutions, and competent administrators to address their everyday needs, yet there develops a powerful quest to transform those very institutions—expelling their bosses, altering rules of the game, and bringing in new blood—as a way to inculcate new political order. People want police to ensure security; they want working factories to provide their jobs and orderly bureaucracy to deliver services; yet they wish to remove the oppressive police force, dismantle exploitative factory administration, and alter bureaucratic bottlenecks. All postrevolutionary Arab states experienced in varied degrees such paradoxical "creative disruptions." Unlike in Egypt, Tunisia, and Yemen, where most institutions of the old regimes remained more or less intact, in Libya there was little semblance of a state left after Qaddafi. Violent revolutionary battles had dismantled much of what had remained, and "Libya was the colonel himself" along with his advisers and self-styled Jamahiriya system.[18] Thus, after the revolution, instead of security carried out by the state, the militias took charge of running checkpoints, patrolling borders, defending airports, and providing a semblance of (in)security. The Libyan civil strife since 2013 resulted largely from the desire of the Islamist armed militias to pursue the law of "political isolation"—that is, to ban the significant personnel of the Qaddafi regime from public office—while the new Libyan officials deemed many of those very personnel necessary to run the country's affairs.

These common paradoxes along with the sabotage of the counterrevolution, capital flight, and desertion of managers and bureaucrats produced disturbing costs to the economy and society. The Libyan economy contracted by a staggering 50 percent, losing some $15 billion as a result of the revolution, according to IMF.[19] Tourism declined sharply in all postrevolutionary states,[20] and foreign investment plunged in Egypt from $6.4 billion in 2010 to $500 million; in Libya, from $3.8 billion to zero; and in Tunisia, fell by 25 percent. At the end of the first year of the revolution, growth rate in Egypt fell from 5 to 1 percent, and in Tunisia, from 3 percent to zero. By 2013, some 15 percent of Egyptians had lost their jobs, while some 750,000 graduates were being added to the job market every year. Thus, three years after Mubarak's downfall, some 73 percent of Egyptians felt "unsafe," and more than 62 percent said their living conditions were worse than the year before;[21] 60 percent of Egypt's young people were hoping to emigrate in search of work.[22]

With the disruptions, welfare downturn, and high expectations comes profound discontent with the very revolutionary leaders who usually project the coming of a promised land but who by default turn "conservative the day after the revolution," as Hannah Arendt once observed.[23] In the Arab postrevolution, popular indignation over a better life merged with a parallel unrest associated with the factional fighting, communal conflicts, gender demands, and student militancy brought daily disorder and instability. Protesters wrote petitions, resorted to street demonstrations, waged labor strikes, and cut off highways and rail tracks, causing massive disruptions.

When such daily disruptions and disorder are mixed with economic strain and dashed hopes, we are likely to see a painful and early disenchantment with the very idea of revolution, bolstering the position of the resentful conservatives and wounded counterrevolutionaries who would victoriously proclaim, "We knew it; we told you; these are the results of revolutions,"[24] disparaging it as "the revolution of the street people,"[25] or longing for the "days of Mubarak."[26] This enhances a general mood in favor of order, stability, and a desire for a resolute, even repressive leader who may emerge from the rank of revolutionaries "to save the revolution" (as in Iran in 1979; or the Libyan general Khalifa Haftar, who crushed the unruly Dawn militias[27]) or arise from the camp of the counterrevolutionaries in the name of "saving the nation," in effect doing away with the whole project of revolution.

Such a trajectory is likely but not inevitable. An inclusive postrevolutionary government with a will to build a national coalition or a country wealthy enough to spend on the welfare of the majority could avert descent into such common disenchantment and its likely authoritarian outcome. But a nation like Egypt with a poor economy, conflict-stricken polity, and confident counterrevolutionaries would be susceptible to the rise of figures like General Sisi and his mission to "restore stability" and "territorial integrity." Of course, such strong but repressive rule may bring calm and confidence to certain constituencies, but it is likely to antagonize many others, such as political youth, the urban poor, and laboring classes, who have just come out of a revolution and mastered the art of protestation. In the end, welfare needs followed by social struggles may come to haunt the very authoritarian rule that emerges from this malaise, as witnessed by increasing labor (1,651 protests in 2014, and 1,117 in 2015) and social protests in Egypt and a new uprising of the poor and unemployed in Tunisia during January 2016.[28]

It seems that only a general trust in the rectitude of governing officials can inculcate in the citizens a measure of understanding, patience, and sacrifice—faculties that are so badly needed in order to get through these difficult paradoxical times. A revolutionary government with a trusted galvanizing leader like Gandhi, Mandela, or Castro could assist in spurring hope, endurance, and popular unity—the kind of charismatic leadership that the Arab revolutions invariably lacked. Whether the Arab revolutions were "leaderless" or "leaderful" only points to the characteristic absence of powerful and unifying spearheads that could have helped ameliorate the painful process through which postrevolutionary transitions invariably undergo.

Good and Bad

These unfortunate paradoxes characterize not just the Arab Spring but almost all revolutions. However, the Arab Spring had its own particular dynamics that left an enduring mark on its transition process, differentiating it from both the revolutionary and nonrevolutionary trajectories. As discussed earlier, what transpired in Tunisia, Egypt, and Yemen (but not Libya, which developed into a NATO-supported war) were not revolutions in the twentieth-century sense of rapid and radical overhaul of the states pushed by popular movements from below. Rather, they were refolutions, powerful revolutionary movements unleashed on the streets that ended up pushing for reform in and through the institutions of the incumbent states. So even though the revolutionaries garnered enormous social and street power, they did not rule or succeed in transforming governmental authority. Thus, most state institutions, ministries, police, intelligence apparatuses, judiciary, military, media, business circles, and networks of the old ruling parties continued to operate in varied capacities.

This means that there are some very positive sides to these nonviolent popular refolutions; they come with far fewer disruptions and less destruction than revolutions that accompany force, violence, and rapid and radical change. It is true that Arab refolutions caused interruptions in the economy, state administration, and normal operations of life, but the loss of life and general disorder were far more severe in Syria and Libya than in Tunisia and Egypt, where for the most part, salaries were paid, water and electricity were available, shops remained open, and supplies were available.[29] Beyond avoiding severe disorder, refolutions also allow for a more open and less repressive outcome with real potential for a pluralist social and political order. Thus, the Arab revolutions remained largely free from the detentions, summary trials, and elimination of old and new opposition members that the revolutionary regimes in Russia, China, and Islamist Iran adopted. Refolutions, in other words, possess the advantage of ensuring orderly transitions and avoiding violence, destruction, and chaos—the evils that dramatically increase the cost of change, where revolutionary excesses and a "reign of terror" can be averted. Unlike revolutionary Iran, where summary trials and executions of agents of the shah's regime and the oppositional leftist revolutionaries became the order of the day, a GCC-sponsored "transitional justice" in Yemen vindicated President Ali Saleh in 2014, despite his atrocities and manipulation of power for some forty years. In Tunisia a belated Truth and Dignity Commission was established to investigate the past governments' repression, but all of the twenty or so senior officials of Ben Ali's regime (including the interior minister and head of the presidential security service) were released from detention fairly quickly.[30] And in Egypt only a few top officials, including President Mubarak and his sons, were tried in controversial hearings, only to be acquitted in December 2014. In sum, few officials of the old regimes were purged or placed behind bars.

But precisely because refolutions fail to substantially change the old state personnel and institutions, the danger of restoration always lingers. The situation in Egypt, where Mubarak's thirty-year rule caused an uprising yet he escaped persecution, points precisely to the perilous potential of refolutions for counterrevolutionary restoration. The Egyptian counterrevolution, led by the military, struck back not only because it had remained vocal and vigilant within the unreformed state but also because it could skillfully surf on the massive wave of popular opposition against Mohamed Morsi—an Islamist ruler they thought was busy building an electoral theocracy and serving the Brotherhood clan rather than the interest of all Egyptians. Already despised by the sizable number of Mubarak supporters, the Brotherhood began rapidly to lose the sympathy of many who had supported Morsi's presidency. By the end of his first year, President Morsi and his patrons were seen as obstacles to deepening the revolution. Thus, opposition to the Brotherhood's rule in practice allied the anti-Mubarak revolutionaries with the pro-Mubarak counterrevolutionaries, who together with millions of disenchanted ordinary Egyptians created the monumental June 30 rebellion, which called for early presidential elections.

The Tamarod movement served as a catalyst to mediate the "alliance" of these strange bedfellows.

This stage in Egypt's revolutionary drama precisely reflected the limits of the refolutions—where the protagonists lacked coercive power to do what they saw the army doing on their behalf. It was the unfortunate predicament of a revolution that enjoyed enormous popular constituency but painfully lacked administrative power, with the consequence that it had to rest on the institutions of the incumbent state—such as the military—to change things. From the revolutionaries' prism, Morsi's forceful ouster served as a catalyst to remove the barriers that had prevented a stalled revolution from moving forward. It served as a desperate midwife for a pregnant nation that was enduring agonizing labor to give birth to a new social order; it needed a dramatic push: revolutionary coercion. But that turned out to be a midwife poised to take the life of the unborn, that is, to terminate the very revolution it claimed to want to save.[31]

Highly likely yes, but restoration is not an inevitable outcome of refolutions. An inclusive postrevolutionary government, capable of negotiating a political pact with competing constituencies, could build enough legitimacy and support to neutralize counterrevolutionary intrigues. In Tunisia, the ruling Islamic Nahda, driven by its own wisdom and the lessons from Egypt, forged a successful pact with labor, liberal, and secular forces, including a sympathizer of the old regime, the Nidaa Tounes. In this bid, al-Nahda dissolved its own majority government in favor of a national technocratic alternative and reached a settlement with all parties for a democratic constitution. This successful accord was due not simply to the neutrality of Tunisia's military but especially to the strong secular sensibilities in Tunisian society that al-Nahda took into account. Unlike the exclusivism of the Islamist Muslim Brothers in Egypt, who were fixated on their majoritarian dogma and the fantasy of establishing Islamist rule, al-Nahda's post-Islamism allowed it to embrace the idea of an inclusive and secular state while insisting on promoting a pious society.

The truth is, and this is a critical point, even if ruling groups such as al-Nahda and the Muslim Brotherhood wanted to monopolize power and establish a majoritarian rule (as the Islamist rulers did in the Iranian revolution), they would not have been able to succeed, precisely because of the de facto pluralism that refolutions tend to engender. In contrast to most twentieth-century revolutions in which the new revolutionary regimes, such as those in Cuba and Iran, could, once they seized the government, monopolize power and wipe out the old and new opposition in the name of "saving the revolution," in refolutions they find themselves surrounded by multiple power centers, including those sheltered in the institutions of the old state, supporters of previous regimes, diverse oppositional media outlets, and a new insurgent civil society. In other words, refolutions are by default pluralist. This de facto diffusion of power can potentially pave the way for an electoral democracy, provided that some sufficient legal, institutional, and social mechanisms are set in place to block the possible monopolization of power through coercion or election by the new rulers and restoration of the counterrevolution. And this may be possible by the incessant mobilization of the citizenry, the revolutionary opposition, not simply in the streets but in the key domains of political and social life where contestation for hegemony takes place. But this is what revolutionaries in Egypt and to a lesser degree in Tunisia avoided, leaving an opening for the rise of the free riders.

Losing to Free Riders

Political contestation and the struggle for hegemony in a society take place in multiple domains: the *state* in the sense of the government, bureaucracy, the military, the state media, and the like; the *political society* embodied in political parties, parliament, or municipality and local governance; the *civil society* as in associational life, NGOs, the syndicates, and collectives at places of work; the *street* in the sense of hegemony over public space, public order, and public opinion expressed in day-to-day idioms and acts; and the *private realm* of the individual, family, taste, and lifestyle. In reality these domains are not separated; they are connected and may overlap, with class, gender, and social clustering running through them. Different modes of state-society relations determine where most of the contestation occurs.

In times of revolution/insurrection, the fiercest battles take place in the streets, the locus where revolutionary breakthrough is achieved. Street politics, then, becomes the most critical battle frame in the exceptional episode of the revolution's life course. This exceptional episode is marked by a swift transformation of consciousness, utopia, and euphoria. It is these extraordinary moments—with their unique spatial, temporal, and cognitive elements—that inspire awe, offer inspiration, and bring the promise of a novel social order. Revolutionaries become masters of the streets at these transitory times; their initiatives, bravery, and sacrifice appear as if they herald the birth of a new historical epoch.

But revolution as insurrection is different from postrevolution—the day after the dictators abdicate. Whereas the street matters most in times of revolution/insurrection, it is the political society and state that reign in the postrevolution. While the exceptional episode, the insurrection, is the work of revolutionaries, postrevolutionary times give rise to free riders—those nonparticipants, the well-wishers, the benign, and the watchers of events or opportunists who assume immediate power the day after the dictators relinquish theirs. They come out, become visible and vocal, and make claims. Most crucially, they become the target of intense mobilization by the already-organized and equally free-riding groups and movements.

A paradox of the postrevolutionary period is that either the revolutionaries (banking on their political capital) impose their agenda through exclusionary populism (as in revolutions in Iran, Russia, China, and Ethiopia) without much regard for the will of the majority by such claims as, "We carried out the revolution, so we have the right to rule." Or if electoral democracy did matter, they might lose the political society to the free-rider majority whose votes can bring nonrevolutionaries to the centers of power. The fact is that revolutionaries are always in a minority, and revolutions are always carried out by a minority (in Egypt, only 11 percent), albeit a spectacular minority, exceptional and extraordinary players who master the art of insurrection.[32] Revolutions are won not because the majority of people fight the regimes but because only a tiny minority remains to resist.

But the street politics of revolutionary times shows its limitations when it is deployed in an electoral democracy. The protests in Cairo's Tahrir Square, Madrid's Puerta del Sol, and New York's Liberty Square were truly the most extraordinary expression of street politics in recent memory. But they were precisely that, *extraordinary*, which in ordinary times reveals their limitations; they cannot be sustained for a long span of time because of high moral and material cost, and their routinization would diminish their clout and efficacy. More to the point, these extraordinary struggles remain short-lived because they are by definition divorced from the business of everyday life. For instance, whereas the mobilization of Zapatistas in Chiapas or *horizontalidad* in Argentina was effectively part of the daily struggle for sustenance (campaign for land, workers' self-management for securing jobs, neighborhood self-rule for ensuring services), the extraordinary street politics of the Occupy movement and Tahrir were divorced from the daily business of ordinary lives and therefore could not be sustained. It is only expected for a poor street vendor in postrevolutionary

Tahrir to state, "I am telling those who are in this square . . . enough is enough! They should think of us; be merciful to us. We want to work; we are tired." For him, "we have nothing to do with the Constitution—their Constitution, our Constitution; their maidan, our maidan! What do I have to do with all this? We want work; we are tired."[33] Consequently, in postrevolutionary moments winners are not those who once created the wonders of Tahrir and its magical power but those who skillfully mobilize the mass of ordinary people, including the free riders, in small towns, farms, factories, and unions and at the ballot box.

It is true that democratic practice is not limited to the ballot box, and recent times have shown that liberal democratic institutions in many countries, including the West, have failed to represent the true wishes of large numbers of their citizens. But this should not be a cause to overcelebrate street politics or to romanticize extralegal acts. On the contrary, these acts are precisely the inescapable corollary of exclusion from, mistrust in, and failure of institutional politics in a volatile revolutionary mode—a tendency increasingly on display in many societies that have experienced popular protests in recent years. In postrevolutionary times, such institutions as political parties, genuine civil society, voting, parliament, and above all rule of law do matter—in fact they are the indispensable, but by no means sufficient, ingredients of building an inclusive polity that the revolutions seemed to aspire.

Whereas revolutionaries continued using the motto "the street is our way," thinking that "we can always come and sit-in [in Tahrir] if we find that our revolution is being hijacked," the religious parties in Tunisia and Egypt began to mobilize the free riders as soon as the dictators fell. Activists of al-Nahda along with its leader Rachid al-Ghannouchi traveled to the provinces, urban neighborhoods, and villages to hold meetings, establish branches, and build networks. Thousands attended these meetings.[34] In Egypt, groups like al-Gama'a al-Islamiyya, banned and banished under Mubarak, as well as the unassuming Salafis, emerged from seclusion and began to mobilize in earnest. The Muslim Brotherhood already had a well-established organization and vast network of cells, cadres, and local leaders throughout the country. They revitalized those networks in a more aggressive fashion in mosques, villages, and neighborhoods, often deploying their messages along with typical populist disbursals— handouts, food, and fuel. When the Gama'a al-Islamiyya held its first free rally in Masjid Adam in Ain Shams of Cairo, some four thousand attended.[35] Through such relentless work far away from Tahrir or Bourguiba Boulevard, the religious parties managed to score impressive victories in the constituent assemblies and parliamentary elections in 2011. They dominated political society through sidelining the left, liberal, and post-Islamist revolutionaries, as well as women, whose mass presence in the revolutions notwithstanding, ended up excluded from the centers of power.[36]

Thus, pushed away from state and political society, and with street politics running its course, the revolutionaries were bound to move into associational life in civil society if they were to continue their political engagement. But even this could not be guaranteed if the new state, once it consolidated itself, extended its surveillance into oppositional civil associations. And it would do so in the name of "safeguarding the revolution." We saw that the SCAF in Egypt in 2011 began to crack down on human rights organizations and nonconformist NGOs, banning some and curtailing others. The SCAF brought some twelve thousand revolutionaries before a military tribunal, subjecting many to prosecution and torture. The crackdown continued after General Sisi seized power in July 2013, boosting the counterrevolutionary efforts to restore the old order and its despised police and intelligence apparatus. It was then that some of the most celebrated revolutionaries, such as Alaa Abd el-Fattah, Ahmed Douma, and Mahinour el-Masry, were put behind bars while Mubarak was set free. Not just civil society organizations but even the sanctuary of the private realm should not be taken for granted, if there is anything to learn from the experience of the Iranian revolution of 1979 (when ordinary citizens were pressed by the new regime to defend the most mundane human rights—what color clothing to wear, what kind of music to listen to, and how much hair to show off beneath headscarves), or surveillance in Egypt of gays and atheists, the sexual assault of women, or scrutiny of social media and private communications.

The story of transition, or "revolution as change," in the Arab Spring has been the tale of conflicts, decline, and disenchantment. But this is not the entire story. The Arab Spring was also a "revolution as movement," that is, those monumental episodes of mobilization, solidarity and sacrifice, shift in consciousness, cognitive break from the past, and imagination of new possibilities—the effects that may keep the transition chapter unfinished and its narrative complex.

11   Revolution and Hope

Nothing as much as revolution simultaneously demands hope, inspires hope, and betrays hope. What then is the wisdom behind engaging in revolutions that may end up in despair? Are revolutions worthy of the enormous efforts needed to make them? Driven by extraordinary courage and commitment, the Arab uprisings championed a revolutionary episode in the world in which the very idea of revolution had ironically been disparaged. Opening a new chapter in the history of the Middle East, the uprisings toppled four entrenched dictators in Tunisia, Egypt, Yemen, and Libya and brought a fifth, Bashar al-Assad, to the brink; they shook the edifice of deep-seated autocrats, kings, and monarchical families, impelling them to buy their citizens' consent through cash or concessions. The sheikh of Kuwait made a cash gift of thirty-five hundred dollars to every citizen along with stacks of food vouchers; the Saudi king went further, pledging in March 2011 a $120 billion increase in social spending to cover housing subsidies, scholarships, pensions, and unemployment benefits; and the monarchs of Jordan and Morocco pushed for political reforms and amending the constitutions to allow for elected prime ministers. Meanwhile, the square politics the uprisings instigated and egalitarian community of maidan they crafted became a global brand, with the "Tahrir moment" imagined as if it were the "future in the present." After years of foreign occupation, domestic repression, and political stagnation, Arab citizens felt a fresh courage and confidence to envision something new for their political futures.

But this early hope and fervor were soon to turn into despair and disenchantment as the revolutions revealed their agonizing anomalies and the counterrevolution waged its sabotage. Rich as movement but poor as change, the Arab Spring lacked the kind of intellectual foundation and social-political radicalism that marked their twentieth-century Cuban, Iranian, and Nicaraguan counterparts. Their spectacular mobilization, inventive tactics, and nonviolent repertoires in Tunisia, Egypt, and Yemen failed to bring a radical break from the old order and meaningful change in the structure of the states. Key institutions of the ancien régimes and the power networks of the elites continued to operate, while the revolutionaries, sidelined by the more organized free riders, were ultimately pushed aside or repressed by the rising counterrevolution. The Arab revolutions occurred at very different political times from those of the 1970s—such as the Marxist insurgency in Yemen, Islamic revolution in Iran, and Sandinista insurrection in Nicaragua, all of which invariably were informed by anti-imperialist, anticapitalist, and social justice sentiments. The Arab Spring emerged in a postsocialist, post-Islamist, and neoliberal climate where the ideas of revolution, distributive justice, social rights, and class politics had been dispelled in favor of the pervasive idioms of civil society, NGOs, individual rights, democracy, and identity politics.

Yet not even these liberal idioms—which in fact had much appeal and import among the citizens suffering from repression and despotic rule—assumed much meaningful traction. The subaltern demands for distributive justice (jobs, land, housing, collective consumption) did not receive concrete support from the political class (whether neoliberal Islamist or secular), and the claims for dignity, democracy, and recognition were likewise frustrated both by intransigent Islamism and the custodians of the old order. But these claims did not disappear; they persisted, causing the postrevolutionary transition to be fraught with paradox, disruption, disenchantment, and counterrevolutionary intrigues. As the rival regional powers, chiefly Saudi Arabia, Iran, Qatar, and UAE, became apprehensive of the specter of democracy and loss of influence, they initiated both covert and overt operations to undermine the revolutions that were already suffering from their own limitations. Even though the revolutions in Tunisia, Egypt, and Yemen were largely peaceful, less repressive, and endowed with real potential for social and political pluralism, their refolutionary character, their failure to set a new social order, made them severely vulnerable in the face of counterrevolutionary restoration. Thus, little changed in the institutions of the old regimes, and the old elites behaved as if nothing like revolutions had swept through their societies. In Yemen, the power structure saw reshuffling of some personnel until the country descended into a civil and proxy war. Tunisia did achieve social and political pluralism, but its continuing neoliberal economy, social disparity, and regional instability posed a real threat to this nascent Arab democracy. The old elites mostly retained their status, disparaging the revolution as the "vengeance" of "street people," and Bouazizi as a nonhero, "scum."[1] And in Egypt, the ascendency of General Sisi to power in July 2013 paved the way for the revival of authoritarian rule, repression of dissent, and neglect of subaltern concerns.

The agony of transition—disruption, decline, and the defiance of the old order—could be expected to spark cynicism and even contempt about these otherwise monumental uprisings that not long before were poised to alter the fate of the region for good. Critics such as the Syrian philosopher Adonis charged revolutionaries with naïveté for limiting themselves to just toppling rulers without causing deep change.[2] Others, such as an Iranian blogger, once envious of the Arab Spring, wondered mockingly why we should be talking about it anymore when "Egypt has turned into semimilitary rule, Tunisian progressives are purged, Sunni-Shi'i dissension rages in Bahrain and Saudi Arabia, while Syria slides into ruin. . . . And Libya? No one remembers where Libya is."[3]

But it was quite a different feeling for the revolutionaries—those protagonists who once held high hopes for their remarkable uprisings but now had to face the vulgar triumphalism of counterrevolution, or the torment of exile and longing for their homeland if they had escaped the routine of arrest and incarceration.[4] A leading activist, frail and forgotten in the despair of exile, lamented that "a lot of us who played a role in history became but footnotes."[5] Deeply disenchanted, others mourned the death of their revolutions. "We thought we could change the world," an Egyptian activist reminisced in the wake of the Rabi'a Adawiyya massacre in June 2013. "How different things feel today. I will not bury our convictions, but that feeling (youthful optimism? naiveté? idealism? foolishness?) is now truly and irrevocably dead."[6]

Despair is neither surprising nor peculiar to the Arab revolutionaries. Most postrevolutionary moments are marked by ecstatic exhilaration followed by deep disappointment and demoralization. Hegel's celebrated work *The Phenomenology of Spirit* (1807) has been described as a historical philosophical mourning for the earlier defeat in the French Revolution. Scores of Russian revolutionaries attempted suicide when Stalin ascended to power in 1922, and despair overtook Iranian revolutionaries as the war with Iraq raged and the revolution under the Islamist state took a repressive turn in the 1980s. It is certainly an understatement to say that revolutions are never calm and clean episodes of transformation; rather, they are marred by inherent paradoxes that make strife and unrest the enduring features of their history. The destructive and despairing aftermath of the Arab revolutions may seem unique. But the conditions in postrevolutionary France, England, Russia, Nicaragua, or Iran were not very different, if not worse. A decade after the 1789 revolution, France sank into a bloody civil war that claimed hundreds of thousands of lives. Tens of thousands perished by execution and incarceration before Napoleon staged a military coup in 1899 to overturn the prospect for a republican France. The English revolution followed years of civil wars and destruction between 1642 and 1651. leaving two hundred thousand dead in a country that had no more than five million people. Soon after the 1917 revolution in Russia, strife erupted in 1918 between the Red Army and the counterrevolutionary "Whites" backed by Britain, the United States, France, Japan, and others, bringing death and devastation to millions of people. The first decade of the Iranian revolution saw an extensive disorder, economic sanctions, and a devastating war waged by neighboring Iraq that cost five hundred thousand lives, ruined cities, population displacement, and economic impairment. And Nicaragua went through a debilitating Contra War backed by US president Reagan, causing massive damage to the economy, society, and people's well-being. Indeed, much earlier, the great revolutionary Rosa Luxemburg had gone so far as to suggest that "revolution is the only form of 'war' in which the ultimate victory can be prepared only by a series of defeats."[7]

Despair and disenchantment usually come as natural reactions when expectations are betrayed and dreams shattered. What is not natural, however, is disengagement. For disengagement forgets that something as momentous as a revolution has happened—something that has unsettled the foundation of the status quo and now could shape a society that is fundamentally different from its prerevolutionary condition. Of course, things will often appear to have gone back to normal as people carry on with their mundane routines—working, shopping, visiting friends, or going on vacations. Those who expect rupture and resistance would no doubt be dispirited by such brutal inertia of the everyday. But one should not be deceived or disheartened by the seeming normalcy, for in substance it may not necessarily be a measure of popular consent or compliance. Rather, it could be driven by the inner force of life itself, expressed in an urge for self-regulation; it could further serve as a technique of survival in rough times, the old-fashioned art of creating one's own reality in the shadow of authoritarian rule, as if the populace is in compliance and the regime in control. But Egypt, Tunisia, and their revolutionary counterparts have experienced an "event" in the sense noted by Alain Badiou, extraordinary social happenings that have impregnated these lands with open-ended possibilities. And it is here in this realm of possibilities that disengagement shed its relevance, whereas revolutionism finds new vistas. Recognizing these possibilities and acting on them is what I call hope. Thus, hope is neither the same as naïve optimism that remains disengaged nor, of course, the blind despair that is entrapped in cynicism. Rather, it is an indispensable moral resource that can guide one toward imagining and working for alternative futures.

But one should also take seriously Badiou's warning that such "condition of infinity," the new consciousness and possibilities, if it fails to translate into alternative polity can vanish before the "finitude," or the deeply entrenched old order and its benefactors, because the old and the entrenched are easier to restore than the new to cultivate.[8] The custodians of the ancien régime, the counterrevolutionaries, would likely remain determined to regain the state machine, monopolize power, restrain genuine civil society, and revive the neoliberal economy. They will likely utter and appropriate the rhetoric of revolution while striving to reconstitute the old order. And in this they may even rely on a survival ideology that blends national chauvinism with neoliberal globalism, on the one hand, and a conservative religiosity and moral politics, on the other. Yet revolutions often stubbornly resist their own ending, for they tend to propel new expectations and outlooks and engender unexpected dynamics. Some thirty-five years after Iran's revolution, its social transformation—by youth, women, and an insurgent new public—continues to deepen in spite, or perhaps because, of the intransigent Islamist state. There are already signs that only after three years in Egypt, the invincible General Sisi and his regime have faced critical challenges. Extraordinary repression has incurred heavy costs, instigating mass riots (as we saw in Darb al-Ahmar against police brutality), individual heroic acts, and elite discord. The general has been criticized in the state media for his failures; students and workers have resumed activism; political prisoners and those in exile are reexamining revolutionary visions in a more systematic fashion; and the state failure in delivering basic necessities has invited mass discontent once again.[9] In May 2015, an indignant Cairo taxi driver, the father of four and resident of the 'ashwa'iyat, who "barely managed life," could exclaim "there is no revolution anymore" when I asked him about the "news of the revolution." But a "second revolution will soon come; this time, the revolution of the hungry." The Arab revolutions may have brought an end to the sinister pattern of lifelong presidencies, and the new awareness they have spurred and the stealthy social change they have caused may disorient the autocratic rule.[10]

These new regimes have to govern a citizenry that has been significantly transformed, while the chief economic, social, and political factors—authoritarian rule, neoliberal economies, exclusion, unemployment, violation of dignity, insurgent urbanity—that lay at the root of the uprisings remain predominantly unaddressed. Large segments of the urban and rural poor, industrial laborers, impoverished middle classes, marginalized and unemployed youth, women and citizens with counter-normal identities have experienced, however briefly, rare moments of feeling free, engaged in unfettered spaces for self-realization, local self-rule, and collective jubilation. As a consequence, some of the most entrenched hierarchies were challenged. Women's extraordinary public presence threatened patriarchal sensibilities, and their public harassment in Egypt produced one of the most genuine movements in the nation's recent history. Revolutionary youths charged their elders with apathy and complicity at the same time that they gained the respect and recognition of the older generation for their own remarkable activism and sacrifice. Workers demanded accountability from bosses, farmers from chiefs, students from mentors, and citizens from the moral and political authorities. The idea and practice of independent unions gained new momentum in both Egypt and Tunisia. There were times when communal solidarity was resurrected ingeniously in the midst of well-organized sectarian bloodshed. These subaltern citizens all lived through revolutionary moments in which "what was right seemed wrong, and what wrong seemed right."

The memories of those extraordinary episodes and the moral resources they generated have become part of the popular consciousness. They could serve as the normative foundation to imagine and build a "good society" of inclusive social order that is concerned with solidarity, egalitarian ethos, and social justice—one that ejects rather than assumes the neoliberal dogma. Even if the reform of authoritarian states needs a different set of painstaking struggles, change in society's sensibilities remains a precondition for far-reaching democratic transformation. In this sense, revolution as such is more than simply regime change and the indispensable reform of the state. The reform of the state—however valuable and critical it may be in its own right—is also meant to foster and facilitate creating a novel, inclusive, and egalitarian social order. Following Gramsci, it should be possible to work on such a project even under the shadow of authoritarian states and neoliberal economies. I have suggested that the idea may begin with building an "active citizenry" endowed with the "art of presence"—a citizenry that possesses the courage and creativity to assert collective will in spite of all odds by circumventing constraints, utilizing what is possible, and discovering new spaces within which to make themselves heard, seen, felt, and realized.[11]

In truth, there is a limit to how much states, even authoritarian ones, can control societies without turning totalitarian, such as communist East Germany, where the secret police (Stasi) kept files on one-third of the total population. Ironically, there may be more favorable spaces to pursue this strategy in such settings as Egypt or Tunisia than under the liberal democratic "hard" states like the United States, where the apparatuses of surveillance, legal or technical, seem to be much more pervasive and detailed than those in the repressive but "soft" states in the Middle East. In the Middle Eastern societies there remain vast informal socioscapes, the "free zones" within which alternative norms and narratives counter to state logic may be instituted. Informal life, the relations and institutions that lie at the margin of state control, make up a vast swath of social existence where some of the most creative (as well as criminal) endeavors take shape, as shown in the circles of cliques, kin members, and friends or among those who operate on the local level in communities and informal worksites. The realms of the art world, intellectual circles, book publishing, cultural production, new social media, independent journalism, the legal and architecture professions, and social work may also produce alternative speech and unorthodox ways of being and doing things. Even state-regulated institutions such as schools, colleges, municipalities, neighborhood associations, city councils, student clubs, workers' unions, and professional syndicates often turn, by critical and creative users, into spaces where some core social and political values are contested. It was in such institutions where the followers of the Turkish spiritual leader Fethullah Gülen found fertile ground to assert their presence and where they challenged the government of Recep Tayyip Erdogan in the early 2010s. After all, how can we explain, as discussed previously, the sudden and surprising upsurge of the Arab revolts at a time when few questioned the invincibility of the Arab regimes and their authoritarian durability without understanding how the active citizenry used, operated, and created their own realities within their "uncivil societies," those socioscapes of cliques and collectives that lay between the Habermasian public and private spheres, while the social and political order appeared as if business was going on as usual?

Active citizenry of this sort, in the meantime, is bound to subvert the ability of the authoritarian state to govern because the state usually rules not from above or outside society but from within by weaving its logic—through norms, relations, and institutions—into the social fabric. Challenging those norms, relations, and institutions would by definition diminish the state's legitimacy and impair its ability to govern. In fact, an active citizenry could go even further to possibly impel and even acclimatize the state to behave in line with the values the subaltern citizens may cultivate in society. It is not surprising that the prohibition law in the United States looked absurd when by the early 1930s numerous citizens were unlawfully consuming alcohol; the law had to change. The absurdity of preventing women from driving should be clear even to the Saudi rulers, who cannot help seeing women capable of doing what men can. An authoritarian state cannot govern for long and with a measure of normalcy a citizenry that moves ahead of its statesmen in ideas and in deeds.

Does this way of thinking mean that we are back to the old ways? In a sense we are if we assume that the old order strives hard to return to business. But something is fundamentally different: These are the old ways in new times—when the old order faces new political subjects and novel subjectivities; when the memories of sacrifice, the taste of triumph, and betrayal of aspirations are likely to turn quiet but lingering mass discontent into periodic social upheavals. These are uncharted political moments loaded with indefinite possibilities in which meaningful social engagement would demand a creative fusion of the old and new ways of doing politics.

But are revolutions worthy of so much love, labor, sorrow, and sacrifice when there is no certainty that they will bring a just and free social order?[12] Is it sensible to be in the business of making revolutions that may end up in despair? These are indeed reasonable questions, but how plausible are they? As the revolutionary leader Leon Trotsky reminds us, in truth "people do not make revolution eagerly any more than they do war. While in war compulsion plays the decisive role, in revolution there is no compulsion except that of circumstances. A revolution takes place only when there is no other way out."[13] In other words, we rarely decide to make revolutions willingly and voluntarily; rather, we are conditioned and compelled to make them.[14] If there is a truism in this peculiar and painful dialectic, then it is only plausible to embrace and deepen the revolutions when they actually occur. For there is much more to these historical events than simply pain and price, and revolutions mean more than just regime change or institutional alteration, though these remain an indispensable part of them. I am thinking of a more complex understanding of revolution along the lines of what Raymond Williams called the "long revolution"—a process that is "difficult" in the sense of being composite and multifaceted; "total," meaning not just political and economic but also social and cultural transformation; and "human," involving the deepest structures of relationships and feelings.[15] Consequently, rather than look for quick results or worry about set demands, we might view the Arab uprisings as long revolutions that may bear fruit in ten or twenty years by establishing new ways of doing things, a new way of thinking about power and citizens' rights. This is not an unreasonable outlook. But at stake are not merely semantic concerns about how to define revolutions but the hard problems of power structures and entrenched interests. However one characterizes the process—as long revolution or as one that begins with the rapid and radical transformation of the state—the crucial question is how to ensure a fundamental shift from the old oligarchy and authoritarian order to inaugurate meaningful democratic and egalitarian change while eschewing violent coercion and repression; how to ensure that the radical impulses of the social, the ideals of inclusion, equity, and justice would remain at the core of the new thinking. These are fundamental and formidable questions for which sensible responses are yet to be determined. One thing, however, is certain: The journey from the oppressive "old" to the liberatory "new" will not come about without relentless struggle and persistent popular engagement both in public and private, in ideas and in practice, individually and collectively. For revolution involves a fundamental rethinking of power, a radical reimagination of our social order, and envisioning a society informed by the ideals of sharing, caring, egalitarian ethos, and inclusive democracy.[16] Indeed, the long revolution may have to begin even when the short revolution ends.

Notes

Chapter 1

1. Misagh Parsa, *Social Origins of the Iranian Revolution* (New Brunswick, NJ: Rutgers University Press, 1989); Mohsen Milani, *The Making of Iran's Islamic Revolution: From Monarchy to Islamic Republic* (Boulder, CO: Westview Press, 1988); Shaul Bakhash, *The Reign of the Ayatollahs: Iran and the Islamic Revolution* (New York: Basic Books, 1990).

2. Ayatollah Ruhollah Khomeini, *Islamic Government*, 3rd ed. (Tehran: Institute for Compilation and Publication of Imam Khomeini's Works, 2008).

3. See Hamid Dabashi, *Theology of Dissent: The Ideological Foundation of the Islamic Revolution in Iran* (New York: Transaction Publishers, 2005).

4. Asef Bayat, *Street Politics: Poor People's Movements in Iran* (New York: Columbia University Press, 1997).

5. Robin Wright, *The Last Great Revolution: Turmoil and Transformation in Iran* (New York: Vintage, 2001).

6. This section draws on Fred Halliday, *Arabia without Sultans* (London: Saqi Books, 2002), pp. 153–226.

7. Fred Halliday, "The People's Democratic Republic of Yemen: The 'Cuban Path' in Arabia," in *Revolutionary Socialist Development in the Third World*, ed. G. White, R. Murray, and C. White (Sussex, UK: Wheatsheaf Books), pp. 35–73.

8. Maxine Molyneux, Aida Yafai, Aisha Mohsen, and Noor Ba'abadd, "Women and Revolution in the People's Democratic Republic of Yemen," *Feminist Review* 1 (1979): 4–20.

9. Halliday, *Arabia without Sultans*, pp. 208–209.

10. Ibid., pp. 320–321; see also John Chalcraft, "Migration and Popular Protests in the Arabian Peninsula and the Gulf in the 1950s and 1960s," in "Labor Migration to the Middle East," special issue, *International Labor and Working-Class History* 79, no. 1 (Spring 2011): 28–47.

11. Halliday, *Arabia without Sultans*, p. 330.

12. Abdel Razzaq Takriti, *Monsoon Revolution: Republicans, Sultans, and Empire in Oman, 1965–1976* (Oxford: Oxford University Press, 2013).

13. Ibid.

14. Fred Halliday reports on the Iranian Marxist Shokrullah Paknejad's relations with the Palestinian militants. See Halliday, *Arabia without Sultans*; see also Maziar Behrooz, *Rebel with a Cause: Left Failure in Iran* (London: I. B. Tauris, 1999). On Islamists' regional connections, like Gholam-Hussein Chamran's to Lebanon, see Roscanack Shaery-Eisenlohr, *Shi'te Lebanon: Transnational Religion and the Making of National Identities* (New York: Columbia University Press, 2008).

15. Henry Weber, *Nicaragua: The Sandinista Revolution* (London: Verso, 1981).

16. *Nicaragua: An Unfinished Revolution*, part 2, Al Jazeera television documentary film, July 27, 2009, https://www.youtube.com/watch?v=URdzoDrp-Ss.

17. Carlos Vilas, *The Sandinista Revolution* (New York: Monthly Review Press, 1986).

18. Asef Bayat, *Work, Politics, and Power* (New York: Monthly Review Press, 1991).

19. Gregory Gause, "Why Middle East Studies Missed the Arab Spring: The Myth of Authoritarian Stability," *Foreign Affairs*, July–August 2011, https://www.foreignaffairs.com/articles/middle-east/2011-07-01/why-middle-east-studies-missed-arab-spring.

20. Adam Hanieh, *Lineages of Revolt: Issues of Contemporary Capitalism in the Middle East* (Chicago: Haymarket Books, 2013), p. 153.

21. Nicholas Noe, "Another Middle Eastern State Could Collapse, and More Cash and Weapons Won't Save It," *Tablet Magazine*, accessed December 11, 2016, http://www.tabletmag.com/jewish-news-and-politics/193723/tunisia-refugee-crisis.

22. "The Protester," special issue, *Time Magazine*, December 26, 2012.

23. See Luiz Inácio Lula de Silva, "The Message of Brazil's Youth," *New York Times*, July 16, 2013.

24. See Manuel Castells, *Networks of Outrage and Hope: Social Movements in the Internet Age* (Cambridge: Polity Press, 2012), p. 160.

25. Martin Gilens and Benjamin Page, "Testing Theories of American Politics: Elites, Interest Groups, and Average Citizens," *Perspectives on Politics* 12, no. 3 (September 2014): 564–581.

26. Todd Gitlin, *Occupy Nation: The Roots, the Spirit, and the Promise of Occupy Wall Street* (New York: itBooks, 2012).

27. Castells, *Networks of Outrage and Hope*, p. 144; Sidney Tarrow, "Why Occupy Wall Street Is Not the Tea Party of the Left," *Foreign Affairs*, October 10, 2011.

28. For an account of anarchist politics, see Richard F. Day, *Gramsci Is Dead: Anarchist Currents in the Newest Social Movements* (London: Pluto Press, 2005).

29. Matt Ford, "A Dictator's Guide to Urban Design," *Atlantic Monthly*, February 2014.

30. But it is important to note that whatever the nature of the OWS, US security officials expressed concerns and carried out thorough surveillance to monitor its activists. Some seventy-eight intelligence-sharing offices known as "fusion centers" (funded by Homeland Security) gathered, shared, and disseminated information about the movement. It produced some four thousand pages of classified e-mails and reports, obtaining information through social media, websites, and police reports. Reporters kept track of details of individual activists, supporters, and recruitment in social media. See Colin Moynihan, "Officials Cast Wide Net in Monitoring Occupy Protests," *New York Times*, May 23, 2014.

31. Saad Eddin Ibrahim, "Thawra om Enqilab? Tasht om Qanat?," *Al-Masry al-Youm*, August 21, 2015.

32. Jack Goldstone, "Understanding the Revolutions of 2011," *Foreign Affairs*, May–June 2011.

33. Jack Goldstone, *Revolutions: A Very Short Introduction* (Oxford: Oxford University Press, 2014), p. 130.

34. Crane Brinton, *The Anatomy of Revolution* (New York: Vintage, 1938).

35. Jeroen Gunning and Ilan Baron, *Why Occupy a Square? People, Protests and Movements in the Egyptian Revolution* (Oxford: Oxford University Press, 2014), pp. 5–8, 211–212.

36. Gilbert Achcar, *The People Want: A Radical Explanation of the Arab Uprising* (Berkeley: University of California Press, 2013), pp. 4, 153.

37. Jean-Pierre Filiu, *From Deep State to Islamic State: The Arab Counter-revolution and Its Jihadi Legacy* (London: Hearst, 2014).

38. The "deep state" is defined as "unaccountable, unelected elites that exert control over elected or civilian officials." See David Faris, "Deep State, Deep Crisis: Egypt and American Policy," *Middle East Policy Council* 20, no. 4 (2013): pp. 99–110.

39. Kamal Zaghbani, "Al-Thawra al-Tunisia: Al-Thawra al-Mobdaiyya," in special issue on the Tunisian revolution, *al-Kitab al-Okhra* 3 (August 2012): 219.

40. Wael Ghoneim, *Revolution 2.0: The Power of the People Is Greater Than the People in Power* (New York: Houghton Mifflin Harcourt, 2012), p. 293.

41. Ivan Krastev, "From Politics to Protest," *Journal of Democracy* 25, no. 4 (October 2014): 6, 16.

42. Ibid., pp. 5–19. Manuel Castells likewise considers the social upheavals since 2011—both the Arab revolutions and Occupy movements—of the same type shaped by our current "network society," so these are "networked social movements" that brought together dissenters through social media. This approach also misses the historical contexts of these different societies, such as Arab countries ruled by autocrats and those governed by liberal democracy. See Castells, *Networks of Outrage and Hope*, pp. x, 220.

43. See video debate between Noam Chomsky and Michel Foucault, "On Human Nature," March 13, 2013, https://www.youtube.com/watch?v=3wfNl2LoGf8.

44. Gauri Viswanathan, ed., *Power, Politics, and Culture: Interviews with Edward Said* (New York: Vintage, 2001), pp. 53–54.

45. Zsuzsa Gille, "Is There a Global Postsocialist Condition?," *Global Society* 24, no. 1 (2010): 9–30.

46. See Jo Freeman, "The Tyranny of Structurelessness," 1970, http://struggle.ws/pdfs/tyranny.pdf; for the resurrection of anarchism in social movements, see Gitlin, *Occupy Nation*, pp. 80–91.

47. Crane Ross, *The Leaderless Revolution: How Ordinary People Will Take Power and Change Politics in the 21st Century* (New York: Blue Rider Press, 2011), p. 59.

48. The US government established dozens of "intelligence-sharing offices" to monitor the activists of the OWS. Only thanks to the efforts of WikiLeaks and Edward Snowden (especially the film *Citizenfour*, directed by Laura Poitras) has the public acquired some limited idea about how the states think in certain domains of political life.

49. Emel Akcali, ed., *Neoliberal Governmentality and the Future of the State in the Middle East and North Africa* (London: Palgrave, 2016).

50. Mitchell Dean, "Rethinking Neoliberalism," *Journal of Sociology* 50, no. 2 (2014): 150–163.

51. The Foucauldian reading has produced a host of discussions on neoliberalism as a form of governmentality; see, for instance, Stuart Hall, "The Neoliberal Revolution," *Cultural Studies* 25, no. 6 (2011): 705–728.

52. See David Harvey, *A Brief History of Neoliberalism* (Oxford: Oxford University Press, 2005); M. Steger and R. K. Roy, *Neoliberalism: A Very Short Introduction* (Oxford: Oxford University Press, 2010).

53. Harvey, *A Brief History of Neoliberalism*.

54. Naomi Klein, *Shock Doctrine: The Rise of Disaster Capitalism* (New York: Random House, 2007).

55. Pierre Dardot and Christian Laval, *The New Way of the World: On Neoliberal Society* (London: Verso, 2014); Thomas Piketty, *Capital in the Twenty-First Century* (Cambridge, MA: Harvard University Press, 2014).

56. Deborah Hardoon, *Wealth: Having It All and Wanting More* (Oxford: Oxfam, 2015), *https://www.oxfam.org/sites/www.oxfam.org/files/file_attachments/ib-wealth-having-all-wanting-more-190115-en.pdf*.

57. The UN and the World Bank report on the state of development in the world in 2013. Anup Shah, "Poverty Facts and Stats," *Global Issues*, January 7, 2013, http://www.globalissues.org/article/26/poverty-facts-and-stats.

58. The average gross national product growth rate for selected Middle Eastern countries during the 1970–1979 period were as follows: Egypt, 7.6 percent; Iran,

22.2 percent; Saudi Arabia, 37.2 percent; Turkey, 15.1 percent; Kuwait, 22.6 percent; Syria, 15.4 percent; Iraq, 28.8 percent; Jordan, 19.6 percent. See "World Tables 1991," in *IMF International Financial Statistics Yearbook 1994, 1996* (Washington, DC: IMF Publications, 1996).

59. Hazem Biblawi, "Rentier State in the Arab World," in *The Arab State*, ed. G. Luciani (London: Routledge, 1990), pp. 49–62.

60. Asef Bayat, "Activism and Social Development in the Middle East," *International Journal of Middle East Studies* 34, no. 1 (2002): 1.

61. Ibid., p. 4.

62. UNDP, *Arab Human Development Reports* (New York: United Nations Development Program, 2002–2009).

63. Hanieh, *Lineage of Revolt*, pp. 145–149.

64. "0.3% of Lebanese Own 50% of Lebanon," *A Separate State of Mind* (blog), posted on February 18, 2015, https://stateofmind13.com/2015/02/18/0-3-of-lebanese -own-50-of-lebanon/.

65. According to a Wealth X report, accessed February 21, 2017, http://www .wealthx.com/reports/.

66. Timothy Mitchell, "Dreamland: The Neoliberalism of Your Desires," in *The Journey to Tahrir: Revolution, Protest, and Social Change in Egypt*, ed. Jeannie Sowers and Chris Toensing (London: Verso, 2012), pp. 224–234; Galal Amin, *Whatever Happened to the Egyptian Revolution?* (Cairo: American University in Cairo Press, 2013). On Amman and Beirut, see Najib Hourani, "Neoliberal Urbanism and the Arab Uprisings: A View from Amman," in special issue of *Journal of Urban Affairs* 36, no. s2 (2014): 650–662, doi:10.1111/juaf.12136.

67. J. Kinninmont, "Bread and Dignity," *World Today*, August–September 2011, pp. 31–33.

68. Alan Richards and John Waterbury, *A Political Economy of the Middle East* (Boulder, CO: Westview Press, 2007), p. 268. For a more thorough analysis, see John Walton and David Seddon, *Free Markets and Food Riots* (London: Blackwell, 1994).

69. Paul Aarts, Pieter van Dijke, Iris Kolman, Jort Statema, and Ghassan Dahhan, *From Resilience to Revolt: Making Sense of the Arab Spring* (Amsterdam: University of Amsterdam, Department of Political Science, 2012), p. 34.

70. Habib Ayeb, "Social and Geopolitical Geography of the Tunisian Revolution," *Review of African Political Economy* 38, no. 129 (September 2011): 473–485.

71. See, for instance, Amin, *Whatever Happened to the Egyptian Revolution?*; Joel Beinin and Frederic Vairel, eds., *Social Movements, Mobilization, and Contestation in the Middle East and North Africa*, 2nd ed. (Stanford, CA: Stanford University Press, 2013); Achcar, *The People Want*; Hanieh, *Lineage of Revolt*; Ayeb, "Social and Geopolitical Geography of the Tunisian Revolution"; Hourani, "Neoliberal Urbanism and the Arab Uprisings," pp. 650–662; Najib Hourani, "Urbanism and

Neoliberal Order: The Development and Redevelopment of Amman," in special issue, *Journal of Urban Affairs* 36, no. s2 (2014): 634–639; Najib Hourani and Ahmed Kanna, "Arab Cities in the Neoliberal Moment," in special issue, *Journal of Urban Affairs* 36, no. s2 (2014): 600–604; Gunning and Baron, *Why Occupy a Square?*

72. Dardot and Laval, *The New Way of the World*. See also W. Larner, "Neoliberalism: Policy, Ideology, Governmentality," *Studies in Political Economy* 63 (2000): 5–26; Hall, "The Neoliberal Revolution," pp. 705–728; Stuart Hall, Doreen Massey, and Michael Rustin, eds., *After Neoliberalism? The Kilburn Manifesto* (London: Lawrence and Wishart, 2013), *https://www.lwbooks.co.uk/soundings/kilburn -manifesto*; Harvey, *A Brief History of Neoliberalism*, pp. 175–176.

73. George Monbiot, "Neoliberalism: The Ideology at the Root of All Our Problems," *The Guardian*, April 15, 2016.

74. Klein, *The Shock Doctrine*.

75. Dardot and Laval, *The New Way of the World*.

76. Pierre Bourdieu, "The Essence of Neoliberalism," *Le Monde diplomatique*, December 1998, http://mondediplo.com/1998/12/08bourdieu.

77. Byung-Cul Han, "Why Revolution Is No Longer Possible," *Open Democracy*, October 23, 2015, https://www.opendemocracy.net/transformation/byung -chul-han/why-revolution-is-no-longer-possible; Colin Crouch, Klaus Eder, and Damian Tambini, eds., *Citizenship, Markets, and the State* (Oxford: Oxford University Press, 2001). The psychologist Paul Verhaeghe has even spoken of the pathology of the neoliberal personality—someone who fiercely competes, is "articulate" in telling lies without guilt, and is "infantilized," jealous of others for trivial things but suffers constant self-doubt and insecurity. See Paul Verhaeghe, "Neoliberalism Has Brought Out the Worst in Us," *The Guardian*, September 29, 2014. "Activist capitalism," according to the *Economist*, is groups of investors "campaigning" to change a firm's strategy to acquire broader participation or remove managers. "Activists are not . . . tree-huggers who dislike what your company does to the atmosphere. They are hedge-funds that seek to shake up your company's management." *The Economist*, February 7, 2015, p. 21.

78. Javier Lewkowicz, "Post-neoliberalism: Lessons from South America," *Open Democracy*, February 9, 2015.

79. J. G. Castañeda, "Latin America's Left Turn," *Foreign Affairs*, June 7, 2006.

80. See a fine study by Murat Arsel, "Between 'Marx and Markets'? The State, the 'Left Turn' and Nature in Ecuador," *Tijdschrift voor Economische en Sociale Geografie* (Journal of economic and social geography),103, no. 2 (2012): 151.

81. Reported in Ellie Mae O'Hagan, "Evo Morales Has Proved That Socialism Doesn't Damage Economies," *The Guardian*, October 14, 2014.

82. Lewkowicz, "Post-neoliberalism."

83. Forrest Colburn and Alberto Trejos, cited in Murat Arsel, "Between Marx and Markets?," p. 151.

84. Arsel, "Between 'Marx and Markets'?," p. 151.

85. Arturo Escobar, "Latin America at a Crossroads," *Cultural Studies* 24 (2010): 1.

86. *The Guardian*, June 11, 2013, opinion page. The mass discontent in Greece and Spain was an important reminder of the deep scars the austerity policies and debt had inflicted on southern Europe, pushing, at least in Greece, for a new government that openly proclaimed its anticapitalism.

87. James Ferguson, *Anti-politics Machine* (Minneapolis: University of Minnesota Press, 1994).

Chapter 2

1. Maziar Behrooz, *Rebels with a Cause: The Failure of the Left in Iran* (London: I. B. Tauris, 2000).

2. Ervand Abrahamian, *Iran between Two Revolutions* (Princeton, NJ: Princeton University Press, 1981), pp. 484–485.

3. Behrooz, *Rebels with a Cause*.

4. Ervand Abrahamian, *Radical Islam: The Mujahedin of Iran* (London: I. B. Tauris, 1989).

5. Ahmad Rezaei, *Nehzat-e Husseini* (Tehran: Mujahedin Khalq Organization, 1976).

6. Abrahamian, *Radical Islam*.

7. Behrooz, *Rebel with a Cause*; Abrahamian, *Iran between Two Revolutions*, p. 480.

8. Nozar Alaolmolki, "The New Iranian Left," *Middle East Journal* 41, no. 2 (Spring 1987): 218–233.

9. Asef Bayat, "Revolution without Movement, Movement without Revolution: Comparing Islamic Activism in Iran and Egypt," *Comparative Studies in Society and History* 40, no. 1 (Spring 1988), pp. 136–169.

10. For a detailed discussion of "Islamic ideology" before the Iranian revolution, see Hamid Dabashi, *Theology of Discontent: The Ideological Foundation of the Islamic Revolution in Iran* (New York: New York University Press, 1993).

11. Ayatollah Ruhollah Khomeini, *Hokumat-e Eslami: Eslam Din-e Siyasat Ast* [Islamic government] (N.p.: N.p., 1970).

12. Sayyid Qutb, *Milestones* (New Delhi: Islamic Book Service, 2002).

13. Ibid.

14. Quoted in Roxanne Euben and Muhammad Qasim Zaman, eds., *Princeton Readings in Islamist Thought: Texts and Contexts from al-Banna to Bin Laden* (Princeton, NJ: Princeton University Press, 2009), p. 143.

15. John Calvert, *Sayyid Qutb and the Origins of Radical Islamism* (New York: Columbia University Press, 2010), p. 16.

16. Sayyid Qutb, "The America I Have Seen," Kashf ul Shubuhat Publications, 1951, https://archive.org/stream/SayyidQutb/The%20America%20I%20have%20seen_djvu.txt.

17. Sayyid Qutb, *Social Justice in Islam* (New York: Islamic Publications International, 2000).

18. Calvert, *Sayyid Qutb*, p. 161.

19. Sayyid Qutb, *Ma'rekah al Islam wa Ra's-al Maliyya*, 14th ed. (Cairo: Dal al-Shorouk, 2006), pp. 109–112.

20. See, for example, Ervand Abrahamian ,"Ali Shariati: Ideologue of the Iranian Revolution," *MERIP Reports* 102 (1982), http://www.merip.org/mer/mer102/ali-shariati-ideologue-iranian-revolution; Mangol Bayat, "Iran's Real Revolutionary Leader," *Christian Science Monitor*, May 24, 1977; Mehdi Abedi, "Ali Shariati: The Architect of the 1970 Islamic Revolution in Iran," *Iranian Studies* 19, no. 3–4 (Summer–Autumn 1986), pp. 229–234.

21. See Hamid Algar, "Preface," in Ali Shariati, *Marxism and Other Western Fallacies* (Berkeley, CA: Mizan Press, 1980).

22. Bayat, "Iran's Real Revolutionary Leader."

23. Parts of this section draw on Asef Bayat, "Karl Marx and Ali Shariati: A Critique of an Islamic Critique of Marxism," *Alif: Journal of Comparative Poetics* 9 (April 1990): 19–41.

24. The earlier writings on Shariati tended to focus more on describing his ideas than on systematic critical evaluation. In the late 1970s a pamphlet appeared in Tehran under a pseudonym, Ali Akbar Akbari (possibly he was Ehsan Tabari, the chief ideologue of the Iranian Communist Party), titled *Barrasi-ye Chand Mas'ale-ye Ijtimaii* (An evaluation of some social issues). This work examines Shariati's critique of a mechanical type of Marxism, ignoring the more critical and sophisticated types.

Some earlier works, in English, that discuss Shariati and his ideas include Bayat, "Iran's Real Revolutionary Leader"; Abedi, "Ali Shariati"; A. Sachedina, "Ali Shariati: Ideologue of the Iranian Revolution," in *Voices of Resurgent Islam*, ed. J. L. Esposito (New York: Oxford University Press, 1983), pp. 191–214; Abrahamian, "Ali Shariati"; Hamid Enayat, *Modern Islamic Political Thought* (Austin: University of Texas Press, 1982), pp. 53–59; Sharokh Akhavi, "Islam, Politics and Society in the Thought of Ayatollah Khomeini, Ayatollah Taliqani and Ali Shariati," *Middle Eastern Studies* 24, no. 4 (October 1988):404–431; Ervand Abrahamian, *Radical Islam: Mujahedin of Iran* (New Haven, CT: Yale University Press, 1989), chap. 4. More recent discussions can be found in Kamran Matin, *Recasting Iranian Modernity: International Relations and Social Change* (London: Routledge, 2013).

25. In a celebration in Istanbul in 2013, the forty-sixth volume of Shariati's col-

lected works was published. At least 70 percent of his works have been translated into Arabic, his book *The Return* is claimed to have sold one hundred thousand copies in Egypt during the 1980s. See interview with Sousan Shariati, Beytoote weblog, 2016, http://www.beytoote.com/news/cultural-news/jnews7142.html.

26. These biographical notes have drawn on Abrahamian, *Radical Islam*, chap. 4.

27. See Abedi, "Ali Shariati," p. 230.

28. As a reaction to those attacks, I, an undergraduate student studying politics, wrote a response and sent it to the mosque that had organized those lively evening lectures. On the last night of the lectures, Ayatollah Mutahhari discussed my letter.

29. Ali Shariati, *Jahatgiri-ye Tabaqati-e Islam* [Class bias of Islam], in *Collected Works* (Tehran: N.p., 1980), 10:16.

30. The English version of the text was published in the United States under the title *Marxism and Other Western Fallacies*. I was able to read the original text in Persian in Tehran in 1977, and I find some considerable differences of tone and emphasis, as well as some omissions between this English version and the original text. For instance, the Persian text ends with this famous disclaimer by Marx: "I am Marx; I am not a Marxist," referring to Marx's frustration with his contemporary Marxists who distorted his ideas. Such a statement does not appear in the book in English. See Bayat, "Karl Marx and Ali Shariati," 19–41.

31. Cited by Abdelkaraim Soroush, public lecture, Queen's University, Kingston, Canada, March 14, 2015.

32. Abrahamian, *Radical Islam*, chap. 4.

33. Shariati, *Marxism and Other Western Fallacies*, p. 21.

34. The notion is quite similar to Marx's Hegelian metaphor of the development of class from being "in itself" to "for itself."

35. Akhavi, "Islam, Politics and Society," p. 407.

36. Ali Shariati, *Entizar* [Awaiting] (Tehran: N.p., 1979), p. 1; Ali Shariati, *What Is to Be Done: The Enlightened Thinkers and an Islamic Renaissance* (Houston, TX: Institute for Research and Islamic Studies, 1986), pp. 9–23.

37. Abrahamian, *Radical Islam*, chap. 4.

38. Muhammad Sahimi, "Shariati on Religious Government," *Tehran Bureau*, August 31, 2009.

39. From Shariati, *Islamology* (N.p., 1972), cited in Abrahamian, *Radical Islam*, p. 117.

40. Ali Shariati, *Jahatgiri-ye Tabaqati-e Islam*, 10:37–38.

41. Ali Shariati, "Bazyabi-ye Huwiyyat-e Irani-Islami," in *Collected Works*, 27:304–305 (translation is mine).

42. J. Nyerere, *Freedom and Unity: "U hum na Umoja"* (London: Oxford University Press, 1962), cited in G. Kitching, *Development and Underdevelopment in Historical Perspective* (London: Methuen, 1982), pp. 64–65.

43. Scholars such as Gavin Kitching used the term to describe a particular development paradigm that stood as an alternative to the "old orthodoxy" by embracing small-scale over large-scale production, agriculture over industry, and rural over urban development. Gavin Kitching, *Development and Underdevelopment in Historical Perspective* (Maidenhead, Berkshire, UK: Open University Press, 1982).

44. W. W. Rostow, *Stages of Economic Growth: A Non-communist Manifesto* (Cambridge: Cambridge University Press, 1960), pp. 4–16.

45. Andre Gunder Frank, *The Development of Underdevelopment* (New York: Monthly Review Press, 1966), and *Capitalism and Underdevelopment in Latin America* (New York: Monthly Review Press, 1967).

46. Jalal Al-i Ahmad's *Gharbzadegi* has been published in English as *Occidentosis: A Plague from the West* (Berkeley, CA: Mizan Press, 1984). The term "westoxification" was first coined by the conservative philosopher Ahmad Farid.

47. Jalal Al-i Ahmad, *Gharbzadegi* (N.p., 1962), p. 49.

48. Khosrow Golsorkhi and eleven other activists sympathizing with the Fedaian Khalq were arrested and charged with plotting to harm members of the royal family in 1972. As their military trial in 1973 was televised live, Golsorkhi and his comrade Karamatollah Daneshian refused to ask for the shah's clemency and were consequently executed. See Behrooz, *Rebels with a Cause*, pp. 69–70.

49. The videos of Golshorki's defense is available online. See "Khosro Golsorkhi," uploaded February 8, 2007, https://www.youtube.com/watch?v=buTlBLGdUfo.

50. According to the cleric Jalal Eddin Farsi, cited by the political scientist Amir Nabavi, pers. comm., July 2016.

Chapter 3

1. Jeff Goodwin and James Jasper, eds., *The Social Movements Reader: Cases and Concepts* (Oxford: Wiley Blackwell, 2015), p. 9.

2. Marina Sitrin, *Everyday Revolution: Horizontalism and Autonomy in Argentina* (London: Zed Books, 2012).

3. I conducted one year of field research in Iran in 1980–1981, including research in fourteen large factories in Tehran, Tabriz, and Arak. See Asef Bayat, *Workers and Revolution in Iran* (London: Zed Books, 1978); Asef Bayat, "Labor and Democracy," in *Post-revolutionary Iran*, ed. Houshang Amirahmadi and Manoucher Parvin (Boulder, CO: Westview Press, 1988), pp. 41–55. Other published works on the factory councils include Saeed Rahnema, "Work Councils in Iran: The Illusion of Worker Control," *Economic and Industrial Democracy* 13, no. 1 (February 1992): 69–94.

4. For details, see Asef Bayat, *Street Politics: Poor People's Movements in Iran* (New York: Columbia University Press, 1997).

5. On city councils, see Kian Tajbakhsh, "Political Decentralization and the

Creation of Local Government in Iran: Consolidation or Transformation of Theo-cratic State," *Social Research* 67, no. 2 (Summer 2000): 377–404; Morad Saghafi, "Tashkil Showra-ha: Mo'jeze-i ke Nashod" [The councils: The miracle that wasn't], *Gofto-Gou* 20 (Summer 1998).

6. This paragraph draws on Ahmad Ashraf, "Dehghanan, Zamin va Enghelab" [Peasants, land, and the revolution], in *Kitab-e Agah: Masa'el-e Arzi va Dehghani* (Tehran: Entesharat-e Agah, 1982).

7. Muhammad Sahimi, "'Cultural Revolution' Redux," *Tehran Bureau*, May 11, 2010.

8. Asghar Schirazi, *The Problem of Land Reform in the Islamic Republic of Iran: Complications and Consequences of an Islamic Reform Policy* (Berlin: Verlag Das Arabische Buch, 1987).

9. Tajbakhsh, "Political Decentralization and the Creation of Local Government in Iran."

10. The story of how I secured the permit (from the Ministry of Labor) to visit the factories needs a separate treatment, but it did involve over two months of being passed around from one government office to another, as no official was prepared to accept the responsibility to authorize the permit. "Factories are explo-sive," they would argue; "your presence would cause strikes." Others denied my request because "who knows, you might be a communist" or a "CIA agent." The response clearly reflected the deep anxiety of state officials about the militancy and unrest that had engulfed the industrial factories in those turbulent times. These were highly charged months to conduct research in Iranian factories; most of them were truly explosive, as officials in the Ministry of Labor had told me. Many times, my own presence there and interviews would cause fights between workers with opposing ideologies. There were also times when I could not com-plete a study because I felt the danger of losing what I had gained. In a large plant in Tabriz, Machine Sazi, with almost all ethnic Azeri workers, the manager had sent a spy to accompany me to report what the workers were saying during inter-views with me. Once as I ended the interviews and prepared to leave for the day, a management assistant informed me that the director wanted to see me before I left. This was not a good sign, I felt. In his large office, the director, following small talk about how he appreciated the research and so on, asked me "if he could listen to recorded tapes" because he "wanted to find out what the workers' complaints are so that we can help them." I explained that I could not give him the tapes, be-cause that would violate the trust workers had placed in talking to me; it is like a doctor who would keep his patients' records confidential." We had a thirty-minute back and forth. In the end, I suggested that I would review the tapes and bring them back the next day, when I was going to research the factory's medical cen-ter. At that time, I knew I would never return, and on the road from the desolate

factory compound, which was covered by heavy snow, I began to run, fearing the plant's guards might follow me and seize the tapes. It certainly felt more secure to seek refuge in a military barrack (in Ajab Shir, where I was given lodging by an officer friend), a potential target of Iraqi warplanes, than roaming around this factory compound while constantly watched.

I was compelled to terminate my field visits to factories when the political mood in the country altered dramatically in the summer of 1981, after the Mujahedin Khalq bombed the headquarter of the Islamic Republic Party, killing seventy-two of its top officials. This was followed by the dramatic escape from the country of deposed President Banisadr and the leader of the Mujahedin to Paris and the start of armed struggle against the Islamic Republic. A mood of terror engulfed the streets, neighborhoods, and workplaces. The industrial sites became the target of widespread repression and arrest. In the Fanoos factory in the Tehran Pars district, I saw the rushed arrival of a dozen armed Pasdaran searching for the shura members to take away. In the Iran Car plant they had taken seventy-three workers in one day. The shura leader, a Mujahedin supporter, had been kidnapped at the factory gate; a few days later he was shot dead. At the height of this security operation, I stopped going to the factories, not knowing precisely what was happening to the places I visited and the people I talked to. All I could do was read the list of detained workers reported in the daily papers to find familiar names of those whom I had met and interviewed weeks or days before in the factories.

11. Bayat, *Workers and Revolution*, pp. 79–81.

12. For my tabulation of workers' protests in postrevolutionary Iran, see ibid., pp. 104–105.

13. My interview with a Shura member, March 1981. All interviews cited here were conducted in the period between January and July 1981 when I was visiting factories for research; also see Bayat, *Workers and Revolution*, pp. 118–119.

14. Ibid.

15. Ibid.

16. Ibid.

17. Ibid., p. 123.

18. Cited in Ahmad Ghotbi, *Kargaran-e Kafsh-e Melli: Agar Iran Hamintor Bemanad Soghout Mikonad* [Workers of Melli Shoe Plant: If Iran remains like this, it will collapse]. (Tehran: N.p., 1980), pp. 28–33.

19. Bayat, *Workers and Revolution in Iran*, p. 125.

20. Cited in *Jumhuri-ye Eslami*, 1981.

21. Hossein Kamali, cited in *Jelve-ye Haqq Ta'ala*, no. 3, 1981.

22. Ayatollah Khomeini, cited in *Kayhan*, June 19, 1983.

23. For details, see Bayat, *Workers and Revolution*, pp. 156–157.

24. I have discussed this in detail in Bayat, *Work, Politics, and Power: An Inter-*

national Perspective on Workers' Control and Self-Management (New York: Monthly Review Press, 1991), chap. 8.

25. Marvin Ortega, "Workers' Participation in the Management of the Agro-Enterprises of the APP," *Latin American Perspectives* 12, no. 2 (Spring 1985) pp. 69–82.

26. G. Ruchwarger, "Workers' Control in Nicaragua," *Against the Current* 2, no. 4 (1984).

27. E. V. K. Fitzgerald, "An Evaluation of the Economic Costs to Nicaragua of US Aggression: 1980–1984," in *The Political Economy of Revolutionary Nicaragua*, ed. R. J. Spalding (London: Allen and Unwin, 1987), pp. 195–216.

28. Michael Raptis, *Revolution and Counter-revolution in Chile* (London: Allison and Busby, 1974), p. 54; J. Espinosa and A. Zimbalist, *Economic Democracy: Workers' Participation in Chilean Industry, 1970–1973* (New York: Academic Press, 1978).

29. Radical politics of this sort was part of the postcolonial political life. In Tanzania, the idea of worker participation had developed out of President Nyerere's Arusha Declaration (1967). In rural areas, it created the program of *ujamaa*, communal agricultural production; in urban areas it brought about nationalization of many industries and the program of worker participation in the management of enterprises, according to Mwongozo, a program that Nyerere used to combat inequality, racism, and arrogance.

30. C. Goodey, R. Ellis, and J. Burke, *Workers' Control in Portuguese Factories* (Nottingham, UK: Institute for Workers' Control, 1980).

31. President Machel, cited in D. Wield, "Mozambique: Late Colonialism and Early Problems of Transition," in *Revolutionary Socialist Development in the Third World*, ed. G. White, R. Murray, and C. White (Brighton, UK: Wheatsheaf Books, 1983), p. 99.

32. Bayat, *Work, Politics, and Power*, pp. 117–119.

33. Eric Hobsbawm, *Forward March of Labor Halted* (London: Verso, 1981); André Gorz, *Farewell to the Working Class* (London: Pluto Press, 1982).

34. See Bayat, "Activism and Social Development in the Middle East."

Chapter 4

Parts of this chapter draw on Asef Bayat, "Islamism and Empire: The Incongruous Nature of Islamist Anti-imperialism," *Socialist Register* 44 (2008): 38–54.

1. Expressed by the ultrarightist commentator Jamie Glazov in "Symposium: The Terror War: How We Can Win," FrontPageMagazine.com, November 15, 2004, http://www.freeman.org/m_online/dec04/glazov.php.

2. See, for instance, Michael Walzer, "Islamism and the Left," *Dissent* (Winter 2015), https://www.dissentmagazine.org/article/islamism-and-the-left; Edward Ellis, "The Left and 'Reactionary Anti-imperialism,'" *Workers' Liberty*, March 30,

2002, http://www.workersliberty.org/story/2005/03/09/left-and-reactionary-anti
-imperialism.

3. Dave Crouch, "The Bolsheviks and Islam," *International Socialism* 110 (Spring 2006): 38.

4. See an interesting critique, for instance, in Chetan Bhatt, "The Fetish of the Margins: Religious Absolutism, Anti-racism and Postcolonial Silence," *New Formations* 59 (Autumn 2006): 98–115.

5. Michael Hardt and Antonio Negri, *Empire* (Cambridge, MA: Harvard University Press, 2000), p. 149; Susan Buck-Morss, *Thinking Past Terror: Islamism and Critical Theory on the Left* (London: Verso, 2003).

6. See Paul Lubeck, "The Islamic Revival: Antinomies of Islamic Movements under Globalization," in *Global Social Movements*, ed. R. Cohen and S. Rai (London: Althone Press, 2000), pp. 146–164.

7. See, for instance, J. Haynes, *Religion in Third World Politics* (Buckingham, UK: Open University Press, 1993); Phil Marfleet, "Globalization and Religious Activism," in *Globalization and the Third World*, ed. Ray Kiely and Phil Marfleet (London: Routledge, 1998), pp. 185–215; John Esposito, "Religion and Global Affairs: Political Challenges," *SAIS Review: A Journal of International Affairs* 18, no. 2 (Summer/Fall 1998): 19–24.

8. Mike Davis, *Planet of Slums* (London: Verso, 2006).

9. Scott Atran, "ISIS Is a Revolution," Aeon, December 15, 2015, https://aeon.co/essays/why-isis-has-the-potential-to-be-a-world-altering-revolution.

10. See Kenneth Pomeranz, "Empire and 'Civilizing Mission': Past and Present," *Daedalus* 134, no. 2 (Spring 2005): 34–35.

11. Niall Ferguson, "The Unconscious Colossus: Limits of (and Alternative to) American Empire," *Daedalus* 134, no. 2 (Spring 2005): 20. See also Niall Ferguson, *Empire: How Britain Made the Modern World* (London: Allen Lane, 2003), p. 358.

12. Interview with David Harvey by Alberto Toscano, *Development and Change Forum* 38 (2007): 1127–1135.

13. See Asef Bayat, *Making Islam Democratic: Social Movements and the Post-Islamist Turn* (Stanford, CA: Stanford University Press, 2007), especially chap. 1.

14. Asef Bayat, "Is There a Future for Islamic Revolutions?," in *Life as Politics: How Ordinary People Change the Middle East*, 2nd ed., by Asef Bayat (Stanford, CA: Stanford University Press, 2013), pp. 241–258. For a fine analysis of al-Qaeda as an ethical movement, see Faisal Devji, *Landscapes of the Jihad: Militancy, Morality, and Modernity* (Ithaca, NY: Cornell University Press, 2005).

15. Asef Bayat, *Post-Islamism: Changing Faces of Political Islam* (New York: Oxford University Press, 2013).

16. Olivier Roy, *Globalized Islam* (New York: Columbia University Press, 2002).

17. Bobby Sayyid, *A Fundamental Fear: Eurocentrism and the Emergence of Islamism* (London: Zed Books, 2004).

18. Taylor Luck, "The Mysterious Islamic Movement Quietly Sweeping the Middle East," *Christian Science Monitor*, December 6, 2015.

19. See Ali Shariati, Shi'e-ye Alavi, Shi'e-ye Safavi (Tehran: N.p., 1979); see also Ali Shariati, *Jahat-guiriye Tabaqati-ye Islam* [Class bias of Islam], in *Collected Works* (Tehran: N.p., 1980).

20. See Ervan Abrahamian, "The Guerrilla Movement in Iran, 1963–77," *MERIP Reports* 86 (March–April 1980); also see Ervan Abrahamian, *Radical Islam: The Iranian Mojahedin* (London: I. B. Tauris, 1989).

21. See Akif, "Al-Wilayat al-Muttahida La Turidu al-Khair lil-Alam al-Islami" [The US does not want the good of the Islamic world], *Ikhwanonline*, February 12, 2006.

22. Esam el-Eryan, "Al-Ikhwan al-Muslimun wa Amrika" [Muslim Brotherhood and the US], *Ikhwanonline*, December 2005.

23. Adel Hussein, "Al-'Awlama wa Sera'atna Ma'a al-Gharb" [Globalization and our conflict with the West], in *Al-Islam wa al-'Awlama* [Islam and globalization], ed. Muhammad Ibrahim Mabruk et al. (Cairo: Dar al-Qawmiya al-'Arabiya, 1999).

24. Ahmad Abdelrahman, "'Al-'Awlama: Wojhat Nazar Islamiya," in Mabruk, *Al-Islam wa al-'Awlama*, pp. 91–100.

25. Mesbah Yazdi, *Tahajom-e Farhagui* [Cultural invasion] (Tehran: N.p., 1997). This volume is translated into Arabic as *Al-Ghazw al-Thiqafi*.

26. Hussein, "Al-'Awlama wa Sera'atna Ma'a al-Gharb."

27. See, for instance, Mahmood Mamdani, *Good Muslims, Bad Muslims* (New York: Pantheon, 2004).

28. Seumas Milne, "Now the Truth Emerges: How the US Fuelled the Rise of ISIS in Syria and Iraq," *The Guardian*, June 3, 2015.

29. See Asef Bayat, "Islamism and the Politics of Fun," *Public Culture* 19, no. 3 (Spring 2009): 433–459.

30. *Entikhab*, 4 Azar 1394/2015.

31. Reported in *Kargozaran*, 17 Ordibehesht 1386/1997, p. 1.

32. For a good analysis, see Kaveh Ehsani, "Iran's Populist Threat to Democracy," *Middle East Report* 241 (Winter 2006): 4–9.

33. Reported in Richard Landes, "Strange Bedfellows: The Islamists and the Far ... What?," *Augean Stables*, May 18, 2006.

34. See Onder Cetin, "The Bosnian Ulema and the Negotiation of Islamic Revivalism in Multi-ethnic Bosnia," unpublished paper, ISIM Seminar, January 23, 2007, Leiden, Netherlands.

35. Nelson Banya, "Zimbabwe Heads for Dark Days as Power Cuts Loom," Reuters News Agency, May 9, 2007.?

36. Mesbah Yazdi, *Tahajom-e Farhangui* [Cultural invasion] (Tehran, N.p., 1997).

37. L. Boff and C. Boff, *Salvation and Liberation* (New York: Orbis Books, 1988), p. 13. The discussions in this section regarding liberation theology in Latin America draws primarily on this book as well as the fine studies by Christian Smith, *The Emergence of Liberation Theology* (Chicago: University of Chicago Press, 1991); and Michael Lowy, *The War of Gods: Religion and Politics in Latin America* (London: Verso, 1996).

38. See Bayat, *Making Islam Democratic*.

39. Gustávo Gutierrez, *A Theology of Liberation* (New York: Orbis Books, 1988); Martin Lee and Pia Gallegos, "Gustavo Gutierrez with the Poor," *Christianity and Crisis* 47, no. 5 (1987): 113–115.

40. Drawn from Bayat, "Islamism and Empire"; for elaboration, see Bayat, *Making Islam Democratic*.

41. Jose Miguez Bonino, *Doing Theology in a Revolutionary Situation* (Philadelphia: Fortress, 1976), p. 88.

42. See Hassan Hanafi, "The Relevance of the Islamic Alternative in Egypt," *Arab Studies Quarterly* 4, no. 1–2 (1982): 54–74. For a concise discussion of Hanafi's ideas, see Elizabeth Kassab, *Contemporary Arab Thought* (New York: Columbia University Press, 2010).

43. See Shariati, *Shi'e-ye Alavi, Shi'e-ye Safavi*; and Shariati, *Jahatguiri-ye Tabaqati-ye Islam*.

44. Abdullahi Jallab, *The First Islamist Republic: Development and Disintegration of Islamism in the Sudan* (Aldershot, UK: Ashgate, 2008), pp. 42–43.

45. Sayyid Qutb, *Ma'rikat al-Islam wa al-Ra'sulmaliya* [Conflict between Islam and capitalism] (Cairo: Dar al-Shorouk, 2006).

46. Bernard Lewis, "Communism and Islam," *International Affairs* 30, no. 1 (1954): 3, 7.

47. Tyler Durden, "Meet The Man Who Funds ISIS: Bilal Erdogan, the Son of Turkey's President," ZeroHedge, November 26, 2015,
http://www.zerohedge.com/news/2015-11-25/meet-man-who-funds-isis-bilal-erdogan-son-turkeys-president.

48. Neşecan Balkan, Erol Balkan, and Ahmet Öncü, eds., *The Neoliberal Landscape and the Rise of the Islamist Capital in Turkey* (New York: Berghahn, 2015). See also Ayse Bugra and Osman Savaskan, *New Capitalism in Turkey: The Relationship between Politics, Religion and Business* (Cheltenham, UK: Edward Elgar, 2014).

49. Yousef al-Qaradawi, *Khitabna al-Islami fi Asr al-Owlama* [Our Islamic discourse in the age of globalization] (Cairo: Al-Shorouk, 2004), pp. 84–85.

50. Eberhard Kienle, "Changed Regimes, Changed Priorities? Economic and Social Policies after the 2011 Elections in Tunisia and Egypt," Working Paper 928 (Cairo: Economic Research Forum, 2015).

51. Kienle, "Changed Regimes, Changed Priorities?," p. 5.

52. Cihan Tugal, *Passive Revolution: Absorbing the Islamic Challenge to Capitalism* (Stanford, CA: Stanford University Press, 2009), pp. 55–56.

53. Ayhan Kaya, "Islamization of Turkey under the AKP Rule: Empowering Family, Faith and Charity," *South European Society and Politics* 20, no. 1 (2015): 47–69.

54. Kienle, "Changed Regimes, Changed Priorities?," p. 25.

55. Mona Atia, "Pious Neoliberalism," Project on Middle East Political Science, September 23, 2014, https://pomeps.org/2014/09/24/pious-neoliberalism/. This draws on her book *Building a House in Heaven: Pious Neoliberalism and Islamic Charity in Egypt* (Minneapolis: University of Minnesota Press, 2013).

56. Atia, "Pious Neoliberalism."

57. Roy, *Globalized Islam.*

58. See, for instance, Graeme Wood, "What ISIS Really Wants," *The Atlantic*, March 2015.

59. The ISIS magazine *Dabiq*, no. 4, accessed February 21, 2017, http://media .clarionproject.org/files/islamic-state/islamic-state-isis-magazine-Issue-4-the -failed-crusade.pdf; for the emergence of ISIS, see Patrick Cockburn, *The Rise of Islamic State: ISIS and the New Sunni Revolution* (London: Verso, 2014).

60. According to the Brookings Institution, there are possibly ninety thousand ISIS Twitter accounts that support its cause and spread its message. Accounts have one thousand followers on average. See Jon Greenberg, "Does the Islamic State Post 90,000 Social Media Messages Each Day," Punditfact, February 19, 2015, http:// www.politifact.com/punditfact/statements/2015/feb/19/hillary-mann-leverett/ cnn-expert-islamic-state-posts-90000-social-media-/.

61. See "The Secret Life of an ISIS Warlord," *Daily Beast*, October 27, 2014.

62. *The Independent*, November 18, 2015.

63. "A Monster Who Led Shabab Mass Killers Is Unmasked," *Daily Nation*, April 5, 2015.

64. Georg Simmel, *On Individuality and Social Forms* (Chicago: University of Chicago Press, 1971).

65. To repudiate the claims of ISIS's "authenticity," even the radical jihadi sheikhs, such as the Jordanian Abu Qatada, Abu Muhammad al-Maqdisi, and especially Abu Mahmud al-Filistini, condemned the ISIS beheadings as a violation of the teachings of Islam.

66. *Dabiq*, no. 7, November 2015, http://media.clarionproject.org/files/islamic -state/islamic-state-dabiq-magazine-issue-7-from-hypocrisy-to-apostasy.pdf, pp. 54–66.

67. Michael Kimmelman, "Street Spared in Paris Attacks Embodies What Terrorists Targeted," *New York Times*, December 2, 2015.

68. Lydia Wilson, "What I Discovered from Interviewing Imprisoned ISIS Fighters," *The Nation*, October 21, 2015; see also Aya Batrawy Paisley Doods and Lori Hinnant, "Leaked ISIS Documents Reveal Recruits Have Poor Grasp of Islamic Faith," *The Independent*, August 16, 2016.

69. According to Erin Saltman, a counter-extremism researcher at the Institute for Strategic Dialogue, cited in Wilson, "What I Discovered."

70. Atran, "ISIS Is a Revolution."

71. The survey was conducted in 2016 in Jordan, Palestine, Tunisia, Algeria, and Morocco. See Mark Tessler, Michael Robins, and Amany Jamal, "What the Ordinary Citizens in the Arab World Really Think about the Islamic State," *Washington Post*, July 27, 2016.

72. See Abu-Ibrahim al-Raqqawi, "Inside the Islamic State 'Capital': No End in Sight to Its Grim Rule," *The Guardian*, February 21, 2015. In Raqqa, women cannot work or study outside the home, cannot leave home alone, nor take a taxi alone; they are constantly watched in public by the morals police; see "Report from the Capital of Daesh: Raqqa Narrated by Women," *Radio Zamaneh*, 26 Esfand 1394/2015, in Persian.

73. See Asef Bayat, "Workless Revolutionaries: The Unemployed Movement in Revolutionary Iran," *International Review of Social History* 42, no. 2 (August 1997): 159–185.

74. See Seymour Hersh, "The Iran Plans," *New Yorker*, April 17, 2006.

75. On the Zapatista movement, see, for instance, Markus Schulz, "Open Futures: Struggle from Below," *OpenDemocracy*, March 17, 2015; also see Markus Schulz, "The Role of the Internet in Transnational Mobilization: A Case Study of the Zapatista Movement, 1994–2005," in *Civil Society: Local and Regional Responses to Global Challenges*, ed. Mark Herkenrath (Münster, Germany: Verlag, 2007), pp. 129–158.

Chapter 5

This chapter is a revised and extended version of Asef Bayat, "Politics in the City Inside Out," *City and Society* 24, no. 2 (2012): 110–128.

1. David Harvey, *A Brief History of Neoliberalism* (Oxford: Oxford University Press, 2005).

2. David Harvey, *Rebel Cities: From the Right to the City to the Urban Revolution* (London: Verso, 2012), p. 22.

3. For an exploration of the neoliberal city in advanced industrialized countries, see Jason Hackworth, *The Neoliberal City: Governance, Ideology and Development in American Urbanism* (Ithaca, NY: Cornell University Press, 2006).

4. See Asef Bayat, "Activism and Social Development in the Middle East," *International Journal of Middle East Studies* 34, no. 1 (February 2002): 1–28.

5. Alejandro Portes, Manuel Castells, and Lauren Benton, eds., *The Informal Economy: Studies in Advanced and Less Developed Countries* (Baltimore: Johns Hopkins University Press, 1989); Alan Gilbert, "Love in the Time of Enhanced Capital Flows: Reflections in the Links between Liberalization and Informality," in *Urban Informality: Transnational Perspectives from the Middle East, Latin America, and South Asia*, ed. A. Roy and N. Alsayyad (Lanham, MD: Lexington Books, 2004), pp. 33–66.

6. Hernando de Soto, "The Free Market Secret of the Arab Revolutions," *Financial Times*, November 8, 2011.

7. An early meticulous analysis can be found in Marsh Posusney, *Labor and the State in Egypt: Workers, Unions, and Economic Restructuring* (New York: Columbia University Press, 1997); see also Iliya Harik and Dennis Sullivan, eds., *Privatization and Liberalization in the Middle East* (Bloomington: Indiana University Press, 1992).

8. For the negative impact of this new economic restructuring social policy in the Middle East, see Massoud Karshenas and Valentine Moghadam, eds., *Social Policy in the Middle East: Economic, Political, and Gender Dynamics* (London: Palgrave Macmillan, 2006).

9. See Mariz Tadros, "NGO-State Relations in Egypt: Welfare Assistance in a Poor Urban Community in Cairo," PhD diss., University of Oxford, 2004; also see United Nations Research Institute for Social Development (UNRISD), "Gendered Ideologies and Practices in Faith-Based Organizations," paper published by UNRISD, Geneva, June 2009.

10. For a fine exploration, see Julia Elyashar, *Markets of Dispossession: NGOs, Economic Development, and the State in Cairo* (Durham, NC: Duke University Press, 2005).

11. Mike Davis, *Planet of Slums* (London: Verso, 2006).

12. Harvey, *Rebel Cities*, pp.18–19.

13. Hernando de Soto, *The Other Path: The Economic Answer to Terrorism* (New York: Basic Books, 1989), and *The Mystery of Capital: Why Capitalism Triumphs in the West but Fails Everywhere Else* (New York: Basic Books, 2003).

14. De Soto, "The Free Market Secret of the Arab Revolutions."

15. See Habib Ayeb, "Social Geography of the Tunisian Revolution," *Review of African Political Economy* 38, no. 129 (September 2011): 473–485; Rabab el-Mahdi and Philip Marfleet, eds., *Egypt: The Moment of Change* (London: Zed Books, 2009). For a general critique of De Soto, see Gilbert, "Love in the Time of Enhanced Capital Flows."

16. According to an ILO report cited in Jumana Al Tamim, "Youth Unemployment in MENA Region Disturbingly High," *Gulf News*, February 7, 2012; and Masood Ahmed, Dominique Guillaume, and Davide Furceri, "Youth Unemployment in the Mena Region," IMF, June 13, 2012, https://www.imf.org/external/np/vc/2012/061312.htm.

17. Alireza Sadeghi, "Everyday Life of the Subsistence Motor Cyclists," unpublished paper, Tehran, 2016.

18. See Kamal Fahmi, *Beyond the Victim: The Politics and Ethics of Empowering Cairo's Street Children* (Cairo: American University in Cairo Press, 2007); for the situation in Africa, see Alicinda Honwana and Filip de Boeck, eds., *Makers and Breakers: Children and Youth in Postcolonial Africa* (Oxford: James Currey, 2005).

19. André Gorz, *Paths to Paradise: On the Liberation from Work* (London: Pluto Press, 1985), and *Farewell to the Working Class* (London: Pluto Press, 1982).

20. See Asef Bayat, *Street Politics: Poor People's Movements in Iran* (New York: Columbia University Press, 1997); also see A. Bayat, "Cairo's Poor: Dilemma of Survival and Solidarity," *Middle East Report* 202 (1996): 7–12; A. Bayat and E. Denis, "Who Is Afraid of Ashwaiyyat? Urban Change and Politics in Egypt," *Environment and Urbanization* 12, no. 2 (2000): 185–199.

21. Aymon Kreil, "Territories of Desire: A Geography of Competing Intimacies in Cairo," *Journal of Middle East Women's Studies* 12, no. 1 (July 2016): 166–180.

22. Ayfer Bartu and B. Kolluoglu, "Emerging Spaces of Neoliberalism: A Gated Town and Public Housing in Istanbul," *New Perspectives on Turkey* 39 (2008): 5–46; Khaled Adham, "Globalization, Neoliberalism, and the New Spaces of Capital in Cairo," *Traditional Dwellings and Settlements Review* 17, no. 1 (2005), http://iaste .berkeley.edu/pdfs/17.1c-Fall05adham-sml.pdf.

23. See Karina Landman and Martin Schönteich, "Urban Fortress: Gated Communities as a Reaction to Crime," *African Security Review* 11, no. 4 (2002): 71–85. Various practices of securitization of modern megacities are fully discussed in Stephen Graham, *Cities under Siege: Military Urbanism* (London: Verso, 2010).

24. On the restriction on the movement of women in the urban expanse, see Shilpa Phadke, "Reinterpreting Public Safety, Risk and Violence: A Gendered Analysis," paper presented at SEPHIS Workshop on Gender and Public Space, Baku, June 2008. See also Michael Sorkin, ed., *Variations on a Theme Park: A New American City and the End of Public Space* (New York: Hill and Wang, 1992), especially M. Sorkin, "Introduction," and David Harvey, "Fortress L.A.: The Militarization of Public Space."

25. The idea of the "right to the city" seems to be more complex than what the current usages suggest. According to Mark Purcell, Lefebvre's original idea is perhaps its most comprehensive formulation: "Lefebvre's right to the city is an argument for profoundly reworking both the social relations of capitalism and the current structure of liberal-democratic citizenship. His right to the city is not a suggestion for reform, nor does it envision a fragmented, tactical, or piecemeal resistance. His idea is instead a call for a radical restructuring of social, political, and economic relations, both in the city and beyond." Mark Purcell, "Excavating Lefebvre: The Right to the City and Its Urban Politics of the Inhabitants," *Geo-*

Journal 58 (2002): 101. This seems to be in line with David Harvey's understanding of Lefebvre. See David Harvey, "The Right to the City," *New Left Review* 53 (2008): 23–40.

26. For a number of case studies, see Asef Bayat and Kees Biekart, eds., "Cities of Extremes," special issue, *Development and Change* 40, no. 5 (2009).

27. Mona Fawaz, "Neoliberal Urbanity and the Right to the City: A View from Beirut's Periphery," in Bayat and Biekart, "Cities of Extremes," pp. 827–852.

28. Harvey, "The Right to the City."

29. Peter Evans, ed., *The Livable Cities? Urban Struggles for Livelihood and Sustainability* (Berkeley: University of California Press), pp. 14–23.

30. For such conclusions, see Dennis Rodgers, "Slum Wars of the 21st Century: Gangs, *Mano Dura*, and the New Urban Geography of Conflict in Central America," in Bayat and Biekart, "Cities of Extremes," pp. 949–976.

31. Mike Davis, "Planet of Slums: Urban Involution and Informal Proletariat," *New Left Review* 26 (March–April 2004): 28.

32. Ibid., p. 206.

33. James Holston, "Spaces of Insurgent Citizenship," in *Cities and Citizenship*, ed. J. Holston (Durham, NC: Duke University Press, 1996), p. 158.

34. Eric Wolf, *Peasant Wars of the Twentieth Century* (Norman: University of Oklahoma Press, 1999)

35. Rodgers, "Slum Wars of the 21st Century." See also Jo Beall, "Cities, Terrorism and Urban Wars in the 21st Century," Working Paper no. 9, London School of Economics, Crisis States Research Centre, 2007.

36. For a detailed analysis, see Asef Bayat, "Radical Religion and the Habitus of the Dispossessed: Does Islamic Militancy Have an Urban Ecology?," *International Journal of Urban and Regional Research* 31, no. 3 (September 2007): 579–590.

37. Rodgers, "Slum Wars of the 21st Century," p. 11; see also K. M. Coleman and D. Stuart, "The Other Parties," in *Nicaragua without Illusions: Regime Transition and Structural Adjustment in the 1990s*, ed. T. W. Walker (Wilmington, DE: Scholarly Resources, 1997), p. 183.

38. See Matthew Gandy, "Learning from Lagos," *New Left Review* 33 (May–June 2005): 51.

39. See Asef Bayat, *Life as Politics: How Ordinary People Change the Middle East* (Stanford, CA: Stanford University Press, 2010), chap. 1.

40. Ibid., chap. 1.

41. For details, see Bayat, *Street Politics*.

42. Bayat, *Life as Politics*, chap. 1.

43. Lisa Wedeen, "The Politics of Deliberation: Qat Chews as Public Sphere in Yemen," *Public Culture* 19, no. 1 (2007): 59–84.

44. Bayat, *Life as Politics*.

45. Amelie Le Renard, *Society of Young Women: Opportunities of Power, Place, and Reform in Saudi Arabia* (Stanford, CA: Stanford University Press, 2014).

46. I have already referred to these nonmovements of the urban poor in terms of the "quiet encroachment of the ordinary." See Bayat, *Street Politics*, p. 1.

47. These observations draw on my studies of the urban poor in Iran and Egypt. See Bayat, *Street Politics*; and Bayat and Denis, "Who Is Afraid of Ash-waiyyat?," pp. 185–199.

48. David Sims, "The Arab Housing Paradox," *Cairo Review* (Fall 2013), https://www.thecairoreview.com/essays/the-arab-housing-paradox/.

49. Asef Bayat, "Cairo's Poor: Dilemmas of Survival and Solidarity," *Middle East Report* 202 (January–February 1997): 7–12.

50. David Sims, *Understanding Cairo: The Logic of a City out of Control* (Cairo: American University in Cairo Press, 2011); Ayse Yonder, *Informal Settlements in Istanbul, Turkey: From Shacks to High-Rises* (Salzburg: Pratt Institute, 2006); Asef Bayat, "Tehran: Paradox City," *New Left Review* 66 (November 2010): 99–122.

51. See, for instance, Mitchell Duneier, *Sidewalk* (New York: Farrar, Straus and Giroux, 1999).

52. See Bayat and Biekart, "Cities of Extremes."

53. Michael Wines, "In Zimbabwe, Homeless Belie Leader's Claim," *New York Times*, November 13, 2005.

54. Steven Erlanger, "Amid Rise of Multiculturalism, Dutch Confront Their Questions of Identity," *New York Times*, August 13, 2011.

55. Partha Chatterjee, *The Politics of the Governed* (New York: Columbia University Press, 2004).

56. For the full elaboration of the concept of nonmovements, see Bayat, *Life as Politics*, chap. 1.

57. For details, see ibid.

Chapter 6

1. Susanne Sahlgren, "Rebels without Shoes: A Visit to South Yemen's Revolution Squares," *Muftah*, April 22, 2014, http://muftah.org/rebels-without-shoes-visit-south-yemens-revolution-squares/#.WH8vovOOqwo.

2. Ibid.

3. Atifa Zaid Alwazir, "The Square of Change in Sana'a: An Incubator for Reform," Arab Reform Initiative, *Arab Reform Brief* 48 (April 2011), https://web.archive.org/web/20140320041152/http://www.arab-reform.net/sites/default/files/ARB_49_A_Zaid_Alwazir_Yemen_ENG.pdf.

4. Nadia Idle and Alex Nunns, eds., *Tweets from Tahrir* (New York: OR Books, 2011), p. 148.

5. Ibid., p. 144.

6. Sahar Keraitim and Samia Mehrez, "Mulid al-Tahrir: Semiotics of a Revolution," in *Translating Egypt's Revolution: The Language of Tahrir*, ed. Samia Mehrez (Cairo: American University in Cairo Press, 2012), pp. 25–67.

7. Ahmad al-Haj, "Thousands of Police Confront Protesters in Yemen," Associated Press, February 16, 2011, http://www.stuff.co.nz/world/africa/4667906/Thousands-of-police-confront-protesters-in-Yemen.

8. Cited by Bernard Rogiere (Cairo's CEDEJ director) at the conference "Youth in Muslim Societies," Boston, April 8–9, 2015.

9. Notable exceptions are Atef Said, "We Ought to Be Here: Historicizing Space and Mobilization in Tahrir Square," *International Sociology* 3, no. 4 (July 2015): 348–366; and Jillian Schwedler and Ryan King, "Political Geography," in *Arab Uprisings Explained: New Contentious Politics in the Middle East*, ed. Marc Lynch (New York: Columbia University Press, 2014), pp. 160–179.

10. D. G. Martin and B. Miller, "Space and Contentious Politics," *Mobilization* 8, no. 2 (2003): 144.

11. See, for instance, Hazem Ziada, "What Brings Them There? Reflections on the Persistent Symbolism of Tahrir Square," *Jadaliyya*, April 2, 2015; Nezar al-Sayyad, "Cairo's Roundabout Revolution," *New York Times*, April 13, 2011; Said, "We Ought to Be Here."

12. See Derek Gregory, "Tahrir: Politics, Publics, and Performances of Space," *Middle East Critique* 22, no. 3 (2013): 235–246.

13. See Jeffery Alexander, *Performative Revolution in Egypt: An Essay in Cultural Power* (New York: Bloomsbury Academic, 2011); Alain Badiou, "Tunisia, Egypt: When an East Wind Sweeps Away the Arrogance of the West," trans. Anindya Bhattacharyya, *Le Monde*, February 18, 2011, https://bato20.com/2011/03/11/badiou-on-the-revolutions-in-egypt-and-tunisia/; Slavoj Žižek, "For Egypt, This Is the Miracle of Tahrir Square," *The Guardian*, February 10, 2011; Helga Tawil-Souri, "Power of Place," *Middle East Journal of Culture and Communication* 5 (2012): 86–95.

14. Farha Ghannam, "The Rise and Decline of a Heterotopic Space: Views from Maidan al-Tahrir," *Jadaliyya*, January 2016.

15. Jeroen Gunning and Ilan Baron, *Why Occupy a Square? People, Protests and Movements in the Egyptian Revolution* (Oxford: Oxford University Press, 2014), p. 259.

16. Manuel Castells, *Networks of Outrage and Hope: Social Movements in the Internet Age* (Cambridge, MA: Polity Press, 2012), p. 144; Sidney Tarrow, "Why Occupy Wall Street Is Not the Tea Party of the Left," *Foreign Affairs*, October 10, 2011; Richard F. Day, *Gramsci Is Dead: Anarchist Currents in Newest Social Movements* (London: Pluto Press, 2005).

17. Victor Turner, *The Ritual Process: Structures and Anti-structures* (Chicago: Aldine, 1969).

18. John Chalcraft, "Horizontalism in the Egyptian Revolutionary Process," *Middle East Report* 262 (2012): 6–11.

19. Marina Sitrin, *Everyday Revolutions: Horizontalism and Autonomy in Argentina* (London: Zed Books, 2012); see also Avi Lewis and Naomi Klein, *The Take*, May 15, 2015, *https://www.youtube.com/watch?v=3-DSu8RPJt8*.

20. Matt Ford, "A Dictator's Guide to Urban Design," *Atlantic Monthly*, February 2014.

21. Interview with a member of Hiz al-Haqq, a splinter group from the Muslim Brotherhood, Cairo, July 2012.

22. Harvey does observe that capitalist urbanization subjugates and dispossesses working people, who should struggle to overturn such an unjust system if they want emancipation. Lefebvre's notion of the "right to the city" does not seem to fulfill this task. Lefebvre presented this notion as a strategy against the Left's unitary working class as agent of change. Lefebvre's agent of change was not simply the industrial proletariat but many different segments of workers in cities, including today's "precariat." Harvey, however, regards the right to the city as the actual strategy of global capital. So the working-class struggle for the right to the city here and there becomes "reformist." Consequently, the liberation lies in the working class questioning and challenging the global capital that is distorting life in our cities. See David Harvey, *Rebel Cities* (London: Verso, 2012), chap. 1.

23. Saskia Sassen, "The Global Street: The Making of the Political," *Globalizations* 8, no. 5 (October 2011): 573–579.

24. Referring to the Der'a uprising, a Syrian military source stated that the "situation" would be handled by "any means necessary. . . . Even if this means that the city is to be burned down." This was followed by dismantling the city's infrastructure such as water, electricity, and phone lines. Reported in Deen Sharp, "Urbicide and the Arrangement of Violence in Syria," in *Beyond the Square: Urbanism and the Arab Uprisings*, ed. Deen Sharp and Clair Penetta (New York: Terreform, 2015), p. 128.

25. Asef Bayat, *Life as Politics: How Ordinary People Change the Middle East* (Stanford, CA: Stanford University Press, 2013), pp. 180–181.

26. Other dreams included a better economy (40 percent) and lower cost of goods (35.5 percent). The survey was conducted by Egyptian National Center for Social and Criminological Research, reported in *Al-Masry al-Youm*, January 18, 2011.

27. Raymond Williams, *The Country and the City* (New York: Oxford University Press, 1973), pp. 165–183.

28. For instance, see Deen Sharp, "Beware of Small Cities," *Jadaliyya*, September 6, 2012.

29. Ferdinand Tönnies, *Community and Society* (Cambridge: Cambridge Uni-

versity Press, 2001); Georg Simmel, "Metropolis and Mental Life," in *On Individuality and Social Forms* (Chicago: University of Chicago Press, 1971), pp. 324–339.

30. See the excellent documentary film *Gabes Labess* (2014), produced and directed by Habib Ayeb, concerning change and deprivation in rural life in Tunisia.

31. Ibid.

32. I have observed similar rural-urban political integration in Iran. In regard to Egypt, see also Lila Abu-Lughod, "Taking Back the Village: Rural Youth in a Moral Revolution," *Middle East Report* 272 (Fall 2015): 12–17.

33. Ellis Goldberg, "The Urban Roots of the Arab Spring,"
April 20, 2014, http://papers.ssrn.com/sol3/papers.cfm?abstract_id=2426960, p. 2.

34. Said, "We Ought to Be Here."

35. See Heghnar Watenpaugh, "Learning from Taqsim Square: Architecture, State Power, Public Space in Istanbul," *Society of Architectural Historians' Blog*, June 11, 2013, http://www.sah.org/publications-and-research/sah-blog/sah-blog/2013/06/11/learning-from-taksim-square-architecture-state-power-and-public-space-in-istanbul.

36. Berna Turam, *Gaining Freedoms: Claiming Space in Istanbul and Berlin* (Stanford, CA: Stanford University Press, 2015).

37. Some analyses tend to look at the history of Tahrir from the prism of the January 25 uprising, extending the particular spatiality of Tahrir as far back as 1919. While tracing the history of struggle at these sites is valuable, there is a danger of reifying the maidan as an essential site of contention rather than historicizing its ecology and sociology. See, for instance, Ziada, "What Brings Them There?"

38. Youssef El Shazli, "A Geography of Revolt in Alexandria, Egypt's Second Capital," *Metro Politics*, February 23, 2016, http://www.metropolitiques.eu/A-Geography-of-Revolt-in.html.

39. Harvey, *Rebel Cities*, pp. 16–17.

40. Following the spread of the Occupy movements in the United States, considered one of the most widespread instances of street politics in the country, Congress passed a bill limiting public protestation. HR347 made it a federal offense punishable by up to ten years to "knowingly" protest in the vicinity of the Secret Service anywhere, whether permanent or mobile, for instance, at such public events as the Super Bowl, election campaign events, or World Bank meetings. More important, it criminalized protests that "impede or disrupt the orderly conduct of the Government business or official functions." Here "disruption" is not defined. See Paul Samakow, "'Anti-Occupy' Law Ends Americans' Right to Protest," *Washington Times*, August 1, 2012.

41. Isam al-Khafaja, "De-urbanizing the Syrian Revolt," Arab Reform Initiative, March 2016.

42. Interview with an anonymous observer, Cairo, May 2015.

43. Matt Ford, "A Dictator's Guide to Urban Design," *Atlantic Monthly*, December 2014.

44. According to the vice president for development and human resources, "the discussions about the transfer of population from Tehran is serious. . . . In the recent sedition [Green Protests] nothing was going on in the provinces. But in Tehran even though only two million, out of forty million, people voted for Mr. Mirhussein Mousawi, they caused trouble in the whole country for eight months." He added that the government has given four months to different institutions to transfer up to 40 percent of their employees from Tehran. BBC Persian, 17 Aban 1389/2010, cited in M. Raha, "Kouch-e Ejbari-ye Jam'iyyat: Tarfand-e Digari Baray-e Rouya-rouii baa Jonbesh-e Sabz," *IranEmrooz*, November 13, 2010.

Chapter 7

Sections of this chapter draw on Asef Bayat, "Arab Spring and Its Surprises," *Development and Change* 44, no. 2 (April 2013): 587–601.

1. Richard Norton-Taylor, "Why Do Revolutions Such as Tunisia's Come by Surprise?," *The Guardian*, February 1, 2011. Former CIA deputy director Michael Morell explicitly acknowledges that US intelligence agencies "failed" to see what was coming to the Arab world. Michael Morell, *The Great War of Our Time* (New York: Twelve Books, 2015), p. 179.

2. Gregory Gause, "Why Middle East Studies Missed the Arab Spring: The Myth of Authoritarian Stability," *Foreign Affairs*, July–August 2011.

3. Alexis de Tocqueville, *The French Revolution and the Old Regime* (Cambridge: Cambridge University Press, 2011), pp. 11–12.

4. Leonard Shapiro, *The Russian Revolutions of 1917: The Origins of Modern Communism* (New York: Basic Books, 1984), pp. 19, 39.

5. Shaul Bakhash, *The Reign of Ayatollahs* (New York: Basic Books, 1984).

6. Cited by YueChim Richard, "On the Surprise Elements of Revolution: Why Tunisia and Egypt?," March 4, 2011, http://www.wangyujian.com/?p=650&lang=en.

7. Interviews with several participants in the uprisings in Tunisia and Egypt, 2011 and 2012.

8. Timur Kuran, "Sparks and Prairie Fires: A Theory of Un-anticipated Political Revolutions," *Public Choice* 61 (1989): 41–74.

9. Charles Kurzman's fine analysis of the Iranian revolution of 1979 shows clearly that, against the structural, economic, and cultural dynamics, people's perception about when to join a protest or their reading about the "viability of change" is essential to the making of revolutions. Since it remains notoriously difficult to determine when such perceptions emerge, and among whom, it becomes almost impossible to predict revolution. See Charles Kurzman, *The Unthinkable Revolution in Iran* (Cambridge, MA: Harvard University Press, 2005).

10. Reported in Amin Allal, "Becoming Revolutionary in Tunisia, 2007–2011," in *Social Movements, Mobilization, and Contestation in the Middle East and North Africa*, 2nd ed., ed. Joel Beinin and Frederic Vairel (Stanford, CA: Stanford University Press, 2013), p. 194.

11. Asef Bayat, *Life as Politics: How Ordinary People Change the Middle East*, 2nd ed. (Stanford, CA: Stanford University Press, 2013).

12. Alexei Yurchak, *Everything Was Forever, Until It Was No More* (Princeton, NJ: Princeton University Press, 2006).

13. Gause, "Why Middle East Studies Missed the Arab Spring."

14. Hannah Arendt, *The Human Condition*, 2nd ed. (Chicago: University of Chicago Press, 1998).

15. For an astute study of surveillance in Tunisia under Ben Ali, see Beatrice Hibou, *The Force of Obedience: The Political Economy of Repression in Tunisia* (Cambridge: Polity Press, 2011).

16. For a documentation of some of these practices, see Bayat, *Life as Politics*; Linda Herrera and Asef Bayat, eds., *Being Young and Muslim: Cultural Politics in the Global South and North* (New York: Oxford University Press, 2013).

17. Jürgen Habermas, *The Structural Transformation of the Public Sphere: An Inquiry into a Category of Bourgeois Society* (Cambridge, MA: MIT Press, 1991).

18. See Taghi Azad Armaki, *Patouq and the Iranian Modernity* (Tehran: Avay-e Nour, 1390/2011).

19. Amelie Le Renard, *Society of Young Women: Opportunities of Power, Place, and Reform in Saudi Arabia* (Stanford, CA: Stanford University Press, 2014).

20. Interview with Abdelrahman, Cairo, June 2013.

21. Pascale Menoret, "Leaving Islamic Activism Behind: Ambiguous Disengagement in Saudi Arabia," in Beinin and Vairel, *Social Movements*, p. 82.

22. Interview with Professor Samiyah, Tunis, July 2011.

23. Interview with a teacher/mentor activist in Tunis, May 2012.

24. Amin Allal, "Becoming Revolutionary in Tunisia, 2007–2011," in Beinin and Vairel, *Social Movements*, pp. 185–204.

25. Interview with Hossam, Alexandria, July 2011.

26. Interview with AbdelRahman, Champaign, Illinois, August 2015.

27. Interview with AbdelRahman, Cairo, June 2013.

28. Narrated in Alia Mossallam, "On the Love of Life and Alaa's Detention," *Mada Masr*, January 4, 2014.

29. Interview with youth activist Abdelrahman Jad, Cairo, March 27, 2011.

30. Marie Duboc, "Egyptian Leftist Intellectuals' Activism from the Margins," in Beinin and Vairel, *Social Movements*, pp. 49–67.

31. For a perceptive analysis, see Elliot Colla, "Solidarity in the Time of Anti-normalization," *Middle East Report* 224 (Fall 2002): 10–15.

32. Habib Ayeb, "Social Geography of the Tunisian Revolution," *Review of African Political Economy* 38, no. 129 (2011): 473–485; Nizar Shaqroun, *Rawaya al-Thawra al-Tunisiya* [A narrative of the Tunisian revolution] (Tunis: Al-Dosari, 2011).

33. Lina Ben Mhenni, "My Arab Spring: Tunisia's Revolution Was a Dream," Al Jazeera, December 17, 2015; interview with Mabrouk Jebahi, Tunis, July 2012.

34. See, for instance, Timothy Mitchell, "Dreamland: The Neoliberalism of Your Desires," in *The Journey to Tahrir: Revolution, Protest, and Social Change in Egypt*, ed. Jeannie Sowers and Chris Toensing (London: Verso, 2012), pp. 224–234.

35. Hazem Biblawi, "The Rentier State in the Arab World," in *The Arab State*, ed. G. Luciani (London: Routledge, 1990), pp. 85–98; Michael Ross, "Does Oil Hinder Democracy?," *World Politics*, April 2001.

36. Kaveh Ehsani, "The Social History of Labor in the Iranian Oil Industry" (PhD diss., University of Leiden, Netherlands, 2014); Timothy Mitchell, *Carbon Democracy: Political Power in the Age of Oil* (London: Verso, 2011).

37. There are of course notable exceptions. Most scholars associated with the journal *Middle East Report* deployed both rigorous political economy approaches and highlighted the role of subaltern groups, notably workers, women, minorities, farmers, artists, and the like. Some of the notable contributors on the Arab countries include Joel Beinin, Zachary Lockman, Diane Singerman, Nadje Ali, Lila Abu-Lughod, Paul Amar, Gilbert Achcar, Sameh Naquib, Habib Ayeb, Reem Saad, Samiah Mehrez, Laleh Khalili, Elliot Cola, Adam Hanieh, and John Chalcraft.

38. United Nations Development Program, *Arab Human Development Report 2004* (New York: United Nations Development Program, 2004), p. 164.

39. Asef Bayat, "Egypt and the Post-Islamist Middle East," *OpenDemocracy*, February 2011.

40. Khalid al-Haddaji, "Hawamish: Al-Thawra al-Tonisiya Thawra Lam Taktamil" [Tunisia's revolution is not completed], in "Kitab al-Thawra 2: Al-Esharat al-Tounisia," special issue, *Al-Kitab al-Okhra*, no. 3 (August 2012).

41. See Asef Bayat, *Making Islam Democratic: Social Movements and the Post-Islamist Turn* (Stanford, CA: Stanford University Press, 2007).

42. For an analysis of post-Islamist trends in Muslim majority countries, see Asef Bayat, ed., *Post-Islamism: The Changing Faces of Political Islam* (Oxford: Oxford University Press, 2013).

43. This "new Arab public" seemed to share many features with their counterparts in the rest of the world. See Kees Biekart and Alan Fowler, "Activism 2010+," *Development and Change* 44, no. 3 (2013): 527–546.

44. The fear is so pronounced that some have called the trend the "Islamist Spring." See, for instance, Yigal Walt, "Islamist Spring Is upon Us," *Ynet News*, June 24, 2012, http://www.ynetnews.com/articles/0,7340,L-4246722,00.html.

45. For a detailed conceptualization and historical accounts of post-Islamism, see Bayat, *Post-Islamism*.

46. Interview with the party spokesman Samir Dilou, Deutschland Kultur, May 18, 2011, http://www.deutschlandradiokultur.de/wir-wollen-keinen gottesstaat.954 .de.html?dram:article_id=146287. See also Francesco Cavatorta and Fabio Merone, "Moderation through Exclusion? The Journey of Tunisian Ennahda from Fundamentalist to Conservative Party," *Democratization* 20, no. 5 (2013): 857–875.

47. Rached Ghannouchi, "From Political Islam to Muslim Democracy: The Ennahda Party and the Future of Tunisia," *Foreign Affairs*, September/October 2016, https://www.foreignaffairs.com/articles/tunisia/political-islam-muslim-democracy.

48. See Hosam Tamam, *Tahawwulat al-Ekhwan al-Muslimin* [Evolution of the Muslim Brotherhood] (Cairo: Maktaba Madbouli, 2010).

49. *El-Shorouk*, "Al-Qotbiyoun Yaseitaroun ala-al-Ekhwan" [Qutb followers will dominate the Brotherhood], December 22, 2009, p. 1.

50. I was present at the conference of the youth of the Muslim Brotherhood in March 2011, where such sentiments were expressed.

51. Ramadan al-Sherbini, "Brotherhood Defectors to Form Apolitical Group," *Gulf News*, January 11, 2013.

52. The value survey interviewed thirty-five hundred Egyptian adults. See Mansoor Moaddel, "What Do Arabs Want?," January 4, 2012, https://www.project -syndicate.org/commentary/what-do-arabs-want?barrier=accessreg.

53. Mohamed Abd El Azim Heba Habib, "Poll Shows Egyptian Opinion after the Revolution," May 26, 2011, http://www.masress.com/en/ youm7en/340346.

54. Interview with taxi driver, Cairo, March 2011.

Chapter 8

Sections of this chapter draw on Asef Bayat, "Revolution in Bad Times," *New Left Review* 80 (March–April 2013): 47–60.

1. Keith Kahn-Harris, "Naming the Movement," *Open Democracy*, June 22, 2011; Alain Badiou, "Tunisia, Egypt: When an East Wind Sweeps Away the Arrogance of the West," trans. Anindya Bhattacharyya, *Le Monde*, February 18, 2011, https:// bat020.com/2011/03/11/badiou-on-the-revolutions-in-egypt-and-tunisia/; Slavoj Žižek, "For Egypt, This Is the Miracle of Tahrir Square," *The Guardian*, February 10, 2011; Michael Hardt and Antonio Negri, "Arabs Are Democracy's New Pioneers," *The Guardian*, February 24, 2011; Paul Mason, *Why It's Kicking Off Everywhere: The New Global Revolutions* (London: Verso, 2012), p. 65.

2. More than seventy countries have experienced major political protests since 2010. See "The Protester: From the Arab Spring to Athens, from Occupy Wall Street to Moscow," *Time*, December 26, 2011.

3. Theda Skocpol, *States and Social Revolutions* (Cambridge: Cambridge University Press, 1979); Crane Brinton, *The Anatomy of Revolution* (New York: Vintage, 1965); Barrington Moore, *Social Origins of Dictatorship and Democracy* (New York: Beacon Press, 1993); Leon Trotsky, *History of the Russian Revolution* (Chicago: Haymarket Books, 2008); Samuel Huntington, *The Third Wave: Democratization in the Late 20th Century* (Norman: University of Oklahoma Press, 1993); G. O'Donnell, P. Schmitter, and L. Whitehead, eds., *Transitions from Authoritarian Rule: Comparative Perspectives* (Baltimore: Johns Hopkins University Press, 1986).

4. Huntington, *The Third Wave*; O'Donnell, Schmitter, and Whitehead, *Transitions from Authoritarian Rule*.

5. Asef Bayat, "The Green Revolt," in *Life as Politics: How Ordinary People Change the Middle East* (Stanford, CA: Stanford University Press, 2013), pp. 284–304.

6. Brinton, *The Anatomy of Revolution*; Trotsky, *History of the Russian Revolution*; Misagh Parsa, *Social Origins of the Iranian Revolution* (New Brunswick, NJ: Rutgers University Press, 1989); Henry Weber, *Nicaragua: The Sandinista Revolution* (London: Verso, 1981); James DeFronzo, *Revolutions and Revolutionary Movements*, 3rd ed. (Boulder, CO: Westview Press, 2007).

7. Victor Sebestyen, *Revolution 1989: The Fall of the Soviet Empire* (New York: Vintage, 2009), pp. 380–400.

8. Recently, some scholars have proposed that the transitions in communist East Germany, Pinochet's Chile, and Marcos's Philippines (as well as the failed attempts in China, Kenya, and Panama) be characterized as "nonviolent revolutions." Placing emphasis on civil and unarmed methods of resistance, the model would include both reformist (Chile) and revolutionary (East Germany) political trajectories and reflects both peaceful (Chile) and not so peaceful (the Philippines) strategies. See Sharon Erickson Nepstad, *Nonviolent Revolutions: Civil Resistance in the Late 20th Century* (New York: Oxford University Press, 2011).

9. Mona El-Ghobashi, "The Praxis of the Egyptian Revolution," *Middle East Report* 258 (2011): 12; Salwa Ismail, "Urban Subalterns in the Arab Revolutions: Cairo and Damascu in Comparative Perspective," *Comparative Studies in Society and History* 55, no. 4 (2013): 872; WikiThawra 2013, https://wikithawra.wordpress.com/author/wikithawra/.

10. The term "refolution" was used first by Timothy Garton Ash in June 1989 to describe the *initial* rounds of political reform in Poland and Hungary, the result of negotiations between the communist authorities and the leaderships of the opposition movements. See Timothy Garton Ash, "Revolution, the Springtime of Two Nations," *New York Review of Books*, June 15, 1989. It is important to stress that Garton Ash's article appeared just after Poland's first free parliamentary elections and before the structural and accelerating changes that rapidly followed—including the dissolution of the Communist Party, the end of the one-party system, the Warsaw

Pact, and constitutional change. If Garton Ash had written his essay a few weeks later, he might have used the term "revolution" instead to describe those significant changes. This is very different from the Arab world in that no Arab dictators during the Arab Spring agreed to far-reaching reform through negotiation; they were either forced out by revolutionary coercion (Ben Ali, Mubarak, Qaddafi) or tried to trick the revolutionaries through a superficial "change," e.g., the military in Egypt after Mubarak or Ali Saleh in Yemen. So, in this book, I clearly use the term "refolution" differently.

11. This is clear in the impressive survey of contemporary Arab thought by Elizabeth Suzanne Kassab, *Contemporary Arab Thought: Cultural Critique in Comparative Perspective* (New York: Columbia University Press, 2010).

12. Asef Bayat, *Making Islam Democratic* (Stanford, CA: Stanford University Press, 2007), p. 180.

13. In the wake of the Kefaya movement, the Egyptian intellectual Amr al-Shobaki warned of the "illusion of revolution" and popular rebellion. He argued the objective is reform and lobbying for reform. See Amr al-Shobaki, "Wahm al-Thawra al-Shab'iyya" [Illusion of the popular revolution], *Al-Masri Al-Youm*, May 10, 2007.

14. Sabry Hafez, "The Novel, Politics, and Islam," *New Left Review*, no. 5, 2nd ser. (September–October 2000): 141. For information on the decline of the activism of the leftist intellectuals in Egypt, see Marie Duboc, "Egyptian Leftist Intellectuals' Activism from the Margins," in *Social Movements, Mobilization, and Contestation in the Middle East and North Africa*, 2nd ed., ed. Joel Beinin and Frederic Vairel (Stanford, CA: Stanford University Press, 2013), pp. 49–67.

15. Samia Mehrez, "Take Them out of the Ball Game: Egypt's Cultural Players in Crisis," *Middle East Report* 219 (Summer 2001): 10–15; Bayat, *Making Islam Democratic*, p. 180.

16. George Lawson, "The Arab Uprisings: Revolution or Protests?," accessed December 23, 2016, http://www.lse.ac.uk/IDEAS/publications/reports/pdf/SR011/FINAL_LSE_IDEAS__TheArabUprisings_Lawson.pdf.

17. Maha Abdelrahman, "In Praise of Organization: Egypt between Activism and Revolution," *Development and Change* 44, no. 3 (May 2013): 572.

18. Interview with Ismail Iskanderani, Alexandria, July 15, 2011. Another organizer of the event acknowledged that "the organizers never expected this to happen." Interview with AbdelRahman Jad, Cairo, March 27, 2011.

19. Interview with cyberactivist Tarek Kahlawi, Tunis, July 2011.

20. Interview with journalist activist Ghassan, Tunis, July 2011.

21. Interview with Abdelrahman, the co-administrator of the We Are All Khaled Said Facebook page, Cairo, July 2013.

22. Wael Ghoneim, quoted in *Tweets from Tahrir*, ed. Nadia Idle and Alex Nunns (New York: OR Books, 2011).

23. Herbert Blumer, "Social Movements," in *Principles of Sociology*, ed. A. Mc-Clung Lee (New York: Barnes and Noble, 1951), p. 202.

24. Charles Tilly, *From Mobilization to Revolution* (Boston: Addison-Wesley, 1978), p. 208.

25. Wael Ghoneim, quoted in Idle and Nunns, *Tweets from Tahrir*, p. 37.

26. Idle and Nunns, *Tweets from Tahrir*, p. 204.

27. Ibid., p. 103.

28. Gamal Eid, *Twists and Turns of the Egyptian Revolution, 2011–2014* (Cairo: Arab Network for Human Rights Information, 2016), p. 18.

29. Idle and Nunns, *Tweets from Tahrir*, p. 156.

30. Eid, *Twists and Turns*, pp. 24–25.

31. Idle and Nunns, *Tweets from Tahrir*, pp. 102, 184.

32. The activist Mustafa Najjar related his observations in the meeting of the Coalition of the Revolutionary Youths held in the al-Ahram Center for Political and Strategic Studies on February 23, 2011; see Amr Hashem Rabi'a, *Thawra 25 January: Qara'a Awwaliyya wa Ru'ya Mustaqbiliyya* [January 25 revolution: An initial interpretation and future prospect] (Cairo: Al-Ahram Center, 2011), p. 429.

33. The regime defenders at the time included Ahmed Shafik, Mubarak's last prime minister. Reported by a member of the Coalition of the Revolutionary Youths in a meeting organized by the al-Ahram Center in Rabi'a, *Thawra 25 January*, p. 429.

34. Mahmoud Salem, "Sandmonkey," quoted in Idle and Nunns, *Tweets from Tahrir*, p. 156. He called for "registering the protesters, getting their names, addresses. and districts. Start organizing them into committees, and they elect leaders."

35. "There is no organization, the people are the ones driving the revolution," stated a protester (ibid., p. 56). This sentiment of antiorganization was quite strong and widespread.

36. Interview with Tarek and Ghassam, Tunis, July 2011.

37. Choukri Hmed, "Abeyance, Networks, Contingency and Structures: History and Origins of the Tunisian Revolution," *Revue française de science politique* 62, no., 5–6 (2012): 48; Dirk Wanrooij, "Revolution in Imbaba" (master's thesis, University of Amsterdam, 2011).

38. Ahmed Ghity, an Egyptian socialist member of April 6 movement, quoted in Rabi'a, *Thawra 25 January*, p. 456. Similar sentiments were expressed by Tunisian activists. Interview with Tarek and Ghassam, Tunis, July 2011.

39. See Wael Ghoneim, *Revolution 2.0: The Power of the People Is Greater Than People in Power* (New York: Houghton Mifflin Harcourt, 2012), pp. 36, 37.

40. Interview with Abdelrahman Mansour, Champaign, Illinois, August 2015.

41. Ghoneim, *Revolution 2.0*, pp. 42, 43, 293, 204–205.

42. From a discussion with twenty-five Youths of the Revolution, quoted in Rabiʿa, *Thawra 25 January*, pp. 435–436.

43. Tamer al-Sadi's testimony, cited in ibid., p. 450.

44. "April 6 Youth Movement," RSS, accessed January 13, 2017, https://shabab6april.wordpress.com/about/shabab-6-april-youth-movement-about-us-in-english/.

45. Walid Shawqi, "Kaifa Tahawul al-Hamish Ela Matn: An al-Ihtijaj wal-Siyassa wa Haraka 6 April" [How the margin moves to the center 6 April], *Mada Masr*, October 29, 2016.

46. Interview with AbdelRahman Mansour, Champaign, Illinois, August 2015.

47. Cited in Mayssoum Sukarieh, "Egyptians between Squares," *Counter Punch*, December 3, 2012, http://www.counterpunch.org/2012/12/03/egyptians-between-squares/.

48. This is clear from the testimonies of twenty-four representatives of the coalition of the Youths of the Revolution in a meeting organized by the al-Ahram Center for Strategic Studies, Cairo; see the proceedings in Rabiʿa, *Thawra 25 January*, p. 450.

49. Idle and Nunns, *Tweets from Tahrir*, p. 220. Other activists came to realize their misunderstandings some five years later. See, for instance, Mohammad Affan, "Filzdikri al-Khamisa lil-Thawrat al-Arabiya: Ma allazdi Fatena Edraka fil-Waqat al-Munasib" [Fifth anniversary of the Arab revolutions], *Edaat*, January 23, 2015.

50. Response by some members of the Coalition of the Revolutionary Youths when asked who they favored as the post-Mubarak president. See Rabiʿa, *Thawra 25 January*, pp. 453, 454–455.

51. Malek Saghiri, "Greetings to the Dawn: Living through the Bittersweet Revolution" [Tunisia], in *Diaries of an Unfinished Revolution*, ed. Layla al-Zubaidi and Mathew Cassel (New York: Penguin Books, 2013), p. 44.

52. Ibid., pp. 43, 45.

53. Interview with Professor Hafid, Tunis, July 22, 2011. For a good discussion of the state of obedience in prerevolutionary Tunisia, see Beatrice Hibou, *The Force of Obedience: The Political Economy of Repression in Tunisia* (Cambridge: Polity Press, 2011).

54. Interview with the activist Abdel-Haqq Zammouri, Tunis, July 25, 2011.

55. Interview with Mehdi Barqoumi, Tunis, July 28, 2011.

56. Bogumila Hall, "Subaltern Rightful Struggles: Comparative Ethnographies of the Bedouin Villagers in the Naqab and the Akhdam Slum Dwellers of Sanaʿa" (PhD diss., European University Institute, Florence, 2016), p. 154.

57. Saghiri, "Greetings to the Dawn," p. 43.

58. Idle and Nunns, *Tweets from Tahrir*, p. 214.

59. April Longley Alley, "Yemen Changes Everything . . . and Nothing," *Journal of Democracy* 24, no. 4 (October 2013): 74–85.

60. Kareem Fahim, "Militants and Politics Bedevil Yemen's New Leaders," *New York Times*, April 21, 2012.

61. Interview with cyberactivist Tarek, Tunis, July 2011.

62. Interview Tarek and Ghassan, Tunis, July 2011.

63. See Tunisian daily *Al-Sabah*, August 16, 2011, www.assabah.com.tn/article-56485.html.

64. Lina Ben Mhenni, "My Arab Spring: Tunisia's Revolution Was a Dream," Al Jazeera, December 17, 2015, http://www.aljazeera.com/news/2015/12/arab-spring-tunisia-revolution-dream-151209062258742.html.

65. Eric Hobsbawm, *Age of Extremes: 1914–1991* (London: Abacus, 1995), p. 439.

66. See, for instance, Ruth Marshal, *Political Spiritualities: The Pentecostal Revolution in Nigeria* (Berkeley: University of California Press, 2009).

67. See James Toth, *Sayyid Qutb: The Life and Legacy of a Radial Islamic Intellectual* (New York: Oxford University Press, 2013); see also John Calver, *Sayyid Qutb and the Origins of Radical Islamism* (New York: Columbia University Press, 2010).

68. See Faisal Devji, *Landscapes of the Jihad: Militancy, Morality, Modernity* (Ithaca, NY: Cornell University Press, 2005).

69. See Asef Bayat, ed., *Post-Islamism: The Changing Faces of Political Islam* (Oxford: Oxford University Press, 2013).

70. See Asef Bayat, "Piety, Privilege, and Egyptian Youth," *ISIM Newsletter*, no. 10, 2002.

71. Hall, *Subaltern Rightful Struggle*, p. 156.

72. Arundhati Roy, "The NGO-ization of Resistance," MASSALIJN, September 4, 2014, http://massalijn.nl/new/the-ngo-ization-of-resistance; Sheila Carapico , *Political Aid and Arab Activism: Democracy Promotion, Justice, and Representation* (Cambridge: Cambridge University Press, 2014), p. 163.

73. Interview with Ahmed, Alexandria, June 2011.

74. For a perceptive discussion of the elitist and conservative politics of the mainstream NGOs in Egypt, see Maha Abdelrahman, *Civil Society Exposed: The Politics of NGOs in Egypt* (Cairo: American University in Cairo Press, 2004). Joel Beinin shows the marginal and even depoliticizing role of civil society in the Egyptian uprising. Joel Beinin, "Civil Society, NGOs, and Egypt's 2011 Popular Uprisings," *South Atlantic Quarterly* 113, no. 2 (Spring 2014): 396–406.

75. Bayat, "Piety, Privilege, and Egyptian Youth."

76. Life Makers had branches in Egypt, Morocco, and the United Kingdom. The initiative was perhaps similar to the programs of the religious leaders Fatullah Gulen's "market Islam" in Turkey and the Indonesian Abdullah Gymnastiar, known as Aa Gym, who held a program of "managing hearts" in Indonesia influenced by the American self-improvement paradigm. Amr Khaled was recognized by *Time* magazine as among the one hundred most influential people in the world in 2007.

77. For a fine analysis of this kind of developmentalist paradigm with respect to the poor, see Julia Elyachar, *The Markets of Dispossession: NGOs, Economic Development, and the State in Cairo* (Durham, NC: Duke University Press, 2005).

78. Islah Jad, "The NGO-ization of the Arab Women's Movements," *IDS Bulletin* 35, no. 4 (2004): 34–42.

79. Mervat Hatem, "Economic and Political Liberation in Egypt and the Demise of State Feminism," *International Journal of Middle East Studies* 24, no. 2 (1992): 231–251.

80. CARE International, *Arab Spring or Arab Autumn: Women's Political Participation in the Uprisings and Beyond* (London: CARE, 2012).

81. See a survey of social policy among the political forces in Egypt, including the New Wafd Party, Free Egyptian Party, Destour Party, Egypt Freedom Party, the leftist Tagammu Party, Egyptian Social Democratic Party, Socialist Popular Alliance, Arab Dignity Party, Strong Egypt Party, Salafi Nour Party, the ruling Freedom and Justice Party (or the Muslim Brotherhood), as well as the youth movements such as the April 6 movement, Youth Movement for Justice and Freedom, and the Coalition of Revolutionary Youths, in Ayman Abdel Maati, "Social Justice: The Road to Complete the Revolution in Egypt (A Case Study of the Demands of the Masses and the Resistance of the Authorities)," in *Social Justice: Concept and Policies after the Arab Revolutions* (Cairo: Arab Forum for Alternatives and Rosa Luxemburg Foundation, 2014), p. 77.

82. Ibid., p. 72.

83. See Fatih al-Shamikhi, "Social Justice in the Light of the Revolutionary Process in Tunisia," in *Social Justice*, p. 92.

84. Ibid.

85. "Ennahda Movement Programme for Freedom, Justice and Development in Tunisia," 2011, http://kurzman.unc.edu/files/2011/06/Nahda_2011_summary_in_English.pdf.

86. Al-Shamikhi, "Social Justice," p. 98.

87. Cited in Habib Ayeb, "Al-Tahmish al-Ijtimaii wal-Iqtisadi wal-Makani le Hayyatein Sha'biein Min Tunis: Al-Sayyida al-Menubiyya Fi Tunis wa Zariq Fi Qabis" [Socioeconomic and spatial marginality in Tunis and Qabis], unpublished paper, Cairo, 2012.

88. Katerina Delacoura, "Islamism and Neoliberalism in the Aftermath of the 2011 Uprisings: The Freedom and Justice Party in Egypt and Nahda in Tunisia," in *Neoliberal Governmentality and the Future of the State in the Middle East and North Africa*, ed. Emel Akcali (London: Palgrave, 2016), pp. 61–83. For the role of European and Arab Gulf States' interventions, see the fine study by Heba Khalil, "Wa Maza an al-Adala al-Ijtimaiyya: Al-Rabi' al-Arabi bein al-Tadakholat al-Orubiyya wa al-Mosa'edat al-Arabiyya" [Why social justice: The Arab Spring between Euro-

pean interventions and Arab assistance], in *Al-Adala al-Ijtemaiyya bein al-Herak al-Sha'bi wal-Masarat al-Syassiya fi al-Boldan al-Arabiyya*, proceedings of workshop, Rabat, September 12–15, 2015 (Cairo: Rwafead, 2016), pp. 157–176.

89. See the fine study by the political scientist Eberhard Kienle, "Changed Regimes, Changed Priorities? Economic and Social Policies after the 2011 Elections in Tunisia and Egypt," Working Paper 928, Economic Research Forum, Cairo, July 2015, p. 25. Hisham Kandil, the prime minister under Morsi, refused the court order to renationalize a number of companies privatized under Mubarak. See Wael Gamal, "Social Justice and the Arab Revolutions," in *Social Justice*, p. 21.

90. Massimo Di Ricco, "The Impeccable Narrative around Tunisian Workers' Syndicate," *Jadaliyya*, January 29, 2016; for a more comprehensive analysis, see Joel Beinin, *Workers and Thieves: Labor Movements and Popular Uprisings in Tunisia and Egypt* (Stanford, CA: Stanford University Press, 2015).

91. Interview with Fatma Ramadan, worker-activist with Egyptian Initiative for Personal Rights, Cairo, June 9, 2013.

92. Ron Nixon, "US Groups Helped Nurture Arab Uprisings," *New York Times*, April 14, 2011; and David Kirkpatrick and David Sanger, "A Tunisian-Egyptian Link That Shook Arab History," *New York Times*, February 13, 2011.

93. Ghoneim, *Revolution 2.0*, pp. 21–23. For a more detailed discussion of this issue, see Linda Herrera, *Revolution in the Age of Social Media: The Egyptian Popular Insurrection and the Internet* (London: Verso, 2014), p. 54.

94. See Herrera, *Revolution in the Age of Social Media*, chap. 2.

95. Tomaz Mastnak, "The Reinvention of Civil Society: Through the Looking Glass of Democracy," *European Journal of Sociology* 46, no. 2 (August 2005): 323–355.

96. The prominent intellectual Adam Michnik has argued that Poles voted for the economic reforms on the assumption that they were voting for socialism without communism, that is, a nontotalitarian distributionist state; see Zsuzsa Gille, "The Hungarian Foie Gras Boycott: Struggles for Moral Sovereignty in Postsocialist Europe," *Eastern European Politics and Societies* 25, no. 1 (February 2011): 114–128. For Hungary, surveys suggest similar sentiments. See Zsuzsa Gille, *Paprika, Foie Gras, and Red Mud: The Politics of Materiality in the European Union* (Bloomington: Indiana University Press, 2016).

97. Juan Linz and Alfred Stepan, *Problems of Democratic Transition and Consolidation* (Baltimore: Johns Hopkins University Press, 1996), pp. 270–271.

98. "From Arab Spring to a Cold Winter," *People's Daily online*, December 29, 2014, http://chinaandthemiddleeast.blogspot.com/2014/12/from-arab-spring-to-cold-winter.html. See also Tariq Ramadan, *Islam and the Arab Awakening* (Oxford: Oxford University Press, 2012), pp. 11–12.

Chapter 9

Parts of this chapter draw on Asef Bayat, "Plebeians of the Arab Spring," *Current Anthropology* 56, no. S11 (October 2015): 33–43.

1. Chris Stephen, "Libya's Arab Spring: The Revolution That Ate Its Children," *The Guardian*, February 16, 2015.

2. *Al-Badil*, March 16, 2013.

3. Peter Beaumont and Patrick Kingsley, "Violent Tide of Salafism Threatens the Arab Spring," *The Guardian*, February 9, 2013.

4. See Kefteji: Tunisian Politics, Media, and Culture, June 11, 2012, https://kefteji .wordpress.com/tag/tunisia/page/4/.

5. *News Wires*, France24.com, October 13, 2013.

6. "Saudi Police Arrest Two over 'Free Hugs,'" Al Jazeera, November 21, 2013, http://www.aljazeera.com/news/middleeast/2013/11/saudi-police-arrest-two-over -free-hugs-20131121164035187159.html.

7. Interview with Hala, Cairo, May 2015.

8. Sheera Frenkel and Maged Atef, "More and More Egyptian Women Are Casting Aside Their Veils," November 7, 2013, https://www.buzzfeed.com/sheera frenkel/more-and-more-egyptian-women-are-casting-aside-their-veils?utm_term =.rkzrjJo6zd#.aqZoPZMLDW. My own interview with Egyptian activists supports the claim.

9. Interview with Hala, Cairo, May 2015.

10. Frenkel and Atef, "More and More Egyptian Women."

11. Interview with Hala, Cairo, May 2015.

12. For a perceptive analysis, see Laleh Khalili, "Women in and after the Arab Spring," Sadighi Annual Lecture pamphlet, Amsterdam, 2013, pp. 62–63. Also see Maya Mikdashi, "Waiting for Alia," *Jadaliyya*, November 20, 2011, http://www.jada liyya.com/pages/index/3208/waiting-for-alia.

13. Bel Trew, "Egypt's Growing Gay-Rights Movement," *Daily Beast*, May 21, 2013.

14. Sarah Carr, "Of Moral Panic and State Security," *Mada Masr*, November 25, 2013; *Aswat Masriyya*, October 13, 2013.

15. "Egypt Prosecutor Orders 7 Held for Homosexuality," Associated Press, September 6, 2014.

16. Nadia Idle and Alex Nunns, eds., *Tweets from Tahrir* (New York: OR Books, 2011), p. 221.

17. Some estimates speak of four million adherents. The two-million figure is based on the Gallup and University of Michigan polls. See Magdy Samann, "Atheist Rise in Egypt," *ZAM Chronicle*, October 17, 2013.

18. Ibid.

19. Carlyle Murphy, "Atheism Explodes in Saudi Arabia despite State-Enforced Ban," *Global Post*, June 12, 2014.

20. Ibid.

21. Murphy, "Atheism Explodes in Saudi Arabia."

22. Diaa Hadid, "Arab Atheists, Though Few, Inch out of the Shadows," *Huffington Post*, March 8, 2013.

23. Mounir Adib, "While Atheisim in Egypt Rises, Backlash Ensues," *Egypt Independent*, September 30, 2013.

24. *Al-Watan*, October 28, 2013.

25. See Shahra Razavi and Anne Jenichen, "Unhappy Marriage of Religion and Politics," special issue, *Third World Quarterly* 31, no. 6 (2010).

26. Cited in Diaa Hadid, "Arab Atheists."

27. Samann, "Atheist Rise in Egypt."

28. *Al-Ahram* daily, June 18, 2014.

29. See an interview with an anonymous member of this secret group: "Anarchists in Egypt, Will the Real Black Bloc Please Stand Up?," Tahrir-ICN, March 3, 2011, tahriricn.wordpress.com/2013/11/03/Egypt-anarchists.

30. Interview with activists of Feminism Attack, in "Tunisia: Feminism Attack! Anarcha-Feminism in Tunisia," Tahrir-ICN, https://tahriricn.wordpress.com/2013/11/04/tunisia-feminism-attack-the-anarchist-feminism-in-tunisia/.

31. Idle and Nunns, *Tweets from Tahrir*, p. 223.

32. Cited in David Kirkpatrick and Mayy el-Sheikh, "In Egypt, a Chasm Grows between Young and Old," *New York Times*, February 16, 2014.

33. "Student Groups Demand Dismissal of Higher Education, Interior Ministers," *Ahram Online*, November 30, 2013, http://english.ahram.org.eg/NewsContent/1/64/87890/Egypt/Politics-/Student-groups-demand-dismissal-of-Egypt-higher-ed.aspx.

34. Stated in a conversation in Champaign, fall 2013.

35. Kirkpatrick and El-Sheikh, "In Egypt, a Chasm Grows."

36. Cited in Christopher de Bellaigue, "Viewpoint: Egypt's Emerging Revolution of the Mind," BBC News Middle East, November 12, 2012, BBC News, http://www.bbc.com/news/world-middle-east-20295572.

37. Vickie Langohr, "This Is Our Square: Fighting Sexual Assault at Cairo Protests," MER 268, accessed December 23, 2016, www.merip.org/mer/mer268/our-square.

38. For a very interesting eyewitness account by an American photojournalist, see Mathew Cassel, Al Jazeera, February 10, 2011. See also Dirk Wanrooij, "The Egyptian Uprising: Imbaba" (master's thesis, University of Amsterdam, 2011).

39. See Asef Bayat, "Does Radical Islam Have an Urban Ecology?," in *Life as*

Politics: How Ordinary People Change the Middle East, 2nd ed. (Stanford, CA: Stanford University Press, 2013), pp. 188–201.

40. Anthony Shadid, "Few Focus on Religion in One Cairo Neighborhood," *New York Times,* February 15, 2011.

41. Cited in Paul Mason, *Why It's Kicking Off Everywhere* (London: Verso, 2012), p. 15.

42. According to Gamal Eid, an activist resident on his Facebook, January 2014.

43. Amnesty International, *"We Are Not Dirt": Forced Evictions in Egypt's Informal Settlements,* 2011, http://amnistia.pt/files/Relatoriosvarios/Egypt_slums_report _August2011.pdf, p. 3.

44. I am grateful to Alaa Abdel-Fattah, a revolutionary activist who brought this point to my attention; Cairo, June 2013.

45. Sara Carr, "Informal Settlement Dwellers Evicted despite Housing Promises," *Al-Masry al-Youm,* July 31, 2011.

46. Interview with Rida and Hayat, Tunis, January 2103.

47. See Nouri Gana, ed., *The Making of the Tunisian Revolution* (Edinburgh: Edinburgh University Press, 2013), introduction.

48. *Al-Maal,* June 11, 2013.

49. *Al-Masry al-Youm,* June 20, 2013.

50. *Ahram online,* November 18, 2012, http://english.ahram.org.eg/.

51. *Al-youm Essabea,* March 17, 2013.

52. *Veto,* May 16, 2013.

53. *Al-youm Essabea,* March 1, 2013.

54. *Al-Badil,* May 23, 2013.

55. *Al-Ahram,* October 5, 2013.

56. *Al-youm Essabea,* May 20, 2013.

57. *Al-Masry al-Youm,* March 14. 2013.

58. Nada Tarbush, "Cairo2050: Urban Dream or Modernist Delusion?," *Journal of International Affairs* 65, no. 2 (2012): 176.

59. Tome Dale, "Cairo's Central Slum under Threat," *Al-Masry al-Youm,* July 5, 2012.

60. Video interview made by the architect Omnia Khalil, June 2012, YouTube.

61. Abdel-Karim al-Jaberi, "Update: Gunfire, Tear Gas Continue in Bulaq," *Al-Masry al-Youm,* July 2, 2012.

62. Abdel Karim al-Jaberi, "Wave of Arrests, Threat of Eviction Plague Ramlet Bulaq," *Al-Masry al-Youm,* August 7, 2012.

63. For a fine discussion of this case, see Omnia Khalil, "The Everyday in Ramlat Bulaq," *Middle East Report* 274 (2015), http://www.merip.org/mer/mer274/ everyday-ramlat-bulaq.

64. Omar Halwa, "Out in the Dark," *Al-Masry al-Youm,* August 5, 2012.

65. *Al-Youm Assabe'a*, May 22, 2013; *Al-Badil*, May 22, 2013.

66. *Al-Shorouk*, May 23, 2013.

67. *Al-Masry al-Youm*, June 7, 2013; *Al-Shorouk*, May 29, 2013.

68. Omar Halawa, "Searching for Water: Residents of Giza Protest Unstable Supply," *Al-Masry al-Youm*, July 23, 2012.

69. *Al-Masry al-Youm*, June 20, 2013.

70. *Al-Youm Assabe'a*, February 9, 2013.

71. *Al-Badil*, March 10, 2013.

72. *Al-Ahram Online*, January 9, 2013.

73. *Al-Ahram*, March 8, 2013; *Al-Balad*, May 29, 2013.

74. *Masr al-Jadid*, 23, 2012.

75. *Al-Masry al-Youm*, May 19, 2013.

76. *Al-Shorouk*, June 11, 2013.

77. *Al-Shorouk*, February 15, 2013.

78. Egyptian Center for Economic and Social Rights, *Special Reports/ECSER: Solidarity Activities during 2013*, 2013, http://ecesr.org/en/2013/12/31/special-reports-ecesr-solidarity-activities-during-2013/. The Egyptian Ministry of Manpower reported that during 2011, workers organized 335 strikes (including 135 sit-ins in the public sector and 123 in the private sector) and 4,460 complaints to the ministry. See *Al-Masry al-Youm*, January 17, 2012.

79. Office of President Morsi, published in a poster and distributed officially, June 2013. In post-Morsi Egypt, labor unrest continued. Between July 1, 2013, and November, the Ministry of Manpower reported 70 cases of labor protests, mostly illegal, in addition to 5,150 collective and 1,746 individual complaints. See *Al-Masry al-Youm*, December 5, 2013.

80. Asef Bayat and Eric Denis, "Who Is Afraid of Ashwaiyyat? Urban Change and Politics in Egypt," *Environment and Urbanization* 12, no. 2 (October 2000): 185–199.

81. Alia Gana, "The Rural and Agricultural Roots of the Tunisian Revolution: When Food Security Matters," *International Journal of Sociology of Agriculture and Food* 19, no. 2 (2012): 201–213.

82. Habib Ayeb, "Rural Revolution in Tunisia: Inaudible Voices," unpublished paper, 2014.

83. Yasmine Moataz Ahmed, "The Union Effect and the State Effect," paper presented at "Conference Tunisia and Egypt: A Comparative Reading of a Revolutionary Process," Tunis, November 9–10, 2012.

84. Lila Abu-Lughod, "Taking Back the Village: Rural Youth in a Moral Revolution," *Middle East Report* 272 (Fall 2014), http://www.merip.org/mer/mer272.

85. David McMurray, "The Bouazizi Effect in Morocco," *Middle East Report Online* 21, February 21, 2013, http://www.merip.org/blog?page=16.

86. *Al-Masry al-Youm*, March 14, 2012.

87. Jano Charbel, "Street Vendors Forming Union to Combat State Crackdown," *Al-Masry al-Youm*, December 9, 2012.

88. Egyptian Initiative for Personal Rights Report, *Economic and Social Justice* (Arabic), December 9, 2012.

89. Abu-Bakr al-Gindi, head of CAPMAS, quoted in *Al-Shorouk*, March 15, 2013.

90. Charbel, "Street Vendors Forming Union."

91. The details of the project are documented in Tadamun: Cairo Urban Solidarity Initiative, "Paving the Streets of Mit Uqba," http://www.tadamun.info/?post_type=initiative&p=488&lang=en&lang=en#.WIAEu_OOrx4.

92. Steve Viney, "Zabaleen Sidelined by Morsi's 'Clean Homeland' Campaign," *Al-Masry al-Youm*, August 14, 2012.

93. Dina Makran-Ebeid, "Old People Are Not Revolutionaries: Labor Struggles between Precarity and Istiqra in a Factory Occupation in Egypt," *Jadaliyya*, January 25, 2015.

94. Esra' Mohammed Ali, "Ehya' Bel-Esm Faqat" [Upgrading in name only], *Al-Masry al-Youm*, April 1, 2013.

95. Wael Gamal, "Blackouts in Egypt Are Also Politics," *Al-Ahram Weekly*, July 31, 2012.

96. Omar Najati, video lecture, American University of Beirut, City Debate lecture series, 2013.

97. Asef Bayat, *Street Politics: Poor People's Movements in Iran* (New York: Columbia University Press, 1997).

98. Interview with Fatma Ramadan, worker activist for Egyptian Initiative for Personal Rights, Cairo, June 9, 2013.

Chapter 10

1. Michelle Dunne and Scott Williamson, "Egypt's Unprecedented Instability by the Numbers," Carnegie Endowment for International Peace, March 24, 2014, http://carnegieendowment.org/2014/03/24/egypt-s-unprecedented-instability-by-numbers-pub-55078.

2. Including Egypt, Tunisia, Libya, Syria, Jordan, and Bahrain; estimated by the HSBC banking giant, cited in *Al-Arabiyya*, October 9, 2013.

3. For a report on the state of the countries undergoing the revolutions in the MENA region, see Transformation Index BTI 2016, "Revolutions in Shambles," http://www.bti-project.org/en/reports/regional-reports/middle-east-and-north-africa/.

4. See, for instance, Gilbert Achcar, *The People Want: A Radical Explanation of the Arab Uprising* (Berkeley: University of California Press, 2013), p. 145; Jean-Pierre

Filiu, *From Deep State to Islamic State: The Arab Counter-revolution and Its Jihadi Legacy* (London: Hearst, 2014). These authors are in opposition to those such as Bernard Lewis, who attribute the setbacks in Arab Spring to the absence of democratic culture.

5. David Kirkpatrick, "Leaked Emirati Emails Could Threaten Peace Talks in Libya," *New York Times*, November 12, 2015.

6. Guido Steinberg, "Leading the Counter-revolution: Saudi Arabia and the Arab Spring," SWP Research Paper (Berlin: German Institute for International and Security Affairs, June 2014). Recently, the Saudi officials admitted that the government has supported radical Islamism, including the Wahhabi trends, since the 1960s as a way to counter secular, socialist, and democratic ideas that threatened the Saudi regime; see Zalmay Khalilzad, "'We Misled You': How the Saudis Are Coming Clean on Funding Terrorism," *Politico*, September 14, 2016, http://www .politico.com/magazine/story/2016/09/saudi-arabia-terrorism-funding-214241.

7. According to Hugh Roberts, primarily the Western powers (United States, United Kingdom, France), the Arab Gulf States (Saudi Arabia, Qatar), and Turkey have hijacked the Syrian revolution because they have insisted on regime change, thus sidelining the nonviolent opposition. Roberts cites a leaked document by the US Defense Intelligence Agency showing that as early as 2012, the United States anticipated ISIS and its establishment of the Caliphate in Iraq and Syria but did nothing to prevent it because it served as a counter to the Assad regime. See Hugh Roberts, "The Hijackers," *London Review of Books* 37, no. 14 (2015), http://www.lrb .co.uk/v37/n14/hugh-roberts/the-hijackers.

8. A WikiLeaks revelation of Hillary Clinton's e-mail suggests that the Israeli government believed that the escalating civil war in neighboring Syria would undermine the regime and keep Iran preoccupied with Syrian affairs. See "Syria, Turkey, Israel, Iran," Hillary Clinton Email Archive, 2012, https://wikileaks.org/ clinton-emails/emailid/12171.

9. See Stephen Walt, "Revolution and War," *World Politics* 44, no. 3 (April 1992): 321–368.

10. See the classic work on revolutionary transitions: Guillermo O'Donnell, Philippe Schmitter, and Lawrence Whitehead, eds., *Transitions from Authoritarian Rule: Comparative Perspective* (Baltimore: Johns Hopkins University Press, 1986).

11. See, for instance, Isobel Coleman and Terra Lawson-Remer, "A User's Guide to Democratic Transitions," *Foreign Policy*, June 18, 2013; Juan Linz and Alfred Stepan, *Problems of Democratic Transition and Consolidation: Southern Europe, South Africa, and Post-communist Europe* (Baltimore: Johns Hopkins University Press, 1996); Samuel Huntington, *The Third Wave: Democratization in the Late Twentieth Century* (Norman: Oklahoma University Press, 1991).

12. Hafez Ghanem, "Egypt's Difficult Transition: Why the International Com-

munity Must Stay Economically Engaged," Brookings Institution, Working Paper 66, January 2014.

13. Coleman and Lawson-Remer, "A User's Guide to Democratic Transitions."

14. See Sergio Bitar and Abraham Lowenthal, eds., *Democratic Transitions: Conversations with World Leaders* (Baltimore: Johns Hopkins University Press, 2015).

15. Huntington, *The Third Wave*, pp.121–124.

16. Crane Brinton, *The Anatomy of Revolution* (New York: Vintage, 1965), pp. 180, 207.

17. Interview with Gamila, medical intern, Tunis, July 23, 2011.

18. M. Boduszynski and D. Pickard, "Tracking the 'Arab Spring': Libya Starts from Scratch," *Journal of Democracy* 24, no. 4 (October 2013): 87.

19. "Arab Spring Economies: Unfinished Business," *The Economist*, February 4, 2012, http://www.economist.com/node/21546018.

20. Egypt suffered a 95 percent decline in income between 2010 and 2013. Egyptian hotels received 14.7 million guests in 2010 but only 9.5 million in 2013. See Patrick Kingsley, "Egypt's Tourism Revenues Fall after Political Upheavals," *The Guardian*, August 29, 2014. In Tunisia, where the tourist industry involved some seven hundred thousand direct and indirect jobs, 60 percent of hotel reservations for the summer of 2011 were canceled.

21. The poll (1,395 people) was conducted by the Egyptian Center for Public Opinion Research, Baseera, in September 2013; reported in "Egyptians' Living Conditions and Their Expectations for the Future: Poll," *Daily News—Egypt*, September 8, 2013.

22. Cited in Hend El-Behary, "More Than Half of Egypt's Youth Want to Emigrate for Work," *Daily News—Egypt*, July 22, 2013.

23. Hannah Arendt, "Reflections: Civil Disobedience," *New Yorker*, September 12, 1970, p. 70.

24. This is how, for instance, the editor in chief of *Alsharq Alawsat* thinks of the Egyptian revolution because of its "chaos." See Tareq al-Hameed, "Hadha Ra'ii" [This is my opinion], *Alsharq Alawsat*, June 27, 2013. See a similar view by a Saudi columnist: Mishari al-Thaidi, http://archive.aawsat.com/leader.asp?section=3&article=705629&issueno=1241.

25. Stated by a number of elite Tunisians who longed for the old order; interview in Tunis, July 22, 2011.

26. See, for instance, "Sowar Mubarak Tajtah al-Shaware" [Mubarak rebels take over the streets], *Al-Arabiyya*, April 24, 2013.

27. See Jon Lee Anderson, "The Unraveling: Letter from Libya," *New Yorker*, February 23, 2015.

28. For Tunisia, see "Tunisia Unemployment Protests Spread to Capital," Al

Jazeera, January 21, 2016, http://www.aljazeera.com/news/2016/01/clashes-spread
ing-tunisia-unemployment-protests-160121190816218.html.

29. The Tunisian activist Rasha was emphatic on this; interview in Tunisia, July
26, 2011.

30. Carlotta Gall, "Release of Ousted Leaders Raises Questions in Tunisia," *International New York Times*, July 18, 2014, p. 5.

31. A poll by Zogby Research Services conducted in September 2013 showed
that 96 percent of Tamarod supporters, 70 percent of the National Salvation
Front, and 60 percent of the April 6 activists supported the military's ousting of
Mohamed Morsi. See Zogby Research Services, "Egyptian Attitudes, September
2013," https://static1.squarespace.com/static/52750dd3e4b08c252c723404/t/5294bf
5de4b013dda087d0e5/1385480029191/Egypt+October+2013+FINAL.pdf. In a conversation on June 12, 2013, in Cairo, Alaa Abdel-Fattah somehow anticipated what
was to come on June 30, when he expressed deep dismay in how the revolutionaries
in their anti-Morsi stands valorized the state institutions that had harbored the
counterrevolution..

32. An Abu Dhabi Gallup organization conducting face-to-face interviews with
one thousand Egyptians in April 2011 found that only 11 percent of Egyptians participated in the uprising (which is rather high) and 83 percent supported it. See
"New Poll Gives Insight into Post-uprising Public Opinion," *Al-Masry al-Youm*,
June 5, 2011. During the Cuban revolution, while a handful of Castro's group took
over the mountains of Sierra Mystera, Che Guevara began to conquer the rest of
the country with 148 men. See Eric Hobsbawm, *The Age of Extremes: The Short
Twentieth Century, 1914–1991* (London: Michael Joseph, 1996), p. 438. John Adams
famously stated that only a third of the population supported the revolutionaries;
just imagine how many were revolutionaries themselves. Adams also believed that
another third supported the British, and the remaining third were neutral. See
George S. Fisher, *The True History of the American Revolution* (Chestnut Hill, MA:
Adamant Media, 2003).

33. Cited in Mayssoum Sukarieh, "Egyptians between Squares," *Counter Punch*,
December 3, 2012; http://www.counterpunch.org/2012/12/03/egyptians-between
-squares/.

34. Marc Lynch, "Tunisia's New al-Nahda," *Foreign Policy*, June 29, 2011.

35. As reported in *Al-Masry al-Youm*, April 16, 2011.

36. Only eight women managed to enter Egypt's parliament of 480 members in
the 2011 elections. See Hania Sholkamy, "Why Women Are at the Heart of Egypt's
Political Triads and Tribulations," *Open Democracy*, January 24, 2012. In Tunisia,
however, thanks to a quota system, the assembly accommodates a more reasonable
number of women deputies.

Chapter 11

Parts of this chapter draw on Asef Bayat, "Revolution and Despair," *Mada Masr*, January 25, 2015.

1. My conversation with a group of old elites, Tunisia, July 2011.

2. "Special Report: The Arab Spring," *The Economist*, July 13, 2013, p. 13.

3. *Radio Fang*, "Parvandeh Bahar Arabi" [The Arab Spring file], 22 Mordad 1392/2013, http://radiofang.org/?p=914.

4. Amr Hamzawai, "Bein Jaza'a wa Hanin" [Between punishment and nostalgia], *Al-Quds al-Arabi*, March 7, 2016, http://www.alquds.co.uk/?p=495457.

5. See the personal account of the leading Egyptian activist, Ahmed Saleh, "How I Went from Leading the Egyptian Revolution to Making Minimum Wage in San Francisco," *Priceonomics*, April 4, 2016, http://priceonomics.com/how-i-went-from-leading-the-egyptian-revolution-to/.

6. Omar Robert Hamilton, "Everything Was Possible," *Mada Masr*, August 17, 2013. According to Shadi Hamid, "The July 3 coup [in Egypt] confirmed the end of the Arab Spring." Shadi Hamid, Middle East observer, quoted in afp, "Arab Spring Legacy in Tatters, Hopes Pinned on Tunisia," *Morocco World News*, December 13, 2013, https://www.moroccoworldnews.com/2013/12/115767/arab-spring-legacy-in-tatters-hopes-pinned-on-tunisia/.

7. Rosa Luxemburg, "Order Prevails in Berlin," *Rote Fahne*, January 14, 1919; https://www.marxists.org/archive/luxemburg/1919/01/14.htm.

8. Cited in Clement Petitjean, "A Present Defaults—Unless the Crowd Declares Itself: Alain Badiou on Ukraine, Egypt and Finitude," Verso, April 23, 2014, http://www.versobooks.com/blogs/1569-a-present-defaults-unless-the-crowd-declares-it self-alain-badiou-on-ukraine-egypt-and-finitude.

9. Part of these new developments are documented in Abdelrahman Mansour and Mohammed Aboalgheit, "Hope without Illusion: Ten Signs of Change in Egypt," *Jadaliyya*, May 12, 2016.

10. Reflecting five years after the Arab uprisings, some thirty political scientists also acknowledge that, despite the prevailing pronouncement of "failure," the revolutions have indeed entailed some important changes in the regional international system, political regimes, and ideas and identities. See "Reflections on the Arab Uprisings: Five Years On," Project on Middle East Political Science, January 20, 2016, http://pomeps.org/2016/01/20/reflections-on-the-arab-uprisings-five-years-on/.

11. For details, see Asef Bayat, *Life as Politics: How Ordinary People Change the Middle East* (Stanford, CA: Stanford University Press, 2013), chap. 1.

12. Such questions abounded in the aftermath of the Arab uprisings; see, for instance, a debate on the sixth anniversary of the Tunisian revolution in Arabic, "Was

the Tunisian Revolution Blessing or Curse?, " Al Jazeera, January 17, 2017, https://www.youtube.com/watch?v=6mbZSKnFemo.

13. Leon Trotsky, *History of the Russian Revolution* (New York: Simon and Schuster, 1932), 3:125. See also Jeff Goodwin, *No Other Way Out: States and Revolutionary Movements* (Cambridge: Cambridge University Press, 2001).

14. In her acclaimed study of "great revolutions," Skocpol comes to the conclusion that revolutions are not made but "happen." See Theda Skocpol, *States and Social Revolutions* (New York: Cambridge University Press, 1979). But as Michael Burawoy argues, Skocpol's conclusion derives from her method of inquiry that "collapses necessary and sufficient conditions" for the occurrence of revolutions. See Michael Burawoy, "Two Methods in Search of Science: Skocpol versus Trotsky," *Theory and Society* 18 (1989): 771.

15. See Raymond Williams, *The Long Revolution* (London: Broadview Press, 2001); Anthony Barnett, "We Live in Revolutionary Times, but What Does This Mean?," *Open Democracy*, December 16, 2011.

16. The irony is that while the neoliberal ideologues, think tanks, and research and development groups invest billions in "utopian" projects, any radical imagination of a humane, rights-based, green, and egalitarian social order is disparaged and dismissed as "utopian." The "Sultans of Silicon Valley," such as Google, invest billions in robotics, driverless cars, and antiaging; Facebook promotes virtual reality equipment; while the venture capitalists like Peter Thiel of PayPal want to extend life to 100 or 120 years, thinking of "abolishing death." Thiel plans to build floating city-states in international waters away from the reach of government regulations—a utopian "unregulated" social existence. "Robber Barons and Silicon Sultans," *The Economist*, January 3, 2005, p. 55.

Index

Abaaoud, Abdelhamid, 87
Abdel-Fatteh, Alaa, 141, 267n44, 272n31
Abdul-Ahad, Faisal, 130
Abdullah, Mohammed Abdirahim, 87
Abrahamian, Ervand, 37, 39
Abu Dhabi, 6
Abu-Lughod, Lila, 198
Abushagur, Mustafa, 150
Abuzar Ghaffari, 36
accumulation by dispossession, 95, 110
Achcar, Gilbert, 15–16
activist capitalism, 234n77
Adams, John, 272n32
Adonis, 221
Afghanistan: economic conditions, 89;
    Mujahedin in, 76; and Soviet Union,
    76
Africa: Pentecostalism in, 102–3, 175
Ahmadinehjad, Mahmoud, 77–78, 84,
    85, 90, 133
Ahmadzadeh, Masoud: *Armed Struggle*, 30
Akif, Mohammad Mahdi, 75
al-Afghani, Jamal al-Din, 35
Alal, Amin, 141
al-Aqqad, Abbas, 83
al-Azhar, 147
Alberta, 185
Al-e Ahmad, Jalal, 47; on "Gharbzadegi"
    (Westoxification), 45

al-Gama'a al-Islamiyya, 139, 172, 188, 217
Algeria, 22, 30, 149; Islamic Salvation
    Front (FIS), 72
Ali, Imam, 38, 43
al-Jihad, 139, 172
Allende, Salvador, 20, 49, 65
Alliance of Youth Movements, 177
Al-Mithaq, 170
al-Qaeda, 72, 76, 78, 90, 147, 148, 172–73
al-Shabaab, 87, 149
Alsharq Alawsat, 271n24
alternative order in urban squares, 115,
    116, 133–34, 153. *See also* cliques (*shil-
    las*); social nonmovements
American Revolution, 11, 272n32
Amr be Marouf wa Nahy an al-Munkar,
    180
anarchism, 13, 19, 154, 184–85, 187
Angola, 7, 49, 65, 66, 170
anticapitalism, 4, 36, 43–45, 46, 80, 81,
    89; in Greece, 235n86; in Iran, 31, 35,
    47–48, 61, 62; in Islamism, 33, 70, 71,
    73, 83; of Marxism, 40, 47, 82, 83; in
    revolutions of 1970s, 1, 7, 11, 26, 29,
    47–48, 62, 220
anticolonialism, 18, 43, 45, 74, 91, 170, 173
antiglobalization, 70, 74, 75, 79, 91
anti-imperialism, 37, 44–45; vs. emanci-
    pation, 91; of Islamism, 26, 29, 31, 69,

Ceaușescu, Nicolae, 156
Central Intelligence Agency (CIA), 2, 136
Césaire, Aimé, 43, 82
Chamorro, Violeta, 207
changes in consciousness, 179–87, 198
Chatterjee, Partha: *Politics of the Governed*, 110
Chávez, Hugo, 24
Chernyshevsky, Nikolay, 34
Chile: Allende government, 20, 49, 65; coup of 1974, 20, 65, 66, 171; neoliberalism in, 20, 171; "refusal to pay" campaigns, 201; transition period in, 208, 258n8
China: income inequality in, 21; Revolution of 1949, 30, 155, 207, 213, 216
Christian democratic parties, 80, 150
Christianity, 34, 81
civil society activism, 174, 178, 220, 262n74
class, 19, 20, 25, 31–32, 118, 220; Shariati on, 41–42, 43, 45, 82
Clinton, Hillary, 270n8
cliques (*shillas*), 140–41, 142, 161, 225
Coalition of the Revolutionary Youths (CRY), 164, 166, 261n48
Cold War, 1, 8, 29, 41, 81, 170; end of, 18, 20, 67, 79, 171, 173; Islamism during, 26, 71, 76, 79, 82, 83, 89
collective identities, 104–5, 122, 144
communism, 19, 23, 34, 69, 73–74, 76, 81, 83–84; collapse of Soviet Union, 136, 137, 171, 207; European revolutions against, 11, 156–57, 171, 178, 207
Conference of the World Council of Churches (1969), 80
consumer culture, 71, 172
contention: in social nonmovements, 106; as spatial, 113, 116, 117, 126–29; between subalterns and authorities, 22–23, 97, 104, 121–23, 138, 139–40

Coptic Church, 147
Correa, Rafael, 24
counter-square strategies, 130, 131, 132, 133
crony capitalism, 23
Cuban Revolution, 5, 6, 80, 155, 159, 207, 214–15, 219, 272n32; influence of, 30, 31, 170. *See also* Castro, Fidel; Guevara, Che
Czechoslovakia, 11, 155

Dabiq, 88
Daneshian, Karamatollah, 238n48
Darwish, Mahmoud, 6
Davis, Mike: *Planet of Slums*, 70; on slums, 101–2
Da'wa, 73, 86
Debray, Régis, 30
deep state, 16, 231n38
democracy, 23, 26, 29, 44, 82, 133, 151, 198, 217, 220, 224; and Arab Spring, 18, 118, 119, 153; and fossil fuels, 146; and Islamism, 73–74, 77, 150; liberal democratic states, 119–20, 153, 231n42; and Muslim Brotherhood, 150; and Occupy movements, 17, 118, 153; popular democracy, 4, 5, 13; social democracy, 20; transition to, 155, 208–9, 215, 216–17, 227, 258n8. *See also* shuras/councils
Democratic Front for the Liberation of Palestine, 171
dependency paradigm, 44–45
De Soto, Hernando, 85, 96
deveiling, 181–82, 185
developmentalism, 20
Diderot, Denis, 40
dignity, 83, 90; as revolutionary demand, 8, 147, 164, 169, 178, 179, 188, 220, 223–24

street vendors, 96–97, 104, 105, 107, 122,
145; Bouazizi, 8, 124, 125, 161, 190,
198, 204, 220–21; in Cairo, 115, 191,
198–200, 216–17; in Tunis, 292
structural change in Arab societies,
143–46
students: activism among, 3, 30, 32, 35,
41, 50–51, 52, 54, 77, 104, 123, 128, 138,
141, 158, 170, 171, 186, 209–10, 223,
224; in Egypt, 128, 139, 141, 143, 158,
186, 223, 224; in Iran, 3, 30, 32, 35, 47,
50–51, 52, 54, 77, 237n28; in Saudi
Arabia, 130; in Tunisia, 138, 161
subalterns, 70, 221, 226, 256n37; contention between authorities and,
22–23, 97, 104, 121–23, 138, 139–40;
contention with authorities, 22–23;
emancipation of, 80, 81, 91; in inside
out cities, 22–23, 96–100, 103, 105,
109, 129; insurgent poor, 187–90, 193;
and Islamism, 76–77, 79, 86, 196, 220;
under neoliberalism, 93–110; nonmovements among, 27, 103, 106–12,
250n46; protests after revolutions,
194–204; role in revolutions, 93, 113,
178, 179, 220; as rural migrants, 106–
8; social justice for, 25, 175, 176, 178,
203, 204; solidarity among, 14, 118,
122, 123, 128, 194, 199–200, 220, 224;
street politics of, 103–10, 122–23, 137;
and survival by repossession, 110–12;
urban subalterns, 22, 26–27, 51,
93–110, 113, 116, 119, 179, 185, 187–90,
194–204. *See also* street vendors; taxi
drivers; women; workers
Sudan, 21, 22, 72, 82–83, 89, 184
Sufism, 40, 180
Sukarno, 170
Suleiman, Omar, 162
survival by repossession, 110–12

Sweden, 21
Sweiris, Najib, 166
Syria: Aleppo, 107, 116, 120, 131; civil war
in, 154, 159, 205, 206, 270n8; Damascus, 131; Der'a, 131, 252n24; Douma,
131; economic conditions, 21, 233n58;
Hama massacre, 116, 120; Hama's
Assi Square, 116; Homs, 116, 120, 130–
31; ISIS in, 86, 89, 180, 246n72, 270n7;
Muslim Brotherhood in, 72; Raqqa,
88, 89, 246n72; Salafism in, 76; street
trade in, 198; uprising of 2011, 10,
16, 23, 78, 116, 154, 156, 207, 212, 219,
252n24, 270n7; Zabadani, 131

Tabari, Ehsan, 236n24
Tabligh, 73
Taha, Mahmoud Mohammed: "Second
Message of Islam", 82–83
Taleqani, Ayatollah Mahmud, 33, 53
Taliban, 76
Tanzania: Arusha Declaration, 170,
241n29; *ujamaa* (familyhood) in, 44,
45–46, 241n29
Tarrow, Sidney, 13
taxi drivers, 98, 145, 151, 223
Tayar Masry Party, 73, 187
Tehran, 30, 31, 35, 113, 124; Arj factory,
55, 57; Aryamehr University, 3; Azmayesh plant, 58, 61; Bloody Friday,
54; Caterpillar plant, 56, 57–58, 59;
contention in, 97, 122, 123; Leyland
Motors, 58, 59; local self-rule in,
52–53; migration to, 121; Pars district,
240n10; Pars Metal factory, 55, 56–57,
58, 62, 63, 64; Philips TV assembly
plant, 56, 57, 58, 60; during revolution of 1979, 6, 74, 90; Revolution
Square, 128; Saipa Citroën car plant,
62–63; Shariati in, 37; subalterns

Twitter, 8, 182, 245n60

ujamaa (familyhood), 44, 45–46, 241n29
Ukraine, 177; Maidan Square, 116; Orange Revolution of 2004–2005, 157–58
unemployment: in Egypt, 97, 99, 122, 200, 210–11; in MENA region, 96–97, 144; in Tunisia, 97, 143
Union of Factory Shuras of the Organization of Industrial Development, 59, 63
Union of the Shuras of the Gilan Province, 59
United Arab Emirates (UAE), 133; counterrevolutionary policies, 206, 220; oil income in, 145–46
United Kingdom, 12, 66, 76, 270n7; inequality in, 21; relations with Iran, 3; relations with Oman, 6; relations with Yemen, 5
United Nations (UN), 21
United States: culture in, 34; empire of, 71, 75, 89; globalization policies, 75; inequality in, 21; vs. Latin America, 24; New Deal, 20; oligarchy in, 13; policies regarding Middle East, 19, 74, 75, 76, 81, 89, 90, 128, 136, 138, 139, 142, 177, 206–7, 270n7; policies regarding Occupy Wall Street (OWS) movement, 231n30, 232n48, 253n40; prohibition in, 226; relations with Cuba, 207; relations with Egypt, 78, 135; relations with Iran, 2, 3, 7, 31, 74; relations with Iraq, 86, 102, 139, 142; relations with Nicaragua, 8, 65; relations with Pakistan, 76; relations with Saudi Arabia, 76, 207; relations with Syria, 76, 206
urbanity: consumption patterns in, 125;

relationship to discontent, 120–24, 197; relationship to revolution, 113–20; spatial flexibility, 127; urban actors, 120; urban amenities/entitlements, 120–21, 144, 194–97, 200, 201–2; urban citizenship, 110, 200, 201–2; urbanization, 51, 144; urban problematics, 120; urban subalterns, 22, 26–27, 51, 93–110, 113, 116, 119, 179, 185, 187–90, 194–204
urban squares, 113, 114–20, 123–24, 126–28, 129–34; alternative order in, 115, 116, 133–34, 153. *See also* Cairo, Tahrir Square; Yemen, Sana'a's Taghir Square
urban streets, 113, 114, 115, 123, 126–27, 128, 129, 130. *See also* street politics
Uruguay, 24
US Agency for International Development (USAID), 25, 175, 177

Venezuela, 24
Verhaeghe, Paul, 234n77
Vidal, Riccardo Cardinal, 157
Vietnam, 30, 31; revolutionaries in, 6, 170
Voltaire, 11, 40

Walesa, Lech, 155
welfare state, 18, 20, 23, 178
Western humanism, 39
Western Orientalism, 37
Westoxification, 35, 45, 75, 238n46
WikiLeaks, 232n48, 270n8
Williams, Raymond: on the long revolution, 226–27; on village vs. city, 123–24
Wolf, Eric, 102
women: activism among, 25, 32, 56, 76, 77, 175, 179, 180–82, 184, 185, 186–87, 224; in Egypt, 175, 181–82,

Stanford Studies in Middle Eastern and Islamic Societies and Cultures

Joel Beinin, Editor

Orit Bashkin, *Impossible Exodus: Iraqi Jews in Israel*
2017

Maha Nassar, *Brothers Apart: Palestinian Citizens of Israel and the Arab World*
2017

Nahid Siamdoust, *Soundtrack of the Revolution: The Politics of Music in Iran*
2017

Laure Guirguis, *Copts and the Security State: Violence, Coercion, and Sectarianism in Contemporary Egypt*
2016

Michael Farquhar, *Circuits of Faith: Migration, Education, and the Wahhabi Mission*
2016

Gilbert Achcar, *Morbid Symptoms: Relapse in the Arab Uprising*
2016

Jacob Mundy, *Imaginative Geographies of Algerian Violence: Conflict Science, Conflict Management, Antipolitics*
2015

Ilana Feldman, *Police Encounters: Security and Surveillance in Gaza under Egyptian Rule*
2015

Tamir Sorek, *Palestinian Commemoration in Israel: Calendars, Monuments, and Martyrs*
2015

Adi Kuntsman and Rebecca L. Stein, *Digital Militarism: Israel's Occupation in the Social Media Age*
2015

Laurie A. Brand, *Official Stories: Politics and National Narratives in Egypt and Algeria*
2014

Kabir Tambar, *The Reckonings of Pluralism: Citizenship and the Demands of History in Turkey*
2014

Diana Allan, *Refugees of the Revolution: Experiences of Palestinian Exile*
2013

Shira Robinson, *Citizen Strangers: Palestinians and the Birth of Israel's Liberal Settler State*
2013

Joel Beinin and Frédéric Vairel, editors, *Social Movements, Mobilization, and Contestation in the Middle East and North Africa*
2013 (Second Edition), 2011

Ariella Azoulay and Adi Ophir, *The One-State Condition: Occupation and Democracy in Israel/Palestine*
2012

Steven Heydemann and Reinoud Leenders, editors, *Middle East Authoritarianisms: Governance, Contestation, and Regime Resilience in Syria and Iran*
2012

Jonathan Marshall, *The Lebanese Connection: Corruption, Civil War, and the International Drug Traffic*
2012

Joshua Stacher, *Adaptable Autocrats: Regime Power in Egypt and Syria*
2012

Bassam Haddad, *Business Networks in Syria: The Political Economy of Authoritarian Resilience*
2011

Noah Coburn, *Bazaar Politics: Power and Pottery in an Afghan Market Town*
2011